THE LIFE OF IAN FLEMING

THE LIFE OF IAN FLEMING

*

JOHN PEARSON

THE COMPANION BOOK CLUB
LONDON

This edition is issued by arrangement with
Jonathan Cape Ltd., London

To Leonard Russell,
who has guided, edited, inspired and
shaped this book, and but for whom . . .

Made and printed in Great Britain
for the Companion Book Club (Odhams Books Ltd.)
by Odhams (Watford) Limited
Watford, Herts.

S.168.UD

CONTENTS

Many people have helped me with personal reminiscences of and information about Ian Fleming, some of them lending letters and all of them giving freely of their time and advice. To list everyone by name here would be impossible, and it would be invidious to select a few. I can only express my deep gratitude to everyone.

Mr Noël Coward has been good enough to let me publish letters and poems by him, hitherto unpublished, and to Mr Paul Gallico go my thanks for allowing me to print a letter by him to Ian Fleming. Copyright and hitherto unpublished letters by Somerset Maugham and Dame Edith Sitwell appear by permission respectively of Mr Spencer Curtis Brown and the executors of the estate of the late Dame Edith Sitwell.

J.P.

ILLUSTRATIONS

CHAPTER ONE

THE FLEMINGS OF NETTLEBED

THERE are ugly houses and ugly houses, but this one is a monster, an architectural tyrannosaurus which has blundered into these Oxfordshire beech woods from another age and somehow become preserved, dead but completely intact. It is a convalescent home now. The grounds flutter with nurses, the windows reflect the grey faces of Londoners brought here to get well, but a monster it remains, and as you turn your car off the main road from Henley-on-Thames to Oxford and peer down the drive between the rhododendrons at this house with its fierce red walls, its elaborate portico, its jagged roofs and chimneys and cornices, you murmur to yourself—who?

Who can have had the money, the energy, the lack of self-consciousness to build Joyce Grove in the first place? Who can have wanted it? And what sort of life can they have led, the people who lived here in this house in its appalling prime?

Within these questions lies much of the boyhood and background of Ian Fleming. For Joyce Grove was the house which his millionaire grandfather Robert Fleming raised as the tribal centre for his family at Nettlebed, near Henley, in 1904, four years before Ian Fleming was born. In many ways the Flemings of Nettlebed were a unique Edwardian family.

The site had been occupied for at least two hundred years already on the day Robert Fleming reached for his architects. There had been a small William and Mary house which had taken its name from Cornet Joyce, one of Oliver Cromwell's men who put his name to the death warrant of Charles the First, and Robert Fleming bought this house and all the land round about. He was then a tall, abstemious man in his early fifties with a fine moustache, a powerful sense of rectitude and a Scots accent, dedicated to country pursuits and to making money rather than spending it. In 1909, five years after he built Joyce Grove, he was to start his own private bank of Robert Fleming and Company at 8 Crosby Square in the City of London (the bank is still there and still flourishing), and he had recently bought a town house in Grosvenor Square, where he could carry on the entertaining that had become expected of him. There was no ostentation in all this. He was a simple-living man who merely happened to have become very rich. It is said that he never took a taxi in his life and that but for the episode of the overcoat his new house at Nettlebed might never have been built at all.

Robert Fleming's overcoat was good but ancient—it had done him sterling service over the years. One afternoon, however, when his wife was mending its slightly frayed cuffs, some friends called, and one of them had the bad manners to say bluntly to Mrs Fleming, 'But isn't it odd for you to be repairing the overcoat of a man who is already a millionaire several times over?'

Possibly she had never before fully understood the extent of her husband's wealth, but from that moment at any rate the days of the unpretentious William and Mary house were numbered. Mrs Robert Fleming had a will of steel, and within a matter of months pickaxes had demolished the mellow brickwork of the house named after the regicide of Nettlebed and the first bold stones of the new Joyce Grove were rising in its place.

Somewhere beneath all that extreme carefulness over such things as taxi fares there must have been a streak of romantic extravagance in Robert Fleming: for by the standards of 1904 his new house was undoubtedly the best that money could buy. No window was left plain if stained glass could possibly be used instead. No balustrade remained uncarved. There was a hint of Chartres, a memory of Spa, an echo of all the most recent châteaux built along the valley of the Loire, with craftsmen brought over from France to achieve the correct effects. There were to be forty-four bedrooms, a great fireplace of Carrara marble weighing eleven tons, and the largest conservatory in south Oxfordshire.

Beautiful it was not, but in its way the new Joyce Grove was ideal for the people for whom it was built: it was comfortable enough and remarkably spacious and it was a symbol of where they stood and what they had accomplished. In just over a quarter of a century the Flemings had accomplished a very great deal.

The story of how Ian Fleming's Scottish grandfather

made his millions would have been appreciated by Samuel Smiles as a demonstration of the Victorian gospel of self-help. One of seven children, he was born in 1845 and brought up in one of the poorest districts of Dundee. The family had originally been farmers in a modest way around Braemar, but Robert's father, John Fleming, seems to have been of an independent and ambitious disposition. Not only did he break away from the Established Kirk and join the Free Church of Scotland, but he left his father's farm, entered the flax industry in Perth, and in 1840 set up his own lint mill on the banks of the Isla at Coupar Angus. Three years later a crisis in the flax industry ruined him, and he was lucky to get a pound-a-week job as overseer in a jute works in Dundee. In those days Dundee had some of the worst slums in Europe. Five of John Fleming's children were to die of diphtheria in the tiny house in Liff Road. The two survivors were Robert and John, and from the Free Church of St David's School in Brown Street they both won scholarships to the Academy section of Dundee High School. 'My brother, Robert', wrote John Fleming later, 'took chiefly mathematics at which he became very proficient.' When they left school at the age of fourteen John was apprenticed to the wood trade and Robert became a clerk with the important Dundee textile firm of Edward Baxter.

What is so striking about the success story of Robert Fleming is its apparent ease and straightforwardness. At the age of twenty-one this frugal, clear-sighted, hard-working Scottish book-keeper was made private secretary to the senior Mr Baxter; at twenty-five he got the chance for which he had clearly been predestined by the stern Calvinist godhead of Dundee. Sent to the United States to represent his firm, he immediately appreciated, with the precision of a mathematician and the assurance of a young man on the make, the investment possibilities which the New World was offering the Old. In the aftermath of the Civil War the pound sterling stood at a premium of from six to eighteen per cent over the dollar; America was crying out for capital; and Dundee, despite its slums, had capital to invest. It was his method of tapping this capital which made him a millionaire.

When he was old and successful Robert Fleming was acknowledged by bankers and financial journalists as the 'Father of Investment Trusts'. This was not strictly true. The principle of joint investment in a number of carefully selected enterprises was known to the Venetians and the medieval German merchants of the Hanseatic towns. But when twenty-eight-year-old Robert Fleming formed the Scottish-American Investment Trust in Dundee in 1873, he was certainly beginning a new chapter in the story of Victorian high finance. Originally he intended to raise £150,000 by public subscription and place the money in a number of American enterprises where the yield would be between ten and twelve per cent instead of the six per cent obtainable on the stock markets of Edinburgh and London. But as on the first day the issue was wildly over-subscribed by enthusiastic Dundonians, the prospectus was withdrawn and a new one for £300,000 substituted. From that moment the Scottish-American Investment Trust and its secretary, Mr Robert Fleming, never looked back, and to this day Robert Fleming and Company advise many well-known investment trusts.

Before Robert died in 1933 he had crossed the Atlantic 128 times. He trafficked on equal terms with Wall Street barons like J. Pierpont Morgan and Jacob Schiff. He completed the financial reconstruction of the Atchison, Topeka and Santa Fe, the Denver and Rio Grande, and the Cuban railroads. 'He had', as his grandson Richard Fleming puts it, 'a sort of sixth sense about how much debt any enterprise could safely stand.' When asked for advice by young men entering on a career in the City he rather depressingly boiled down all his experience into the words, 'Lairn to say no, laddie. Lairn to say no.'

During the last half of the nineteenth century the incursion of new, wealthy, self-made Scottish families like the Tennants and the Macmillans brought an exotic element into the placid mainstream of English society. With a Scots-loving Queen upon the throne these northern nabobs, with their tartans, their accents and their money-bags, were accepted and quietly absorbed. But although they could become Anglicized these families were not English—least of all the Flemings. 'Never forget you're a Scot,' Ian Fleming's mother would repeat to him when he was a child. In the circumstances he was hardly likely to, for the Flemings were always something of a clan: even today they gather as a family every August at Black Mount, an Argyllshire deer-forest of some 100,000 acres originally bought by Robert Fleming and today jointly owned by his surviving son and daughter. The impressive old Scottish millionaire at the head of the tribe into which Ian Fleming was born was a man who, like all good Dundonians, seems emotionally never to have left his native city; and his wife, Ian Fleming's redoubtable grandmother, who celebrated her seventieth birthday by grassing a couple of stags, was also Scottish. Clearly the vast success of the investment trust movement which made Robert Fleming such a name in the City of London left the granite core of the Flemings' Scottishness unscratched. The two sons, Valentine and Philip, were sent to Eton and Oxford and groomed to take their place in society and the family business. But the family itself remained a solid, closely integrated Scots family with a physical toughness rare in the south, a Calvinistic sense of the passionate importance of achievement, and great carefulness with money.

Ian Fleming's father, Valentine Fleming, appears as one of those rare, slightly baffling Edwardian figures of whom nothing but good is ever spoken. From his father he had inherited his physical strength, his family sense and his love of the accepted sports of a country gentleman. At Eton he rowed in the eight. At Magdalen College, Oxford, he took a second in history and only missed his rowing blue because of a boil on a crucial spot at a crucial moment. He read for the Bar but never practised, and he listed his recreations for *Who's Who* as 'deerstalking, salmon-fishing, fox-hunting, hunts a pack of basset hounds'. The only Fleming characteristic he seemed to lack was ambition, but as a rich young man this hardly mattered: he was universally liked and had an acceptable willingness to do whatever was expected of him. Though not deeply interested in politics he became an exceedingly conscientious M.P. for South Oxfordshire. He loved the countryside but dutifully took his place in his father's office in Crosby Square. He was a pacific man but accepted a commission in the Oxfordshire Yeomanry and used to train his men in the grounds of Joyce Grove. As a Fleming the one untypical act of his life came at two thirty on the afternoon of Friday, February 18th, 1906, when at the age of twenty-four he married Miss Evelyn St Croix Rose at St Paul's Church, Knightsbridge.

Young Miss Rose was not one of those restrained, tweedy, county girls. She was a bird of paradise, with very large eyes and a high natural colouring which must have been particularly striking in the days before women wore make-up as a matter of course. The portraits Augustus John painted of her when she was in her forties show a Goyaesque beauty, hard, strong-featured, the self-absorbed face of an acknowledged prima donna used to getting her own way as very beautiful, very rich women usually do. Her family was of Irish, Scots and Huguenot descent; apart from John of Gaunt, whom she always claimed as one of her forbears, her most distinguished ancestor was Sir Richard Quain, a surgeon from County Cork who became Physician-Extraordinary to Queen Victoria and editor of the famous *Dictionary of Medicine*.

The bride and the groom seem to have exemplified D. H. Lawrence's requisite for a satisfactory marriage in that they were as different as two people can be. Where he was cautious she was extravagant. Where he was temperate she was passionate and given to outbursts of sudden devotion and equally sudden rejection. She was demanding, beautiful, and a law to herself. He was honourable, kindly and remarkably concerned with his duty to society. Yet as sometimes happens in such marriages of opposites they seem to have been devoted to each other: Valentine Fleming was one of the few people who ever knew how to handle the remarkable woman he had taken as his wife.

In the high Edwardian style Robert Fleming settled something more than a quarter of a million pounds sterling on his son, and Valentine Fleming used part of it to buy a country place at Ipsden in Oxfordshire, a mock-Gothic, fairy palace of a house whose beech woods, in the period phrase, marched with the beech woods of Joyce Grove. There was stabling for the horses, kennelling for the basset hounds, several hundred acres of rough shooting and that vital proximity to the head of the family which allowed the tribe to remain intact. The following year the first son, Peter, was born.

Soon afterwards Valentine Fleming took a short lease on 27 Green Street, off Park Lane. It was here, in Mayfair, on May 28th, 1908, slightly less than twelve months after the birth of her first son, that Evelyn St Croix Fleming was brought to bed of another child, again a boy. He weighed nearly nine pounds and was given the good Scots name of Ian, followed by Lancaster, in memory of John of Gaunt. All his life the two names were to symbolize the curious mixture of genes he had inherited from the two very different sides of his family.

CHAPTER TWO

THE DIFFICULT ONE

IAN LANCASTER FLEMING was a large, healthy, exceedingly naughty child. Nannies adored him, parents and grandparents were devoted to him. With Peter and, in due time, the two younger brothers, Richard and Michael, he was brought up in the large house at Ipsden in a sort of woodland paradise, and it is hard to think of more pleasurable circumstances and surroundings for a small boy. Yet almost from the start Ian Fleming seems to have been the difficult one of the family, the one for whom allowances had to be made. The restlessness which followed him through life began early.

Around the age of four he took against porridge and began emptying it over the top of the nursery wardrobe, until the smell or the fungus finally revealed what Master Ian had been doing with his breakfast. At five he objected to dumplings, and when he put them down the lavatory and found that they would not flush away he tried to force them down with one of the weights from a grandfather clock. The dumplings remained, the pan was shattered.

He must have been a spoiled, humorous, strong-willed boy; for the world he reacted against with such evident disapproval was as ordered, comfortable, and successful as only the upper reaches of late Edwardian England knew how to be. The family business was prospering. In 1909, with the private banking house of Robert Fleming and Company successfully established, Ian's grandfather was already shrewdly backing the Anglo-Persian Oil Company in addition to American railroads.

Valentine Fleming was prospering too. Since his election as Tory M.P. for South Oxfordshire in 1910 (the seat had formerly been held by a Liberal, Philip Morrell, husband of Lady Ottoline Morrell) his circle of friends had widened, and his fellow M.P. and brother officer in the Oxfordshire Yeomanry, Winston Churchill, would sometimes join his week-end shooting parties.

Mrs Valentine Fleming was busy as mother and hostess. The house in Green Street was given up. In its place the Valentine Flemings bought Pitt House, a Georgian mansion on the brow of Hampstead Heath, where the Elder Pitt, the Earl of Chatham, had lived during his attacks of melancholy, 'shutting himself off from all communication with the outside world, even from his own family and servants'. Despite these sombre associations the house and its superb situation seem to have suited Mrs Fleming. It was ideal for her four young children, and her husband had to travel no more than five or six miles to get to the House of Commons. She liked to give musical parties at Pitt House, and she herself was a talented violinist.

Ian Fleming seems to have been the only member of the family to react against all this, and his childhood was to leave him with a set of antipathies which lasted for life. They consisted in the main of precisely those things the rest of the clan loved best. He hated horses and he disliked dogs. He had a horror of family gatherings, particularly at Christmas, and would do almost anything to avoid having to go near Scotland—'all those wet rhododendrons and people with hair on their cheeks sitting round peat fires wrapped in plaid blankets'. He had no interest in politics, no ear for music, and according to his brother Peter, 'no feeling for land'. He was a good shot and a good walker but he never took to any of those sports which the rest of the Flemings seemed to live for. 'Well, Uncle Phil,' he is supposed to have remarked one year at Black Mount, 'if I *have* to make a choice I suppose I would rather catch no salmon than shoot no grouse.'

Evidently from the start he had one of those natures for which the world is uncomfortable in whatever shape they find it; and during the next few years the world had no intention of making things any easier for him.

First came the war. In August 1914, not long after his second son's sixth birthday, Captain Valentine Fleming rode off at the head of C Squadron of the Oxfordshire Yeomanry for France, and in December he was promoted major. From now on, with her husband away most of the time in France, it was Mrs Valentine Fleming who had to bring up the family. She took this very seriously, and in 1915, when she had to find a boarding school for her two eldest sons—aged eight and seven—she set off on a whirlwind tour to see for herself and settled on Durnford School, near

16

Swanage, in the Isle of Purbeck. It was a singular choice and one which was to have repercussions on the character of her second son. For at that time Durnford School was unlike any other successful preparatory school in England.

It had been founded in 1893 by an immensely stout short man called Tom Pellatt, and the more successful the school became the more it reflected Pellatt's extrovert and eccentric view of life. It occupied a large Jacobean house of Purbeck stone, and Pellatt presided over the establishment more like some rumbustious eighteenth-century Dorset squire than a twentieth-century prep-school headmaster. According to his daughter, Hester Chapman, the novelist and historian, 'When he came to Durnford after a spell as a junior master at Marlborough, he had the completely novel idea for those days that boys should be happy at school. As he was something of a schoolboy himself, he was remarkably successful.'

He blasted out a natural pool in the rocks where the boys used to swim naked every morning, and he gave them an extraordinary amount of freedom, aiding and abetting them in many of their escapades. Corfe Castle was near by, and the boys were free to explore that whole stretch of romantic smugglers' country.

But for all this there was a price to be paid, particularly by new boys. The freedom Pellatt believed in led to a good deal of bullying. Food was rough, dormitories unheated, and few allowances were made for gently nurtured eight-year-olds packed off from fond families for the first time in their lives.

Ian Fleming wrote to his mother:

Dear Miewy,
I am afraid that I do not like school very much. I do not know what form im in im in so many. I am afraid I have not made many friends, they are so dirty and unreverent.

Things seem to have got worse before they got better, for a little later he was writing:

My dear Mum,
I don't like school half so much now. Thanks for the knife, here is a map that I drew at lessons some of the boys are beastly. We have eight hours lissons some of the boys say that we are beasts. Peter is a great help to me. We are aloud knives.
Lots of love and lots of X X X
from Ian

One thing he soon learned at Durnford was to give as little

17

as possible of himself away. For the rest of his life he was always wary of people who tried to get too close.

Yet once he had learned this precocious lesson in survival Durnford had much to offer. Intellectually he seemed no match for his brother Peter, who was already being tipped as a natural for an Eton scholarship. But he was good at games, he was popular, and he was to become a favourite of Tom Pellatt's—and this despite the trouble with Mrs Val about young Ian's teeth. At the beginning of the second term he brought a letter from his mother:

Dear Mr Pellatt,
Would you please make sure that Ian cleans his teeth properly. They were quite green when he arrived home from school last term . . .

Hester Chapman remembers her father going scarlet with rage when he read it—no mother had ever written such a letter to him before. 'Pack the boy's trunk,' he shouted. 'I won't be written to like this by anyone.' But as usual Mrs Val was to get her way. Mr Pellatt calmed down, and for the rest of his time at Durnford Ian Fleming cleaned his teeth.

At the school a great premium was placed on daring and initiative—the boys' raids on the larder and the orchard were almost a legitimate school activity; and it was now that Ian Fleming received his introduction to Sapper, the author of the Bulldog Drummond books and the creator of the character whom Fleming often acknowledged as the true spiritual forerunner of James Bond.

Every Sunday evening the headmaster's wife used to invite the entire school into her drawing-room before dinner. Sitting on the sofa, and with one of the boys stroking her feet, she would read a story. For years the favourite book had been John Meade Falkner's *Moonfleet*, but just around the time Ian Fleming arrived she decided to add some new stories and picked among others on the first of the Bulldog Drummond books. It was an instant success. Mr Pellatt used to take his bath while the reading was in progress, and when he had finished he would shout down, 'Do stop reading—I'm very hungry and want my dinner.' This became the cue for the whole school to shout back, 'Oh! Shut up!' As Hester Chapman says, 'It was that sort of school.' And on Sunday nights, while the headmaster was in his bath and the headmaster's wife was having her feet stroked on the sofa, Ian Fleming went along with Sapper, while on his own account

VALENTINE FLEMING.

AN APPRECIATION.

"W. S. C." writes of the death of Major Valentine Fleming, M.P., who, as announced in *The Times* on Wednesday, was killed in action:—

This news will cause sorrow in Oxfordshire and in the House of Commons and wherever the member of the Henley Division was well known. Valentine Fleming was one of those younger Conservatives who easily and naturally combine loyalty to party ties with a broad liberal outlook upon affairs and a total absence of class prejudice. He was most earnest and sincere in his desire to make things better for the great body of the people, and had cleared his mind of all particularist tendencies. He was a man of thoughtful and tolerant opinions, which were not the less strongly or clearly held because they were not loudly or frequently asserted. The violence of faction and the fierce tumults which swayed our political life up to the very threshold of the Great War, caused him a keen distress. He could not share the extravagant passions with which the rival parties confronted each other. He felt acutely that neither was wholly right in policy and that both were wrong in mood. Although he could probably have held the Henley Division as long as he cared to fight it, he decided to withdraw from public life rather than become involved in conflicts whose bitterness seemed so far to exceed the practical issues at stake. Friends were not wanting on both sides of the House to urge him to remain and to encourage him to display the solid abilities he possessed. It is possible we should have prevailed. He shared the hopes to which so many of his generation respond of a better, fairer, more efficient public life and Parliamentary system arising out of these trials. But events have pursued a different course.

As a Yeomanry officer he always took the greatest pains to fit himself for military duties. There was scarcely an instructional course open before the war to the Territorial Forces of which he had not availed himself, and on mobilization there were few more competent civilian soldiers of his rank. The Oxfordshire Hussars were the first, or almost, the first Yeomanry regiment to come under the fire of the enemy, and in the first battle of Ypres acquitted themselves with credit. He had been nearly three years in France, a squadron leader or second in command, and had been twice mentioned in dispatches, before the shell which ended his life found him. From the beginning his letters showed the deep emotions which the devastation and carnage of the struggle aroused in his breast. But the strength and buoyancy of his nature were proofs against the sombre realizations of his mind. He never for a moment flagged or wearied or lost his spirits. Alert, methodical, resolute, untiring he did his work, whether perilous or dull, without the slightest sign of strain or stress to the end. "We all of us," writes a brother officer, "were devoted to him. The loss to the regiment is indescribable. He was, as you know, absolutely our best officer, utterly fearless, full of resource, and perfectly magnificent with his men." His passion in sport was deer-stalking in his much-loved native Scotland. He rode well and sometimes brilliantly to hounds, and was always a gay and excellent companion. He had everything in the world to make him happy; a delightful home life, active interesting expanding business occupations, contented disposition, a loyable and charming personality. He had more. He had that foundation of spontaneous and almost unconscious self-suppression in the discharge of what he conceived to be his duty without which happiness, however full, is precarious and imperfect. That these qualities are not singular in this generation does not lessen the loss of those in whom they shine. As the war lengthens and intensifies and the extending lists appear, it seems as if one watched at night a well-loved city whose lights, which burn so bright, which burn so true, are extinguished in the distance in the darkness one by one.

Churchill and Fleming's Father. This appreciation in *The Times* of Major Valentine Fleming, M.P., was written by Winston Churchill in May 1917 and inscribed by him. It hung in Ian Fleming's bedroom at his London home at 16 Victoria Square.

Winston S. Churchill

he was soon reading everything he could lay hands on by Sax Rohmer, Buchan, Poe, and Robert Louis Stevenson.

But even as a very young boy at Durnford he was already managing to convey the impression of moodiness and uncertainty which was to recur for the rest of his life.

While he was at Durnford he saw his father occasionally: as a Member of Parliament Major Fleming was sometimes recalled from France for debates at Westminster, and one of his periods of leave usually coincided with the family holiday in Scotland. He was a fond father and particularly attached to his second son. He called him Johnny and usually found time to write a postcard from France when the boy was going back to school. The last one arrived at Pitt House in 1917 at the end of the Easter holidays, when Major Valentine Fleming and his brother Captain Philip Fleming were in Picardy:

My dear Johnny,

In the wood where we slept last night were wild boars. I killed a snake but not a poisonous one. A hedgehog came into Philip's shelter one night . . .

After that the Major was too busy to write again. His squadron had taken over the dangerous outpost of Gillemont Farm, and at one a.m. on May 20th, 1917, suspecting that trouble was brewing, he sent a reassuring message to Headquarters, 'My squadron holds its locality.' At three a.m. the Germans opened up with a hurricane bombardment, including gas shells, and half an hour later he and a second-lieutenant were killed instantaneously.

Peter Fleming had been in hospital having his tonsils out, and Mrs Fleming had collected him and taken him home to Pitt House. 'As we arrived', he says, 'my aunt came rushing out of the front door with a telegram for my mother. I had no idea what was in it. I remember being hustled off to bed and for the rest of that night I could hear people crying in the house. Early next morning I was packed off back to school.'

No one knows what effect the news had on Ian Fleming. He always said that he could never remember his father, but he can hardly have avoided the legend of his death. Winston Churchill wrote the appreciation in *The Times*:

As the war lengthens and intensifies and the extending lists appear, it seems as if one watched at night a well-loved city whose lights, which burn so bright, which burn so true, are extinguished in the distance in the darkness one by one . . .

There was a posthumous award of a D.S.O.; and the German shell which ended the life of Valentine Fleming meant that his sons grew up with a dead hero for a father.

Yet the influence of Valentine Fleming was not confined to the memory of his heroism and death. In November 1917, when his will was proved, his gross estate stood at £265,596. He bequeathed his wife all his 'carriages, motors, horses, harness and stable furniture'; he left her Pitt House 'absolutely for her own use and benefit'. Almost all the rest of his estate was to be invested to form a trust fund, and the trustees were directed 'to pay the said income to my wife during her life, so long as she shall remain my widow', her share being fixed at £3,000 a year if she remarried; and although, subject to his wife's interests, his children were to benefit equally, he gave her sweeping powers to alter this if she thought fit—in effect she could disinherit any of the children if she wanted to.

Wittingly or unwittingly the will of Major Valentine Fleming left his thirty-two-year-old wife rich, powerful and with a strong incentive not to marry again.

CHAPTER THREE

VICTOR LUDORUM

I

THE only sign of nostalgia Ian Fleming ever showed for the five years he spent at Eton came rather late in life, when he donated a silver trophy called the James Bond Cup to the Old Etonian Golfing Society. It was gratefully accepted. When it arrived it was found to be in the shape of a large silver chamber-pot. It was a wry little joke and not very well received, for Old Etonians tend to take their school rather seriously; Fleming never did.

When he wrote *The Times* obituary in *You Only Live Twice* for 'Commander James Bond, C.M.G., R.N.V.R., missing, believed killed while on an official mission to Japan', he recorded that Bond's 'career at Eton was brief and undistinguished and, after only two halves, as a result, it pains me to record, of some alleged trouble with one of the boys' maids, his aunt was requested to remove him'. Fleming's own Eton career was neither brief nor undistinguished, but as usual with everything about James Bond there were distinct resemblances between Fleming and his creation.

At Eton, the Timbralls is a large sombre building on the Slough road, overlooking School Field. Built in 1860 with much of the red-brick solemnity of Keble College, Oxford, it lacks the creepered mellowness of the older Eton houses. When Ian Fleming arrived there in the autumn term of 1921 it had recently been taken over by a new housemaster, E. V. Slater; and Slater, 'an abrupt, red-faced bachelor with a loud voice and a liking for port', as one member of his house remembers him, had already decided that the place, with its forty boys, was going to improve its position in the Eton hierarchy. When he was appointed it was 'one of the most despised houses in the school', and Ian Fleming arrived to find Slater hard at work converting it into the best. It was not the sort of atmosphere he took to, and 'Sam' Slater was scarcely the man to bring out the best in him.

At Durnford Tom Pellatt had grown very fond of him.

In a reference he wrote for Fleming a few years later he referred to him as 'almost a son to me'. People at Durnford had made allowances for the moodiness of Fleming Minor and appreciated his sense of fun and his flights of imagination. He was a personality in his own right. In Slater's house things were different. For Slater was an obsessively straightforward character. Lord Caccia, who was British Ambassador at Washington from 1956 to 1961, was in his house at the same time as Ian and Peter Fleming, and he spoke of Slater in his address to the school when he was installed as Provost of Eton, referring to his 'contempt for self-delusion, for pretence that we or things are other than we known them to be'. This was not an attitude likely to generate much warmth in a potential thriller-writer, and as Lord Caccia says, 'Slater would have looked at Ian Fleming and detected James Bond in minuscule.'

At thirteen Fleming, already tall for his age, was strikingly good looking, and he was quite conscious of his looks. 'Even in those days', says Peter Fleming, 'Ian had considerable panache.' Throughout his time at Eton he took considerable trouble with his appearance, dressing with that touch of premeditated unconcern which stayed with him for the rest of his life. According to Chester Beatty, the financier, who was in Slater's house with him, the housemaster used to become enraged by Fleming's use of Trumper's most expensive and strongest-scented hair oil. This was not the sort of character Slater wanted in his house, and in time a battle of wills developed between the two of them.

'I'm going to break you, Fleming,' Slater is supposed to have said at one moment of high stress, and at Eton it was a serious matter for a boy to incur the antagonism of his housemaster.

At the same time, Ian Fleming's problems were not confined to Sam Slater. In 1921 Mrs Val Fleming was a rich, beautiful widow and—thanks to the provisions of her husband's will—likely to remain one. In many ways she was an exceptional mother: the death of her husband had given her a role to play, and she performed it with indomitable energy and high seriousness. As a hero's widow she lived for her family, determined to be both father and mother to her four boys. She was equally determined that her four boys should be a credit to her and the family. She had a great way with children, took infinite trouble with them, and placed great emphasis on their obligation to succeed and on their

23

duties as young gentlemen. She did her best to instil into them all a sense of pride in their family and in their father. 'Remember you're Flemings' was one of her constant standbys in moments of family crisis, and she taught her sons to end their prayers, 'and please, God, make us like father.'

When her children behaved no one could be more loving and gracious to them than the beautiful Mrs Val. But when they disobeyed the emotional penalties were severe; it must have seemed as if they were betraying mother, family and the ghost of a dead father.

Ian Fleming was not a particularly obedient child, and Mrs Val was hardly the woman to understand his failings. Something of the uncomprehending relationship between the mother and the small son comes through in the story Fleming told of how he found his first treasure—he was a compulsive treasure-hunter all his life—at the age of nine. That summer the family were on holiday at St Ives, Cornwall, and he was searching the caves for amethyst quartz. One afternoon he found in a cave a lump of ambergris 'as big as a child's football'. He knew it was ambergris from the adventure books he had been reading—it was real treasure: 'Now I would be rich and I would be able to live on Cadbury's milk chocolate flakes and I would not have to go back to my private school or indeed do any more work at all. I had found the short cut out of all my childish woes.' He carried it back to the Tregenna Castle Hotel in the lap of his grey jersey, but the ambergris began to melt and soon he was a dreadful sight. 'What did I care? There would be no scoldings or punishments ever again.'

Mrs Fleming was having tea with an admirer in the Palm Court when her son arrived with his treasure and let it fall with a soft squelch at her feet. 'What is it, darling?' she asked. 'What a mess you've got your clothes into.'

'It's ambergris,' he replied. 'It's worth £1,000 an ounce and there must be two pounds of it. How much does that make? I'm never going back to school.'

It was then that one of the waiters explained that the ambergris was really a lump of very rancid butter from a supply ship that had been torpedoed off the coast. Mrs Fleming was not amused.

Small lapses like these were apt to fall below the exacting standard of behaviour she set and were the more tiresome because of the impeccability of the eldest son. For Peter Fleming, grave beyond his years and taking his duties as head of the family with admirable seriousness, already seemed the embodiment of the finest Fleming virtues; and once the boys were at Eton, Peter's success was so notable that Ian was inevitably outclassed and outdistanced.

'Even to his contemporaries,' says Lord Caccia, 'Peter Fleming was completely outstanding. It wasn't just what he did but the style in which he did it. He had a degree of *gravitas* unusual for his years.' At Eton Peter won all the prizes. He was admired and envied. He became Captain of the Oppidans (otherwise the top boy of the whole school except for the seventy scholars), and in 1926 he was to depart in a blaze of glory for Christ Church, Oxford. Altogether it was the sort of overwhelming success that no younger brother could hope to compete with, and it meant of course that throughout his time at Eton Ian Fleming was very much in his brother's shadow, Fleming Minor to the gilded Fleming Major.

This need hardly have mattered. The two younger brothers, Richard and Michael, both followed to Slater's house and managed perfectly well. Neither achieved Peter's distinction, but Richard became head of the house and Master of the Beagles and Michael was an extremely popular extrovert who sailed through Eton without a care or an enemy in the world. But Ian Fleming was too close to his brother to avoid being scorched by his success. Since early childhood the two of them, despite a real devotion which continued throughout their lives, had been struggling and competing with each other, as first and second sons born so close together invariably do; and then the death of their father had subtly changed things. Ian Fleming has described how he started 'hero-worshipping my elder brother Peter, who had to become head of the family at the age of ten, when our father was killed in 1917'; and once they were at Eton in the same house and with only a year between them the situation must have become a curious one. For it meant for Ian Fleming that the elder brother he had been in the habit of competing with was not only immensely successful but also his acknowledged hero and the head of his family.

Ian Fleming solved that impasse in the only way he could: he no longer competed. He seems to have opted out of a competition he could never win had he even wanted to do so. Since lessons and scholarship were ruled out as a means of getting the personal success he needed, he took little trouble with them. At the same time, he was never one to

25

accept failure. 'The Flemings', says a close friend of the family, 'are people who believe in success.' And since Ian Fleming could not win success as a respectable, hard-working member of his house, he found other ways of achieving distinction. One was to concentrate on being an individual —a bit of a dandy, a bit of an eccentric—and to establish personal ascendancy over his school-fellows on his own terms. It was not difficult. He was a born actor.

Rupert Hart-Davis, the publisher, remembers him as 'something of a swell, walking down late with his friend Lord Willoughby de Eresby for a breakfast of buttered eggs at a place called the Red House near the river.' Lord Caccia says that 'after forty years you forget most of the boys you were at school with, but with Ian the impression remains that this was a boy who was unlike any other.'

He was admired for his wit, for his caustic turn of phrase, but his withdrawn periods continued; he developed the habit of keeping himself to himself, and he liked to spend at least a part of the day alone. He was popular, but most people were a little wary of him—it probably suited him that way.

Predictably, the one legitimate school activity at which he excelled was the one in which his brother could not beat him. In later life Ian Fleming always said that the reason why he was successful at athletics was that he happened to mature earlier than most boys—he was certainly one of the most precocious athletes Eton can have known. For whereas Peter was physically rather a late developer, because of colitis contracted as a child, Ian was exceptionally strong. It was his strength which accounted for his earliest success on the football field in Eton's Field Game (as opposed to the Wall Game).

The football he played for his house team, when he was only fourteen, against boys sometimes three or four years older, drew this report:

Still a lower boy with an exceptionally long kick for his age. He seems to suffer from nerves a bit before a match, and varies tremendously, some days playing brilliantly but on others amazingly badly. On these days he appears to lose his head completely. If he can overcome his nervousness he should be very good one day . . .

It was three years after this that Ian Fleming collided head-on, during a football game, with Henry Douglas-Home, brother of the future Prime Minister; and Fleming broke his nose so badly that he had to have a small copper plate inserted. While his mother lamented that his nose spoiled his looks, he complained that the copper plate gave him headaches. Whatever Mrs Val may have said, this spectacularly broken nose really completed his appearance, giving to those too perfect features a touch of battered nobility.

Perhaps it was that team games never suited his isolated spirit, but at any rate Fleming mi never fulfilled his promise as a footballer or cricketer. Instead, quite suddenly, and to almost everyone's surprise, he emerged as an extraordinary athlete. There are two sets of sports at Eton, one for juniors (under sixteen) and the other for seniors. His really astonishing feat, never equalled before or since, was to win every single event in the 1924 junior sports except the high jump and the 100 yards—the mile, the half-mile, the quarter-mile, the 220 yards, the hurdles, the long jump, throwing the cricket ball, and the steeplechase as well. As a senior he set another record by becoming the only boy in living memory to have been Victor Ludorum—champion of the games—two years in succession; for he was Victor Ludorum in 1925 (while still under seventeen) and again in 1926 (while under eighteen). In this last year, because of the operation on his nose, he was not allowed to compete in the mile, half-mile, quarter-mile or steeplechase. Fleming, in short, proved to be the best athlete—one of style, strength, and will power—that Eton had seen for generations.

In the blurb, which he drafted himself, for the original edition of *Casino Royale*, Fleming said: 'Like his brother Peter—a more famous author—he was educated at Eton, where he was Victor Ludorum two years in succession, a distinction only once equalled—presumably, he suggests, by another second son trying to compensate for a brilliant elder brother.'

Yet all this athletic success did not really compensate for all his brother's success. Presumably it earned him the coveted distinction of getting elected to the Eton Society, otherwise Pop, a self-elected club of some twenty older boys chosen for their athletic prowess, charm, and natural authority who enforce school discipline and in return enjoy special privileges, particularly of dress. But at Eton athletics have never carried the prestige attached to membership of the cricket eleven or the rowing eight, and at home it was all treated as rather a joke. Grannie Fleming was supposed to have told one of her friends at Cannes that she had just heard that her grandson Ian had been made Victor Ludendorff at Eton. 'Yes, and little Richard', Peter Fleming added artfully, 'has won the Eton knitting prize.'

Mrs Val was pleased but not appeased; her mind was still not easy about her second son. She had sold Pitt House in 1923 and was now living in Turner's House, Cheyne Walk, Chelsea: a beautiful house right on the river, with Turner's big studio at the back, decorated now with gold wallpaper. It was a superb place for entertaining. She liked celebrities and for a while gave very good parties: one of her lions was Augustus John, who had already painted several of the portraits of her which hung on the studio walls.

Mrs Fleming valued her social success without becoming its slave or relaxing her superintendence of the boys. Certainly the news of Ian's success in the Victor Ludorum can hardly have compensated for the yellow tickets he had been collecting for bad work or the story she heard that the Head Master had given him a birching five minutes before he set off to win the cross-country race. It was now that she began to fear that Ian would somehow let the family down and that he was all set to become the black sheep of the Flemings.

Children have a habit of living up to the fears of their parents, and there seems something almost deliberate in the way Ian Fleming allowed himself to go to pieces during his last year at Eton. Normally, after the age of sixteen, any boy of reasonable ability went on to prepare for university. Mrs Fleming decided against this: she felt that the best thing for her wayward son would be a career in the Army— a good Scots regiment like the Black Watch would be highly suitable, and he looked very fine in the kilt. For this he would first have to go to the Royal Military College at Sandhurst, and in order to prepare for the Sandhurst examination Ian Fleming was placed, at the age of sixteen, in the Army Class at Eton.

'This was an unheard-of thing for someone like Ian,' says his friend Hilary Bray, whose name Fleming was later to appropriate for one of his characters. 'In those days the Army Class was the very bottom of the school, the wastepaper basket for none but the dullest boys.' Yet for someone like Fleming there may have been a certain satisfaction in having his role of black sheep confirmed and in being able to withdraw entirely from the struggle to succeed. For it was now that a streak of real irresponsibility began to show. Very likely he no longer cared greatly what happened. But Mr Slater did.

There was trouble about a car. Boys were not allowed cars during term-time, but Ian Fleming, who owned an old khaki-coloured Standard tourer, found somewhere to garage it in Windsor and used it for illicit trips to London whenever there was a chance to escape. His friend Ivar Bryce remembers playing truant with him one afternoon and driving up to the Wembley Exhibition, which King George V had just opened.

There was also trouble with girls. Like motor-cars, they were forbidden in term-time, and once again the red-faced Mr Slater found out. He managed to avoid the scandal of expelling the boy. Luckily, Mrs Val agreed that it might be best for Ian to leave school a term early to go to a cramming establishment specializing in getting boys through the Sandhurst examination—there was a Colonel Trevor at Newport Pagnell who was highly spoken of. And after that, before embarking on his first term at Sandhurst in September, he could go abroad, to the Austrian Tyrol, to study; Lord Ellesmere's nephew had been sent to a highly satisfactory establishment there. It was settled. Like many a boy before him, like a latter-day Steerforth, Ian Fleming left school under a cloud.

II

There is an undeniable elegance and precision about the Royal Military College (it is now called Academy), with its smoothly gravelled parade ground, its well-regulated shrubberies, the calm-pillared Georgian dignity of Old Building Square. Away from the buildings, though, people have noticed an odd resemblance between those miles of scrubby heathland around Camberley and the sparse, bitter lands of Prussia: and in the autumn of 1926, when Gentleman Cadet Ian Lancaster Fleming joined No. 5 Company under Major the Lord Ailwyn, D.S.O., M.C., Sandhurst still had something of the atmosphere of a highly disciplined Prussian military academy. As soon as he set foot in the place Cadet Fleming must have realized what a mistake it had been ever to think of becoming a soldier. The first six weeks did nothing to make him change his mind.

It was a searing disappointment, for after the setbacks of

Eton he had arrived at Sandhurst with a sense of justifiable achievement. He must have worked hard at Newport Pagnell, for he passed sixth for the whole country in the Sandhurst entrance examination and was awarded a prize cadetship. When he left, Colonel Trevor had written enthusiastically about him to Mrs Val: 'He is an exceptionally nice fellow to live with—manly and sensible beyond his years. Here he is quite a triton among minnows. He ought to make an *excellent* soldier, provided always that the Ladies don't ruin him.' That last sentence might have given Mrs Val a moment's uneasiness, but to start with at any rate it was not the Ladies who were the trouble.

If some malevolent deity had tried to create an environment specially calculated to bring out the worst in Ian Fleming it would inevitably have contained a strong element of the spirit of the old Sandhurst. During his first six weeks Cadet Fleming was on the square for most of the day being knocked into shape by the Guards drill instructors for whom Sandhurst was famous: the standard of drill was exceptionally high and the cadets were expected to approach it during this preliminary period. When not being drilled Cadet Fleming found himself being submitted to intensive physical training, fitted for his various uniforms, tested as a horseman. It was after a 'horrible experience in the Cavalry School at Sandhurst' that Fleming said how profoundly he 'agreed with whoever said that horses are dangerous at both ends and uncomfortable in the middle'.

It must all have come as a shock to a boy who had already begun to bridle against so tolerant and individualistic a school as Eton. In those days the aim of the first term at Sandhurst was to turn simple schoolboys into a set of eager, pugnacious, games-playing, rifle-slapping self-denying automata. Discipline was strict, keenness a god. Practically from the moment Cadet Fleming left his pillow in the morning to his returning to it at night his time was in mortgage to the college. Infringement of the rules was serious. A missed roll call or a speck of fluff on a tunic meant 'losing one's name' and with it one's meagre privileges. For a while Cadet Fleming tried to make the best of things, but for one of his temperament there was not a great deal to make the best of. He soon gave up the struggle.

Perhaps he hoped to be thrown out; perhaps he was past caring. He took the minimum of trouble with his work and fled whenever he could. It was always possible to persuade the Cadet Corporal to sign you in at the evening roll call if you were prepared to take the risk, and there was a girl in Camberley he had grown quite fond of. Finally, after an evening trip to London in his Standard, Cadet Fleming was caught climbing into college and all privileges were stopped for his intermediate term. As this meant virtual confinement to barracks for six months he seems to have decided that the time had come for his military career to draw to a close.

In May 1927, wearing Sandhurst's pale-blue shorts and regulation singlet, he represented the college in the Woolwich-Sandhurst-Cranwell athletics match at Queens Club. The Central Band of the Royal Air Force, by permission of the Air Council, played selections from Waldteufel and Puccini, and Cadet Fleming, the only Old Etonian to compete, came second in the 120 yards hurdle with a time of 16½ seconds. It was the last time he ever ran in a race and almost the last part he played as a Gentleman Cadet.

'He could do really well if only he would realize that as he is at Sandhurst he might just as well make the best of what is, to him, a bad job and settle down . . .' wrote Major the Lord Ailwyn at the end of that term's report. But Cadet Fleming had no intention now of trying to make the best of a lifetime as a regular Army officer. He dropped a postcard to the Commandant, Major-General C. E. Corkran, C.B., C.M.G., telling him so.

It is hard not to feel sorry for Mrs Val when she heard that her second son was not going to be a soldier after all. After the trouble at Eton it had seemed like a genuine solution, and the tartan of the Black Watch would have suited him so well.

She was extremely upset and must have asked herself whatever was to become of this difficult, good-looking son of hers. Perhaps he wondered himself.

CHAPTER FOUR

THE GOLDEN TIME

In the mid-1920s the travel agents had yet to come to Kitzbühel. Tucked away in its valley in the shadow of the towering Kitzbüheler Horn, it was a picturesque, sleepy little Tyrolean market town, one which has now been buried for good beneath the booming international ski resort of today. In 1926 the Grand Hotel, with its two hundred bedrooms, was not very old, the north end of the town was still dominated by the fifteenth-century church of St Andreas, and what visitors there were arrived mainly in the summer, a snobbish, wealthy little crowd from Vienna whose smart talk and fast living could still sometimes raise the eyebrows of the local people.

These summer residents took little notice of an English couple named Forbes Dennis who had settled in the neighbourhood. They were not wealthy like most English visitors, and they seemed very serious—to the young things from Vienna this made them appear rather odd. Besides, it appeared that they were running some kind of idealistic educational establishment, first at a villa called the Waldschütz and then at a large chalet, the Tennerhof, on the opposite slope. Forbes Dennis was a tall, aristocratic-looking Scot who had been badly wounded in the war; his wife was a benign but striking-looking woman with brilliant eyes and a great halo of prematurely white hair. She was of Quaker stock, had run a boys' club in the East End of London when she was seventeen, had recently come through an attack of tuberculosis, and was the author of several novels (including one, *Old Wine*, which had attracted considerable attention) under her maiden name of Phyllis Bottome.

After a great deal of earnest thought the Forbes Dennises had decided to undertake an experiment in education, and for this purpose they established themselves in Kitzbühel in 1924. In those days there were always a number of young men of good family who needed to learn German to complete

In the junior sports
at Eton Ian Fleming
won eight events
out of ten in 1924,
including the mile
(*above*). As a senior
he was Victor
Ludorum twice
running, in 1925
and 1926; here he is
shown winning the
long jump in the
latter year

After Eton and Sandhurst Fleming lived a student life at Kitzbühel in the Austrian Tyrol—'that golden time when the sun always shone'. Attracted to the young Englishman were the girls on holiday from Vienna. The friend next to him (*below*) is Lisl Popper

their education or to enter business or the Foreign Office, and Forbes Dennis was an excellent linguist. He also knew the sort of people—his family was well-connected—who would entrust their sons to his care during these formative months of late adolescence, and after the Waldschütz the Tennerhof, with its apple trees, its pure air and its spacious pine-smelling interior, was the perfect setting for the experiment he had in mind.

It was not intended to be a mere language-cramming establishment. Without children of their own, the Forbes Dennises were great idealists with an aggressive sympathy for the young. They were anxious to find out how big a part psychology and educational theory could play in curing the ills of nations, and the Tennerhof—part community, part educational laboratory—was to be the visible expression of all they believed in.

Lord Ellesmere sent his nephew Cyril Egerton as one of the first pupils, and it was through Mrs Egerton that the Forbes Dennises came to be mentioned to Mrs Val Fleming. She was interested because it sounded exactly the place to keep young Ian out of mischief. So it was that on a bright July morning he stepped off the Arlberg Express and took in Kitzbühel. He seems to have played things very cool.

Forbes Dennis was at the station to meet him. 'My first impression of Ian was that he was very good-looking, very arrogant, very Etonian and very prickly. What the French call *difficile*. It was almost impossible to get through his defences, and he showed no great inclination to work. We were reading André Maurois's *Ariel* in French, and Ian made a great show of not liking it. I learned later that he wrote to his mother complaining that he was being worked far too hard.'

With Sandhurst before him it was inevitable that these few weeks at Kitzbühel should have appeared to Fleming as a mere interlude. He wore a dark-blue shirt—the first in the history of the place—and made a great impression on the young girls in the Café Reisch. He swam a lot in the Schwarzsee and climbed the Kitzbüheler Horn before dawn to watch the sun rise over the Eastern Alps. He preferred all this to André Maurois.

Yet, as it turned out, Kitzbühel was to become more than just a passing incident in his life or simply a place for a holiday. For in the following spring, while an increasingly frustrated Cadet Fleming was stamping and saluting his way across the rainswept parade grounds of Camberley, Ernan Forbes Dennis made a journey the results of which were to influence Ian Fleming for the rest of his life. It happened in this way.

As the experiment grew the Forbes Dennises began to feel the need for expert advice in dealing with some of the problem adolescents who came their way. They had heard that in Vienna there was a doctor called Alfred Adler who specialized in such work, and Forbes Dennis decided to pay him a visit.

At this time the fame of Adler was still confined almost entirely to his native Vienna. It was sixteen years since he had broken away from Freud, but the bitterness between the Freudians and the Adlerians remained, and while Freud was becoming an international figure Adler had worked on in Vienna as a specialist in nervous diseases, building up a small group of disciples and delivering his weekly lectures at the *Volksheim*. Apart from the clash in temperament between the two men, the real source of their break was to be found in a fundamental disagreement over the psychology of nervous disease. Adler had come to dispute Freud's insistence on the primary importance of infantile sexuality; instead he believed that neuroses should be traced to the early struggles of the developing infant to assert his personality against his environment—particularly the environment of the home and the family. 'Every neurosis', he had proclaimed in the first of the original twelve tenets of his *Individual Psychology* of 1913, 'can be understood as an attempt to free oneself from a feeling of inferiority in order to gain a feeling of superiority', and the remainder of his work and life was concerned with building on the implications of this central idea.

Forbes Dennis knew little of this when he called on Adler at his consulting-room in the old quarter of Vienna. 'All I saw was this funny, tubby little man who offered me a cigarette and asked what I wanted. I tried to explain and he asked me if I'd read any of his books. I said, "No. Have you written any?" And he pointed to a shelf above his head. When I'd scribbled down a few titles he told me to read them and then come back in a year's time. That was my first interview with Alfred Adler.'

For Forbes Dennis and for his wife as well this was to be the start of a great friendship: Forbes Dennis was to become one of the closest admirers of Adler and Phyllis Bottome his official biographer. To begin with they both grappled with Adler's lectures in the original German during their spare time at Kitzbühel. They were greatly impressed; and it was at this point that the two eldest Fleming boys arrived. For Peter came to Kitzbühel that summer only a month or two before the crestfallen Ian arrived from Sandhurst. If Alfred Adler had picked the young men in person it is hard to think of an apter pair as a demonstration of his theories on first and second sons.

Peter Fleming arrived during the long vacation of 1927 from Christ Church. At nineteen he felt the need to brush up his German, and Forbes Dennis found him the perfect pupil, with a 'wonderfully disciplined intelligence which went through German like a razor through butter'. Even then Forbes Dennis was struck by the contrast between this and what he remembered of Ian from the previous summer. 'Peter was the sort of thoroughbred who comes out of the stable glossy, confident, superior to all the other horses, a natural winner. Whereas Ian had been the sort of horse that arrives sweating and nervous at the starting-post, more likely to throw its rider than win its race.'

Forbes Dennis was to have a chance of observing the contrast between these two ill-matched brothers in greater detail; for it was not long after Peter Fleming had returned to England that he heard of Ian's disgrace. Forbes Dennis wrote to Mrs Fleming asking for news, and she told him that she was terribly worried: with this Sandhurst business on top of all the trouble at Eton she could see no future for Ian at all. She was determined that all her sons should be a credit to her and the family. If they were not she would rather have nothing to do with them, and she had practically made up her mind to send Ian off with a one-way ticket to Australia.

For Forbes Dennis this was the sort of challenge his experiment existed to cope with: 'I said, "Why not send him out to us for the winter and I'll see what we can do—then you can decide his future for yourself." '

So Ian Fleming boarded the Arlberg Express a second time and came back to Kitzbühel a sadder and sorrier figure than he had left it.

On the surface he was more difficult than ever—rude, resentful, determined to make the most of his disgrace. Underneath he was bored and chronically disappointed. 'He was like a weathercock as one mood chased another,' says Forbes Dennis. 'He couldn't give himself a chance. He had no workable aim at all to his life and all the usefulness had been squeezed out of him. He was immensely frustrated —who wouldn't be after trying to compete with an unbeatable brother like Peter? There he was, caught between his burning ambition and his constant disappointment. By the time he came to us, all he could really do successfully was to make a nuisance of himself. For he was a rebel, like most second sons.'

'We were all terribly excited when Ian arrived,' recalls one of the pupils at this time, 'and he made an enormous impression on Phyllis. He was like someone straight out of a novel, and he seemed the living proof of all her new Adlerian theories.'

For Adler believed that a child's first five years were the most important period of its life, and that during it he was apt to take a so-called *Gegenspieler*, a person to compete with at all costs in an endless neurotic duel. This *Gegenspieler* could be a parent, but more often, as Phyllis Bottome puts it in a book on Adler, 'the *Gegenspieler* is a contemporary brother or sister by whom the child has felt dethroned or otherwise outdistanced. The danger of the situation', she continues, 'lies in its unconsciousness; as well as in the fact that in almost any intimate relationship that follows, the child as he develops into the man will build up the same perpetual antagonism between himself and any beloved person.'

This in itself is interesting enough, yet it was only the start of what Adler had to say. The second tenet of his doctrine held that the struggle with these feelings of inferiority led to the steady isolation of the subject from the world around him. The world at large gets 'pushed aside by a mechanism consisting of hypersensitiveness and intolerance'. 'Thus estranged from reality,' continues tenet number four, 'the neurotic man lives a life of imagination and fantasy and employs a number of devices for enabling him to side-step the demands of reality, and for reaching out towards an ideal situation which would free him from any service to the community and absolve him from responsibility.' 'These exemptions and privileges of illness and suffering', continues tenet number five, 'give him a substitute for his original hazardous goal of superiority.'

It would be going too far to think of Ian Fleming as a neurotic even at this depressed and unhappy period of his life, yet whatever the rights and wrongs of this Adlerian analysis the parallels it shows with Fleming's attitudes when he came to Kitzbühel are not unremarkable, and they were hardly likely to be overlooked by the two highly intelligent apprentice Adlerians whom Mrs Valentine Fleming had entrusted with his care. At any rate, with sympathy and much common sense they set to work to help him according to the best Adlerian principles. They knew that what Alfred Adler called 'Social interest' had led to his attention being switched to child-guidance and education and that though he continued with his adult patients he was working to get at potential neurotics while they were still malleable—in the schools.

'To cure a neurosis,' Adler had written, 'it is necessary to change completely the whole upbringing of the patient and turn him definitely and unconditionally back into human society.' It was what they tried to do. Of course, Kitzbühel and the mountains must have helped a lot, and now that he was living abroad and his elder brother was up at Oxford, Fleming was out of the daunting orbit of his family for the first time in his life. Undoubtedly he would have come to terms with a lot of his difficulties in his own time; as it was, the most important thing Ernan Forbes Dennis and Phyllis Bottome did for him was to supply the aim and encouragement he had never found back in England.

Fleming was always touchingly grateful for this. In 1960 Phyllis Bottome wrote to him about his books and in his reply he thanked her and added, 'My life with you both is one of my most cherished memories, and heavens knows where I should be today without Ernan.' For it was Ernan Forbes Dennis who got him to work. 'At first', says Forbes Dennis, 'he had a terribly difficult time settling to it—until then the intellect had been Peter's zone. But once he did, he began to work very creditably. I then set an aim for him and decided on the Foreign Service.' This was exceedingly ambitious at a time when the Foreign Office examination was highly competitive and only a very few candidates from the best colleges at Oxford and Cambridge were normally accepted. 'But for someone with Ian's extreme ambition it had to be an important aim or nothing. At the same time as I advised him on his syllabus I picked on as many subjects as I could in order to get him interested in educating himself. Until then he was really very ignorant.'

The next few years were to provide Fleming with the equivalent of the university education he had missed by being sent to Sandhurst, and the course Forbes Dennis worked out for him was much wider and certainly more cosmopolitan than anything he would have acquired at an English university. In languages he seems to have inherited the same gift as Peter: his German was to be impeccable, his French fluent, and when later on he decided to learn Russian he picked it up with great facility.

More important than languages were books, and now for the first time in his life Fleming really began to read. He also conceived a passionate interest in books as objects—he loved the feel of a book, the style of its type, the excitement of a jacket—which was to last him the rest of his life. He described his early enthusiasm for reading and collecting in the chapter on Vienna in *Thrilling Cities*:

> I remember in those days before the war reading, thanks to the encouragement of the Forbes Dennises, the works of Kafka, Musil, the Zweigs, Arthur Schnitzler, Werfel, Rilke, von Hofmannsthal, and those bizarre psychologists Weininger and Groddeck—let alone the writings of Adler and Freud—and buying first editions (I used to collect them) illustrated by Kokoschka and Kubin.

Apart from German literature, he started on the set books of the London University English degree course—Shakespeare, Swift, Pope and Tennyson—and read a lot of French in his spare time. According to one of his Kitzbühel girl friends his favourite writer then was Perret, author of *Le Caporal Épinglé*, and he was an early devotee of Simenon's crime stories. Another girl friend recalls his taking several paper-bound Simenons with him on a motoring holiday through Switzerland, reading at a great rate as she drove and throwing the books out of the window as they were finished.

Once Fleming's interest was roused its range became quite impressive, and Forbes Dennis soon began extending the syllabus. 'The choice of subjects you could offer for the Foreign Office examination was very wide, and as I advised Ian I tried to give him subjects which would complete his education and also suit his temperament. So I centred his reading on the idea of studying the struggles of the individual throughout the ages to improve himself and better his conditions of life.' In this manner Fleming studied social history, anthropology and the history of science and technology, subjects in which he retained a lingering interest all his life. Yet the most lasting result of this idea of Forbes Dennis's was the remarkable library—now known as the Fleming Collection—which Fleming started to build up soon after he left the Tennerhof for good.

On one thing at least Forbes Dennis could congratulate himself: he had taught the weathercock to work. And it was his wife who made the young man begin to write. Fleming wrote in a letter to Phyllis Bottome not long before she died in 1963:

Looking back, I am sure that your influence had a great deal to do with the fact that, at any rate, three of us later became successful writers, and I remember clearly writing a rather bizarre short story for you which you criticized kindly and which was in fact the first thing I ever wrote.

These 'three successful writers' were Ralph Arnold, the novelist and publisher, Nigel Dennis—Ernan Forbes Dennis's nephew and the author of *Cards of Identity*—and of course Fleming himself.

All three were at the Tennerhof at the same time, all three came under the powerful influence of Phyllis Bottome. She was a woman of extraordinary enthusiasms, a born romantic whose feeling for the extremes of human emotion must have matched something in Fleming's own volatile nineteen-year-old nature. Her mornings she spent in seclusion writing her novels (Fleming rejoiced when in 1937 she made a great hit with *The Mortal Storm*); in the afternoon she rested and in the evening she appeared downstairs for dinner. It was then that she was at her best, and as she talked with the boys at dinner she loved to elaborate on imaginary happenings and grotesque characters in the village, building them up into extravagant tales of gothic adventure. Some of the boys followed her example, and Fleming was particularly good at it. He invented an endless story about Graf Schlick, the local lord of the manor who lived in the big castle at the end of the valley, and had him committing the most terrible crimes and perpetrating unspeakable tortures. At the end of one of these stories, when the Graf had performed multiple villainies upon some unprotesting virgin, retribution caught up with him. Unknown to him the girl suffered from leprosy, and Fleming closed his epic with a bloodcurdling account of how, at that very moment, the Graf was writhing in the last agonies of his just yet awful fate in the Schloss on the other side of the valley.

As well as encouraging the pupils of the Tennerhof to exercise their imaginations in this way Phyllis Bottome insisted on some of them putting anecdotes on paper. The short story Fleming referred to in his letter was called 'Death, on Two Occasions', and it was a remarkable tale to come from a nineteen-year-old author. It showed that Fleming already possessed that unusual combination of qualities which brought him success when he started writing about James Bond nearly a quarter of a century later. The sense of doom and melancholy was there; so was his fascination with the danger hiding behind everyday things. When Phyllis Bottome read the story she must have wondered just where this mixed-up young man's talent was going to land him.

Clearly the first stage of the Forbes Dennises' therapy was working—Fleming was rapidly gathering confidence in his own ability. But difficulties remained, as Forbes Dennis indicated in a letter he wrote to Mrs Valentine Fleming in the spring of 1928, replying to her anxious inquiry whether or not Ian really was a suitable candidate for the Diplomatic Service. In his reply he gave this thumbnail sketch of the young man:

Ian's qualities are considerable; his general intelligence is above the average; he has imagination and originality, with the power of self-expression. He has excellent taste, a love of books, and a definite desire both for truth and for knowledge. He is virile and ambitious; generous and kind-hearted.

But he is nineteen and going through the most difficult period of his development. With unusual physical and intellectual maturity he has not yet acquired mental discipline or working philosophy.

He therefore lacks stability and direction. His ambitions are considerable but vague. He has not yet learnt to enjoy work or to subordinate his impulses to his permanent aims, nor has he yet grown out of the schoolboy's fear of authority and the mental dishonesty which such fear often produces. This coupled with the strength of his desires, often make him fall below his theoretically high standards of conduct.

These facts should not cause dismay. He requires time to learn to handle a complex personality.

Somewhere within this complex personality Forbes Dennis saw the reactions of a badly spoilt child. 'I could only suppose', he says, 'that it was the father who was originally responsible—unconsciously, of course. That, after all, is usually the pattern you get in these cases of a family with an outstanding elder son. The father tries to make up for the mother's devotion to the eldest, and in Ian's case the father's death when the boy was nine must have made it worse.'

Whatever the cause, Fleming certainly was to exhibit all the symptoms of the badly spoilt child during the settling-in period at the Tennerhof. Although he was not by nature extravagant, he got into trouble with his mother for over-spending his allowance, and it was stopped; but when Forbes Dennis suggested to Mrs Fleming that she should give him a bonus of five pounds a month he kept within it. At times, feeling sorry for himself or in a mood of black melancholy, he would retire completely into his shell, often climbing the Kitzbüheler Horn alone and then coming down to a late solitary breakfast at a little café at the foot of the mountain. Forbes Dennis met him there on one occasion, and Fleming pointed to his half-finished breakfast. 'There, Ernan— scrambled eggs and coffee,' he sighed. 'The only two things in the whole world that never let you down.'

Forbes Dennis's theory was that much of Fleming's rest-lessness and extreme behaviour was part of a struggle to beat this sense of the inevitable disappointment at the heart of things. 'Ian was inclined to do everything to excess in a desperate attempt to get through to a mythical place where everything would be all right at last, where nothing would ever let him down again. And of course it never was and it never could be. In those days at the Tennerhof we used to read Ibsen a lot in German, and whenever we read *A Doll's House* I could never stop thinking how like Nora Ian was —that beautiful, unhappy girl who was always waiting for something *das Wunderbare* to happen, and who was always disappointed because it never did.'

Both Forbes Dennis and his wife were anxious for Fleming to meet Adler, but although Fleming read him and was immensely impressed he showed a notable lack of enthusiasm about a meeting. When Fleming finally did agree Adler was in America and he saw another Adlerian, Dr Seif. It was not a success. 'In Adler's psychology', says Forbes Dennis, 'there is always such an immediate reaction to having to face the truth about oneself that many people are thrown right off. Ian was. With his fears and his impatience he was not the man to take to any sort of real treatment. It might have just worked if he had seen Adler himself—Adler had such a sense of humour and reality that he might have been able to get through to him. But Seif couldn't manage it and Ian sat there in front of him and refused to speak.'

So there was no question of Adlerian aid for Ian Fleming, and the contradictions of his highly contradictory nature remained unresolved; instead what Kitzbühel and the Tennerhof did was to teach him to live with them. Here they succeeded. In that clear Alpine air, away from the restraints and heavy-handedness of England, all Fleming's vitality and high spirits came bubbling up and he began to enjoy the part which Phyllis Bottome, Ernan Forbes Dennis and Adler's Individual Psychology alloted him.

'When Ian turned up at the Tennerhof,' says Ralph Arnold, 'he seemed to be in quite appalling disgrace. He went out of his way to tell us all about it, and it was not until some time later, when I had learned what a born romantic he was, that I began to suspect that he might be rather enjoying the role. Several times I heard him going over the details of how he had left Sandhurst, how abominably his family thought he had behaved, how despicable his conduct seemed in his mother's eyes, and how he had been banished to the Tennerhof as a result. We were all very young and impressionable, and of course in no time at all Ian had established himself as the Tennerhof's prize exhibit, a sort of high romantic exile. And before long, old Ian was playing up his new role like nobody's business. The romantic, the practical joker, the fantasist in him all received an enormous fillip from the attention he was getting. Like his brother Peter, Ian was a natural-born actor and suddenly he found that this aura, this dark cloud of family disapproval, could be used. In that tiny picturesque Austrian village there was this slender, extraordinarily good-looking young Englishman who had been sent into exile for quarrelling with his family and the harsh inhuman world of a military academy. Before long I'm sure that's how he saw himself as he strode round Kitzbühel in his dark-blue shirt and heard people point him out and whisper with awe, "That's the man who insulted the commandant of his academy on a point of principle and was disowned by his family for ever." '

By freeing him of his feelings of inferiority, Kitzbühel was giving him a unique chance to enjoy his fantasy for all it was worth and to establish his personal ascendancy as well. Before long he was having the time of his life. Years later, when he was ill and famous, he wrote a letter to a friend in which he referred to these early days at Kitzbühel as 'that golden time when the sun always shone', and throughout the rest of his life he seems to have looked back on these years as the happiest of all. He loved the Austrian Tyrol and its great lonely mountains. He loved its people, who reminded him in some curiously sentimental way of the Highlanders of Scotland. He loved the skiing and the climbing and the freedom. And he loved the girls.

Fleming was an amorist by nature, but up to now the English girls he had known seem to have been either prudish or mercenary, boring or a source of trouble, and his frequently expressed objections to Englishwomen—that they never wash and have no idea how to make love properly—seem to have begun even before he came to Austria. It was all so different in Kitzbühel. No mothers to worry about, no families to offend, no moral codes to outrage, no entanglements that could not be forgotten by breakfast time. He looked at the girls and they fell into his lap.

During that first year at Kitzbühel he had three regular girl friends and any number of incidental affairs. In later life some women were powerfully attracted to him and some were not, but here his success was apparently universal. 'He was irresistible to women,' remarks Ralph Arnold, 'and he was the only man I have ever known who was.'

'He was quite ruthless about girls,' says one of the women who knew him then—'or perhaps a more apt word is absent-minded. Women were all a bit of a joke for Ian, a treat to enjoy but not to make any sort of fuss about afterwards. Of course, in those days this was a very unusual attitude to find in an Englishman, but I can assure you that it was very normal on the Continent and particularly in Vienna. Ian seemed to get the idea straight away and he behaved exactly as any young Viennese with his looks and his means would have been expected to behave.'

Conventional morality seemed to present him with no particular problem. 'Ian was totally amoral in sex,' says a former girl friend. Sometimes his association with these easy, eager girls from Vienna got him into trouble. On one occasion he was threatened with expulsion from the Tennerhof and there was a tearful repentance scene with Phyllis Bottome. Something must have gone wrong there: usually he managed to avoid hurting the gentle Forbes Dennises. It was—or it became—part of his system to keep his friendships locked away in separate cupboards. Nearly everyone who knew him well comments on the way he seemed to enjoy compartmentalizing his life, keeping his various sets of friends rigorously apart, so that those to whom he was very close in one role would not be aware of those equally close to him in another.

At any rate, he now began to enjoy two quite separate existences at Kitzbühel—one with the Forbes Dennises up at the Tennerhof, the other with the young things he met at the Café Reisch and with whom he swam and skied and walked and climbed and made love. To this second group Fleming seemed an altogether different creature from the clever, troubled young man of the Tennerhof.

Lisl Popper, the lifelong friend to whom he left £500 in his will, says, 'All the things people said about Ian later—his gloom, his melancholy, his solitariness—frankly amaze me. To all of us who knew him in Kitzbühel he was exactly the opposite—gay, carefree, terribly happy, the most exciting and vital sort of person. Not like an Englishman at all.' Later, summing up his sexual experience of those years, he wrote, somewhat ungratefully, 'Technique in bed is important, but alone it is the scornful coupling that makes the affairs of Austrians with Anglo-Saxons so fragmentary and in the end so distasteful.'

All the same, as he grew older he liked to remember the golden life of Kitzbühel, and it generated the nostalgia for the mountains and winter sports which was to appear in his books. It was now that he learned to ski. Apart from golf it was the only sport he ever really loved. He took to it with almost instant success and was soon skiing with such verve that Ralph Arnold was greatly impressed.

'Difficult to ski?' Fleming replied when Arnold asked him how on earth he had picked it up in so short a time. 'But, my dear fellow, surely it *can't* be difficult to ski? One just skis. One falls over or one doesn't fall over. It's as simple as that.'

Lisl Popper was less impressed than Arnold: 'Ian wasn't a good skier because he was a wild skier. He loved taking risks, and sometimes he got away with them and sometimes he fell very heavily. It wasn't pretty skiing, but for Ian it must have been exciting all right.'

This craving for excitement was not confined to skiing or to other material things. At Kitzbühel that 'life of imagination and fantasy' which Adler had written about was disclosed for the first time, and a few people were permitted to share it. 'Ian was always contriving situations,' says Ralph

44

Arnold, 'and then making life fit into them. He'd suggest hiring a car and taking a couple of girls off somewhere for the day on a trip, and almost at once it became fun because Ian made it fun. He'd invent a plot for us. We were being pursued down the mountain road by a car-load of dangerous international agents and we would finally destroy them because it turned out that we had a gun concealed along the exhaust pipe of our car.'

Arnold remembers driving with his friend in Fleming's old Standard tourer up a narrow mountain road in the wake of a large lorry loaded with heavy machinery precariously roped to the body. It was impossible for the car to pass, and to cover his impatience Fleming began inventing an elaborate situation of gangsters and a pair of British agents —the agents, outnumbered and outgunned, were in the lorry, the crooks in the car behind. As soon as the lorry reached the top of the narrow road the agents were for it. What were they to do? Fleming changed down to bottom gear as he explained the trick which Sir Hugo Drax in *Moonraker* was to employ some twenty-five years later from the Bowater lorry against James Bond's Bentley on Charing Hill. 'Simple, my dear fellow,' he said to Arnold. 'Climb out on the back of the lorry and slice through the ropes. Just think what would happen to us now if those ropes went and that machinery came crashing down. We'd all be smashed to smithereens.'

In fact, soon after this, reality took over and the Standard *was* smashed, in a manner appropriate to one of James Bond's private adventures. It happened on the light railway that used to run between Munich and Kufstein, crossing the main road on the way to Kitzbühel: as it was almost a toy train with one pair of coaches and a brightly polished engine, it had never been thought necessary to build a proper level-crossing for it. In summer, however, the corn grew very high, and anyone driving fast towards Kitzbühel was unable to see the track until the last minute. On this particular evening Fleming was driving to the Tennerhof from Munich, a matter of sixty miles, and he must have been rattling along at top speed in the Standard, for neither he nor the engine driver spotted each other until it was too late. The engine ploughed right through the front of the car, carrying remnants of it fifty yards along the track. Fleming was uninjured but badly shaken. For the rest of his life he seems to have sensed something dangerous and strangely exciting about light railways, and that small lethal railway of Scaramanga's in *The Man with the Golden Gun* carried on where the Munich–Kufstein train left off.

During his early months at the Tennerhof Fleming had another escape which he stored up and used with suitable embellishments in the avalanche scene in *On Her Majesty's Secret Service*. Not long after he had learned to ski one of the slopes above the Tennerhof was placed out of bounds because of the danger of avalanches. It immediately fascinated him, as risk and danger always did, and for several days he watched the empty slope until he became obsessed by the challenge. Even as a young man he was never one to rush needlessly into peril for the fun of it—his sense of danger was unusually sharp. When he finally took his skis and swept down the forbidden slopes he must have felt death very close to him: for the avalanche did start and he was buried up to his shoulders, but for once the fall was lighter than usual and he escaped with a few bruises and a twisted ankle. He was reckoned to have been very lucky, and next day his reputation as a wild romantic figure was greater than ever among the girls of the Café Reisch.

There was something in all this besides mere playing with danger. It was at Kitzbühel that several discerning friends began to comment on an element of self-denial and self-mortification which was beginning to appear in many of his escapades. His friend Selby Armitage says: 'Ian always had a frantic love of luxury. He longed for comfort, women, rich food and expensive cars. At the same time the more he enjoyed these things, the more he seemed to need to punish himself for doing so. This made his life a battle between self-indulgence and self-mortification. The more he enjoyed himself, the more he needed to punish himself afterwards.'

When Fleming was in his forties he was able to play out these feelings in his books, balancing James Bond's pleasures with the pains which earned them, the bed against the bastinado, the caviare against the carpet beater. At the age of nineteen, not having invented James Bond, Fleming had only himself to be hard on, and he was.

With the strain and the physical gruelling he imposed on himself, it must have been like the athletic feats for the double Victor Ludorum at Eton all over again. There was the same grim endurance, the same determined expression on the long thin face, the same pleasure in the pain he knew that he could bear. His body was very strong, and he enjoyed

46

staying up all night at a party and setting off into the mountains while it was still dark in order to reach the highest peaks as dawn was breaking. He delighted in the ice-cold waters of the lake, in the effort of long ski runs across hard country. Even so, his favourite self-discipline was always climbing. 'He positively seemed to enjoy the pain and the discomfort of it,' says one of his friends. 'I was climbing with him once when he was out of practice and he began to get a terrible cramp in his legs. Far from giving up and resting, Ian insisted on going on, with sweat pouring down his face and a look of terrible satisfaction as he overcame what must have been the most dreadful pain.'

All his life mountains represented something of immense importance to Fleming: a way of proving that his will was still in command of his body, a means of atoning for the formless sense of guilt he carried about with him and of asserting his identity through striving and harsh achievement, a way of punishing his body for the softness it succumbed to so easily. Even in his last years, when illness had put an end to most of the temptations he might have punished himself for, he would still struggle, sweating, purple in the face, to the top of Big Spruce, the 1200-foot peak that juts above the Bryce farm in Vermont.

It was at Kitzbühel that Fleming's cult of personal toughness really began, without, then or later, being the expression of a genuine inner toughness. Fleming was not a hard man—quite the reverse. He had an abnormally high sense of risk and danger, an unusual awareness of pain, he was hypersensitive, lacked confidence and found temptation irresistible. But as the snail has developed its shell to protect its vulnerability and its privacy, so now in late adolescence Fleming assumed his own shell of toughness to keep potential intruders at bay.

'Ian', says an old Etonian who knew him most of his life, 'was odd with everyone—terribly unpredictable. Even with old friends who wished him well that defence mechanism of his would spring into action and he would have to get in the first crack. I think he just felt that his fellow men didn't really like him.'

At Kitzbühel this unease usually showed itself in a certain surface ruthlessness, in a purposeful unconcern for people's feelings which cropped up particularly in his passion for practical jokes. Ralph Arnold remembers Fleming coming to him early one morning at the Tennerhof and announcing,

'Ralph, I've put you down for the Kitzbühel tennis tournament.' 'I was,' says Arnold, 'no good at all at tennis, so I told him I had no intention of playing anyone. "Now, now, Ralph," said Ian, "that's simply no way to speak. A lot's at stake in this. You must pull yourself together and get some sneakers and a pair of decent white flannels. We simply must put up a bit of a show, and it's all up to you."

'I should have known better, but I was rather taken in by all this, and I asked who I was supposed to be playing.

'"A fellow called Herr Bosch."

'"Is he any good?"

'"No—good heavens no. The man's an old ruin and anyone who knows how to hold a racquet could beat him."

'So off to the courts I go, only to find to my horror that waiting for me is not merely the biggest crowd I have ever seen in Kitzbühel but also Herr Bosch himself and that he is a quite alarming gentleman, much younger and more aggressive than I had ever supposed. It turned out later that he was Tyrolean champion or something of the sort, and to get the crowd to come and make the joke a bit more pointed Ian had passed word round that I was Southern Counties grass-court finalist. Of course, I got a terrible licking—the memory of it still haunts me. Afterwards Ian was so charming and amusing about it all that it was impossible to be really angry with him. Somehow he made it all right as he always could.'

CHAPTER FIVE

THE GIRL IN GENEVA

THIS Kitzbühel life went on for a year. Then Forbes Dennis decided that the time had come for Fleming to go to Munich, to continue his studies in a German family and at the same time become an external student of Munich University.

It is odd how little impression Munich and Ian Fleming seem to have made on each other, considering that at this time the Nazi party had its headquarters here and Hitler was improving the organization of his Brown House and looking for the opportunity to deal a real blow at the German Republic. But as usual Fleming steered clear of politics and kept himself to himself. There is no evidence that he ever attended a lecture at Munich University, although he certainly enrolled and wrote, as will be seen, of the 'turmoil' of his work there, and later was in the habit of describing it as one of his two *almae matres*.

In fact, in Munich he seems to have carried on more or less the same sort of student life as he led at the Tennerhof. He continued to read a lot. He charmed his hosts, who still remember him as the most delightful student ever to stay in their house. He began learning Russian. His spells of black melancholy became less frequent.

Now that he was alone in Munich he showed for the first time that he was capable of coping with life on his own, and it was at this point that his character and his way of life took on a pattern that was to be emphasized later on—urbanity and a certain aloofness against a background of comfort and ease, care with money, a handful of real friends kept carefully apart from a handful of mistresses, periods of extreme vitality combined with periods of sloth, solitariness and despair, an eagerness to get into the intellectual swim provided not too much hard work was required to stay there. It is unlikely that he would have described himself as happy, but he certainly enjoyed himself now in his own way. Significantly, there were no more short stories; and still more significantly, relations seem to have been entirely restored with Mama.

At the end of November 1929, she fulfilled a long-standing promise and descended upon Munich to see how he was getting on. Fleming described what happened in an assured, slightly priggish letter to old Lady Sackville at Knole:

Thank you most awfully for your letter which arrived with Mama, and which I would have answered before but for the turmoil of work into which I was swept, when Mama left, at the University. She tells me you are not very well—England at this time of the year is enough to make anybody ill—why not go abroad and have a rest—it did Mama a lot of good, or so she says, and you would anyway escape the November weather?

Yes. I am much too apt to be affected by externals. They force themselves so much upon one that it is difficult to ignore them unless one is a hermit or a fanatic of some sort, in which case one is generally a large brain with a tiny little forgotten body attached. But when one is fairly equal parts brain and body—as I am—neither half is strong enough to exclude the other, so consequently at least half my life is made up of externals, which always try their best to intrude on my poor other half—however, it's better than extremes in either direction.

Mama was looking awfully well when she left, and I got a proud postcard from Dover to say that she had conquered the bad crossing and not been ill. She was most energetic here, and rushed from gallery to gallery flourishing her ten words of German with an intrepidity and unselfconsciousness which put my inborn fear of foreigners to shame.

She bought, of course, all sorts of ridiculous things for all of us, and spent the whole time running out of money, until I had to be quite firm about further expenditure—she tips everybody colossally—waiters, servants, everyone, and I'm sure the whole of Munich was sorry she went. She still forms a topic of admiring comment in the family where I am here.

I can hear my Russian teacher coming down the passage, and now I shall have to explain why I haven't learnt my verbs—I hope you don't mind being an excuse.

Thank you again more than I can say for your letter, and do take my advice about going abroad.

This attitude of tolerant amazement at his remarkable parent was one that Fleming tried to maintain for the rest of his life. Already he seems to have recognized her as a unique creation, and on this occasion his air of benign responsibility for her was justified. For between the forays into the art galleries and the full-scale offensives on the shops he seems to have convinced her that he would make a splendid diplomat. As a result his allowance was to continue and his name was to go forward for the Foreign Office examination.

In July he had returned to Kitzbühel to discuss the future with Forbes Dennis, who for the first time began to believe that Fleming really had a chance in the examination, provided he improved his French. Geneva was the nearest place for this, and Forbes Dennis arranged things, putting forward Fleming's name as an external student at Geneva University and recommending a pension in the rue de Lausanne kept by a professor's widow—'terribly respectable, the very acme of student pensions in Geneva'.

It was hardly the place for Ian Fleming, and he soon moved into a room at the Hotel du Lac along the shores of Lake Geneva at Coppet, and then into a room of his own at Mies. Indeed here, in Geneva, he showed a supreme capacity for pleasing himself and doing virtually what he liked. Geneva seems to have fascinated him; that 'clean, tidy, God-fearing city of Calvin' brought out the same feelings of love-hate that he felt for the Calvinist cities of Scotland.

As he was to write when he included it, somewhat oddly, in his round-up of *Thrilling Cities* of the world:

The beautiful lake, plus the highest fountain in the world and the Rhône that thunders so majestically through the town—all this and Mont Blanc too, do not make Geneva a happy town. The spirit of Calvin, expressed in the ugly and uncompromising cathedral that dominates the city, seems to brood like a thunderous conscience over the inhabitants. In the rue des Granges, adjoining the cathedral, the great patrician families, the de Candoles, de Saussures, Pictets, set a frightening tone of respectability and strait-laced behaviour from which the lesser Genevese take their example.

In 1929 he seems to have taken on the probity, reserve and rectitude of the inhabitants of Geneva almost single-handed. If they remained that way by the time he left at the end of 1930 it was not his fault. For there was something about Geneva that obsessed him:

. . . the quality that makes a thriller-writer want to take a tin-opener and find out what goes on behind the façade, behind the great families who keep the banner of Calvin flying behind the lace curtains in their fortresses in the rue des Granges, the secrets behind the bronze grilles of the great Swiss banking corporations, the hidden turmoil behind the beautiful, bland face of the country.

Geneva was a small world, and Fleming made a great impression on the group of students, junior diplomats and wealthy young Genevese who formed what one of them called, even as late as 1930, the *jeunesse dorée* of Geneva. At last he was really free. There was no one to criticize, no one to intrude on his private world. He could keep to himself when he wanted to or enjoy himself entirely on his own terms. And now at twenty-one he began to show that strange off-hand glamour which stuck with him for the rest of his life. 'There was always something faintly glittering about him,' says one of his friends. To Forbes Dennis he suddenly appeared 'half Faust, half Byron'. And his friend Martin Hill says that he 'wanted to do everything, taste everything, read everything. You just mentioned something to Ian, and he immediately had to do it. He wasn't particularly popular among the solider citizens of Geneva. None of us was really. But Ian was always the one who stood out, with his black Buick, his Old Etonian tie and his compulsion to kid anyone who was old or stuffy or who took himself too seriously.'

Geneva was an odd completion to an odd education, but it was the only sort of student life which Fleming could have endured or that would have endured him. Instead of the restraints of English university life there were long days on the lake, skiing expeditions to the mountains, picnics in the woods behind Coppet. Again, no one remembers his attending a lecture at the university, but his French improved and he carried on with his Russian, reading Lermontov and Turgenev in the original with a devoted White Russian named Maslov who addressed him as 'Ivan Valentinovitch'.

He was as attractive to the girls of Geneva as he had been to the girls of Kitzbühel—more so, perhaps, for this saturnine young Englishman with, as one of them said, the 'cruel face' (Bond in due course was to have a cruel face), must have held an irresistible appeal to those carefully nurtured puritan maidens. But soon, instead of a succession of light-hearted, Austrian-style affairs, Ian Fleming began going steady. It was a new phenomenon and his friends asked themselves how long it would last.

The girl was young, pretty and amusing—a French-Swiss Protestant whose father was an extremely respectable landowner near Geneva. Perhaps Ian Fleming was not every Swiss landowner's ideal as a suitor for a marriageable

Küsnacht•Zürich
Seestrasse 228   29. Nov. 29.

J. Fleming, Esq., rue Toepffer, Genève.

Dear Sir,

I give you my authorization for trans-
lating my speech on Paracelsus with the understanding that you give
me information about your agreement with the publisher, as I want
to reserve the right to reproduce the paper in a collection of
papers to be published at a later date. I'm glad you made the acquaintance of Mrs. Keller. She is indeed quite capable of giving
you a fair idea of my work.

Sincerely yours

C.G. Jung

Jung writes to Fleming. While a student at Geneva University Fleming sought permission to translate a lecture by Jung on Paracelsus. Later he showed his translation to Edith Sitwell, and they planned to write a joint book on the sixteenth-century Swiss physician and philosopher.

daughter, but the girl was high-spirited, her mother succumbed to the Fleming charm, and at the age of twenty-one Ian Fleming found himself unofficially engaged.

Perhaps he was genuinely in love, perhaps it was a new role to play, perhaps the sheer impossibility of marriage appealed to his natural romanticism. For he had no prospects until he had passed the Foreign Office examination and he was hardly the man for love in a garret. To support a wife in the style to which *he* was accustomed would require considerable help from his family; but it was to be several months before the news of the engagement filtered back from Switzerland to Mrs Val in Chelsea, and in the meantime Fleming continued in the unusual role of the fond and reasonably faithful fiancé. Otherwise the prospect of marriage scarcely changed him.

To those he met he still appeared a sophisticated, knowing young intellectual with a taste for anything new enough to capture his attention. 'His room,' says one friend, 'used to be so untidy that I thought it must be intentional. It was always littered with ashtrays, grey flannel trousers, old love letters, uncleaned shoes and parcels of books which had just arrived by post from London or Vienna. There would be the latest novels of Huxley and D. H. Lawrence and Thomas Mann. He got terribly excited by *The Magic Mountain* when it came out. And he subscribed to all the avant garde literary magazines of the day.'

The one thing he did not do was to write anything of his own. But he had great theories and ideas about the novel he was *going* to write and used to send long earnest letters on the subject to his friend Selby Armitage back in London. Years later, when Armitage showed them to him, Fleming became very embarrassed, asked for them back, and apparently destroyed them. They were not among his papers after his death.

While Fleming was a student at Geneva it seemed as if his future was already mapped out: a cultured dilettante, a highbrow littérateur of private means, eccentric tastes, and no conceivable interest in anything that could appeal to the public in general. He collected his first editions and prints by Kokoschka and Picasso. He spoke to Einstein at a League of Nations reception and was very impressed; he bought an old passport that had belonged to Mussolini; through Forbes Dennis he received written permission from Jung to translate a lecture he had delivered on that famous forerunner of modern science, Paracelsus. Fleming never said why this particular lecture of Jung's caught his imagination, but the translation was duly completed, and although it was never published he was to show it years later to Edith Sitwell and suggest it as the basis for a joint book on Paracelsus.

But, culture apart, Fleming now had his future to worry about, particularly since he was thinking of marriage, and by the autumn of 1930 next summer's Foreign Office examination began to loom. Some of his friends thought the mere idea of Ian Fleming as a diplomat patently absurd, but he suddenly started taking it seriously: far more was at stake for him than any of the *jeunesse dorée* of Geneva can have suspected. He started work on the special subjects like psychology and anthropology which Forbes Dennis had suggested. He took a temporary job with the Bureau of Intellectual Co-operation of the League of Nations to gain some experience as an international civil servant. His

French accent improved. And when he returned to London that Christmas he found that his mother was now rather excited at the prospect of having a diplomat for a son. Perhaps things were working out after all—Ian would look far better as an ambassador than an army officer. She even agreed to meet the young lady from Geneva; although she insisted that they were far too young to think of marriage he could certainly invite her over if he wanted to.

Everything really depended on his passing the examination: he could redeem the past and guarantee his future. Mrs Val had confidence in him now. All that was needed was the sort of effort he had once put into becoming Victor Ludorum.

His Majesty's Commissioners for the Civil Service examined sixty-two applicants for the Foreign Office and Diplomatic Service that year, and the examinations, held in Burlington Gardens, were spread out over ten days. The competition was extreme. As usual, some of the brightest of that year's young men from Oxford and Cambridge were sitting, and it was no secret that only two or three places would be offered.

When the examination was over there was a four-week wait for the results. Ian Fleming came twenty-fifth out of the sixty-two. He got his lowest marks for his English essay—twenty out of a hundred.

It was a failure, as we shall see, that changed his life and helped to wreck his idea of marriage.

CHAPTER SIX

THE WATCHER AT THE TRIAL

I

BEFORE the war the most exciting train in Europe was the Nord-Express, which left Berlin Central at six p.m. for Warsaw and Moscow, where it made the connection with the Trans-Siberian Express. As Fleming climbed aboard it on the evening of April 6th, 1933, in his black-and-white check suit and with his two grey suitcases and his Imperial portable, it must have been a memorable moment in his life: at last he was on to a real adventure.

It had all been arranged with supreme efficiency—the precise instructions, the £200 in blue-and-yellow travellers' cheques, the official identity card with his photograph and the endorsement from the Foreign Office, the visa in his passport with the red stamps and the Cyrillic characters.

He had caught the morning Lufthansa flight from Croydon to Berlin—this in itself was still an adventure in those days. The big, lumbering three-engined Junkers aircraft took five hours for the journey across the North Sea and Holland, and passengers were given sandwiches and thermos coffee to keep up their spirits. At Berlin they had arranged for a car to meet him, and when he was safely aboard the train for Warsaw and Moscow he found they had even booked him a place at the first sitting in the *Speisewagen*. He was hungry and the food was good. Then came a first-class sleeper to himself as the great train ran eastwards across the plains of Prussia. Always a light sleeper, he woke just after midnight when the train halted for its scheduled sixty-four-minute stop in the empty, dimly lit station at Poznan. At dawn, when they reached Warsaw, he strolled up and down the platform looking on as most of the passengers left. For the rest of the day he sat alone in his compartment reading Turgenev and watching the unfamiliar country and the small grey towns through the carriage window as the train trundled on farther and farther east.

By late afternoon it had begun to snow; and just after six the train, still on time, passed the two red-and-white posts marking the border between Poland and Russia and slowed down to walking pace. It stopped altogether at the small dingy station with its newly built customs house and the hammer and sickle and 'Workers of the World Unite' painted on its drab walls in four languages. The first part of Fleming's journey was over, and the Moscow train was waiting on the other platform. There were porters here but they were not allowed to accept tips—it was a demonstration to visitors that Russia was trying to abolish every form of bribery. The customs men and the police who inspected this particular visitor's papers made no difficulty, and the Russian guard in his grey, neck-buttoning tunic was friendly enough as he showed Fleming to his private compartment on the Moscow train.

This train was to be his first taste of the endless contrasts he was to find in this land of contrasts. The Moscow express still used Victorian-style carriages which had somehow survived the Revolution, and Fleming's compartment had brass and mahogany fittings, massive Staffordshire wash-basin and neatly appointed table with lace-fringed tablecloth and rose silk shaded lamp. There was no need to book a place in the dining-car of this train: only foreigners and high Party members could afford a meal, and he had it almost entirely to himself. The pound was worth ten roubles at the official rate but, because of inflation, sold unofficially for more than two hundred in Moscow.

Night falls quickly in April in this part of the world, but Fleming had just a chance to see the flat snow-covered countryside—an unending landscape of fir and birch—of White Russia, which was still in the grip of the famine of that terrible winter in which many thousands had died. At ten next morning—a cold sharp day even for Moscow at that time of the year—the express steamed into the Byelo Russky station. Not bothering to pause to unpack his overcoat, Fleming looked eagerly for the man who was to meet him on the platform. He was an American and only a couple of years older than Fleming, a cheerful humorous young man called Robin Kinkead.

'I've booked you in at National Hotel,' he said, as they shook hands. 'Of course, it's not the Ritz, but it's better than anywhere else in Moscow. At least they've got a bar, and you sometimes get hot water.'

The young man had a black seven-seater Lincoln waiting outside the station, and they drove off in it along Tverskaya

57

Street, now Gorki Street. As Fleming looked out at the long melancholy streets, the crowded trams, the whole incredibly drab Moscow scene with the empty shops, the big pictures of Lenin, and the squat, badly dressed Muscovites, he must suddenly have realized how incongruous he appeared. For he turned to Kinkead and began to apologize for his check suit. 'You see, my dear fellow, I had it made some time ago at the Fifty Shilling tailors. I'd always wanted to try one of their suits, but since I got it I've never quite had the nerve to wear it. Somehow I thought I might get away with it out here.' Kinkead seemed delighted. 'It's fine—everyone thinks that you English always wear check suits.'

They laughed and began to talk about the business on hand.

II

The failure in the Foreign Office examination of 1931 had been a serious setback for Ian Fleming, worse in its way than anything that had happened at Eton or Sandhurst. It shook his confidence and was such a blow to his pride that for the rest of his life he was to cover up the full extent of his defeat by explaining that he had come seventh—virtually a pass mark—in a year when, purely through bad luck, only five candidates were accepted.

It also meant that he had had to look to his mother for money and somewhere to live. After four years of freedom abroad it can hardly have been easy for him to have settled back, as he did, into the matriarchal routine of Cheyne Walk, particularly with Mrs Val doing her best to make him keep regular hours and stay within his slender allowance. 'If there's one subject we have more arguments about than sex it's money,' he confided wearily to his friend Percy Muir.

It was an uneasy relationship for both of them, for they resembled each other in their egoism and their strength of purpose. Sometimes he would win simply by making her laugh; but if a genuine point of principle arose she could always get her way in the end, and if it had come to a show-down there was always the authority of his father's will allowing her to cut him out of his inheritance.

At any rate, deep maternal disapproval finally wrecked his engagement. When his fiancée came to Cheyne Walk Mrs Val made it quite clear what she thought about the girl and the idea of the marriage. If she was not very subtle about it she seems at least to have known her son better than he knew himself. There were tears and there were recriminations, but when the girl returned to Geneva Ian Fleming did not travel with her. He must have found it very humiliating even if, possibly, he was conscious of a feeling of slight relief. To his men friends he was very bitter about it all: after this he would never dream of marrying anyone. 'I'm going to be quite bloody-minded about women from now on,' he told Ralph Arnold. 'I'm just going to take what I want without any scruples at all.'

Bitter he may have been; but he stayed on in Cheyne Walk, and it was through his mother that he finally got a job that really suited him. Sir Roderick Jones, the head of Reuters, agreed to see him: he liked the look of him and offered him a six months' trial with the news agency at a salary of £300 a year. The young man was lucky. Reuters was being rejuvenated at the time, and although he was without journalistic experience Fleming was exactly the sort of energetic, sophisticated, reasonably cultivated young man whom Roderick Jones was after. For more than a year Fleming worked in the news room of the old Reuters building in Carmelite Street, by the Embankment, getting on particularly well with the news editor, Bernard Rickatson-Hatt, another of Jones's discoveries. The work was mostly the routine sub-editing of the avalanche of foreign copy which descended on the agency from every quarter of the globe, but occasionally Fleming would be offered a reporting job—twice he covered motor-racing at Brooklands. Then something much more exciting turned up. It was what took him to Moscow and gave him an opportunity to show what he could really do.

III

The trial of the six British engineers of the Metropolitan-Vickers Electrical Company, arrested by the O.G.P.U. in March 1933, on charges of espionage and wrecking, is now part of history, taking its place with the great purges and the State trials which followed as part of the ice age which Stalin imposed on the Russian nation in the mid-'thirties. But to this day it remains something of a mystery. The pattern was to become familiar enough: the sudden arrests, the startling accusations, the fantastic confessions undisclosed until the prisoners finally appeared before the military judge, whose chief task in court was merely to demonstrate their guilt to the world. Justice in the Western sense of the word did not arise in these trials: Soviet justice was admittedly an expression of State policy and supported whatever political objectives it happened to be pursuing at the time.

What was odd was for this to have happened to six employees of a foreign firm like Metropolitan-Vickers, with its long business associations with Russia and its present contracts on which something of the success of the wildly ambitious Five-Year Plan, with its aim of turning the Soviet Union into a great modern industrial State, depended. What was odder still was for the trial to have taken the course it did.

The whole affair opened dramatically on the night of Saturday, March 11th, 1933, when a crowd of agents of the O.G.P.U., which existed to combat counter-revolutionary activities, raided the company's compound at Perlovka, near Moscow, swarming into the dining-room and calling out for Alan Monkhouse, Metrovick's chief electrical engineer in the Soviet Union, and Leslie Thornton, who was responsible for building and maintaining the plant supplied by the company.

At two fifteen a.m. they arrested the two Englishmen and various Russian nationals living in the compound, including Anna Sergeevna Kutuzova, Monkhouse's secretary. Next morning they arrested two other Metrovick employees in Moscow, John Cushny and W. L. MacDonald. No official mention of these activities was conveyed to the British Embassy, and when Mr William Strang (now Lord Strang), the Counsellor, began to make sharp inquiries of the Commissariat for Foreign Affairs he was coolly told that two other Metrovick engineers, Gregory and de Nordwall, were also in custody, along with a large number of Soviet citizens.

At about two a.m. on March 14th Strang was summoned to the Commissariat and told that the reason for the arrests was that breakdowns in four big power stations were the result of wrecking activities carried out by State employees actively aided by engineers of the British company. (Later the charges against the six Metrovick men were extended to include espionage and bribery.) The astonished Mr Strang, who is grave in appearance but charming in manner, also learned that Monkhouse and de Nordwall had just been released on their written undertaking not to leave Moscow. These high-handed goings-on understandably outraged the British Ambassador, a spirited gentleman named Sir Esmond Ovey, and when Vyshinsky, the Soviet Public Prosecutor, indicated that the engineers would be tried at a special session of the Supreme Court of the U.S.S.R. his advice to Sir John Simon, Foreign Secretary in Ramsay MacDonald's National Government, was couched in language vigorous to the point of violence. Believing as he did that a shocking frame-up was being prepared, Ovey was all for demanding the release of the prisoners without trial and for the severance of diplomatic relations if it came to a real showdown.

In Britain the news of the arrests produced instant uproar, certainly far louder than anything the Russians can have expected. It was a shock to the prevalent feeling that revolutionary Russia was settling down and desired stable foreign relations, an impression furthered by the generally moderate attitude of Litvinov, the Commissar for Foreign Affairs. These wholesale arrests seemed to destroy such cosy illusions, and the British reaction brought about a crisis in Anglo-Soviet relations almost overnight, with such emotional accompaniments as bishops praying on the B.B.C. for God himself to look after the imprisoned men.

No one knew then—and perhaps no one can say with any certainty today—whether or not the arrests were a considered act of foreign policy, designed as a reprisal against what the Soviet Government regarded as British discrimination against Russian trade; for the unwillingness of Russia to improve the balance of trade had caused the United Kingdom to serve notice on her that the existing commercial agreement would lapse on April 17th, 1933. More probably the running was made by the O.G.P.U. itself, who to demonstrate its power to the Russian people and indeed to the whole world had taken advantage of the prevailing disgruntlement with Britain to force the issue. At any rate, the British Government responded to the arrests by deciding to ask Parliament for power to exclude Soviet imports when the existing Anglo-Soviet agreement expired in a matter of days.

It is clear that the Kremlin was completely taken aback by the violent reaction of the British people and by the threat of a trade embargo. It seems equally clear that on Stalin's orders there was a rapid move to back down. All of

61

the accused except MacDonald were rather hastily released on bail from the Lubianka prison, and the charges were never pressed as powerfully as the original ballyhoo suggested they would be. Litvinov also made some conciliatory gestures to Sir Esmond Ovey, but the Ambassador remained unappeased. At the end of March he was instructed by Sir John Simon to return home immediately for consultation. He never went back to Moscow. William Strang took charge of the Embassy and was left with the nerve-racking job of trying to make sense of the incredibly disordered legal process which was to culminate without any great enthusiasm, in a trial mounted for a world audience.

With so much excitement in Britain about the trial Reuters recognized the necessity of securing the fullest possible coverage. At this time the big news agencies were at each other's throats and the two largest American organizations, United Press and the International News Service (with which a competitor of Reuters, the Central News of London, had a tie-up), were known to be planning to give the Moscow trial the full treatment. Most big British papers were expected to send special correspondents of their own.

For Reuters' New Editor, Bernard Rickatson-Hatt, renowned in his office for his furious energy, his clipped speech, his eyeglass, and his pride in a great British regiment in which he had served, the situation was one which called for a do-or-die effort, and on April 5th he issued a special 'Editorial Order' to the entire office:

The forthcoming trial in Moscow of the arrested British engineers will be a story of supreme importance to Reuters. Our subscribers both in London and the provinces are counting on us for first-class coverage. *Everything depends on getting in first.*

Before this Rickatson-Hatt had sent Kinkead, Reuters' regular man in Moscow, one of his celebrated terse telegrams:

I AM SENDING YOU IAN FLEMING ONE OF OUR ABLEST YOUNG MEN TO HELP COVERAGE OF TRIAL

Ian Fleming was being thrown in at the deep end.

The National Hotel, where he stayed in Moscow, was a monstrous building, featureless, vast, with a perpetual smell of cabbage in the corridors and a constant sense of doom in the restaurant, even if Tolstoy used to lunch there. Yet it was by no means entirely a disaster area and had amenities rare in Moscow at this time. It was warm, the service was reasonably good, there was an American bar—the city had only one other—which served Scotch whisky, French vermouth and Gordon's gin, no matter if the prices were grossly inflated. This bar, run by a plump lady from Odessa who was in the habit of warning her customers of the harrowing dangers of alcoholism, was the regular meeting place of foreign correspondents in Moscow, and it was here that twenty-five-year-old Ian Fleming met his rivals for the first time. They were a formidably expert crew for an inexperienced reporter to be up against on his first foreign assignment.

Among the agency men was the alert Eugene Lyons (now a senior editor with *Reader's Digest*), who as United Press and consequently British United Press representative was a rival of Reuters. Associated Press exchanged stories with Reuters, and with Linton Wells, of the International News Service, there was not quite the same do-or-die competition as with United Press. But Linton Wells's assistant, Mikhailov, had a temporary job with Reuters' chief rival, Central News of London, and this made him dangerous.

Apart from the agency men there were a number of old Moscow hands: distinguished correspondents like A. T. Cholerton, the blackbearded representative of the *Daily Telegraph*, and Walter Duranty of the *New York Times*. A. J. Cummings had come out to report the trial for the *News Chronicle*. Malcolm Muggeridge, now nearing the end of his storm-tossed career on the *Manchester Guardian*, had just left Moscow in a frenzy of frustration at the attitude both of his editors in England and the censors in Russia. The *Daily Express* was without a special correspondent: he had been refused a visa by the Russians at the last moment.

As Fleming was introduced to the Press corps in the bar of the National Hotel and was served his first sixteen-rouble martini by the old girl from Odessa he must have felt certain qualms, especially with Rickatson-Hatt's battle-order buzzing in his ears: 'Everything depends on getting in first.'

But this was the sort of talk and the sort of situation to appeal to him. There was not a correspondent that evening in the bar of the National Hotel who was not his superior in journalistic experience and knowledge of the Russians. But there can have been no one there who was even his equal in hunger for excitement, in vitality, natural ingenuity and joy at winning. All these characteristics of his were to be shown to the full in the next few weeks.

On that first evening Fleming dined with Cholerton and soon picked up the baffling mixture of rumour and surmise which formed the background to the trial. Cholerton was well informed as always. But there were aspects of this business about which neither he nor any of the other foreign correspondents knew a thing. One of them was highly sensational. It was that two of the British engineers—Thornton, the head of the company's erection staff, and MacDonald, who was still in the Lubianka—had made confessions. The first had admitted to being the co-director of spying operations on Soviet territory and named twenty-seven Metrovick employees as his accomplices; the second, MacDonald, had confessed to trying to disorganize the supply of electricity at one of the new power stations, hoping thereby to interfere with military production.

From the first William Strang had taken the view that the six engineers were innocent victims of a classic O.G.P.U. frame-up, caught in a mesh of forced confessions. On April 10th he interviewed a haggard, numbed Thornton and heard what he had expected to hear. 'Thornton agreed', says Strang, 'that he wrote the statements. He denied that there was any truth in them. He explained that he wrote them under examination when he was too tired to care what he wrote. As he said later, they had been pieced together and he had set them down under dictation when he had been reduced to such a state that he would have signed his own death warrant.' By the end of the interview Strang had given Thornton new courage: he was to plead not guilty on all counts.

The case of MacDonald was more mysterious. Not one of his colleagues believed the resolute club-footed little man to be guilty of wrecking or spying or anything else. Yet now he was apathetic and fatalistic, and Strang made little impression on him. The fact was that the O.G.P.U. had arrested someone for whom MacDonald cared deeply—his old Russian housekeeper Ryabova. She was their hostage.

Altogether it was clear to Strang that in court Vyshinsky would bring his heaviest pressure on MacDonald and Thornton. He awaited the event with his usual calm; but in his heart he must have cursed what he calls the Russian passion for excess.

Ian Fleming's mother, Mrs Valentine Fleming, was painted at least three times by Augustus John. When she died at 79 in 1964 she left her collection of paintings and drawings by John to various members of her family

In 1930, when attending Geneva University, Ian Fleming became unofficially engaged to a French-Swiss girl, the daughter of a landowner

IV

In the final days before the trial opened the foreign correspondents began to dry up—they had exhausted the rumours and there were no hard facts. It was at this point that Fleming demonstrated two of his advantages over the old Moscow hands of the National Hotel. Fresh from Britain, he understood better than they how avid newspaper readers at home were for information about Moscow; and he also had a curiously ingenious imagination which could suggest danger and conspiracy in the most humdrum surroundings.

'Tonight', he wrote as he sat at his typewriter in his big bedroom on the sixth floor, hammering out his first Moscow dispatch for Reuters, 'thousands of enemies of the Soviet State are skulking in cellars, gnashing their teeth.' When he showed the report to Kinkead and asked him to put it on the wire to London, the startled resident correspondent of Reuters pointed out that even if these skulking enemies really did exist it was a positive fact that very few houses in Moscow possessed cellars. 'My dear fellow,' replied Fleming cheerfully, 'don't let's worry too much about that. It's the sense of the thing that matters, and evil-doers always gnash their teeth and skulk in cellars.'

Another fill-in story he sent off began with the knowledge-able line, 'When the big hands of Moscow's three hundred electric clocks reach the hour of six . . .'

'How do you know there are three hundred?' Kinkead asked.

'How do you know there aren't?' said Fleming.

Back in London, in the absence of anything more substantial, stories like these were highly appreciated. And while he was keeping up a flow of copy he found time to become surprisingly popular with the rest of the correspondents, particularly the Americans. It was after being up half the night shooting craps with some of them that he proved himself alert enough, on the day before the trial began, to get an excellent little exclusive story. He approached William Strang and asked to be allowed to interview the five bailed engineers in the company compound at Perlovka. Predictably, Strang refused permission. Fleming went off to the compound, nevertheless, and wrote a story about this curious log cabin settlement where the accused wandering restlessly around awaiting their fate.

It was just what Reuters needed at that moment, and back from the battling Hatt came a grateful cable:

CONGRATULATIONS YOUR LOGCABIN STORY STOP WE SCORED HEAVILY OPPOSITIONWISE

It must have been a comfort to Fleming on the eve of his first big assignment; next morning at noon he took his seat on the Press benches in the hall of the former Moscow Noblemen's Club, now the House of Trade Unions, determined to give the opposition a run for their money.

Throughout the seven days of the trial he was to show most of the qualities of a successful popular journalist. Gone was the *Angst*-ridden young dilettante of Vienna and Munich, the student of the best contemporary German writers who had put all his adolescent unhappiness into tortured little stories of disillusion and death. He realized now that it wasn't so much the quality of his writing that mattered as the ability to carry several million newspaper readers with him into his private world of high Buchanesque adventure.

The Soviet refusal to allow the *Daily Express* reporter a visa turned out to be a stroke of good fortune for Fleming, for it meant that on the morning after the proceedings opened its front page lead story was under his own by-line, an unusual thing to happen to any news agency reporter in those days or these.

The military judge, Vassili Ulrich, sat on a stage erected at one end of the hall and was assisted by ten experts. He already had a fearsome reputation in Russia as the most merciless instrument of Stalin's terror—Cholerton described him as 'the Russian Judge Jeffreys'—and there was something about his mole-like inscrutability and false smile as he whispered into his microphone from behind a pile of papers that fascinated Fleming.

There was also Andrei Vyshinsky, the brick-shaped, bespectacled Prosecutor, who in 1953 was to find a wider stage for his denunciations of the West as Permanent Representative of the U.S.S.R. at the United Nations. As Fleming predicted, Vyshinsky quickly emerged as the dominating character of the court-room.

And there were the prisoners: Thornton, tired and grey-faced; Monkhouse, his boss, a good-looking, confident New Zealander; the sturdy pair, de Nordwall and Cushny; Gregory, a tough, rhetorical Welshman who was to challenge

Vyshinsky on the legality of the whole trial; and MacDonald, gaunt and nervous after his three weeks in the Lubianka, with his pale eyes and his club foot and his little goatee beard.

MacDonald was called first and pleaded guilty, to the audible pleasure of the four hundred Soviet citizens who had been specially selected to attend the trial. Thornton came next, and his repudiation of his confession brought Vyshinsky storming into operation; thereafter Thornton was his chief target. The four other prisoners put up strong defences, and even MacDonald came to life twice, on one occasion denying the evidence of a terrorized Russian prisoner who had worked with him and on the other throwing the proceedings into confusion by recanting everything. The court was immediately adjourned; but when the session was resumed MacDonald tonelessly confirmed his original testimony. He said later, when he was leaving Russia for ever, that in the interval he had been told that his housekeeper Ryabova would be shot at once if he persisted in repudiating his confession.

V

As Fleming watched from the Press benches he was having the rare chance for those days of witnessing the operation of a Police State at first hand. The man who was to write *From Russia, With Love* at least had this glimpse of people like Ulrich and Vyshinsky in action, heard the woman secretary Anna Sergeevna Kutuzova make fantastic allegations against her friend and colleague Thornton, and saw the effect the O.G.P.U. had on MacDonald and the eleven terrified Russians who were supposed to have been the accomplices of the English.

But apart from the enigma of the trial Fleming was obsessed with the idea of beating the other agency correspondents by getting in first. It was a challenge which brought out all his natural competitiveness.

During the early days he drove himself hard, cabling more frequently than anyone else. The routine procedure was for him to sit in court with Kinkead until they had enough material for a story, when one of them would make his way to the Press room on the floor below and there quickly type out a short message for transmission to London. By sending these telegrams at intervals throughout the day's proceedings, which lasted until ten p.m., Kinkead and Fleming kept Rickatson-Hatt supplied with the blow-by-blow material he needed for the successive editions of the London and provincial evening papers. Deliberately, Fleming moved around, keeping an eye on the other correspondents, especially Lyons of the United Press, seeing that nothing had been altered in the layout of the place—he knew where every telephone was, how the near-by cable office operated, who the staff were. Sending a report back to London was a somewhat complicated business. Every story had to be typed in duplicate in the Press room and taken upstairs for the censors' approval. This was vital. Each page had to be stamped and signed before it could be taken to the cable office two blocks away. The telegraph girls strictly checked the sheets for the censors' approval, and because of the shortage of operators the stories were sent out one after the other and not simultaneously. So it was that in the battle for deadlines the first reporter to reach the cable office with a story complete with the censors' red stamp and signature was the winner. All the agency men wanted, of course, to be first with the result of the trial, and most of them tried, by means of silk stockings and boxes of chocolates, to establish special relationships with the girls in the cable office. Fleming discovered early that this was quite useless, and while his rivals were still flirting with the girls he was purposefully cultivating the three principal Russian censors. The senior of them was Umansky, the O.G.P.U. head of censorship, a solemn, humourless man already far advanced in the Party and Soviet Ambassador to the United States from 1940 to 1941; his deputy was Podolsky, a bizarre figure with enormous beard and completely shaven head; and the third was one Mironov, sleepy, bespectacled, who had been educated in Paris and spoke excellent English and who appeared to Fleming altogether too soft and bourgeois a figure to last in Stalinist Russia. (He was right. Mironov and Podolsky were both to disappear within two years in the great purges.)

Fleming got on quite well with Mironov, even striking up a friendship of sorts; and he decided that on the closing day of the trial he would try to make discreet use of this most civilized of the three censors.

On the sixth day Vyshinsky made the final speech for the prosecution—a long, vituperative attack in which he singled out poor Thornton, who had not only repudiated his confession but as a first-rate engineer had made the Prosecutor look ridiculous by tearing to pieces the charges of wrecking. 'So far as this country is concerned, Thornton,' Vyshinsky bellowed, 'your only use would be to manure the soil of our Soviet fields.' With these words the proceedings of the fantastic Metropolitan-Vickers trial virtually ended. When the court met on the final day Judge Ulrich smiled and shuffled his papers for the last time, then whispered into his microphone that he and his colleagues would retire to consider their verdict. The long wait started.

After consultation with S. P. Richardson of Associated Press and Linton Wells of I.N.S., Fleming had evolved a strategy. He immediately typed two stories, one suitable for a verdict of guilty and the other for acquittal, hoping to get both contingency stories censored in advance. It was a highly irregular proceeding, and when he rushed off to try it on Mironov he was met with a point-blank refusal. In this emergency, with the Hatt battle-cry echoing in his head, Fleming turned the full battery of his charm and persuasiveness on the censor. Surely there was nothing actively wrong in putting the censors' stamp on both stories on the absolute understanding that as soon as the verdict was announced the correct one would be offered for dispatch? At last, very reluctantly, Mironov gave way.

Now Fleming worked fast. He had two helpers standing by, a man and a boy. The man was given both stamped stories and told to station himself at the cable office. The boy, a fourteen-year-old nephew of Kinkead's Russian interpreter, was to wait below a window within easy reach of Fleming in court, and when a message giving the verdict was dropped to him he was to rush it to the cable office, where the other helper would pick out the appropriate report and fill in the gaps before sending it off.

To the details of the plan Fleming the perfectionist paid the same attention as he was to pay to detail in his books. They ranged from tennis shoes for the boy to a dash to the cable office by Kinkead, as soon as he could get out of court, to make sure that nothing had gone wrong. Fleming himself was to wait in the court-room building, watching the telephones. It was highly unlikely that anyone would succeed in getting on to London—the delay in those days was formidable. Indeed, the whole Russian telephone service was extraordinarily erratic; and in addition to the usual hazards the censor was listening-in, and he was apt to cut off conversations at a moment's notice. All the same, Fleming wanted to be sure. He might even have to take drastic action himself.

The long wait for Judge Ulrich and the members of the court went on. A sense of anticlimax hung about the hall. Lawyers, guards, journalists, spectators yawned their way through the long afternoon and into the evening. At last Kinkead left the court for a hurried meal and when he returned the wife of Mikhailov of the Central News (she had no pass for the trial) called out to him as he was about to enter the main door: Central News had been telephoning her husband from London—would Kinkead please tell him that they wanted him to ring back? Reuters' resident correspondent in Moscow no doubt permitted himself a slight smile at the optimism of Reuters' chief rival in London and passed the message on.

An hour or so later the buzz went round that Judge Ulrich and his colleagues were soon to return. As the pass-holders pushed in, Ian Fleming pushed out, himself filled with the passion for excess and bent on action which up to now he had regarded as something to be resorted to only in an emergency. The telephones were downstairs. Before he returned to court he had put them all out of action save the one on which Mikhailov was still patiently waiting to get through to London.

Fleming was back in his seat by the window in good time to hear Judge Ulrich—still smiling—announce judgment: *Thornton*—three years' deprivation of liberty; *Mac-Donald*—two years' deprivation of liberty. (On July 1st, 1933, as the result of William Strang's persistence and a deal between Litvinov and Sir John Simon, the two men were freed and expelled from Russia.) *Monkhouse, de Nordwall* and *Cushny*—to be deported from the U.S.S.R. and prohibited from re-entering for five years. *Gregory*—acquitted.

The leniency of the sentences took everyone by surprise, and in the ensuing hubbub Fleming had no difficulty in scribbling them out, checking them with his interpreter, and dropping the paper out of the window to the boy in the tennis shoes.

Everything went with the smoothness of one of Fleming's own plots, and Reuters' story was easily the first to be cabled from Moscow. Together Kinkead and Fleming, con-gratulating themselves on a good night's work, drove off to

Stalin says No. In 1933 Fleming tried to secure a world scoop by interviewing Stalin. At least his collecting instincts were gratified when he won this signed letter of refusal.

the National Hotel to celebrate, late as the hour was, with caviare and pink champagne. They were wondering whether to order a second bottle when a night porter with a wooden leg stumped into the bedroom with a telegram. Fleming opened the small blue envelope, looked puzzled for a moment, and then began laughing. He had a powerful, irresistible laugh, and without knowing quite why Kinkead joined in. 'That settles it,' said Fleming. 'We simply must have a second bottle now. But I still don't see how the devil it happened.'

He passed the cable to Kinkead. It was from Rickatson-Hatt in London:

CENTRAL NEWS BEAT YOU WITH VERDICT BY TWENTY MINUTES STOP REQUEST EXPLANATION IMMEDIATELY

Next day they found out that Fleming had overlooked one thing—Judge Ulrich's microphone. It had relayed the sentences over the loudspeaker system throughout the whole building, and Mikhailov, doggedly waiting for his call to Central News, had noted them down. Ten minutes later, by a hundred to one chance, he found himself connected with his News Desk in London. He had scooped everyone by a fluke.

The story soon got round; and as Fleming treated it as a huge joke everyone else did so as well—he never found it hard to laugh at himself when things backfired. So it was that just two days after this brash young outsider from London in his Fifty-Shilling suit had been tearing out telephone cords to prevent his rivals from getting their stories back to London, those same rivals sent this telegram to the head of Reuters:

SIR RODERICK JONES EYE SHOULD LIKE YOU TO KNOW THAT WE FELLOW JOURNALISTS OF IAN FLEMING WHOM NONE OF US HAD EVER MET BEFORE HIS APPEARANCE HERE COVER METVICKERS TRIAL NOT ONLY CONSIDER HIM A PUKHA [sic] CHAP PERSONALLY BUT HAVE EXTREMELY HIGH OPINION OF HIS JOURNALISTIC ABILITY STOP HE HAS GIVEN US ALL A RUN FOR OUR MONEY

It was an unusual tribute.

Fleming had more than a week left in Moscow, and he tried to make the most of it. With visions, however misty, of a world scoop, he joined forces with S. P. Richardson of Associated Press and applied for an interview with Stalin. When this was refused in a letter from Stalin himself, on the ground that he was too busy, they asked Litvinov for an interview or exclusive statement on the 'foreign trade relations of the U.S.S.R.'. Back from the Commissar for Foreign Affairs came a long but distinctly dusty answer, the gist of which was that trial or no trial the Soviet would continue to trade with any country abroad that suited its book.

Fleming had done his best. It was time to go. On the night before he left he shot craps with Richardson for the signed original of Stalin's letter and won. But he took something much more valuable out of Russia. As he sat on the morning of April 23rd, 1933, in that empty Victorian dining-car, spending his last roubles on his last Russian meal, with the old grey train scuttling on towards the Polish border, he carried with him memories which were to yield unexpected dividends in a quarter of a century's time.

But in 1933 the world of S M E R S H and James Bond was not even a minute figment in his imagination, and life had nothing more exciting to offer than the dull routine of Carmelite Street, where he resumed his job of sub-editing the inexhaustible flow of copy, brought in wire baskets into the great dusty newsroom on the first floor of Reuters' building.

However, his Russian experiences gave him a certain distinction, and Sir Robert Vansittart, Permanent Under-Secretary at the Foreign Office, arranged for him to report his impressions of Moscow and the trial to a number of anonymous gentlemen in a room in the Foreign Office. There was little he could tell them that they would not have known already, for there was no question at this stage of Ian Fleming's being any sort of espionage or intelligence expert. Yet the interview evidently got his name on to the files as someone with first-hand experience of Russia who might be of use one day should the need arise.

Sir Roderick Jones's attention was on him too. At the end of September he was summoned to the chairman's office and offered a plum job—Reuters' Far-Eastern correspondent with an office in Shanghai. For a journalist of only twenty-five it was the chance of a lifetime, and Fleming appeared enthusiastic and flattered. Jones explained that the post would not become vacant until the end of the year and that in the meantime he wanted Fleming to go to Berlin to see how the office there was run and to put his German to good use by interviewing Hitler.

It would have been an interesting encounter, but it was not to be. In October Ian Fleming resigned from Reuters, announcing his change of mind in this sorrowful letter to Sir Roderick Jones:

Just a week after our conversation, when I was about to write and accept the post you offered me, a business man with whom I am only slightly acquainted asked me to see him and offered me what at first sight appeared a quite exceptional post in his firm of merchant bankers. The gist of the offer was that he himself intended to retire and that he offered me his partnership in the firm after two years of learning the business.

Fleming stressed the financial advantages of the offer: it would be 'quite remarkably remunerative', and he would reach, before he was thirty, 'a position which it is unusual to attain before the age of fifty, if at all'.

He also conveyed the impression that there had been some sort of pressure from his family—Robert Fleming's and a director of Barings, the merchant bankers, had urged him to accept. He was terribly sad about it all because his two years in Reuters had been among the happiest of his life.

To Rickatson-Hatt he wrote a still more hangdog letter, again stressing the inescapable arguments of financial reward and family duty. However, if there was one quality

Ian Fleming had possessed since childhood, it was a resolute incapacity to do what he did not want to do. If he had decided to become a merchant banker instead of going to Shanghai it was nobody's decision but his own.

And yet it *does* seem odd. Shanghai should have been just the place for this adventure-loving young romantic. It was strange that he gave it up for a blue pinstripe suit and a desk in the City. There was a reason, though.

CHAPTER SEVEN

THE SOLITARY AND THE *CERCLE*

I

THE old banker Robert Fleming was eighty-eight when he made his last journey south from Scotland in August 1933. His old age had been as vigorous as the rest of his life: in his mid-seventies he was still stalking deer, and at seventy-three 'he brought off a remarkable right and left, killing a Royal and a fourteen-pointer, the two stags weighing between them forty-three stone.' But by the end he had grown very feeble, and he was gratefully leaving the affairs of the family to his wife and of the business to his son Philip. The heart attack which killed him occurred at his house at Black Mount in Argyllshire, and the body travelled on the overnight train to King's Cross.

When it reached Nettlebed the gardeners from Joyce Grove had already had time to line the grave with moss and heather, and South Oxfordshire was gathered to bury him in style. The shops in Nettlebed closed for the day; the family, the local gentry and the villagers filled the church; and when the service was over and the muffled bells of Nettlebed rang a peal of grandsire doubles, two generals, a viscount, a baron and a High Court judge followed the family to the graveside. It was a tribute to the position and the wealth of the Flemings. An era was over, and to Ian Fleming, as he stood beside his black-veiled mother as one of the principal mourners, it must have seemed as if his days of dependence would be over as well. For Robert Fleming had been devoted to all his grandchildren: he must have made some provision for the four sons of Major Val, if only to offset the effect of their father's will.

But he had not. In his anxious old age, perhaps, he had simply failed to understand their predicament, and the whole of his fortune of nearly three million pounds was left in trust for his widow and then passed to his second son Philip, who had already been appointed chairman of Robert Fleming and Company. For Ian Fleming the terms of his grandfather's will must have appeared as yet another of those periodic disappointments which always managed to fall on him when the going was good. Pessimist as he was, he would have suspected that this was one more sign that the world was still against him. The ambergris was still turning into rancid butter.

Not that such disappointments depressed him for long, and it was now that he thought he saw the chance to make his own fortune in the City. The death of his grandfather and the shock of his will made up his mind for him, and he resigned from Reuters a few weeks later: his six years first in merchant banking and then as a stockbroker began.

One of the things about Ian Fleming that never ceased to puzzle people who knew him well was his curious attitude to money. His closest friend in the years just before the war was Gerald Coke, one of the trustees of Covent Garden and formerly chairman of Rio Tinto. 'The odd thing about Ian', he says, 'is that he really had everything he could possibly have wanted—looks, brains, enough money and position. Yet he was never satisfied. He always behaved as if he were permanently deprived.'

Alaric Jacob, the writer and broadcaster, who knew Fleming well during his time at Reuters, noted the same paradox, and when he put him into his book *Scenes from a Bourgeois Life* (1949) under the pseudonym of Hugo Dropmore, he pointed out how odd it was that such a civilized and good-looking young man should have bothered with the dull, wealthy world of London financiers when he 'knew all about Gertrude Stein and Rilke, played bridge beautifully and skied like a ghost . . . This young man, so aristocratically *dégagé*, so courteous and well informed, could if he wished have enjoyed the best company in London. But he seemed to solicit not even the second best, but that of the more boorish finance capitalists.'

All his adult life Fleming was fascinated by the world of the very rich and yet he was not a straightforward money snob. He was a financial romantic: it was as if the promise of treasure, of extreme wealth, symbolized for him the happiness and security and position that had been offered by the Fleming millions and then snatched away by the wills of his father and his grandfather.

The irony of it all was that although he had such high romantic notions about wealth he soon discovered that he was not particularly good at accumulating it. The prospects he had written so enthusiastically about to Sir Roderick

Jones when he left Reuters never materialized at the merchant bankers he joined, Cull and Co. in Bishopsgate, who may have been dazzled by his family connection with Robert Fleming and Company. Within less than two years he had moved on to Rowe and Pitman, where he was to remain a junior partner, nominally at any rate, until 1945.

Rowe and Pitman are still one of the solidest and most important stockbroking firms in the City of London, whose clients include Rolls-Royce, the Diamond Corporation, and most of the banks and big insurance companies. Superficially the life of a junior partner drawing his annual percentage of the profit from such a prosperous firm seems to have suited Fleming. The family name still gave him a certain status in the City and the work of keeping in touch with his clients was not onerous. He never drew less than £2,000 a year and was perfectly entitled to speculate on his own account. 'Today,' says his friend Hilary Bray, who worked in the same office, 'Ian wouldn't have a chance of getting away with life at Rowe and Pitman as he did in the days when he was there. He was accepted on the old boy basis because of his connections with Robert Fleming. Nowadays he would have to learn a great deal of Stock Exchange law and the technique of finance, but then he was virtually able to write his own part.'

He not only wrote the part—he also acted it with his usual skill. 'Whenever I saw Ian towards the end of his time in the City,' says Cyril Connolly, 'he gave the impression of being a playboy business man with all the money and all the friends he could possibly want. I met him once in Brook Street. He was wearing a blue suit and an Eton Ramblers tie and his appearance was so absolutely correct that it made me think of someone out of a Wodehouse novel.'

In fact, he had found himself a comfortable niche at Rowe and Pitman, where one of his regular jobs was writing up the monthly news-sheet. Hugo Pitman, the senior partner, became his close friend and patron, and he was popular in the office. All the same his six years in the City can scarcely be counted a success. The big money he had been hoping for never materialized, and it was soon clear that he lacked entirely the right temperament and ability.

'As a stockbroker,' says Hugh Vivian-Smith, who was also at Rowe and Pitman with him, 'old Ian really must have been among the world's worst.' He lacked staying power, and the minutiae of money-making bored him—he was never much more than an amateur. 'I never *could* understand what was meant by a sixty-fourth of a point,' he once explained apologetically. Though he was fascinated by a romantic idea of the tycoon and the millionaire, everyday reality in the shape of most of the clients he had to work with was a very different matter.

'Ian's job,' says Vivian-Smith, 'consisted basically in keeping contact with his clients, advising them, and bringing in fresh business.' He soon seems to have worked out his own private way of doing this. 'Normally he would take his client out to lunch—usually White's Club or somewhere in the City—and he'd take a great deal of trouble to make sure that the food was as good as he could get. Over the lobster or the tournedos he'd start talking rather knowledgeably about what he called the strategy of investments—he used to enjoy theorizing about money. Then after lunch he would bring the client along to the office, turn him over to the client investment section, and that would be that.'

But if the City never offered Ian Fleming a fortune equal to that of his grandfather's, it did give him something almost as valuable—independence and the chance to leave home at last.

II

No. 22A Ebury Street was one of the oddest private houses in London—it was a setting rather than a home. Sir Oswald Mosley, the leader of the British fascist movement, had lived there for a while and after he moved out it was as if the place was waiting for a new tenant with a sufficient sense of the theatrical to live up to it. It would have made a good spot for a Black Mass or a meeting of the Hellfire Club.

From the outside it looked like a chapel—a splendid, slightly cracked, cream-painted stucco façade, two towering Doric pillars, a pious commemorative tablet unveiled by Viscount Milton in 1830. Since piety had given it up, No. 22A had been used as a school, a night-club and a furniture store, and Fleming saw its possibilities at once. 'But Ian, darling, how stupid wanting to live in a dirty old church,' said Mrs Val. But this time he got his way and against the unlikely background of this former Strict Baptist chapel and literary institute a new episode in his private life began.

78

It was the perfect place for him and it immediately contributed to the legend he seemed to be building around himself. He employed a lady interior decorator from Berlin to help with the details, but the form which the interior took was entirely his own idea. The big meeting hall of the chapel remained intact. There were no windows, and he had the walls painted grey; indirect lighting was installed and the skylight filled in with dark-blue glass. He fitted a lavatory in the alcove which had once contained the altar; a large black sofa was placed in the centre of the room and a fire kept burning even in mid-summer. The gallery was just wide enough to take a small dining-table, and his bedroom lay beyond. It must have been a lonely and oppressive house, and it was here that he entertained his women, his friends, and the members of the *Cercle*.

The *Cercle*, or to give it the full Fleming title, *Le Cercle gastronomique et des jeux de hasard*, was, like his house, another expression of the odd way of life Ian Fleming worked out for himself as a young man in his late twenties. The members were a well-to-do gang of youngish Old Etonians-about-Town and the purpose of the society or club was to allow them to dine well two or three times a month, indulge in a little bridge at half-a-crown a hundred, and spend their week-ends playing golf together. But when Fleming founded the *Cercle* with his friend Gerald Coke, half the fun of it for him lay in building an elaborate myth around these very ordinary activities.

Coke, an amiable and rather conventional young man, simply wanted to gather together a few friends, but this was not enough for Fleming and it all had to be turned into a carefully ordered ritual. He took a lot of trouble finding a suitable name for the club and the one he finally chose emphasized its gastronomic side: members must start improving their palates by enjoying a very special menu whenever they dined.

At the Tennerhof at Kitzbühel Phyllis Bottome had invented an imaginary dining-club, and Fleming had been particularly good at suggesting exotic meals for it. With the *Cercle* there was more than an echo of those youthful fantasies. Boredom was always his great enemy, but with a little imagination the most drab situation could be given a shining veneer of excitement. Before members of the *Cercle* dined at Ebury Street he would spend hours discussing the ideal menu, but all too frequently these meals turned out to be Barmecide feasts, perhaps because Fleming was never really interested in food and wine—it was the *idea* of the perfect meal that excited him. 'I always used to tell Ian,' says Coke, 'that what he really liked to eat was *œuf à la coq* and a good slice of chocolate cake.'

To golf and bridge his attitude seems to have been somewhat similar. He was not a sophisticated player of either game: what he wanted was simple schoolboy excitement and he pursued it with insatiable energy. 'His bridge,' says Coke, 'was erratic and unconventional. He could play well but he would always take too many risks to be a really reliable partner.' And already he was fascinated by the idea (but not, significantly, by the reality) of cheating at cards: Coke remembers Fleming one evening in Ebury Street trying to reconstruct from memory the entire Culbertson hand which was later to figure in the bridge battle in *Moonraker*.

It was Fleming's restless and imaginative temperament which really made him the moving spirit of the *Cercle*, even if most of its members were slightly older than he was. Apart from Coke, the regular members included Sir George Duff-Dunbar, lawyer and collector of Wedgwood and one of the four people to whom Fleming left £500 in his will*; John Fox-Strangways, an eccentric member of the family of Charles James Fox who, war-wrecked as he was, pathetically tried to kick Aneurin Bevan, the Socialist leader, down the steps of White's Club in 1951 and gave the second half of his name to the head of the Caribbean branch of the Secret Service in *Live and Let Die* and *Dr No*; David Nicol, a City wine merchant, who like Fox-Strangways had been at Eton with Fleming; and Dr Jack Beal, who was to be Fleming's doctor for the rest of his life.

During the week they would take it in turns to play bridge at each other's clubs. Occasionally they dined at Ebury Street, and at week-ends they would often drive off to play golf together. Sometimes they went to Le Touquet and combined their golf with a visit to the Casino, but even in those days Fleming's favourite week-end was to stay at the Guilford Hotel at Sandwich Bay and play over the course of the Royal St. George's which, under the name of the Royal St Marks, would one day be the scene of James Bond's battle with Goldfinger.

In the *Cercle* Fleming was the one who provided most of the fun and excitement, keeping the rest on their toes:

* The others were Mrs Lisl Popper, William Plomer and Robert Harling.

he was a sort of prima donna among them, just as his mother had been in her circle of friends. 'He was always so up to date and novel in his ideas,' says Dr Beal, 'and if something came up that he didn't know about he always managed to imply that it wasn't really worth bothering with anyhow.'

But although the *Cercle* gave him that position of ascendancy he had sought even as a schoolboy, it never seems to have broken down the barriers he had carefully erected. None of the members, as far as one can judge, felt they really knew him. They were the supporting cast for the leading role he had given himself, and for all his crackling vitality and gaiety the impression persists that underneath lay an isolated and unhappy man.

He never spoke of writing now. His brother Peter Fleming, after extraordinary travels through the jungles of Brazil and the wastes of Mongolia, had scored a great success with his two books, *Brazilian Adventure* and *News from Tartary*. Here was the genuine man of action, the effortless elder brother's achievement all over again, and when a friend from the Kitzbühel days asked Ian Fleming about his own writing there was a swift shrug and the reply, 'My brother Peter's the writer in the family and he's really terribly good at it.'

Indeed, Ian Fleming seemed by now to have shrugged off most of the intellectualism of his early twenties. That phase was over and apparently forgotten. 'In all the time I knew him we never once discussed what you might call the eternal verities,' says Coke. 'He was of course a complete materialist and lived entirely in the present. His ambitions in those days? Very simple, I should think. He wanted to make a great deal of money and live on his own terms in considerable comfort for the rest of his life.'

Yet there was one thread of his earliest intellectual interests which did survive—his collector's feeling for books. Perhaps there was a touch of nostalgia in the way this young stockbroker still loved the feel and the aura of first editions: if there was, he managed to combine it with a touch of shrewd Dundee business sense that would have been worthy of old Robert Fleming himself. For it was during his time in the City that he built up the book collection which was to prove the canniest financial investment of his life.

It all began with his friend Percy Muir, whom Fleming had met in the Kitzbühel days. Muir was then a partner in Dulau's bookshop in Bond Street and Fleming, on holiday from the Tennerhof, had walked in to buy a book of D. H. Lawrence's poems. They discussed first editions generally and their friendship began. They went on holiday together; and when Fleming was in Geneva he asked Muir to send him regular parcels of the latest books. Then when Muir became a partner in Elkin Mathews, the rare-book dealers (Fleming himself became a partner later on), the young stockbroker had a chance to observe some of the spectacular increases in the value of contemporary first editions. It was a lesson hardly likely to be lost on his keen and money-conscious mind, but it was not until he had left Reuters that he had enough money of his own to take much advantage of it. When he did he was to show a flash of typical Fleming originality which was to pay off handsomely.

At the beginning of 1935, just after he had joined Rowe and Pitman, Fleming wrote to Muir saying that he wanted to spend £250 on starting a collection of books marking what he called the 'milestones of human progress', or, as he put it on another occasion, 'books that have started something'. There was to be none of the triviality of subject matter which annoyed him in most collections; his was to be concerned with social and scientific and medical significance—books on motor cars and miners' lamps and zip-fasteners and tuberculosis and the theory of relativity.

He was not worried about appearance or readability. The only criteria he laid down were that the subjects must be important and the books themselves first editions—any work published after 1800 would qualify. He made one other condition, and that too was typical; As Muir puts it, 'He was not prepared to do any research. That was for me to do.'

Even in the mid-'thirties £250 was a modest sum on which to found an ambitious collection, and Muir decided to limit it to the great scientific discoveries of the nineteenth century followed by historically important pronouncements. But once he began looking for the books which this uncon-ventional client had broadly specified the true originality of the idea was revealed. Muir found that none of the recog-nized rare-book dealers were interested in such works; and when he approached booksellers specializing in medical and scientific books he discovered that to them 'first editions were largely out-of-date textbooks to be thrown away. Their clients wanted up-to-date editions.'

Fleming the amateur had done what every serious collector dreams of doing: he had hit on a genuine collectors' blind spot. For the next four years he and Muir proceeded to exploit it. For four pounds they picked up one of the remaining copies of Madame Curie's historic doctorate thesis of 1903 which told the world that she had isolated radium. They bought a copy of Koch's paper on the tubercle bacillus for five pounds. Other unusual rarities they picked up for next to nothing included first editions of Sir Humphry Davy on fire-damp in coalmines, Pitman on shorthand, and Freud on the interpretation of dreams.

By the beginning of 1939 Fleming's total expenditure was still not much over £2,000, while his collection was already an important one. By now he was beginning to refer to it with offhand pride as 'one of the foremost collections of scientific and political thought in the world', and after the war, when asked by an American rare-book dealer how much he would take for it, he gave the arbitrary figure of £100,000.

By then, however, he had really lost interest in the collection except as a purely financial investment and a hedge against inflation. He had had his bright idea and moved on, as he always did. In his Ebury Street days he went to great trouble to have the books cased in expensive black boxes stamped in gold with the arms of the Flemings, and in this way they became part of the décor—part of the scenery almost for the lonely performance which he was electing to play.

CHAPTER EIGHT

PRIVATE AND PUBLIC

I

'He was extraordinarily good-looking in those days, and the first time I had supper with him in his house in Ebury Street he was sitting on a sofa in the middle of that strange room with shelf upon shelf of the book collection around him in all those forbidding-looking shiny black boxes. It was July, but there was a large coal fire which he always kept burning even in high summer. He had a giggly Irish maid who showed me in, but he didn't get up, didn't say a thing. He just sat there on the sofa staring into the fire with an expression of quite extraordinary sadness on his face. He took no notice of me at all and he was obviously expecting me to sit there like a mouse and then do exactly as I was told. But I said "I'm damned if I'm taking this", and forced him to talk and said I wanted something to eat. He bucked up then, produced a bottle of champagne and we had supper by candlelight at the small table in the gallery with the "Skaters' Waltz" playing rather loudly on his radiogram in the background. I remember how he cracked up the supper as if it was something terribly special, but all it was was black coffee and kedgeree and more champagne. It all struck me as very strange. I knew no other young man in London who seemed so comfortable or so eccentric or who had quite such an original way of entertaining a young girl.'

This is how one of Fleming's pre-war girl friends describes an evening spent with him in the summer of 1936. By then he had had time to carry out his threat made after the breaking-off of his engagement and generally seems to have treated his women with all the ruthlessness he had promised. There was a Rumanian countess and an American heiress and a marquess's daughter, a large lady nicknamed the 'galloping bedstead', and the daughter of a Midlands business man whose brother appeared dramatically at Ebury Street one wet Wednesday afternoon with a riding crop. Fortunately the girl had got wind of what was happening and she and Fleming spent the day at Brighton.

Some women adored him, and this was fatal. Adoration bored him. Bored with a woman, no one could be more elusive, more cold, if necessary more brutal, than Ian Fleming. The kindness which was an undoubted part of his character did not extend to the women who loved him.

Adoring women were also a source of danger, for they could be indiscreet and attempt to entangle him; and he had no intention of becoming entangled. On the whole he was discreet in his affairs, usually avoiding gossip, recriminations, scenes, emotional excesses. He kept his friends and his mistresses apart. His name was not mentioned in a divorce case until he was forty-two.

But despite his discretion Ian Fleming as a young man acquired a fearsome reputation, and like most reputations of its sort it both exaggerated and over-simplified the facts. He was something more than a philanderer, something less than a rake.

One reason for his notoriety was that among people he knew he was completely free from the usual English prudery and reticence about sex. He was deeply, almost obsessively, interested in the subject. He was entirely deficient in any sense of sexual shame or guilt. If he met a woman at a party who interested him he might quite likely suggest carnal relations on half-an-hour's acquaintance, but if he was refused he would be cheerfully unconcerned.

Among conventional Englishmen such behaviour was unusual, and he seems to have played the part of the unprincipled seducer with the same slightly stagy gusto that he brought to all his other activities. His appearance was on his side: tall, saturnine, hollow-cheeked, his face lop-sided with its magnificently broken nose, his brow half-covered by that thoughtful comma of black hair which he was to pass on to his hero, he looked as if he had walked straight out of the pages of *The Romantic Agony*.

'Some women thought his looks terribly sinister,' says one of his admirers from those days. 'Others felt they hid great depths of intensity and suffering and feeling. Whatever their reaction he wasn't a man to whom women could remain indifferent.'

His restlessness and volatility added to the total effect. 'He struck me as being terribly complex,' says another woman, 'and this is always exciting. He was like one of those children's play-blocks with a different picture on each side, and you never knew which side you would come across when you met him.' 'When I first saw him,' says yet another, 'I felt that there was something of the wild animal about him—something restless and uncaged and untrappable.'

In all this Fleming exerted a very powerful appeal on certain women. He had not the sort of charm and good looks to bowl over all of them: some felt he was sinister, others objected to his rudeness, his apparent insensitivity. 'I felt that any relationship with Ian would simply be too dangerous and too difficult' is how one woman summed it up.

But to those who found him attractive and were not frightened off by the risks he was clearly irresistible, and there were always enough of such women to go round. Like James Bond he never had to work hard for them.

In Switzerland an Englishwoman who met him one morning tried to assault him the same afternoon on a ski lift. And the girl whose brother had come stalking into town with his riding crop was to put up with almost every possible sort of slight and cruelty from him before being killed, like a true prototype Bond heroine, in a London air-raid.

At the same time it is hard not to detect an element of play-acting in Fleming's role as the great Byronic seducer. It was too studied, too much like his other personal fantasies, to be entirely credible, and although he certainly drew on memories from these years for some of James Bond's more impressive sexual exploits, his own attitude to women was nothing like as simple and uncomplicated as Bond's. Several of his more perceptive friends have noticed this. 'The trouble with Ian,' said Miss Rosamond Lehmann, borrowing a quotation from Elizabeth Bowen, 'is that he gets off with women because he can't get on with them.'

For like most determined philanderers he was a womanizer who did not really like women. 'Ian's attitude to women always fascinated me,' says one of his close male friends. 'He was so obsessed with them, he made such an issue over sex, that he always made me think of the man who denounces the demon rum because he feels guilty for wanting to get drunk. His exasperation came because he couldn't take them or leave them alone.'

It was this attitude that helped to prevent his affairs from turning into any deeper relationship. Real friendship could exist only among men—women were there to be slept with and then forgotten. 'Men want a woman,' Fleming wrote with some truth, 'whom they can turn on and off like a light switch.'

'For Ian,' says one of his Kitzbühel girl friends, 'women were like fish cakes. Mind you, he was very fond of fish cakes, but he never pretended that there was any great mystique about eating them.'

'Women,' he wrote in one of his notebooks, 'have their uses for the relief of tension' and for giving a momentary relief from loneliness. 'The only time people are not alone is just after making love. Then the warmth and languor and gratitude turn them into happy animals. But soon the mind starts to work again and they become again lonely human beings.'

'The mind starts to work again'—that was the trouble, for that was the one thing he distrusted. When women's minds started to work they lost that animal capacity for giving the happiness and relief which he needed from them.

The distrust of women who tried to mix intellect with sex was particularly marked at this period of his life. 'Some women,' he wrote, 'respond to the whip, some to the kiss. Most of them like a mixture of both, but none of them answer to the mind alone, to the intellectual demand, unless they are man dressed as woman.'

For the intellect, according to the strict logic of his philosophy, was the preserve of the male. Women had to remain 'happy animals'—animals to be petted, bought presents for, made a fuss of—but not to be accepted as real human beings at all; for him it was only men who could be allowed the luxury of independent thought, only men who were fit objects of real friendship.

It is tempting to relate all this to the oddities of Fleming's upbringing, education and class. For certainly this distrust of women, this anxiety to keep them firmly in their place, was common enough in the upper-class Edwardian England of his boyhood. And the attitude to women displayed in his books is far closer to the attitude of Buchan or Sapper than he probably realized. Richard Hannay idealizes his women, Bond sleeps with them, but both acts are a device for keeping women out of the real man's world where action and comradeship and life occur.

But if Fleming's general attitude to women was—and still is—common enough, it is one that most reasonably intelligent men grow out of or compromise with. Until his marriage Fleming never did. 'He looked on women,' says one of his pre-war girl friends, 'just as a schoolboy does, as remote, mysterious beings. He could never hope to understand them, but if he was lucky he felt he might occasionally shoot one down.'

What was more remarkable still was the way he managed to maintain this attitude so resolutely through a multitude of affairs until it became as basic to his way of life as it was to be to James Bond's. In many ways it suited him perfectly. That curious routine at Ebury Street of kedgeree, candle-light and no complications meant that he was free to keep his solitude and free to be master of himself. By limiting women to the role of fish cakes, by refusing to accept that a mistress could also have a mind, he remained safe from love and all its uncomfortable complexities and safe from being found out. He could maintain his mystery.

Part of his fear was the normal male fear of marrying, and he made it quite clear that he never intended to do so if he could possibly help it. 'I couldn't bear my wife's eyes gradually going dull after the honeymoon and only lighting up again when she talked to her friends,' he wrote. His idea of the only possible wife was a woman who was 'double-jointed, and who knew when to keep quiet and make *sauce béarnaise*'. And about children his verdict was, 'The main danger of breeding is that you may double the strengths but you may also double the weaknesses.'

But his fear of women went beyond this, and he took elaborate steps to make sure that no sexual relationship ever developed to the point where he had to give anything of himself away. In order to achieve this he resolutely refused to recognize his women as full and independent human beings. 'A woman,' he wrote, 'should be an illusion,' and any fleshly frailty distressed him. In Capri he completely disowned one girl he had liked the look of after she retired for a few moments behind a rock. He had, as another girl friend of his put it, 'a remarkable phobia about bodily things. He worked himself up into a frenzy when I took an aspirin once for a headache, and I'm certain he would never have tied up a cut finger for me. I feel he would also have preferred me not to eat and drink as well.'

This curiously disembodied way of regarding his women had certain advantages. Jealousy never troubled him. 'I told him once that I had spent the night with a marvellous man and had had breakfast with him afterwards,' says one woman from this period. 'All Ian bothered to ask me was what kind of jam he gave me with my toast.'

Along with this lack of jealousy went an almost Swiftian abhorrence of physical female defects. 'The trouble is,' he told Miss Barbara Griggs in an interview published in the *Evening Standard* as late as April 1960, 'that women simply are not clean—absolutely filthy,' he went on, 'the whole lot of them. Englishwomen simply do not wash and scrub enough.' Frenchwomen, he conceded, generally *were* better on this score, but usually had 'hideous bodies and skins' all the same. And just to show that he was not biased against the Old World he described with equal distaste how an American woman he had known had always leapt out of bed after making love and 'gargled vigorously with a strong mouthwash'.

For Fleming the most important result of regarding women as illusions rather than as human beings was that it gave him an excuse for treating them without feeling. He felt justified in being as ruthless or as cynical as the occasion demanded.

'The older women are best, because they always think they may be doing it for the last time.'

'The woman likes the door to be forced.'

'You think more of the kiss than of the mouth—you want the thing and not the person.'

'As long as a woman's flesh is clean and healthy what does it matter what shape she is.'

These are some of the reflections which this sensitive, fundamentally kindly man was to record in one of his notebooks.

With beliefs such as these he was able to keep clear of entanglements, build up his fantasies, pay off a lot of old scores against his mother beneath the guise of women in general, and maintain his solitary introvert's life in his lonely book-lined chapel.

But for all this there was a price that had to be paid. One part of it was that he would never really understand women at all, and it is because of this that all his heroines from Vesper Lynd to Kissy Suzuki remain the same tedious two-dimensional cardboard creatures.

This would have mattered less if he had enjoyed himself, but he never gives the impression that his long succession of affairs ever gave him any great happiness. Quite the contrary. There is something distinctly anguished about those silences

89

he imposed on his mistresses, those sudden changes of affection, that anxious restlessness. It was not until long after the war that he told one of his mistresses that she was the first woman he had spent an entire night in bed with.

Some people who knew him well believe that the reason for all this was that Fleming was essentially a puritan and an idealist and that he was always longing for a woman who matched some childhood dream of chastity and beauty. It was this endles search, they maintain, which lay behind his womanizing, and it was his endless disgust when women succumbed to him that drove him away in search of others. 'Never forget,' says one of his close friends, 'that behind Ian stood the Galahad figure of his father. As the black sheep, Ian had learned to rebel against him but never to reject him, and the older he got the more the puritanical side of his nature disapproved of what the rest of him was up to.'

Certainly there was a strong vein of instinctive puritanism in Fleming—it showed, for example, in his dislike of nail varnish and lipstick on women, and he could easily be shocked by the behaviour of the teenage daughters of his friends. During the last years of his life he clearly believed that his illness was some sort of retribution for the 'indulgences' of his youth.

But the trouble lay deeper even than this. It lay in that solitary dream world which he had constructed and of which even sex had had to become a part. In this world of unreality he would never risk revealing himself to another human being. Ultimately there was no relief from the interminable ego. He was bored and he was alone with his boredom and not even sex could provide a lasting escape. For it was now, in the years just before the war, that he began to talk for the first time of the subject which later in life was to become his particular *bête noire*—*accidie,* 'that awful boredom', as he wrote, 'which would engulf whole towns in the Middle Ages, and which, because it was a denial of life itself, was made an offence against God by the Church.'

It was this boredom, this 'denial of life itself', which was the source of his periods of black melancholy, and it was a boredom that finally destroyed his relations with women. He described the process quite unsentimentally in *Casino Royale*:

With most women his manner was a mixture of taciturnity and passion. The lengthy approaches to a seduction bored him almost as much as the subsequent mess of disentanglement. He found something grisly in the inevitability of the pattern of each affair. The conventional parabola—sentiment, the touch of the hand, the kiss, the passionate kiss, the feel of the body, the climax in bed, then more bed, then less bed, then the boredom, the tears and the final bitterness—was to him shameful and hypocritical.

And as he was to write, with still greater candour, in one of his notebooks, when he was describing a man's progress from woman to woman, 'What happens is that, as with drugs, he needs a stronger shot each time, and women are just women. The consumption of one woman is the consumption of all. You can't double the dose.'

II

The private life of Ian Fleming was a very private affair. But in public he had friends and contacts now in many spheres, not least in Whitehall. In the Foreign Office they had not forgotten his private report on the Vickers trial, and Sir Robert Vansittart, whom he met occasionally, had his eye on him. (So had Lord Kemsley, the newspaper proprietor, with whom Fleming played bridge and went yachting.) Vansittart knew that war was a certainty and thought that when it came someone with this young man's background and experience and knowledge of Russia could be very useful.

Fleming was still a stockbroker when he returned to Moscow in the spring of 1939: a stockbroker and a reserve subaltern in the Black Watch mysteriously seconded to *The Times*. On this occasion he entered Russia in an official Pullman specially dispatched by Litvinov, the Commissar for Foreign Affairs, to the Polish frontier. As the train steamed off towards Moscow Fleming tucked into a breakfast of caviare, cream and Russian pancakes served by Litvinov's white-gloved butler.

It was a bizarre occasion. Mr R. S. Hudson, Secretary for Overseas Trade in the Chamberlain Government, was leading a Trade Mission to Russia and Poland which no one believed in. Fleming was going with it officially for *The Times* and unofficially for the Foreign Office. According to a recent article in *Pravda* the real purpose of his journey was to spy for British Intelligence, and it is true that he made the same impression on Mr Sefton Delmer, who was reporting the mission for the *Daily Express* and who met Fleming for the first time over that indigestible breakfast in the

Pullman. 'As soon as I saw him,' says Delmer, 'I knew he was on some intelligence job or other. He was so much the type they used to use in those days and he made such a determined show of typing away whenever the Russians were looking that it was clear he was no ordinary journalist.' The truth seems to be that Fleming was asked to keep his eyes and ears open and prepare an estimate, on his return, of potential Russian military strength and morale.

To *The Times* he sent a stereotyped interview with the Polish Prime Minister and two or three dull little snippets of journalism. Evidently Fleming's heart wasn't in this part of the job. Yet the Special Correspondent of *The Times* enjoyed himself during his five days in Moscow, even if he did insist that it was 'just like the Gorbals' in Glasgow. According to Delmer he seemed to be acting the part of one of the Secret Service men he had read about in Phillips Oppenheim. With a suitable air of mystery he took the *Daily Express* correspondent off one wet evening on a long and fruitless attempt to discover Litvinov's private flat. Finally, just to prove to Delmer that he was an old Moscow hand, he took him to the National Hotel, where they booked suite 107 and picked up a pair of young ladies from Odessa. Next morning Fleming left the bottom half of his silk pyjamas as a present for his girl. The two men were lucky, perhaps: it was in suite 107 in 1961 that Fleming's friend Commander Anthony Courtney, then a widower, was secretly photographed with a Russian woman by the Russian secret police.

But if Fleming's attempts to probe the secret life of Moscow were rudimentary, he did have the opportunity of observing the Soviet leaders at work. The discussions on the Anglo-Soviet trade agreement took place inside the Kremlin, and as he watched Mikoyan and Litvinov presenting the Russian case he was seeing an aspect of Soviet leadership very different from what he remembered of Vyshinsky's vituperation from the Prosecutor's desk at the Metro-Vickers trial. The bomb-proof devices with which Stalin's court surrounded itself appealed profoundly to his imagination.

On March 26th the mission had its final meeting with Mikoyan before boarding Litvinov's caviare-encumbered Pullman once more for the Finnish frontier and home. Fleming had preferred to join Delmer on the Warsaw Express, and as soon as he was back in Ebury Street he began to write his report. He headed it, 'Russia's Strength. Some cautionary notes,' and opened with an interesting confession: 'The writer returned from Soviet Russia last week. He has no political prejudices whatever.'

Considering how short had been his stay and how meagre his sources the report was a minor *tour de force*; where facts were lacking his imagination was more than adequate to fill the gap, and it was written with the fine Buchanesque relish of a man who had found his right element at last. It is hard to believe that it was any more misleading than most of the intelligence reports sent back by genuine British agents at the time—it was certainly more readable.

It was near the end, when he gave his own estimate of the Russian soldier, that he showed his real flair:

It is impossible to judge these men by English standards. Their fatalism, their lack of critical standards, their general unawareness are all foreign to our character and a source of exasperation to us. In attempting to estimate their value as allies we can only say that their courage is high and that the breaking point of their morale is high. British and French liaison officers who may be called upon to work in Russia will be appalled by the task which will confront them: they will be confounded with administrative chaos such as they never dreamt of: they will flounder in a Sargasso Sea of all the red tape in the world. But when the moment comes for action they will realize that these tough grey-faced little men (the average height of the army is 5′ 5″) are a vastly different force from the ill-equipped gun fodder of 1914.

If a man who could roll off phrases like these in an obscure intelligence report was probably of dubious value as a spy, there was not a great deal more he needed to learn in the business of becoming a thriller-writer.

CHAPTER NINE

FLEMING'S WAR

I

> But if the politicians make mistakes it isn't from lack of good
> instruction to guide their steps. If I had a big proposition to
> handle and could have my pick of helpers I'd plump for the
> Intelligence Department of the British Admiralty.
>
> John Buchan: *Greenmantle*

SINCE they built New Zealand House on that corner site
where Haymarket sweeps into Pall Mall, the Carlton Grill
has become one of the lost landmarks of London. But it
really died one night in 1940 when a German thousand-kilo
bomb brought the rest of the Carlton Hotel crashing down
into its famous gold-and-white interior, burying the rococo
side-tables, destroying the big portrait of King Edward VIII
as Prince of Wales, and scattering the ghosts of the generals
and actors and politicians who had dined and gossiped
and plotted here since the turn of the century. Before the
war the Carlton Grill, a brisk five-minute walk across the
Horse Guards and up the Duke of York steps, was almost an
annex of Whitehall, and when the Rear-Admiral decided
one May morning in 1939 that the time had come for him
to meet Mr Ian Fleming (who had now settled down to
stockbroking again after that odd visit to Russia and
Poland), the Carlton Grill was the obvious place to suggest.
It was sufficiently discreet; the tables were wide enough apart
for one not to be overheard; the food and the wines were
better than at most of the clubs in Pall Mall or St James's.
The Rear-Admiral believed in doing things well, and much
could depend on this first meeting. A lot of people had taken
a lot of trouble finding him the man he needed. The moment
had come to look him over.

Not that Fleming had any idea what was involved or
where this first lunch was to lead him when he paid off his
taxi and went through the hotel foyer and down the stairs
to meet his mysterious host: he had spoken to him only
once, on the telephone, and he had to ask Henri Mittaz, the
grill-room's *maître d'hôtel*, to show him Admiral Godfrey's
table. To his surprise he saw sitting there a dapper, elderly

figure with a neat white beard whom he knew well already, Admiral Aubrey Hugh-Smith, brother of Lance Hugh-Smith, the senior partner in his own stockbroking firm of Rowe and Pitman; and it was Admiral Hugh-Smith who introduced him to his host, a tall, rubicund naval officer in a dark-grey suit who briskly thanked Fleming for coming and began to order lunch. It was a strange situation for this reserve subaltern in the Black Watch to find himself in, unexpectedly being given lunch by a brace of admirals.

Neither of them explained at any stage of the meal what was exactly in mind nor how Admiral Godfrey had come to invite the young man to the Carlton Grill in the first place. If they had, Ian Fleming would have been excited and flattered: what with one thing and another he was becoming very popular in Whitehall. He would also have seen the funny side of it, for he was there on the direct recommendation of the Governor of the Bank of England—the flamboyant and dictatorial Montagu Norman. Fleming had never met Norman, but behind the scenes the Governor had been taking a lot of trouble on the young man's behalf during the last week or two. It was an odd role for a banker.

It had all begun with the recent appointment of Rear-Admiral John Godfrey to the post of Director of Naval Intelligence at the Admiralty. During his thirty years in the Royal Navy he had been Deputy Director of the Plans Division at the Admiralty and commanded the battle-cruiser *Repulse*. His reputation was that of a decisive and unusually imaginative officer, but this was his first experience in intelligence work and he was deeply aware of the importance of the position he now occupied. In Room 38 in the West Block of the Admiralty, ground floor, he sat behind the desk of Admiral Sir Reginald 'Blinker' Hall, who during the First World War had built up the Naval Intelligence Division into the most efficient organization of its sort in the world. Hall was a determined, ruthless and vital little man, and his department at the Admiralty had become the centre of a complex yet self-contained network of technical experts, cartographers, reporters, interrogators, cryptographers and spies whose entire purpose was to see that the Royal Navy was better informed than the enemy. With its efficiency and its determined use of the latest techniques it had become the first full-scale modern intelligence organization. And it had belonged to the Navy. A tradition had been established.

When Admiral Godfrey was appointed Director of Naval Intelligence at the beginning of 1939 the department had shrunk to a peacetime ghost of its wartime splendour. Now, with a fresh war around the corner, the time had come to rebuild it, and the memory of N.I.D.'s successes was there to suggest how it should be done and what would be expected of it. Sir Reginald Hall was still alive to give the new D.N.I. his advice—and incidentally to lend him his flat at No. 36 Curzon Street—and Rear-Admiral Godfrey began to earmark the men he would need.

One of the lessons Sir Reginald Hall had learned was that intelligence organizations require talents not necessarily found among service officers. Much of his success had been due to the use he had made of the outlandish, the unorthodox and the inspired—he had employed brains wherever he could find them. Admiral Godfrey was eager to do the same, and since his appointment he had been hard at work as a talent scout, discovering dons and scientists, journalists and lawyers who might one day be of use to him. By the time he met Fleming he had about 130 names on his short-list.

There was still one important post the D.N.I. had to fill within his embryo empire, and here again Godfrey was to consult precedent. During the first war one of the key men in N.I.D. had been a stockbroker called Claude Serocold. Admiral Hall had chosen him to act as his personal assistant, and as the unorthodox, unseamanlike organization grew, Serocold became invaluable. As a stockbroker he possessed experience and aptitudes which Hall lacked and he had friends and contacts in the most unlikely places. When it was necessary he could get on with almost anybody, and much of the cohesion of Admiral Hall's heterogeneous department came from the tact and skill of his personal assistant.

When Admiral Godfrey spoke to Admiral Hall about the appointment of his own personal assistant, the former D.N.I. said that he could not do better than choose another stockbroker. Godfrey was without personal knowledge of the City so, as he says, 'I consulted Serocold and Admiral Aubrey Hugh-Smith and talked again to Admiral Hall about the filling of this appointment in war. They gave the matter much thought and advised me to consult Montagu Norman and Edward Peacock, chairman of the merchant bank of Barings.'

Far from being surprised by this unusual request, Norman

seems to have taken it very seriously and tackled it with customary energy. He asked for a few days to think it over. Godfrey suggested that he should call on him at the Bank of England to discuss it. 'No sir,' replied Norman. 'Your time is far more valuable than mine. I shall call on you.'

So the Governor of the Bank of England drove from the City to Horse Guards Parade in his large grey Lincoln. He had always been a man of decision and few words, and when he was shown into Room 38 he came straight to the point. 'Admiral,' he said, 'I think we've found the man you want. His name is Ian Fleming and he is a junior partner in the firm of Rowe and Pitman, stockbrokers in the City of London.' They shook hands. The interview was over.

Godfrey never knew exactly how Montagu Norman reached this somewhat startling decision nor whom he in his turn had consulted. Norman did not know Fleming personally and so must have relied on the recommendations of a number of others before he could have been quite so sure of the man he was putting forward. It is interesting that he gave Godfrey no alternative names.

The usual mode of entry to the misty world of intelligence is by knowing somebody who knows somebody, and there was an impressive cluster of people around Montagu Norman and N.I.D. who knew Ian Fleming well. It is interesting that Admiral Hugh-Smith, who knew him through Rowe and Pitman, had served as Deputy D.N.I. under Sir Reginald Hall during the first war. Baring Brothers, the chairman of which Rear-Admiral Godfrey had also consulted, had very strong ties with the firm of Robert Fleming. Hugo Pitman, the other senior partner of Rowe and Pitman and an important figure in the City, was a devoted friend of Fleming's, and Sir Claude Serocold, the former personal assistant to the D.N.I., whom Godfrey had already consulted, had known the Fleming family for years.

Despite the impressive nature of Fleming's candidature, Godfrey had no intention of making up his mind irremediably. He was predictably impressed at the Carlton Grill meeting, for at thirty-one Ian Fleming was a striking young man. The charm, the vitality, the sense of adventure and enthusiasm of his early twenties had remained intact. He had acquired something else during his time in the City —a certain confidence and air of authority which during the years ahead was to carry him through many a tense encounter with officers considerably his senior.

But Godfrey wanted a chance to see him at work, and during that first lunch at the Carlton Grill the only reference he made to the future was to suggest that Fleming might care to hold himself in readiness for a very special post in time of war. It was highly nebulous and all the more exciting for that. Naturally Fleming soon found out Godfrey's position at the Admiralty, and during those last few months of peace he must have enjoyed the surreptitious importance he had suddenly assumed. Everything was beginning to unfold in the best adventure-book style.

A few days after the lunch an official letter arrived for Fleming. It made him little the wiser but heightened the suspense:

Sir,

I am commanded by My Lords Commissioners of the Admiralty to thank you for the offer of your services to the Admiralty and to inform you that as they would probably desire to avail themselves of your offer should hostilities break out, My Lords have given directions that you should be earmarked for service under the Admiralty in the event of emergency.

I am, Sir,

Your obedient servant,
N. MACLEOD,
Secretary of the Admiralty

Then Admiral Godfrey telephoned again, suggesting another meeting, this time in the Admiralty itself. He was still vague about Fleming's precise duties but said if he could square it with Rowe and Pitman it would be very useful if he could start working at the Admiralty on a part-time basis, in order to get the feel of the place.

This presented no difficulty, and during July Fleming began visiting the Admiralty three or four afternoons a week. It was highly secret. During the mornings he was still a stockbroker. But after lunch at White's in St James's Street he would stroll along the Mall, present his temporary pass to the retired sergeant of Marines at the small desk just inside the discreet entrance at the Admiralty Quadrangle, and walk along the corridor to the left until he reached a large black door with the number 39 in white numerals. Here he would enter without knocking, and it would often be late before he reappeared.

During the war Room 39 was to become something of a legend, and as it was also to be the scene of the greater part of Ian Fleming's war it is worth a glance. When Fleming first saw it the room itself was already a relic of an older, statelier Admiralty which had been on its way out when the first dreadnoughts were coming in: a large, uncomfortable, mid-nineteenth-century office with high, elaborate ceiling, iron radiators, cream-painted walls and a heavy black marble fireplace fed by anonymous men with large coal scuttles from the Ministry of Works. It was on the ground floor and its two large sashed windows gazed out on the gravelled meadow of Horse Guards Parade. The First Sea Lord had his office directly overhead, the private entrance to No. 10 Downing Street was just visible on the opposite side of the square, and beyond that stretched the Foreign Office, the Treasury and the whole grey back of Whitehall.

Throughout the war it was the nerve centre of the Naval Intelligence Division, originating, sifting, co-ordinating the day-to-day work. If the enemy developed a new torpedo or planted another minefield, if maps were needed for a stretch of North German coast or details were wanted of a particular U-boat commander, if an agent was reporting on the harbour facilities at Kiel or a check was needed on the range of German bombers from Hamburg, action of some sort would sooner or later follow in Room 39. While Godfrey was building up this machine Fleming was quietly learning how it worked during those early summer afternoons when he slipped away from the City. 'He had a remarkable power of assimilating the details of any organization,' says Godfrey, 'and I arranged for him to be shown everything. Within a month he had a better all-round picture of N.I.D. and its place in the Admiralty than most of the people who had been there for years.'

For Admiral Godfrey this was more than enough. He had found Serocold's successor. On July 26th Ian Fleming was appointed a Lieutenant (special branch) in the Royal Naval Volunteer Reserve, and the Admiral explained just what his duties were to be when war broke out. They were considerably more than is normally understood by the term personal assistant, and in fulfilling them Fleming finally discovered the one job for which he was ideally suited, the one career in which he was to be completely at home and in which every side of his complex and contradictory nature could be made the most of; by the time war was declared he had already created an indispensable place for himself.

'From the beginning,' says Admiral Godfrey, 'my idea was that I would tell Ian everything so that if anything happened

99

to me there would be one man who would know what was going on—he could ensure the continuity of the department. I also used him a lot to represent me on important routine inter-departmental conferences.' These included subjects like propaganda, Press, subversive activities and political warfare—the sort of intricate, time-consuming committee work for which the D.N.I. himself had insufficient time but which was found fascinating by his conscientious and highly trusted P.A. Soon Fleming had become the wartime executive *par excellence,* representing and directing, co-ordinating, liaising and reporting along Whitehall's rabbit-run of power. Throughout the war his desk stayed in the same place—on the far side of Room 39 by the window and the green baize door behind which, in Room 38, the Admiral worked in his lonely splendour, summoning whichever member of his staff he required by two, three or four bursts from the buzzer on his desk.

The hubbub and discomfort of Room 39 steadily increased. At the peak of the war one captain, seven commanders, two lieutenants, two male civilian assistants and four women secretaries somehow worked there; and in the middle of it all Fleming managed to act as the buffer, the fixer, the reporter and the personal representative of the man in Room 38.

'Ian had enormous flair, imagination and ability to get on with people,' says Admiral Sir Norman Denning, a post-war D.N.I. who saw a lot of him during the war. 'He would have been no use in a routine Admiralty appointment, but he was perfect for this one job. He could fix anyone or anything if it was really necessary.'

He could also be surprisingly tactful. 'He learnt, perhaps sooner than I,' says Admiral Godfrey, 'that intelligence may be a sticky commodity which sometimes needs sugar coating and that the purveyor of bad tidings is unwelcome. How to reconcile sugar coating and bad tidings with speed is an aptitude possessed by few.' Fleming evidently did. But he seems to have combined this with a total lack of awe for the admirals and generals and air marshals he found himself working with. 'There are only two people you should ever call "Sir",' he once told his friend Philip Brownrigg, 'God and the King'. And he maintained this attitude throughout his Admiralty career. 'He was,' says John Godfrey, 'completely devoid of "very senior officer veneration".' 'As a wavy navy chap,' says another friend, 'old Ian just didn't care. If there was a job to be done he would speak to the First Sea Lord in exactly the same way as he would speak to his driver. And the remarkable thing about him was that he would always get away with it. He just had a way with him.'

It was because he had a way with him that Godfrey was able to make the use of him that he did. When it was necessary for Naval Intelligence to work with the Air Ministry it would be Lieutenant Fleming who sat in on the preliminary committees. When the time came to co-ordinate propaganda attacking the morale of enemy U-boat crews, Fleming attended that committee as well. And earlier, when the First Lord himself, already champing at the inaction of the early weeks of war, sent down his dangerously barbed inquiries to the Director of Naval Intelligence, it was Lieutenant Fleming who would usually end up drafting the replies. 'Pray why is nothing being done about the enemy shipping in Vigo harbour?' Churchill would ask, and in his precise yet deceptively lethargic manner Fleming would dictate a suitable reply to one of the women secretaries. And as Godfrey's confidence in his P.A. increased, Fleming was given considerable discretion in vetting fresh personnel for N.I.D. The only part of Naval Intelligence Fleming had nothing to do with during these early months of the war was that which would have bored him anyhow, namely the detailed plotting of the movement and position of every enemy vessel; this was directed in the big underground map room in the Citadel.

Apart from this Fleming had a finger in virtually everything, and before the war had lasted many months this reserve lieutenant knew more secrets and had more real power than most of the senior officers in all three Services with whom he came into contact. Godfrey saw the incongruity as well as the danger of this situation, and used his influence to ensure that Fleming's promotion to lieutenant-commander and then to full commander went forward as fast as possible. For once he had chosen Fleming and put his trust in him, he never seems to have had even a momentary qualm. Indeed, there is a touching modesty in the tribute he was to pay Fleming after his death: 'I once said that Ian should have been the D.N.I. and I his naval adviser. If he had been ten years older and I ten years younger this might have had the elements of a workable proposition.'

Inevitably, Fleming's position caused occasional resentment and jealousy: some felt that this gilded newcomer from the reserve had altogether more power than was good for him. But the one thing no one could deny was his dedication. He was loyal to John Godfrey in the way he always could be to men he respected and who were older than himself; and Godfrey in his turn understood how to treat him and get the best from him. 'I soon realized that Ian's weakness was that he couldn't be bothered to persuade people who weren't interested and that he wasn't naturally good at following things through. But I wouldn't let him get away with just flinging in a few ideas and then leaving someone else to do the hard work. "Ian," I'd say, "you've got to fix every detail down to the last button." And in the end he did too.'

Everyone agrees that Fleming rapidly developed a surprising feeling for the Navy. The oddly persuasive trappings of the Admiralty intensified that same pre-1914 brand of now unfashionable patriotism which he passed on to James Bond. There is an extreme example of this in an anonymous letter he sent to *The Times* in July 1940 arising from the wiping out of a squadron of obsolete R.A.F. Gladiator biplanes in the defence of Narvik. Fleming seemed to think the time had come for a special award for units which were totally destroyed in battle:

It occurs to me that a suitable award of this kind would be the presentation by His Majesty the King of the Union Jack which, on the day of the event, was flying or was ready to be flown from the flagstaff of the Houses of Parliament. This is certainly the most famous flag flying in the Empire. It has a great significance for us and great associations in all our hearts. It is to keep that particular flag flying that our men are dying and our units sacrificing themselves. There could be no more simple or romantic symbol of the gratitude of the Empire and no greater heritage for a wardroom or an officers' mess. I hope the idea or its equivalent will be adopted.

Your obedient servant,
AN OFFICER

Altogether Fleming was in his element at the Admiralty. Yet the tension, the aloofness, the loneliness, the alienation of others were still there, and many of the people with whom he worked closely in Room 39 were to feel at the end that he had never been one of them at all. One of them writes:

In a sense he repelled happiness in the innocent forms in which it manifested itself in Room 39. Indeed, there were moments when quite amusing little remarks were being hurled across the room and Ian was not and had no intention of being 'with it'. I am not sure there were not moments when one even felt a trifle ashamed of being so light-hearted.

Throughout the war the man who saw most of him was a solicitor named Edward Merrett, Admiral Godfrey's secretary, who sat at the next desk. Just before he died in March 1966 Merrett said: 'The first time I saw him I put Ian Fleming down as a withdrawn and unhappy man, and I never changed my mind about that. I thought his attitude was very much that of the typical Old Etonian, that same withdrawn superiority, and I have never forgotten the way he used that remark of his, "Well, there it is." Anything he was bored with or tired of would be terminated with "Well, there it is." '

All the same, withdrawn, lonely, aloof though he still may have been underneath, he seemed transformed to certain people who remembered him from before the war as 'someone rather dim in the City who happened to be Peter Fleming's brother'.

'During the war,' says Cyril Connolly, 'Ian, whom I always liked, seemed to have become terribly grand. For me he suddenly had all the attraction the genuine man of action often holds for the intellectual. He was far too important to ring up at the Admiralty, but I used to see him from time to time at White's or the Étoile, and he always seemed to be with someone or other immensely important—a general or a field-marshal or something—and when he greeted one, one would feel rather like a delicate monkey being put through its tricks. "Look, General"—or "Admiral"—he'd say, "this is Connolly, who publishes a perfectly ghastly magazine full of subversive rubbish written by a lot of long-haired drivelling conchies. Of course, all of them will soon be inside for seven years under 18B so perhaps you'd better subscribe to the thing now while you've got a chance just to see the sort of outrageous stuff that can get by in a country like this during wartime." And,' adds Connolly, 'grudgingly, laughingly, the man would be pushed into taking out a subscription for *Horizon*.'

Perhaps Fleming was a little too immaculate and handsome in that discreet blue uniform. Perhaps he seemed just a little too pleased with himself. At any rate, it was about now that a wag gave him a nickname that was to stick for a long time to come. He had been invited to a party in Mayfair and had arrived late from the Admiralty. 'Aha!' said someone maliciously as he came in, 'if it isn't the chocolate sailor.'

II

It would be grossly unfair to regard Ian Fleming, even at the beginning of the war, as a playboy sailor. But the impression was around, possibly invented and fostered by those who looked sourly at his influence at the Admiralty and his access to a social set not greatly frequented by young R.N.V.R. lieutenants.

It was noted, for example, that he was present at a party which Lady O'Neill gave for her friends at the Dorchester Hotel on the first New Year's Eve of the war. Duff Cooper, the Minister of Information, was there with his wife Diana. So was Lord Rothermere, who was to marry Lady O'Neill after her husband Shane was killed in action. Loelia, Duchess of Westminster, arrived, as did Brendan Bracken. All things considered, it was a remarkably cheerful evening, with the best joke coming by proxy from the legendary General Carton de Wiart, who had led the British Military Mission to Poland and, when that country was overrun by the Germans, had made his way out through Rumania. 'I was told,' he had remarked to Lady O'Neill, 'that in Bucharest I would find pimps, pansies and musicians. I found no musicians.'

At this early stage in the war Ian Fleming was often at the Dorchester. The place was crowded with the rich and the famous, some of whom had shut their London houses and all of whom must have felt comforted by the story that had got round that the steel and concrete construction of the hotel offered superior protection against Hitler's bombs—which, as it happened, were to be delayed for another nine months or so. To this 'gilded bird-cage of the rich', as Anne O'Neill called it, Fleming went to dine in the restaurant or play bridge with Lord and Lady Kemsley and Lord Rothermere. The O'Neills used the Dorchester when they were in London, and Fleming, who was now their friend, met them there. Through Anne O'Neill, who knew everyone and was passionately interested in what was going on, he must have had a better idea of political gossip at the top than most of the admirals and generals he met in the conference rooms of Whitehall during the day.

Inside knowledge always fascinated him, and with it he combined an almost mystical feeling of veneration for the Royal Navy. The resulting enthusiasm which he felt for his job also tapped that industrious, serious side of his nature which so few of his friends knew anything about.

But there was the other side—the dreamer, the ever-present black sheep who was always longing for adventure, for movement, for the fertile promise of excitement. This too was catered for by the war. For that winter Fleming must have recognized the boyhood tang of Buchan and Jules Verne which wafted around the corridors and committee rooms of Whitehall. London was full of secret organizations. Private armies were forming everywhere. The geniuses and the crackpots were getting their chance at last. Whitehall was thronged with them. Innovation being in the air, one revolutionary in a thick tweed suit had plans to freeze the clouds, moor them along the coast of Southern England and use them as platforms for anti-aircraft guns. Another had a scheme for a chain of heavily fortified Allied icebergs in the North Atlantic. Even the First Lord of the Admiralty had pet plans which left fiction far behind.

For Fleming in the middle of it all it must have seemed like his youthful fantasies at Kitzbühel all over again, with the machine-guns hidden in the exhaust pipes of fast sports cars and the prospect of long brave battles with enemy agents again in the mountain passes above Munich. 'What nonsense they were,' he wrote nostalgically when the war was long behind him, 'those romantic, Red Indian daydreams so many of us indulged in at the beginning of the war—to blow up the Iron Gates of the Danube, to parachute into Berlin and assassinate Hitler and all the rest.' But nonsense or not he was thrilled—his imagination had never needed much encouragement.

The fantasist in Fleming fed on contacts between Naval Intelligence and the cloak-and-dagger world of the Special Operations Executive, an organization set up in the war to carry out irregular operations such as the parachuting of men and weapons to resistance movements in Occupied Europe. For although Lieutenant Fleming was officially an outside observer at the conferences which went on inside those anonymous-looking heavily guarded office blocks at

Baker Street and elsewhere, he was emotionally very much a part of them. The experience was to be immensely useful when fourteen years later he began the life-story of James Bond. Of course, there was no secret agent quite like James Bond, nor was there any organization calling itself simply the Secret Service. But Fleming did have considerable contact with what is commonly called the Secret Service: M.I.6 (Military Intelligence, Section 6), the cover title given to the British Secret Intelligence Service, which works under the supervision of the Foreign Office. He was also in touch with M.I.5, the security service responsible for counter-espionage, under the Home Office.

But although Fleming was strictly an outsider in these worlds, he seems to have become very much involved in spirit with the 'black' world of the Special Operations Executive. His brother Peter had already been recruited by the S.O.E. for special work in the Middle East, and blowing up the Iron Gates and assassinating Hitler were both S.O.E. pipe-dreams which were scrutinized in complete seriousness in the earlier days of the war. In this climate Fleming inevitably worked out a private undercover adventure of his own. He described it all in 1960 when he drove up the coast of North Germany past *The Riddle of the Sands* landscape of the Frisian Islands, on his way to write about the night life of Hamburg:

The last time I had paid serious attention to these island names—Wangerooge, Spiekeroog, Nordeney, Borkum—was when, as a young Lieutenant R.N.V.R., I had studied them endlessly on Admiralty charts and put up a succession of plans whereby I and an equally intrepid wireless operator should be transported to the group by submarine and there dig ourselves in, to report the sailings of U-boats and the movements of the German fleet.

(This idea of digging in and surveying the enemy through periscopes was a favourite daydream. Apart from a variant of it which he suggested, as we shall see in a moment, for the Dieppe raid, he was to use it again as the basis of the plot of his short story 'From a View to a Kill', where a gang of Russian spies bury themselves in the woods near SHAPE headquarters at St Germain.)

Everything in those foolhardy minutes on Admiralty dockets was thought out, everything provided for. There would be a pedal generator for the wireless set, we would live on shell-fish, my excellent (as I claimed) knowledge of German would be enough to bluff our way out of trouble in case some inquisitive fisherman turned up.

Nothing came of it, though—perhaps nothing was really intended to come of it; it was hardly likely that Admiral Godfrey would have risked his highly valued personal assistant on a North Sea island with a periscope and a pedal generator. It was at the desk that the true task of this P.A. lay, and during all these exciting months, when so much was in the air, the restless, romantic side of Fleming had to make do with the fiction writer's *faute de mieux*—he could dream but not do, plan but not perform.

'A lot of Ian's ideas,' says Admiral Denning, 'were just plain crazy. One had to accept this element of wildness in all his thinking. But a lot of his far-fetched ideas had just that glimmer of possibility in them that made you think twice before you threw them in the wastepaper basket. Just before the Dieppe raid, for instance, he had the idea of sinking a great block of concrete with men inside it in the English Channel to keep watch on the harbour through periscopes. We never did it, of course, but it *might* have worked.'

Another early idea of his was that the Germans might have been installing listening devices on a number of off-shore wrecks along the English coast to transmit the engine noise of passing Allied shipping to their U-boats. No one had thought of this disquieting possibility before; and just to put the Admiralty's mind at rest a detailed search of wrecked ships along the Kent coast was duly made.

He also evolved a scheme for bringing the German battle fleet out of harbour. 'Why not,' he suggested, 'send a cruiser into the Heligoland Bight with an extremely powerful transmitter beamed to the German Navy's wavelength? It could keep up a torrent of abuse, challenging the German Naval commanders by name to come out and do something about it. No sailor likes to be accused of cowardice, and Germans are always particularly touchy.' For a few days Fleming's suggestion was given a lot of thought, but finally it had to be dropped because no cruiser with a powerful enough transmitter was available.

During these early months in Room 39 what Fleming really longed for was not so much action as adventure, a genuine dramatic role; and at the beginning of June 1940, on the eve of the French surrender, he finally got his chance.

By then the lightning German attack through the Low

Countries and Northern France had already occurred, and Paris was expected to fall at any moment. The French Army was finished but the Navy, under Admiral Darlan, was still very much a power to be reckoned with—it was the fourth largest navy in the world, highly efficient and with modern ships. The Admiralty, during those days of chaos, was vitally concerned to know what would become of it. Churchill himself had grave qualms when he remembered how Darlan had replied to a toast at an Admiralty banquet in his honour the previous December by reminding his British hosts that his own great-grandfather had been killed at Trafalgar. The French Navy was devoted to Darlan, but Darlan was far from devoted to Britain. So far he had refused to give the order, so desperately desired by Churchill, for the French warships to sail to British ports.

As long as Paris held out, the Admiralty had a tenuous radio link with the French Admiral through the British Embassy there. By the second week in June Darlan had already withdrawn his rear headquarters from Paris to the big Château d'Artigny (built by Coty, the scent king) at Montbazon, near Tours, and although a French-speaking British naval officer, Captain C. S. Holland, was with him to represent the Admiralty, there seemed no way of maintaining this communication once the teleprinter link between London and the British Embassy was lost by the fall of Paris. At this point Fleming came up with an idea. He suggested to Godfrey that he, Fleming, should be sent off immediately to Montbazon, along with a wireless operator, with orders to stay as close as possible to Admiral Darlan until he made up his mind. 'I cannot imagine what made me suggest this,' Fleming wrote later, 'except perhaps my usual desire to escape from Room 39 and get some fresh air.'

Somewhat to his surprise, Admiral Godfrey agreed: and on June 13th the R.A.F. flew a wireless operator and Fleming to Le Bourget. He carried with him an official letter from the Air Ministry to the British Air Attaché in Paris optimistically requesting that Lieutenant I. L. Fleming be given return passage by air to London on any date that suited him.

From Paris the two men made their way to Tours and Montbazon by road, and at the château—a grandiose affair which is now one of the most luxurious and expensive hotels in France—found the expected chaos. Darlan was still refusing to commit himself, and much of the time passed in repetitious argument between him and Captain Holland, who was trying to persuade the Admiral that the situation was now so grave that he had to leave for England immediately.

Through his radio operator Fleming was able to keep in touch with London, and on June 15th he passed on to Darlan an official message urging him yet again to bring over his fleet and explaining that preparations were already being made to receive him and his ships. Still playing for time, Darlan wrote his reply to the British Government and handed it to Fleming for transmission back to London:

I have shown the message to Commandant Auphan who found it too pessimistic. The Germans are only in the south of Paris and it is not yet a question of burning harbour installations. The port of Cherbourg, the first threatened by the long range plan, will be energetically defended by Admiral Abrial.

As for the *Richelieu* and the *Jean Bart* [two incomplete great battleships], they will go to England if the risk from the air is too serious or if anything really grave occurs. The French Admiralty is grateful for these preparations to welcome these ships or others if it is necessary, but i·s not counting on using them except in the last resort. For the moment the war at sea will go on as before.

This was practically the last Fleming saw of Darlan, for German dive-bombers, a little too well-informed for comfort, attacked the château and Darlan and his staff disappeared in the direction of Bordeaux with Lieutenant Fleming and wireless operator in hot pursuit. In keeping up with a highly mobile quarry Fleming was full of initiative, and it was a disappointment to him to be turned away from the job and told to help with the British evacuation from Bordeaux instead.

Perhaps the Admiralty gave up too easily. He certainly thought that his place should have been beside Admiral Darlan until a genuine decision was reached. Yet in that event he would have missed a strange and moving episode in his life. For in Bordeaux the actor *manqué* in Ian Fleming suddenly discovered the drama he missed in Room 39 and assumed a role which only he could have played. Virtually without orders, he found himself a key figure in one of the oddest episodes of the French defeat.

By the time he arrived there, Bordeaux and the estuary of the Gironde offered the best escape route from the whole of Western France, and everyone anxious to get away had funnelled into the town. It was crammed. The French and British General Staffs were there. The British Ambassador arrived with a large party from the Embassy in Paris. The First Lord of the Admiralty, Mr A. V. Alexander, landed in a flying-boat in yet another attempt to make Darlan see sense. De Gaulle got away by air to Britain on June 14th. Officials of all kinds and servicemen and hordes of refugees, many of them rich British nationals, were all clamouring to get away too.

One of the few precise instructions Fleming did receive over his private radio was to make sure that a large dump of aero engines and spares was prevented from falling into enemy hands. Getting these engines back to England immediately became a challenge to his ingenuity. Documents and dumps of war material were already smouldering on the outskirts of the city, for senior diplomats and others were jettisoning all but their most vital belongings. Such behaviour was not Fleming's line at all. As a uniformed British naval officer he exerted a mixture of casually delivered bluff and effortless authority on the captain of a ship which was to sail for England that same afternoon. No matter if V.I.P.s were crowding the vessel, those several dozen large packing cases on the dockside had to be put aboard straightaway. He was not in a position to tell the captain exactly what they contained: enough to say that the British Government had been in contact with him by radio to make sure that they reached England safely. The captain understood, and the engines arrived home two days later. Peter Smithers—later Conservative M.P. for Winchester and today Secretary-General of the Council for Europe—remembers arriving in Bordeaux as a naval lieutenant with the British Naval Attaché, meeting Fleming there, and going with him to a farewell dinner which the British and French General Staffs held in the Chapon Fin restaurant in Bordeaux, then one of the greatest restaurants in France. Fleming was immensely touched by the occasion. Until the meal actually began an air of appalling disaster hung about the strange, grotto-like interior with the tree growing up the middle. Then grim satisfaction took hold of the sombre diners as they began to realize that the Chapon Fin was bringing out—at its own expense—its finest wines and its most renowned food. It was the grand finale. All that remained was for everyone present to eat and drink his way out in style.

In Bordeaux the British Embassy party had made their headquarters in the old Consulate General, and on the night they left for Arcachon, some twenty-five miles away, where a British cruiser, the *Arethusa*, was waiting to take them off, Fleming and Smithers wandered round the deserted building, taking a final look at this last piece of official British territory in France. Fleming's security-conscious nose was soon smelling out quantities of papers which should be kept from the Germans, and he and Smithers worked late into the night in the empty consulate; then when the last file was a blackened cinder in the courtyard below they turned out the lights, locked the door and left. Even then Fleming's sense of symmetry was concerned about the key— what was to be done with it? Smithers suggested leaving it with the American Consul in Bordeaux, but when they approached him he began to make difficulties, saying that he had no authority to receive it. By now Fleming was in no mood to argue diplomatic niceties. Before the American could do anything about it he had thrust the large key into his pocket, thanked him for his trouble and disappeared into the night.

But before going to Arcachon himself, Fleming got involved in the plight of the many hundreds of British civilians, refugees from the South of France and elsewhere, who had made a dash for the coast, their cars piled high with their possessions. Out in the estuary, beyond the Point Verdon, were seven or eight neutral vessels, whose bewildered captains had an unparalleled view of the bombing and the chaos on shore. It was Fleming who persuaded those captains to evacuate the refugees, in a sudden torrent of argument, pleading, warning and command. At last, when he had won his point, the evacuation began from the little harbour at Point Verdon under his personal control. Many of the British were well-to-do expatriates who had stayed on in France when war broke out, hoping for the best. Now their Bentleys and their Rolls-Royces, crammed with their most precious belongings, were abandoned on the quay, and they themselves, grimy, sweating and fearful, had surrendered themselves to the orders of the good-looking naval officer who had stationed himself at the top of the narrow stone steps leading down to the water where the tenders were waiting. There was no time for a general scrutiny of passports or papers. The rules were all *ad hoc*. There were tears from some of the women when Fleming ordained that no one could take aboard more possessions than he could carry in his own two hands. If anyone felt like arguing he made him stand aside. Peter Smithers was there to help and gradually the refugees got away.

It went on throughout the afternoon and into the long summer evening. As each small boatload pushed off and headed out across the estuary to where the ships were anchored, the sweating refugees shouted their goodbyes, and Fleming, impassive at the top of the stone stairs, gave just the faintest nod in return. From time to time German bombers came, but nothing stopped the evacuation, and by dusk nearly all the refugees were away. Then came a *coup de théâtre*. The last boat was nearly filled when motor-horns were heard in the distance; and over the cobblestones rolled a cavalcade of enormous motor cars carrying King Zog of Albania, his family, and mountains of luggage, including the crown jewels of Albania. Somehow Fleming managed to get the royal party safely off. The day's work over, he watched the ships' smoke against the grey of the dusk, then strolled back along the deserted main quay speculating on the glee of the German troops when they came upon King Zog's very imperial motor cars, not to mention the Rolls-Royces and Bentleys abandoned by the English.

He knew that his own brief role in the tragedy was almost over. The French had signed their armistice with the Germans. Relations between the British and Admiral Darlan had worsened. H.M.S. *Arethusa* was waiting off Arcachon to take away the British Ambassador, and when she sailed Lieutenant Fleming would sail in her.

But before that he had had a last suggestion to make. He had been talking to the Minister at the British Embassy in Paris about the difficulty of satisfying the pride and allaying the suspicions of Admiral Darlan. 'Now why,' he said thoughtfully, 'doesn't His Majesty's Government offer Admiral Darlan the Isle of Wight for the duration of the war and make it French territory under the French flag for the entire period?'

The Minister smiled bleakly. Two weeks later Admiral Somerville's Force H. was bombarding Darlan's ships off the coast at Oran. 'From that moment,' wrote Fleming a long time afterwards, 'I thought I had better stick to my duties as a Lieutenant R.N.V.R., and leave the conduct of the war to older and conceivably wiser heads.'

III

WHEN Sefton Delmer of the *Daily Express* saw Room 39
for the first time, in the early days of the war, it reminded
him of an Arab bank he had seen somewhere in Tangier
or Beirut. There were the same tightly packed desks and
never-diminishing piles of paper, the same din of telephones
and typewriters as the harassed staff tried to scrabble
through. Ian Fleming, a sort of 'chief clerk' as Delmer saw
him, sat slightly aloof from the rest of the room in a haze
of cigarette smoke at his desk by the window, 'guarding
the glass door to the boss's room'.

Like all the others in that room, Fleming was an
administrator. But he was an administrator with a difference.
'He always tended to be presented with the unusual jobs
that no ordinary department would take responsibility for,'
says Admiral Denning. One such job was the affair of the
German air-sea rescue launch.

Early in the Battle of Britain N.I.D. received details of
a new high-powered launch which the Germans had based
along the coasts of Holland and Northern France and with
which they were rescuing the crews of German and Allied
aircraft shot down in the Channel. Fleming dreamed up the
idea that the ciphers on board ought to be captured—they
would be of real general value to our cryptographers. The
proposal was approved and inevitably the job went to him.
As there was general agreement that the launches were too
fast and too cautious to be caught with any certainty by
an ordinary British motor torpedo boat, Fleming decided
to set a trap. It was to be rather an elaborate one. He needed
a captured German aircraft, a determined German-speaking
British crew and the chance of staging a dummy crash somewhere in the Channel near the French coast. Given proper
organization and rehearsal, he felt that the counterfeit
airmen ought to be able to lure out one of the launches
and overpower the crew before the Germans realized what
was hitting them. He himself would take charge of the
actual operation, and Peter Smithers, who on his return
from France had joined N.I.D. on Fleming's recommendation, would be his chief accomplice. When Admiral Godfrey
gave qualified assent to the plan, Smithers, at first understandably wary, found himself swept along by Fleming's
enthusiasm.

Off they went to Churchill's the gunsmiths in Orange Street to choose better weapons than the Admiralty-issue revolvers. They needed authentic German flying kit: again it had to be personally selected, at a depot where captured enemy uniforms and equipment were stored in an R.A.F. hangar. There is a story that Peter Fleming was with his unit near Canterbury at the time, and that one afternoon the orderly-sergeant rushed into his office to report that a German airman was in the officers' mess asking for Major Fleming—it was, says the legend, Ian Fleming high-spiritedly taking an airing in his German flying kit. It is an invention. The idea that at that time (or at any other period of the war) anyone could go about dressed in German uniform without being apprehended is foolish; and the implication that Fleming was, in effect, showing-off is unjust. It is true that when he met his brother—and stayed the night with him in Kent—he had his German kit with him in a suitcase, but nobody but Peter Fleming knew what he was up to. The project was still provisionally on (he had been to Beaverbrook, the Minister for Aircraft Production, to see if he could conjure up a German bomber), and he was now on his way to various R.A.F. and anti-aircraft H.Q.s to look into the problems of arranging a *laissez-passer* for the aircraft. He was going to fly in it himself and, after it had belly-landed, take charge of the operation. In the end no one was able to produce the ironmongery—captured bombers were in short supply. The idea suddenly dropped dead.

Other ironmongery—guns and knives and gadgets—held a peculiar fascination for Fleming. He became extremely attached to a small commando fighting knife which he bought from Wilkinsons and carried with him on most of his foreign assignments. These knives were named after the Earl of Suffolk, a member of S.O.E. who was killed in 1941 during a bomb-disposal operation, and although Fleming used to laugh about his and say how useful it was for opening his letters and cutting his nails, he had it engraved with his name and rank along the blade and could become eloquent about it on occasion.

A more sophisticated little weapon that also appealed to Fleming was a fountain pen which could eject a sizeable cloud of tear gas when you pressed the clip. He sometimes carried one with him. 'Of course,' he explained to another member of N.I.D., 'you're not confined to tear gas. It will take a cyanide cartridge too, but naturally you don't fit one of those except on really dangerous missions.'

The pen was kept loaded with tear gas on the off-chance of his meeting an enemy agent face to face; nothing suggests that he actually did so, but he was allowed such remarkable latitude in following up his own leads that it was not entirely impossible. His routine contacts with the undercover society of Special Operations made him an ex-officio member of the cloak-and-dagger world, where all this was rather taken for granted. He visited S.O.E.'s newly founded school for subversion at Aston House, near Knebworth, in Hertfordshire, one of the first of the sabotage schools set up to train the agents and resistance fighters who were soon to be parachuting into Occupied Europe. It must have been a place after Fleming's own heart and one that set in train more of his Red Indian daydreams.

The arrival of enemy agents in Britain was a subject which occupied him increasingly, even if it occasionally involved him in comedy. For example, Peter Fleming has related how, as the German invasion scare was growing, he and his brother were officially informed that Southend was in peril: a letter, purporting to come from a German agent, and bearing every mark of authenticity, warned that in the small hours of Whit Sunday 1940 a battalion of parachute troops was to descend on the resort. The Chiefs of Staff hurriedly made plans to deal with the raid, and as not a word could be said to the newspapers the two Flemings got themselves accredited Official Eye-witnesses, to report the Battle of Southend for posterity and confound the inevitably lying reports of Dr Goebbels. On the Saturday they rushed off to Southend in a staff car and joined a party of naval officers stationed on the roof of a large hotel on the seafront, keeping their vigil throughout the evening to the sound of 'The Lambeth Walk' from the blacked-out ballroom below. But nothing happened; and as dawn broke on Whit Sunday the two Official Eye-witnesses drove back to London, speculating in general on the strangeness of human affairs and in particular on the perversity of whoever had written the warning letter.

Occasions like these were only a small part of Fleming's life at the time, but they must have given him a certain relief from the desk work that took up so much of his time in Room 39. In this connection a note of stern judiciality was struck by Admiral Godfrey's secretary, Edward Merrett.

'You mustn't get the wrong idea about Ian's service with N.I.D.,' he insisted. 'He wasn't James Bond. He was a pen-pusher like all of us. All through the war I thought of him as a collector of rare books. Of course, he *knew* everything that was going on, but he never seemed to show any real inclination to take part in it. If he was secretly longing for action I never saw any sign of it. In short, Ian's war had plenty of sweat and toil and tears but no real blood.'

For the most part Fleming managed to avoid genuine discomfort too. When he was bombed out of Ebury Street he moved into the Carlton Hotel—'I notice,' remarked Shane O'Neill at the time, 'that the orchid has finally left the orchid house.' He had already arranged—it was a Flemingesque touch—that the Bodleian Library at Oxford rather than the more ponderous British Museum should have the honour of looking after the Fleming Collection for the duration, and now that the books had gone, and his pre-war bachelor's life and furniture along with them, Ebury Street belonged in any case to the past. One of the few items from it that did remain was the sister of the man with the riding crop. She, as devoted and in love with him as on the day they had disappeared to Brighton together, was now a dispatch-rider in a dashing uniform. It made no difference. Fleming had never been impressed by dashing ladies who adored him but wanted to marry him.

Real friendship continued to be something that was possible only with men, and for Fleming friendship was always an active and not a static relationship. A friend was there to be helped or to be used, and throughout the war he helped a number of his friends into N.I.D. In return the Navy used them very thoroughly indeed.

It was Fleming who introduced Sefton Delmer to Admiral Godfrey in the autumn of 1939 and so paved the way for the 'black propaganda' radio station—the *Atlantiksender* which Delmer and N.I.D. devised early in 1943 to feed programmes and news items to German U-boat crews. The idea of hoaxing the enemy and sapping their morale with a radio station which pretended to be on their side appealed to the imagination of Fleming—it was the sort of idea he might have had himself. On a number of occasions he broadcast for Delmer from the secret transmitter in the village of Aspley Guise, in Bedfordshire.

He was also closely involved with the small Naval

Propaganda Section which Godfrey set up to worry the German Navy. This was very much his sort of group. In charge of it was Lieutenant Donald McLachlan, later first editor of the *Sunday Telegraph*. McLachlan's deputy for a time was Robert Harling, typographer and novelist, now editor of *House and Garden*. It was Fleming who had first brought Harling to N.I.D. from active service in a sloop in the Atlantic, among other things to design the department's intelligence reports. The literary style of these reports had always been distinguished: Charles Morgan, the novelist, Hilary St George Saunders, the historian, and William Plomer had all helped to write them. But their physical appearance offended the publisher *manqué* in Fleming, and it was typical of him to have done something so practical about it.

All his life Fleming prided himself on knowing the right man to go to in any situation. He usually did, too. But when Hitler's deputy, Rudolf Hess, made his mysterious parachute descent in Scotland in May 1941, Fleming surpassed himself by appealing to one of the most notorious men in the whole of the British Isles. For many years he had been fascinated by the legend of wickedness which had attached itself to the name of Aleister Crowley, necromancer, black magician and the Great Beast 666. This immensely ugly old diabolist and self-advertiser had thrown himself into certain more unsavoury areas of the occult with a gusto that must have appealed to Fleming, and when the interrogators from British Intelligence began trying to make sense of the neurotic and highly superstitious Hess he got the idea that Crowley might be able to help and tracked him down to a place near Torquay, where he was living harmlessly on his own and writing patriotic poetry to encourage the war effort. He seems to have had no difficulty in persuading the old gentleman to put his gifts at the disposal of the nation, for a brief formal note sealed with cabbalistic signs arrived, through the 'usual channels', for the Director of Naval Intelligence:

Sir:
   If it is true that Herr Hess is much influenced by astrology and Magick, my services might be of use to the Department in case he should not be willing to do what you wish. I have the honour to be, Sir,

Your obedient servant,
ALEISTER CROWLEY

Included with the letter was a poem, printed like a penny tract, entitled 'England Stand Fast'.

It is a pity that this had to be one of Fleming's bright ideas which never came off: understandably, there was hilarity in the department at the idea of the Great Beast 666 doing his bit for Britain. Fleming preserved the old man's letter and poem and filed away the Great Beast himself for future use. He always knew a good villain when he saw one.

His friendship with a remarkable Australian named Sidney Cotton was altogether more useful to the nation. When war broke out this inventor, man of action, and eccentric near-genius was one of the country's few experts in high-altitude photography. He offered his aircraft and his own laboratory at Heston Airport and his know-how to the Air Ministry, but its officials hardly recognized his true potential. The Admiralty did, and Sidney Cotton became a useful friend of Room 39.

'Ian had an odd sort of imagination,' says Cotton. 'Always given to flights of fancy. "Sidney," he said once, "suppose the Huns are using Southern Ireland as a base for U-boats— they'd need only one or two small bays along some deserted stretch of coastline . . ."' It all ended with Cotton photographing the entire coast of Southern Ireland from two thousand feet. The pictures supported other evidence that there were no bases.

Fleming passed on to some fresh conundrum.

IV

Nineteen forty-one was a key year in the naval career of Commander Ian Fleming. It was then that he came nearest to living that life of high adventure he had always dreamed of: after a year like this nothing would ever be quite the same again.

It began in February with a short trip to Tangier to check on Naval Intelligence in North Africa. This was the sort of adventure he loved. He was on his own at last on a secret mission across the neutral no-man's land of wartime Europe. The London winter was behind him; so was the clatter and the tension of Room 39. He carried the commando fighting knife and the fountain pen with the cyanide cartridge, but he travelled as a civilian, wearing a dark-blue suit and Old Etonian tie and carrying an official diplomatic courier's passport. It was a splendid, archaic-looking document, and

Courier's Passport.

THIS PASSPORT IS ONLY
GOOD FOR THE JOURNEY
SPECIFIED AND MUST BE
GIVEN UP WITH THE
DESPATCHES.

Valid for a journey
to Gibraltar and
return to Madrid
16 February 1941.

777

Renewed and valid
for a journey to London
via Lisbon
26 February 1941.

Rother Renetee

By His Britannic Majesty's

Minister
at
Madrid.

Le Toussigné

Ministre de S. M.
Britannique à
Madrid

These are to request and
require, in the Name of His Majesty,
all those whom it may concern to allow

prie et requiert au nom de Sa Majesté
tous ceux à qui il appartiendra de laisser
passer librement

Mr. Ian Lancaster Fleming

charged with Despatches to pass freely
without let or hindrance, and to afford
him every assistance and protection
of which he may stand in need.

chargé de Dépêches et de lui accorder en
toute occasion l'aide et la protection dont
il pourra avoir besoin

Given at Madrid the sixteenth day of February 1941.

Robert Renetee

Secret Mission. In February 1941, carrying this courier's passport,
Fleming went off on a trip to Tangier to check on Naval Intelligence in North Africa.

as he made the exciting wartime journey by plane to Lisbon, then across to Madrid, down to Gibraltar and over the narrow strait to the international city of Tangier before returning to Madrid, he must have felt that he was stepping into the pages of Maugham's *Ashenden* at last.

It was not a hazardous mission, but Fleming was not the man to become mousey about it all. At Tangier he and a young British attaché created a minor diplomatic incident by daubing an enormous V sign on the main runway of the international airport. It was judged a silly thing to do and he got into hot water with the Admiralty. He was more discreet in Lisbon, where enemies could watch each other in the restaurants and the dividing line between a spy and a diplomat was anybody's guess. At the beginning of June he was to have the chance of looking more closely at Lisbon. He was there with the D.N.I. himself, and they were en route for the United States.

This American visit was one of some consequence. British Naval Intelligence felt the time had come to establish closer relations with its opposite number in the United States while recognizing that liaison of this sort called for careful handling. There was an Anglo-U.S. agreement not to conduct secret intelligence activities against each other, but for the British Admiralty to move closer to U.S. Naval Intelligence would call for considerable tact and diplomacy, and Godfrey had no doubt that his hand would be strengthened if his invaluable personal assistant accompanied him on this top secret mission to Washington.

In those days the quickest and surest way to New York was by the big six-engined Clipper flying boats which made the journey from Lisbon via the Azores in just under twenty-two hours. It was a highly convenient route in particular for the D.N.I., since it gave him the chance of making contact with his own people in Lisbon on the way.

On their first night in Lisbon Godfrey and Fleming dined in style at the big luxury Aviz Hotel, but on the following evening they decided to eat in their Estoril hotel and then take a look at the casino. They found it to be a grey-walled, melancholy-looking building along the estuary of the Tagus, but it holds a special place among the many casinos where Ian Fleming chanced his luck during his long and cautious career as a gambler. For it was here that he played out the scene which was to grow in his imagination for eleven years until it formed the plot of his first book, *Casino Royale*.

Fleming himself has described how it all happened: how he got the idea of James Bond's baccarat battle with Le Chiffre from a game he himself played here in deadly earnest against a group of Nazis. According to this account he suddenly got the idea of striking a blow at Germany by winning as much money off his opponents as he could, but patriotism was not enough and his gesture ended with a total casino victory for the Germans.

The reality seems to have been rather different. It was a decidedly dismal evening at the casino—only a handful of Portuguese were present, the stakes were low, the croupiers were bored. The Admiral was not impressed.

Fleming, however, refused to submit to the depressing atmosphere. This was his first visit to a casino since the beginning of the war, it was a treat to which he had been looking forward. He began to play with the careful concentration he always put into his gambling, and Admiral Godfrey says that he noticed 'a strange sort of glazed look' coming over his eyes. The game progressed. Then Fleming whispered to Godfrey, 'Just suppose those fellows were German agents—what a coup it would be if we cleaned them out entirely!'

It was not a thought that particularly appealed to the Admiral—he found it impossible to translate those sombre Portuguese in their dark suits into Nazi agents. But Fleming liked the idea and played a long, unsuccessful game until he was completely cleaned out. He filed away the details of the evening in his memory. Next day he and the Admiral boarded the flying boat in the estuary of the Tagus and left for the United States.

They were ready to slip into New York, two anonymous Englishmen, one in a grey suit and one in a blue. But as they went ashore from the flying boat Press photographers began to crouch round them. Although they soon realized that it was their elegant fellow-passenger Madame Schiaparelli who was attracting the cameras, the damage was done. That evening the chief of British Naval Intelligence was to be seen in the background of all the Press photographs of the famous French couturière arriving in New York. If just one smart picture editor had recognized Godfrey and singled him out the Admiral's delicate mission might have been torpedoed in port.

As it was, the D.N.I. and his personal assistant made a discouraging beginning with the head of the Federal Bureau of Investigation, J. Edgar Hoover. Fleming was later to describe their reception:

Hoover, a chunky enigmatic man with slow eyes and a trap of a mouth, received us graciously, listened with close attention (and a witness) to our exposé of certain security problems, and expressed himself firmly but politely as being uninterested in our mission ... Hoover's negative response was soft as a cat's paw. With the air of doing us a favour he had us piloted through the F.B.I. Laboratory and Record Department and down to the basement shooting range, where at that time his men had their training in the three basic F.B.I. weapons—pistol, automatic shotgun and sub-machine gun. Even now I can hear the shattering roar of the Thompsons in the big dark cellar as the instructor demonstrated on the trick targets. Then with a firm, dry handclasp we were shown the door.

However, Hoover's firm, dry brush-off was not quite as decisive as it seemed. Godfrey went on to discover that there were *two* solid men in America 'in the confusion of fledgling intelligence organizations'. One was Hoover. The other was the Canadian millionaire Sir William Stephenson, whose British Security Co-ordination represented British Intelligence in the U.S. 'Hoover,' said Fleming, 'had his channels with Bill Stephenson, and his common-sense, legalistic mind told him it would be unwise to open separate channels with us. He was, of course, quite right. Our constitutional link with the American Intelligence could only lie with the Office of Naval Intelligence of the Navy Department.'

But if Hoover was taking a strictly legal view of the British mission the attitude of the other 'solid man' could hardly have been more different. For Sir William Stephenson—known variously as 'Little Bill' and the 'Quiet Canadian'—lacked Hoover's sense of the over-riding importance of constitutional niceties. He could be an inspired opportunist in a good cause, and already, in June 1941, his office on the thirty-sixth floor of the Rockefeller Center in New York had become the headquarters of the complex British Intelligence network he had been building up throughout North and South America. Working closely but unofficially with the Americans, he had, as Fleming wrote, already rendered 'innumerable services to the Royal Navy which could not have been asked for, let alone executed, through normal channels.'

And when the British D.N.I. and his personal assistant arrived in New York he was at their disposal with hospitality, advice and an office, complete with secretary, next door to his own.

Fleming was a confirmed hero-worshipper all his life, and his heroes—Lord Beaverbrook, Noël Coward, Somerset Maugham—embodied certain qualities of success he admired but always felt he lacked himself. Now Stephenson joined the team: within a day or two he had stepped straight into Fleming's private Pantheon. For Fleming, Stephenson was almost everything a hero should be. He was very tough —First World War fighter-pilot, M.C. and D.F.C., and European lightweight amateur boxing champion. He was very rich—first million before the age of thirty from his invention of the first successful radio photograph transmitter. He was single-minded and patriotic and a man of few words. He mixed the 'largest dry martinis in America and served them in quart glasses'. To the creator of James Bond this man was 'one of the great secret agents of the last war'.

'From the start,' says Stephenson, 'Ian was always fascinated by gadgets and equipment. In those days we were building up our mechanical coding equipment which was ultimately handling thousands of messages a day, and he used to spend hours watching exactly how we did it.' By now Stephenson's organization in New York was also stepping up its subversive operations against German interests in South America, and Fleming had a chance of seeing something of the whole elaborate box of tricks which the Quiet Canadian had been developing. For Stephenson was a master of the technology of subversion. Station M., the laboratory he had set up in Canada under cover of the Canadian Broadcasting Corporation, claimed to be able to 'reproduce faultlessly the imprint of any typewriter on earth'. It specialized in all known forms of forgery—the polite phrase was 'fabrication of letters'—and some unknown forms as well.

To the young naval commander from N.I.D. much of this was new and all of it was fascinating. But Stephenson did not confine himself to theory—there was even a little action. Fleming was to remember it for a long time to come, and when he wrote *Casino Royale* and described the two missions which had earned his hero his double-O classification—his licence to kill—one of them was the shooting of a Japanese cipher expert in the Rockefeller Center in New York. The idea of the double-O came from Whitehall's official classification of top secret documents. The death of the Japanese was a highly exaggerated account of the adventure in which Fleming took part with Sir William Stephenson. If there was no killing there was certainly a Japanese cipher expert. He was on the staff of the Japanese Consul-General in New York, whose office happened to be in the Rockefeller Center on the floor below Stephenson's.

Stephenson knew that coded messages were being transmitted from this office back to Tokyo by short-wave radio and he decided that the time had come to find out more. The visitor was provided with a neat demonstration of the organization in action.

Fleming was a bystander while the Consul's office was cased, the duplicate keys prepared, the movements of the cipher expert studied. He joined in more satisfyingly at three in the morning when Stephenson with two of his assistants let him into the office to borrow the Japanese code books for an hour or so. The safe presented little difficulty, and it took no time at all to get the code books microfilmed upstairs and returned to their exact place. To Stephenson it was a straightforward operation; to Fleming a great and gleeful adventure, one all the more precious because it had happened in New York.

He would always grumble about New York—the rush and the rudeness, the pitiful food, the trash in the shops, the complexions of the women—but it became what it was to remain for the rest of his life, one of his three favourite cities in the world. He got to know the few odd bars and dives to which over the years he remained touchingly faithful. One was called Robert's, on 54th Street, and another, opposite Stephenson's apartment, was the Hickory House, where Fleming enjoyed sitting alone drinking his bourbon and branch water and listening to the well-made brunette who was the chief attraction of the place. She was known as the hot harpist, and as she harped away into the small hours her most devoted listener would be the solitary, bourbon-drinking Ian Fleming.

Fleming had first visited New York in 1938 with Hugo Pitman, and now, however exciting he found these wartime visits, his real mission in June 1941 lay in Washington. It was there that the Navy Department had its Office of Naval Intelligence and Godfrey knew that only in Washington could he find the real solution to his problems. Yet, as Stephenson had already found, it was not all that easy. The Americans were not unwilling to help in matters of intelligence and counter-espionage, but there was no single person or department with such authority and organization as British Intelligence needed to work with. In fact, in these months before Pearl Harbour there was still no American secret service. Instead there was rivalry between the information departments of the Navy, the Army and the State Department; and Hoover, though he was in general friendly to Stephenson, could also be extremely touchy about the rights and duties of the F.B.I. The answer to the whole situation according to Stephenson lay in trying to persuade the Americans to set up a secret service organization of their own and to ensure that if and when they did the man at the head would be someone with whom he and the British Government could work. When Godfrey and Fleming arrived in the United States he was on the point of succeeding in this.

For a long time he had been coaching and pushing his candidate for the post: General 'Wild Bill' Donovan, Roosevelt's former legal aide and a close friend and associate of Stephenson's. Donovan, a famous divorce lawyer and a good friend of Britain, already knew more of the secrets and inner workings of Stephenson's organization than any other American. The British Government recognized him as someone on whom they could rely, and he was of course high on the list of people whom Godfrey had to see in Washington.

As it turned out, the appointment was in the bag: Godfrey was assured by the White House that America was in the very act of setting up her own secret service and that it would be able to give the British Admiralty the help it wanted. The President made it known that its head would be General Donovan.

For Godfrey this was highly satisfactory news; he was already very friendly with the short, plump lawyer with the Southern drawl whom he had entertained in England. Fleming for his part found General Donovan irresistible and wanted to do everything in his power to help him, even if he had to disregard red tape in the process. The stage was set for a notable episode in his career.

On June 18th, 1941, according to Sir William Stephenson's biographer, Montgomery Hyde, 'Donovan was received by the President and after a long discussion agreed to accept the office of Co-ordinator of Information, his duties to include the collection of all forms of intelligence and the planning of various covert offensive operations.' About this time Fleming went to ground for a couple of days. When he finally left Washington he took with him a present from General Donovan. It was a ·38 Police Positive Colt revolver with the inscription, 'For Special Services'. After the war Fleming would occasionally tell his friends that it was given to him by the father of the American Secret Service, without divulging what the special services were. He enjoyed puzzling people with small mysteries and hoarded the secrets of his past.

A few years before he died, however, he did write two letters which throw new light on the relationship between the fantasy world of James Bond and the real world of modern espionage. For Ian Fleming claimed, casually but quite unequivocally, that he had a hand in creating the American Secret Service—and he wasn't using the term in the American sense and referring to the body of men who, under the Treasury Department, guard the President and his family.

The first time he mentioned it was in a letter to Colonel Rex Applegate, a former U.S. army officer who worked in Washington with General Donovan when his organization was still known as Co-ordination of Information. (Out of this evolved first the O.S.S.—the Office of Strategic Services —and then the present massive and world-wide organization called the Central Intelligence Agency, otherwise the C.I.A.) Applegate had sent Fleming a copy of his book *Manhandling Techniques for Police and Military*. In his letter of thanks, written in March 1957, Fleming said:

It is quite possible that we came across each other during the war. General Donovan was a close personal friend of mine and, as a matter of fact, in 1941 I spent some time with him in his house in Washington writing the original charter of the O.S.S.

He was even more specific when writing on May 8th, 1962, to Cornelius Ryan, author of *The Longest Day*, who was just starting work, Fleming had heard, on the official biography of General Donovan: 'I wonder if during your researches you came across my memorandum to Bill on how to create an American Secret Service? This was in fact the cornerstone of the future O.S.S.' Secret services are never anxious to emphasize their connection with myths and fantasies about them such as Fleming wrote, and when Mr Ryan finally produces his book it will be interesting to see if the document survived.

It seems undeniable that Fleming, quite unofficially and without reference to Admiral Godfrey, did give General Donovan, as a man with a heart-warming belief in the ability of Britain to survive, the benefit of his advice, and that his paper formed the 'special services' for which he received the revolver.

According to Fleming's close friend Ivar Bryce, who was in Washington at the time, working for Sir William Stephenson, 'Ian wrote out the charter for the American C.O.I. at General Donovan's request. He wrote it in long-hand in a room in the British Embassy and it took him just over two days. He wrote it as a sort of imaginary exercise, describing in detail all the arrangements necessary for financing, paying, organizing, controlling and training a secret service in a country which had never had one before. It explained how this secret service fitted in with the other Departments of State. And it included a mass of practical detail on how much use could be made of diplomatic sources of intelligence, how agents could be run in the field, how records could be kept, and how liaison could be established with other governments.' It was the sort of exercise in imaginative non-fiction that Fleming was always good at; it also seems to have worked.

This was fact, not fantasy. But on another transatlantic visit later in the war Fleming found himself deep in a series of situations which might have come straight out of one of his own fictions. Again it was Sir William Stephenson who was responsible.

Not far from Toronto, on the shores of Lake Ontario, lies the town of Oshawa, and here Stephenson had bought a farmhouse. It suited him for a number of reasons. It was isolated and easy to reach from the United States. There was room for a number of new temporary huts and outbuildings and the lake was a great advantage. For Stephenson had been running up quite an establishment here, and by the time he invited Fleming to see it this country retreat of a millionaire had become the foremost training ground for sabotage and subversion in the New World.

It was part of a plan Stephenson had worked out with General Donovan to bring on a cadre of highly trained Allied agents and so ensure that the new U.S. Secret Service did not lack the right men. Fleming suggested that he spend a few days there as a trainee. It was to prove a formidable experience. Stephenson had planned the course at Oshawa with characteristic thoroughness and toughness, and although the school was to have imitators it remained in many ways unique.

The training staff were odd but highly competent. Murphy, the firearms instructor, and Colonel Wallace, the unarmed combat expert, had learned their specialities in the Shanghai police. Some of the experts in safe-blowing, lock-picking and housebreaking had tested their skills the dangerous way. For practising the higher technology of espionage—the use of ciphers, the planting of explosive and incendiary devices, the proper use of the latest developments in radio and listening devices—Stephenson employed men he had trained himself at Station M. But Oshawa did not neglect the do-it-yourself side of the business, and it taught its agents to survive when they had nothing except their wits and the clothes they stood up in. All this appealed very strongly to Fleming. Although he was theoretically only an observer, he took part in all the exercises with great seriousness and energy. According to Stephenson he was one of the best pupils the school ever had.

He got his highest marks on the underwater exercise. A derelict tanker moored on the lake was used for limpet mine instruction; the final test came at night with a long underwater swim rather like the one James Bond performed in *Live and Let Die* when he fixed the limpet mine to the hull of the *Secatur*. Stephenson recalls that Ian Fleming was every bit as good as his hero and was one of the few trainees who succeeded in getting the mine firmly into place and escaping without detection.

This was not his only success. Always a good shot, he enjoyed working with the various small-arms, and he took to the sub-machine gun with extraordinary relish. The judo and the other self-defence exercises made a strong appeal to his cult of personal toughness, and he did well at the agents' initiative exercise towards the end of the course. This was an elaborate game of bluff devised by Stephenson. With all the Toronto police alerted the trainees had to plant an imaginary bomb at one of a number of strategic points in the city. Fleming and several others were assigned the Toronto power station, but the place was heavily guarded and when the agents tried to sneak in hidden in coal trucks or disguised as stokers they were soon nailed. Fleming was the only one of them to succeed. He put on his best suit, rang up the managing director, explained that he was a

The girl seen here was Fleming's friend for a long time. She became a dispatch rider in the war and was killed in the Blitz

During the war Room 39 became something of a legend. . . . In the middle of it all Fleming acted as the buffer, the fixer, the reporter and the personal representative of the Director of Naval Intelligence

A drawing by Augustus John, 1942

visiting British engineer, and arranged an appointment for that afternoon.

Altogether Fleming struck it rich at Oshawa. The school not only provided him with a lot of tricks which he was to pass on to James Bond, but it helped him to decide, when the time came to decide, just what kind of an agent Bond must be.

Much of the atmosphere of Oshawa went into the books —the subversive gimmickry of Station M., the sado-romantic toughness of the unarmed combat sessions, the expertise borrowed from the New York underworld. Fleming was the perfect pupil—once again he was living fiction. And since his experience of an agent's life was confined to places like Oshawa and to missions like his trip to Tangier it all went to reinforce his dream of the bold, romantic, extrovert secret agent's life he was to give to James Bond.

But what is interesting is that, despite all his success on the course, none of his instructors, not even Stephenson, seemed to think that he would ever have made a satisfactory agent in the field.

'The trouble,' says Stephenson, 'was that although Ian was an outstanding trainee he just hadn't got the temperament for an agent or a genuine man of action. I'm not saying that he lacked courage—he had a great deal. But he had far too much imagination. Look what happened at the end of the course. One of the instructors I'd recruited was this top armed combat man with the Shanghai police, and as a sort of finale he used to put on a special performance for the trainees. We used to book him a room in a cheap downtown hotel in Toronto—nothing but a table and a chair and a single light bulb—and then we'd give the trainee the name of this hotel and the room number and say that the man staying there was a dangerous enemy agent who had to be destroyed. It would all be as realistic as possible—after all, this was exactly the sort of mission an agent might be called on to perform in the field, and we'd try to pressure him into thinking that it was a genuine killing. It was a test of nerve really, a test to decide whether he really was ruthless enough to kill a man when it came down to it. All right—the trainee would have his instructions and a normal police ·38 revolver which he'd load himself. From then on we'd watch him to see exactly what he did—we even had a peep-hole through the wall into the hotel bedroom where the instructor was waiting. Now one of the tricks this instructor had picked up was the ability to dodge a bullet—a sort of circus trick. If you fired at him from five yards he knew how to divert you sufficiently for the shot to go wide. Extraordinary man. Well, after the success Ian had been having on the course we were all interested to know what would happen, and I briefed him myself. I made sure his gun was loaded. I told him that the games were over now and this was serious. "Open that door, draw fast and shoot straight," I told him. "It'll be his life or yours." Several of us were at the hotel watching when Ian arrived. He got as far as the landing, and there he waited a long time. Then he went away. He apologized about it afterwards. "You know," he said, "I just couldn't open that door. I couldn't kill a man that way." '

Touchingly—and sensibly—he was bowing out of one area of the dangerous world of the Quiet Canadian.

V

During the late summer of 1941, from his desk in Room 39, Commander Ian Fleming began to study the career of a certain Nazi. He was a large, bull-like man in his early thirties who had already risen through the Studenten Freikorps and the illegal peacetime Austrian Nazi party to a position of importance in the war machine of the Third Reich. Although it was to be two years before Obersturmbandfuehrer Otto Skorzeny (who was to become the inspirer of Sir Hugo Drax in *Moonraker*) carried out his daring aerial rescue of Mussolini, he was already specializing in a type of operation which the Allies had so far ignored. Fleming was one of the few to spot its importance.

It all began with the loss of the island of Crete during May 1941. There were a number of sombre lessons to be learned in Whitehall from the onslaught of Goering's fanatical 11th Airborne Division and how it toppled General Freyberg and his 25,000 hard-bitten Commonwealth troops. It was the first time in history that a campaign had relied entirely on airborne forces. Though the Royal Navy controlled the waters round Crete (as far as the Luftwaffe permitted) the island had fallen to the Germans.

It was when British Naval Intelligence began to study the defeat that Fleming's interest in Skorzeny really began. For he saw that the man had clearly been given a special role. Although he had landed with the first wave of German troops he and his group had taken no part in the main fighting. It seemed to Fleming that Skorzeny's targets had been the British headquarters at Maleme and Heraklion and that he had one simple objective—to grab as much British secret material as he and his men could lay their hands on. They had concentrated on maps, divisional orders, codes and equipment—obviously they knew what to look for; they were in fact the first Intelligence Commandos. It dawned on Fleming that this was an idea which N.I.D. could well afford to copy. Appropriating it and adapting it he came up with his own inimitable version of an Intelligence Commando. It was to be known as No. 30 Assault Unit— or as Fleming liked to say 'My Red Indians'. Under his direction they were to become one of the most remarkable small private armies of the last war.

But all this took time, and the second half of 1941 was particularly frenzied in Room 39: the battle of the Atlantic was coming to a climax and N.I.D.'s major concern was with U-boats; in this as in other matters Fleming seems to have been given any unusual jobs or inquiries that were going. Usually he would reply by pulling one of his own unique ideas out of the hat. Sometimes it worked. One which did not was the lunch party he gave at Scott's Restaurant in Piccadilly early in the war.

In those days Albert Baker, Scott's head waiter, knew Fleming by sight as an occasional customer. One lunch-time Fleming arrived in civilian clothes with three other men and took a table in the grill-room. Baker began to get suspicious, for there was something disconcerting about two of Mr Fleming's guests. Their clothes did not fit them and they looked ill at ease. Somehow they were noticeably out of their element.

Fleming gave the order, chose the wine, and called for large whiskies as an apéritif; the two awkward guests remained mum. But soon the whole group were talking animatedly, and when Albert Baker served the second course he heard something of their conversation. As he said afterwards, you can recognize German without necessarily understanding it, and ordinary people don't chat away to each other in German in the heart of London in the middle of a world war. Before he served the cheese Albert Baker did his duty. He telephoned Scotland Yard.

Fleming and the three other men drank a lot and finished up with coffee and large brandies. Then just when the grill-room was preparing to close a number of fresh faces appeared at the tables round about, ordering drinks and studying the menu in a constrained fashion. They were not the faces of late lunchers. They were the faces of detectives, and they were there to try to listen to the conversation of the quartet. When the four men left the detectives left too, walking smartly out of the restaurant into crowded Coventry Street.

Fleming himself related what it was all about: 'I have never received a free mouthful of food or drink from any restaurant in the world and I therefore don't care what I say, short of libel, of any place where you consume food and drink. I don't even know the name of any restaurateur or head waiter in London, and I regard name-dropping in restaurants as a vulgar affectation. To be absolutely accurate, I do know the name of the head waiter on the first floor at Scott's. It is Baker, and I know it because he did his best to have me arrested as a German spy at the beginning of the war. I and a fellow officer from the Submarine Service were trying to get the first captain and navigator we had captured from a U-boat drunk at Scott's so as to worm out of them how they avoided our minefields in the Skagerrak. They had been "allowed out" of their prison camp for a day's "sight-seeing" in London and we were playing the rather clumsy role of brother officers talking chummily about the sea with other brother officers whom we were only fighting because of the politicians. Baker, then a waiter in the downstairs grill-room, became suspicious of our extraordinary conduct and extremely loose talk and by about half past three we were encircled by harmless-looking couples picking at bits of fish. It was only when we got back to the Admiralty, befuddled and no wiser about the Skagerrak, that a furious Director of Naval Intelligence told us that the only result of our secret mission was to mobilize half the narks of the Special Branch of Scotland Yard.'

Unabashed, Fleming tried again. When the *Bismarck* was sunk he learned that one of its gunnery officers, a certain Kapitänleutnant von Ostheim, was among the prisoners. He had met von Ostheim in London before the war and remembered him as an engaging young naval attaché at the German Embassy with a reputation for good living; and he persuaded himself that the most likely way to get the prisoner to talk was to demonstrate to him that London still bore some resemblance to the happy and elegant place which he had so enjoyed in 1938. Accordingly he planned a night out for the German: the prisoner was to see his old flat in Eaton Square and go to his favourite London restaurant, the Écu de France in Jermyn Street. And Fleming borrowed a house —a very beautiful house near Sloane Square—where von Ostheim could be entertained after dinner.

But once again, as so often with Fleming's more ingenious plans, the idea was superior to the execution. The Kapitän-leutnant was brought to London in civilian clothes from the prisoner-of-war camp in Bushey Park. Fleming met him and then sent him off to Eaton Square and the Écu de France with a pair of agreeable young German-speaking British naval officers. All three had a splendid dinner, but by the time they arrived at the house near Sloane Square, which Fleming had had wired for sound, the German had drunk so much that he could hardly make sense, let alone bandy secrets. All that Fleming had at the end of his carefully planned evening was a memorable recording of one incoherently happy German naval officer.

Fleming could always laugh when some stratagem misfired —he had plenty more to choose from. At the beginning of 1942 his mind returned to the more serious subject of Otto Skorzeny and his group of Intelligence Commandos. Naval Intelligence was now involved in early plans for the first of the full-scale commando raids on the French coast—the attack on the harbour installations at St Nazaire—and as early as this Fleming was arguing the case for a small group of specially trained 'intelligence scavengers' to go in with the first wave of the attack. The idea was still premature, but when plans were made for the big raid on Dieppe he was given his chance. It was too late for anything very elaborate. All he could do was to pick two naval lieutenants, provide them with a covering force of ten extremely ferocious Royal Marines, and brief them to fight their way to German Headquarters.

Fleming asked for permission to go with the party but Godfrey judged him too valuable to risk, and indeed there was a standing order that officers with access to certain types of classified intelligence material were never to be exposed to risk of capture. Fleming was therefore confined to an observer's role aboard one of the ships. Not that his Intelligence Commandos played a much more effective part at Dieppe; when the Canadians were held up and the attack began to go wrong none of them succeeded in getting ashore.

Still, the idea remained alive, and in the summer of 1942, as plans went ahead for the Anglo-American invasion of North Africa, Fleming was told to see to it that his small assault unit was ready. He took a deep breath. Its men would be his men. They would depend on him for their training, their orders, their success, even their lives; and he, planning and directing in the background, could live the war through them. Once again he was 'creating fiction' and turning his dream into reality.

As the TORCH landings were scheduled for the beginning of November he had to move rapidly. At this early stage he worked with Captain 'Red' Ryder, who won a V.C. as naval commander of the St Nazaire raid, to get his little group of 'Red Indians' into shape. Dunstan Curtis, who had commanded the leading ship in the raid on St Nazaire, was appointed joint commanding officer with Quentin Riley, the Antarctic explorer; and early in the autumn Curtis and the seven Royal Marines of 30 Assault Unit received the full Fleming treatment.

They seem to have enjoyed themselves: Ian Fleming's instant agent course had that particular blend of imagination and attention to detail which was to distinguish his books, and it drew freely on his Oshawa experiences. First he hustled the unit along to Scotland Yard, where he had engaged an elderly chief inspector to take it through the theory and practice of blowing safes, picking locks and breaking and entering. After that Fleming's commandos were packed off to a large house in Buckinghamshire for a series of demonstrations in the use of gelignite, plastic explosive, booby traps, minefields and small-arms weapons. That was the rough stuff. More important were the sessions devoted to the recognition and capture of the treasure trove of modern war—ciphers, code books, intelligence reports, secret orders, new weapons, radar sets. And this was very much Fleming's own department.

'At this stage,' says Dunstan Curtis, 'Ian was immensely excited. You'd have thought he was the one who was going on the trip. It was an enormous adventure for him.' Curtis was also struck by Fleming's hastily acquired but impressively detailed knowledge of Algiers. 'He must have given an extraordinary amount of thought to this particular show. He had organized air pictures and maps and models to show us exactly where we would land and what to go for. He knew where the enemy H.Q. was. He told us what troops were there, what they were up to and what we ought to find.'

He was also good at looking after his own people, and saw to it from the beginning that each member of his little unit had that special status which only top Admiralty priority could give. They were his men and they enjoyed his protection. Again it is an interesting sidelight on the power this young R.N.V.R. Commander had won himself that, despite frequent objections from local commanders of troops, 30 A.U. was always to have its own direct line to the Admiralty.

It was this imaginative involvement with his Red Indians which made Fleming the ideal intelligence impresario. On November 8th, while he sweated it out in Whitehall, the big Anglo-American invasion fleet was steaming towards Algiers. Thirty Assault Unit was aboard H.M.S. *Sheffield*, sharing the forward decks with the burly Swedish-Americans of the Minnesota Regiment, and like the hybrids they were the men of the unit went on their first active mission wearing the uniforms of American G.I.s and the caps of British naval officers.

In Room 39 Fleming would soon have news of how the two British destroyers, H.M.S. *Malcolm* and H.M.S. *Broke,* had come in close under the guns of the harbour and how the Vichy French who were manning them had seriously damaged *Broke;* of how the landing in the harbour had been called off and how his Red Indians had gone ashore from *Malcolm* to the west of Algiers at a place called Sidi Ferruch.

It was here the unit discovered that the maps and the planning and the papier mâché models no longer meant very much. No one seemed to have anything but a cloudy idea of where they were or what was happening. Fleming's carefully briefed Red Indians had to extemporize. Within a matter of minutes they found themselves a French lorry with some petrol in its tank, commandeered the vehicle and its driver at gun-point and set off on a zigzag course through Algiers until they managed to find the large white villa on its outskirts which the Italians had been using as their naval headquarters.

Then at last Fleming's theories and plans proved themselves. The months of training paid off. Surprised by the invasion, the Italians had not burnt their files or buried their code books, and 30 A.U. ransacked the entire headquarters according to the best Fleming principles. Within a matter

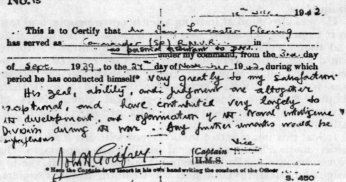

No. 15

.... 194 2.

.. This is to Certify that _Mr. Ian Lancaster Fleming_

has served as _Commander (Sp) R.N.V.R._ in ____

—as personal assistant to D.N.I.— under my command, from the 3rd. day

of _Sept._ 19 39., to the 21st day of _November_ 19 42., during which

period he has conducted himself* _very greatly to my satisfaction._

His zeal, ability, and judgment are altogether exceptional, and have contributed very largely to its development, and organisation of NI. Naval Intelligence Division during its war. Any further remarks would be superfluous

John H Godfrey   { Vice Captain ────
                         { H.M.S. ────

* Here the Captain is to insert in his own handwriting the conduct of the Officer . . . .

S. 450

Admiral Godfrey's Tribute. On leaving N.I.D. in December 1942, Godfrey acknowledged that Fleming had 'contributed very largely to the development and organization of the Naval Intelligence Division during the war'

of hours the loot was on its way top priority to Gibraltar, whence it was flown to the Admiralty in London. Fleming was there to deal with it. It was a great moment. For once in his life reality transcended fantasy.

The total haul from Algiers was impressive—the current German and Italian ciphers, the order of battle of the enemy fleets, and a mass of other information sufficient to keep N.I.D.'s experts busy. And now that his private army had proved themselves Fleming could begin to build, recruiting new members and extending the whole range of his intelligence network as he pieced together the sort of desirable information he could put on the agenda.

Soon he got the Unit reinforced with a squad of Royal Marines, to provide its defence and fire power. It was given its own transport, and its status as the direct representative of the Admiralty in London was confirmed. As Fleming's men went about their business they continued to wear their naval caps and khaki battledress. It was the first chapter in the strange saga of the sailors in jeeps.

This success of his brain-child came at an important moment for Fleming, for in November 1942 the familiar climate of Room 39 had changed abruptly. Rear-Admiral

John Godfrey, Fleming's friend, patron and commanding officer, vacated the post of Director of Naval Intelligence and became Flag Officer, Royal Indian Navy, being succeeded by Commodore E. G. N. Rushbrooke.

Though Fleming was greatly to extend the success of his Red Indians, this was the high-water mark of his career at the Admiralty. For the remainder of the war the Commander was to perform his duties as conscientiously as ever. But the days of real power were almost over. Fleming was no longer the D.N.I.'s right hand—he was simply his personal assistant.

It was sad. But real sorrow descended on Fleming when he lost his faithful and much-misused girl friend, the dispatch-rider, whom he had asked to collect two hundred Morland Specials before the shop in Grosvenor Street shut for the evening. It was the last thing she did for him. That night, while he was playing bridge at the Dorchester, the Germans raided London and a bomb-fragment pierced the roof of the house where the girl lay asleep in bed, killing her instantly. It was the sort of swift death which Fleming was to inflict on one or two of James Bond's heroines when their usefulness was over.

He was summoned by the police to identify the body and found himself severely shaken. Remorse was succeeded by sentimentality, and he held the girl tenaciously in his memory. 'Nostalgia is dangerous,' he was later to write in his notebook, 'unless you are certain of never seeing the subject of your nostalgia again.'

Meanwhile Fleming's sailors in jeeps were driving the hot victorious miles eastwards along the coast of North Africa as the Anglo-American Army went forward to meet Montgomery's Eighth Army. In Bône, Sousse and Sfax they kept up their hunt for enemy secrets, and by the time the two armies met in April 1943, 30 Assault Unit had already captured one of its prize exhibits of the war—a completely up-to-date map of the enemy minefields and defences of the coast of Sicily. It was a considerable asset when the invasion of Sicily began.

For Fleming there was one danger in success on this scale—the unit could soon be so important that it might easily pass entirely out of his control. For the rest of the war he was to fight hard to make sure that he kept his position at the head of what he regarded as his private army. The unit was split into two, and the half which went off on the Allied invasion of Sicily and Italy under Quentin Riley achieved virtual independence of the Admiralty, but the other half returned to England to train for the invasion of Europe, and Fleming was soon as involved with its plans and training as he had been before Algiers.

The unit needed more personnel: here Fleming was in his element, as he was still able to carry on his recruitment campaign for 30 A.U. much as he liked. He enjoyed being able to offer adventure to men of whom he approved. Robert Harling was one. He had just returned from a long one-man mission through Syria for N.I.D., and now he became the Unit's expert on mines and minefields. Ralph Izzard, the writer and broadcaster, was another. One of the few who refused Fleming was his boyhood friend Selby Armitage, who had turned from stockbroking to bomb disposal and for his services was awarded the George Cross and the George Medal; with a mistrust of all Fleming's schemes which dated back to childhood, he thought that 30 A.U. must be one more piece of madcap fantasy.

Perhaps it was. Perhaps Fleming was still in search of that ideal role which only he could play. Nevertheless, he earned the loyalty of his Red Indians, even their affection.

While the Unit was training for D-Day it was inevitable that something of Fleming's control of 30 A.U. should pass to others. But the impression he left on its members was always much the same—the lean, good-looking commander with the faint smile and the constant cigarette, standing on the edge of things and pausing to offer a sardonic, half-humorous word of encouragement before disappearing back to the place where the decisions were made and the real power lay. Back in the Admiralty, as methodical as ever, Fleming began as D-Day approached to mark the target areas on a large-scale map of Western Europe. Each potential enemy secret weapon had its own symbol. At Trondheim in Norway he indicated the spot where agents reported the Germans to be storing their latest pattern of magnetic mine. Small crosses along the French coast confirmed where German radar installations had been reported. V-1 launching sites were shown in the Pas de Calais, along with airfields, harbours and factories where the latest German equipment might be found. For 30 A.U. was concerned now not just with ciphers and maps but with the entire range of the enemy's armoury.

Fleming visited his Red Indians—they numbered by now about 150—in England for the last time just before D-Day to give them their final instructions in person. They would go in to the Arromanches beachhead and their task would be to reach the big German radar station before the enemy had a chance to destroy it. Before he left he gave Dunstan Curtis a detailed shopping list of several dozen top-secret pieces of German equipment which would be gratefully received back in Room 39.

At Arromanches 30 A.U. was a great success. It reached the radar station exactly as planned. But after this one success the pickings became disappointing for several months. The Germans proved a tidy-minded enemy who methodically blew up every important installation and carried away those code books and packing cases marked *Geheim* for which Fleming was waiting so anxiously in Room 39. And to add to his frustrations his Red Indians seemed to be abandoning the very role he had assigned them. The spirited part 30 A.U. played when it joined the Americans in the capture of Cherbourg showed him how easy it would be for it to turn into a normal fighting commando and how easily it could achieve virtual independence of the Admiralty.

Another problem was that the Unit, with its contingent of rampageous and red-blooded young Marines, began earning quite a reputation for itself. According to Robert Harling, these Marines were 'merry, courageous, amoral, loyal, lying toughs, hugely disinclined to take no for an answer from foe or fraülein', and it was Fleming himself who renamed them 30 Indecent Assault Unit.

He was not a patient man, and his relations with 30 A.U. during the capture of Cherbourg are revealing. For when the men in his Unit were behaving with a dash and independence which would have done credit to James Bond himself, Fleming reacted with all the touchiness and exasperation that old M. was to show when the best-laid plans were disregarded by bungling subordinates. Beneath the exasperation there seems to lie the passionate disappointment of the symmetrist whose tidy vision of things has once again been reduced by reality to chaos.

On August 15th he heard from Curtis that various pieces of German radar equipment and a number of the latest German weapons were captured and ready for shipment to England. He arranged for a high-speed launch to make the crossing to Cherbourg the following night to collect them, but in all the disorder of the freshly captured city no contact was made and it came back empty. Next day, from his desk in Whitehall, Commander Fleming delivered a truly Nelsonian broadside at the commanding officer of 30 Assault Unit. 'Great trouble,' he began, 'was taken to lay this craft on as you desired and it is indeed disappointing that the Unit should have failed D.D.O.D.(1) in its side of the arrangements . . . To put it mildly, D.D.O.D.(1) is fed to the back teeth.' Fleming's real complaint, however, was that 30 A.U. was not paying sufficient attention to his orders and that the men in the field seemed to think they knew better than the men at headquarters:

I urge you not to continue questioning the decisions of D.N.I. and A.N.C.X.F. under whose orders you operate. The position in Brittany and also in regard to Paris is perfectly clear here and we are fully informed on the progress of the campaign. Why you should imagine that this is not so, which is the only possible excuse for your attitude, I cannot understand. The duties of the Unit and its immediate role are also planned on the basis of more information than you can ever possess in the field.

One thing is certain and that is that unless the Unit obeys its orders without question during the future stages of the campaign it will be quite impossible for me or Captain Lewes to prevent higher authority intervening drastically.

Fleming was always an efficient executive and the disorder and untidiness of actual battle never ceased to disturb him. One of the few contacts he made with his men in the field occurred at Carteret as the Allied armies were re-grouping before the big push to the north-east. Fleming arrived there suddenly with Captain Rushbrooke, and something about his well-turned-out appearance served to emphasize the gulf that lay between him and the battle-stained men of action in his Unit. Fleming was not particularly tactful either. 'But my dear fellow, the stuff's undrinkable!' he said of some captured enemy cognac. It was later, while he was sitting by the roadside eating his K ration with Robert Harling, that he said, when asked what he intended to do after the war was over. 'Why, write the spy story to end all spy stories.'

'I almost choked on my Spam,' said Harling. But Harling, with his confident enjoyment of life and his hilarious cynicism, was to become one of the few men with whom Fleming felt completely at ease.

It was not long after Fleming's visit that 30 A.U. made contact with General Patton on the road to Paris, and the sight of British officers in naval caps driving jeeps in the middle of his army gave him what appeared to be a painful and sudden crick in the neck. He stopped his car. He took one of his ivory-handled six-shooters from its holster and raspingly inquired who in the hell those sonofabitches in fancy hats thought they were. When told he made the memorable reply, 'I like no navy men. But if it has to be the navy why isn't it the United States goddam Navy?' He drove off.

Partly to avoid further trouble with Patton, 30 A.U. attached itself to General Leclerc's Army for the advance on Paris, and in this way the Unit became among the first troops to enter the capital. They made good use of this advantage, for in the Admiralty it had long been known that the German Navy had set up its headquarters in the opulent Rothschild mansion on the boulevard Lannes. Thirty A.U. liberated it. They came at the right moment and had the place to themselves, complete with the files, the coding machines, the charts, and the line of battle of the German fleet, even if there wasn't much of it left by then. It was quite a haul, and the only real damage occurred when an eager member of the Unit tried to carry out Fleming's instructions on how to blow a safe with gelignite.

With Europe opening up to the Allied armies the treasure hunt Fleming had been planning for so long began in earnest. He provided the directions from Whitehall and 30 A.U. did its best to find and snatch his secret Black List material from the retreating Germans.

At last his skill as an intelligence executive was proving itself. He was painstaking and imaginative and most of the tip-offs he sent produced results. Sometimes he even provided names and addresses. Ralph Izzard received a cryptic, M. like order from Fleming to pick up a certain professor—an expert in liquid oxygen—from a house near Tours. The address was correct, the professor was at home and turned out to be a statuesque brunette in her mid-thirties. Another of Fleming's addresses sent the Unit driving off to a mushroom farm near a place called Houeilles. At first it looked like any other mushroom farm, but when they investigated they found that the Germans had turned the cellars into a carefully concealed store for torpedoes. The prize exhibit was the latest German acoustic homing torpedo—a neat piece of nautical technology several years ahead of anything the Allies had at the time.

It was around this time that Fleming's relations with the Unit became considerably simplified. A regular Royal

Marine officer, Colonel Humphrey Quill, was put in charge of its day-to-day running, and as the Allied armies moved up into Holland Fleming's Red Indians were to pass under the direct control of the Naval C.-in-C. of the Allied Expeditionary Force, Admiral Sir Bertram Ramsay. But although this meant that Fleming's close emotional ties with the Unit declined he remained the chief link with the Admiralty in London and continued to enjoy the vicarious excitement of living its adventures through the reports its members gave him whenever they were back in London. He was particularly pleased with the story Ralph Izzard told of how the Unit finally discovered the first German one-man submarine, placed by Fleming on the Black List but never sighted by any reliable witness. During the advance through southern Holland one of these midgets was found washed up on the beach of Walcheren. Izzard inspected it and excitedly telephoned Admiral Ramsay with the news: the first German one-man submarine had been found. 'Nonsense,' replied the Admiral. 'There's no such thing as a one-man submarine.'

'Very well, sir,' replied Izzard, 'I'll have it sent round to your headquarters immediately,' and he had the submarine —the Germans called it the 'Master'—loaded on to a tank transporter and shipped off like a tiny steel whale. It arrived as the Admiral was finishing breakfast. He was still unimpressed. 'The thing's a toy,' he said.

'I suggest, sir,' said Izzard, thinking of something, 'that you just have a look down the periscope.' The Admiral did so. And staring at him from the other end of the periscope was the still open eye of the dead German submariner who had been killed when his vessel foundered. In the excitement of the discovery Izzard had forgotten about him.

All the same, during the last months of the war Fleming's involvement with his Red Indians was not entirely a matter of listening to their exploits when they returned to London. Thirty Assault Unit was to have its grand finale and Fleming played a great part in it. As the invading armies stormed their way into Germany both the Americans and the British were trying to snatch whatever secrets they could from the ruin of the Third Reich. The treasure hunters had reached the treasure, but everything depended on knowing where to look and what to look for; and Fleming's Black List of wanted enemy equipment became the catalogue for 30 A.U.'s final shopping spree. It was his directions that led the Unit to the Walterwercke, the big submarine works in Hamburg where Herr Walter had developed his hydrogen-peroxide-driven boat. The next point of interest on Fleming's industrial map of North Germany was the torpedo experimental station at Eckernforder, and again 30 A.U. knew where to go and what to look for; there was much to be learned here, and by the time the Unit had taken what it wanted the Russian armies were fewer than twenty miles away.

Then with the hunt almost over Fleming himself had the chance he wanted to be in at the kill. It was a strangely symbolic ending to Fleming's war.

For several months vague reports had been reaching Room 39 about a castle at a place called Tambach, deep in the forests of Württemberg. No one could be sure what was happening, but it appeared that an elderly admiral was in charge and that for months lorry loads of documents had been arriving there. Fleming set his book collector's heart on getting to the castle of Tambach. An expedition was arranged, and on the eve of the German surrender he joined Trevor Glanville, 30 A.U.'s expert on enemy documentation, and they made the long drive to Tambach. There they found the old admiral in a state of high excitement. In the grounds of the Schloss a huge pyre had been prepared on the dried-out bed of the lake. It consisted of the entire German naval archives since 1870. With the Russian advance the admiral was preparing to go down with his documents.

Perhaps his nerve failed him at the last moment. Or perhaps the villages of Tambach had stolen the ration of petrol which the German High Command had allocated for burning the archives. Anyway, the pyre was never lit and Fleming and the stricken old enemy admiral got on well together. The result was that when Fleming left Tambach he brought the whole of the official German naval archives with him. There were many tons of them, and he arranged for a fishery protection vessel to bring them back from Hamburg to London. The old admiral came too, and at Fleming's suggestion he spent the next few months in London helping to edit the German naval archives in a small office in the Admiralty.

Fleming's last signal to the Unit had the authentic Fleming touch: 'Find immediately the twelve top German naval commanders and make each one write ten thousand words on why Germany lost the war at sea.'

VI

In the last twelve months of the war Fleming began to think of an escape route: once he was free of the Navy he would leave England for good and find his paradise, his lotus-eating land. He discovered it sooner than he thought.

In the autumn of 1944 he had to go to Washington for routine liaison with the U.S. Navy Department's Office of Intelligence and after that to Kingston, Jamaica, to represent the D.N.I. at a special conference about the German U-boat menace in the Caribbean. Before he left Washington Fleming met Ivar Bryce again—Bryce was still in Sir William Stephenson's set-up—and Fleming saw the chance of another of those expeditions he had first planned with his friend when they were at Eton.

All his life Fleming had a wonderful offhand ability to reorganize his friends' lives on the spur of the moment—it was part of his charm. All his restlessness and energy would be at their disposal and while the fit lasted life would become the sort of clear, schoolboy adventure which he loved. Not that Bryce needed any urging to go with him to Jamaica: his second wife had lived there and they still had a house, Bellevue, one of the most beautiful and famous of the island's old houses, on the slopes of the Blue Mountains. He had not seen it since the war.

What did startle Bryce was the efficiency with which Fleming managed to clear his journey with his superiors. Within thirty-six hours Bryce had been officially ordered to Kingston and he and Fleming were aboard the Silver Meteor as it pulled out of Pennsylvania railroad station en route for Miami.

This was Ian Fleming's first experience of the train journey which James Bond took with Solitaire in *Live and Let Die*. It was a journey he loved, with the power of the diesels, the efficiency of the big stainless steel carriages and the poetry of the long run south. At Miami the treat continued and they dined on soft-shelled stone crabs cooked in butter at a restaurant called Joe's along Miami Beach. But from then on everything went wrong. They flew on to Jamaica, and by the time they had reached the Myrtle Bank Hotel in Kingston Bryce was regretting the trip. November is never a month for Jamaica, even at the best of times. It is the month of the monsoon, and in the afternoons, as the humidity creeps up, it often seems as if the whole damp green island is washing away in the unending downpour.

Besides, in 1944 the run-down, clapped-out old city of Kingston was a study in threadbare melancholy. The past colonial splendours of the Myrtle Bank Hotel, with its drooping palms and sad dank verandas, seemed unlikely to impress the comfort-loving commander, who was attending the conference on the U-boat menace, held in the heavily guarded hotel ballroom, while the rain dripped, the fans turned fruitlessly and his regulation blue naval serge soaked up the steady sweat of the Caribbean autumn.

The conference went on for three days. It was hard work. On the last evening, when it was almost dark, Bryce suggested a hurried visit to his house high up on a shelf of the Blue Mountains. They hired an aged Austin which Bryce drove.

Bellevue is a house with a history. Fleming's hero, Admiral Lord Nelson, had stayed there when mounting expeditions, and from its beautiful eighteenth-century rooms he must have seen exposed before him the southern coast of Jamaica and an unmatched immensity of the Caribbean. But like the rest of Jamaica, Bellevue was hardly at its best in 1944, and when they reached it they found the paint peeling and the fences broken and the giant trees looking menacing in the rain. The only person at home was a very old, slightly deaf Jamaican housekeeper who followed them round making plaintive noises and muttering, 'Dearie me, Mr Bryce sir, dearie me!' It was something of a Charles Addams situation.

When they asked for something to drink all the old girl could find was a dusty bottle of grenadine syrup. The furniture had been put away, but Fleming brought in a couple of old cast-iron chairs from the balcony and they sat on them in silence, drinking grenadine and watching the rain. The water trickled noisily from broken gutters. Below them were coffee-woods and tropical trees, a scene to Fleming at once beautiful and inexpressibly melancholy.

This one evening was his sole excursion during the whole of his three-day stay. With the conference over he and Bryce had to fly straight back to Washington. Fleming was silent for most of the journey, but just before the plane landed he turned to Bryce and said, 'I've made up my mind. I'm going to live the rest of my life in Jamaica.'

Bryce was amazed. He had looked on the trip as a failure.

'Could you please arrange to buy me a good patch of land?' Fleming went on. 'I'll want about fifteen acres. There must be cliffs of some sort and a secret bay and no roads between the house and the shore. When you've fixed it for me I'll build a house and write and live here.'

Bryce knew when Fleming meant business, and accordingly he wrote to an old Jamaican land agent called Reggie Acquart giving him the specifications exactly as Fleming had outlined them. A few days later a reply came back from Jamaica. 'I've found you a place on the North Shore on the old donkey race track at Oracabessa.'

'As Reggie described it in his letter,' says Bryce, 'it sounded exactly the place Ian had in mind. Acquart said the owner wanted £2,000 sterling for it. I wired to Ian in London. His reply came the following morning. He said, "Buy it." '

It was then that Fleming (who resembled Proust's Swann in this respect) started a new compartment in his life of many compartments. He had always taken trouble with the details of his dreams, and this was to be the greatest of them all. He spent hours looking at the Admiralty charts of Jamaica until he knew the jagged outline of the North Shore almost as well as he knew the walk down St James's Street and along the Mall which he took in the morning from his new flat in Berkeley Square.

When Bryce sent photographs of the property, with its hidden beach, its cliffs and the overgrown wilderness behind, Fleming's dream took more tangible shape. It was then at his desk in Room 39 that the commander started to plan his house and it was on his office pad that he sketched out the details. It seemed very practical but a trifle dull and spartan—a low roof set with thick local shingles, one vast living-room with big windows, slatted jalousies instead of glass, no bathrooms or hot water, and three unadorned four-square bedrooms.

Once Fleming had bought his land and designed his house the Admiralty seemed to go out of its way to help him realize his vision. At the end of 1944 it sent him on his travels again —this time to Colombo, Ceylon, and then on to Australia to report on Naval Intelligence in the Far East—and somehow his rute home inevitably lay through Jamaica. He was there at the beginning of March 1945.

This time the island was at its best, with long blue days and starlit nights. He stayed with the William Stephensons at Hillowton, their big white house with the cool rooms and the scented garden overlooking the green horseshoe of Montego Bay. While he was there he put the finishing touches to the plans for his own house and showed them to Lady Stephenson.

'It looks beautiful, Ian,' she said, guardedly. 'But what about cupboards in the bedrooms for the people's clothes?'

'I'm not worrying about cupboards. All you need really are a few nails.'

While he was staying at Hillowton he found a builder and accepted his quotation of £2,000 to build the house. And finally, to complete the occasion, Ivar Bryce arrived on leave from Washington and the two of them drove out to inspect the land at Oracabessa and decide on a name for the house. It was a beautiful morning and Fleming, full of excitement, insisted on borrowing the Stephensons' jeep. When they reached Oracabessa they rattled their way down the track leading to the banana port and walked across to the edge of the cliff with the tiny bay beneath. Fleming reached it first. 'Look,' he shouted back to Bryce. 'This place has everything.' And then, according to an interview which Fleming gave to an American magazine, when they looked down at the sea there was a young Jamaican girl swimming naked in the clear water. Maybe. But it sounds just a little imaginative: most Jamaican girls, being Methodists, would shrink from swimming without a costume.

At any rate, it is somehow typical of Fleming that on his first excited visit to his new property he should have been chiefly preoccupied with what to call the place. Anne Rothermere, who was to marry Fleming in 1952, suggested 'Shamelady', the name of the plant which grows wild along Jamaica's whole North Shore—a sensitive plant, she said ironically, and one which curls up if touched; another of their friends, Alastair Forbes, made a good punning suggestion, 'Rum Cove'. Finally Fleming settled on 'Goldeneye'. He had picked the perfect name to go with the myth he was to spin around his house.

And as with all the best myths there is an appropriate mystery which he seems to have done his best to perpetuate. Sometimes he insisted that he took the name from Carson McCullers's novel *Reflections in a Golden Eye*. Sometimes he said it came from Operation Goldeneye, the Allied plan he worked on in 1940 to provide for the defence of Gibraltar if the Germans tried to invade through Spain. He had recently bought a print of a goldeneye duck. He remembered, too, that Oracabessa was Spanish for 'head of gold', and, most potent of all, in the garden there was a strange Spanish tomb with a golden eye in a golden head.

Whatever its origins the name was important for a man who had always known the value of a good title. For as he wrote in a letter many years later, 'When I came to Jamaica, I was determined that one day Goldeneye would be better known than any of the great houses that had been there so long and achieved nothing.'

It happened. But before that both he and Goldeneye had a long way to go.

CHAPTER TEN

THE LIFE FOR TREATS

I

WHEN Commander Ian Lancaster Fleming, R.N.V.R., was officially released from His Majesty's Service on November 10th, 1945, with fifty-six days' resettlement leave, he threw off the dust of Whitehall, his gold-peaked cap and his much-travelled heavy naval commander's greatcoat for ever. Still undecided about his future, he gave his address as care of Glyn Mills Bank, 67 Lombard Street.

It was a melancholy going in one respect; for in the share-out of decorations which had accompanied victory his name had been noticeably absent. Several people, aware of his peculiar contribution, had tried to do something about it, but in the end the only country which did reward his services was Denmark, though not for any very gratifying reason. The Danish Government had simply asked one of Fleming's subordinates, Mr William Todd (formerly Thos. Cook's man in Egypt, currently the Admiralty's Scandinavian expert) for the names of a few people deserving of their gratitude. Todd, a kindly man, had added his superior's name to the list, and Fleming was awarded the Commander's Cross of the Order of the Dannebrog.

But his real trouble was that the six-and-a-half years he had spent in the Admiralty had established a pattern for his life which it was difficult to break. Despite the frustrations and the tensions, his strange job, with its unusual combination of power, travel, mystery, intrigue and respectability, had satisfied the demands of his complex nature like nothing before. It had given the fantasist in him the time of its life while finding a use for his solid Scots banker side, with its capacity for hard work, loyalty and devotion to a cause.

As he knew quite well, it was going to be hard to find anything as satisfying again. Despite his talk about making a dash for it to the tropics and spending the rest of his life at Goldeneye writing books and lying in the sun, he knew there was really no chance of this and never seriously pursued it except as one more daydream to fall back on in moments of depression or high excitement. In any case, behind the occasional arrogance, the veneer of effortless assurance, he was still surprisingly diffident, and apart from that one by-line in the *Daily Express* in 1933 for his story on the Moscow trial had never put his name to a word he had written.

This lack of confidence helps to explain why he did not begin his books now that he had the time and the opportunity. For the house at Oracabessa was nearing completion, and for anyone who really wanted to write, nothing could have been easier than to slip away for a year or two to try out his talent. But he was reluctant to commit himself wholeheartedly to anything as precarious as the career of a full-time writer.

All the same, there was no question now of going back to the sort of life which had circled so emptily around the Ebury Street orchid house before the war. Those six years at the Admiralty had changed him. He had ambition now. He enjoyed power. He had influential friends. He was thirty-eight and it was time he made his way in the world.

He discussed it all with certain of his friends. Should he go back into the City and try to make a fortune? The idea of the money still appealed to him but the City no longer did. Should he try to continue in intelligence work in some form or another? At one point before leaving the Admiralty he considered this and even discussed with Stephenson whether to stay on in the Navy or attempt to transfer to M.I.5 or M.I.6 on the strength of his wartime experience.

But again, probably wisely, he made no real attempt to do so. Certainly the day-to-day contact with those professionally humdrum characters who are the backbone of the real Secret Service would have seemed a tedious anticlimax after his Red Indians and the wartime variety-show of Room 39.

Instead, with considerable foresight and self-knowledge, he plumped for the one career which seemed to promise exactly what he needed. He accepted an offer from Lord Kemsley to organize a Foreign News Service for his chain of national and provincial newspapers at a starting salary of £5,000 a year plus expenses. As an additional bonus he coolly insisted on a clause being included in the contract under which he was guaranteed a minimum of two months' paid holiday a year, so that for at least a sixth of his life he would be able to realize his dream and escape to the sun and the warm seas of Goldeneye while the rest of London suffered its way through the last cruel months of winter. Here, as usual, he was entirely egocentric. All his life he nimbly side-stepped the dull, the drab, all the routine duties that exhaust ordinary people.

At the same time he felt that as the favoured but independent protégé of a Press Lord hoping to extend his empire with the coming of peace he might find a purpose to life and one which would cancel out the futility of those empty pre-war days in the City. He could also set out really to enjoy himself now; his health had never been better; he had sufficient money—never enough, of course, for his emotional needs, for the constant desire to *be* wealthy—but he had received his share of the profits as a junior partner in Rowe and Pitman throughout the war and there was enough for his new car, his tailor's bills, his shirts at £3 10s. a time from Turnbull and Asser in Jermyn Street, his lunches at Scott's, and the rent of £450 a year on his newly acquired flat in Montagu Square.

Not that Fleming was an extravagant man. In this period of national austerity he proved that he could live something aproaching the life of a millionaire on his £5,000 a year, plus the dividends from what he was later to call his 'meagre portfolio' and with occasional presents from his mother. Few men of his age can have ended the war by reconciling worldly ambition and the pursuit of pleasure quite so successfully.

These were the flush years, the years when he had the chance of living the life most young men dream of but few have the money or the wit or the capacity or the selfishness to achieve. His flat in Montagu Square was comfortable, almost opulent; and here his love-affairs continued with the same rapidity as before the war although, it seemed, with even less danger of his becoming seriously entangled with any one woman. More than ever now he was keeping love of any sort out of his relations with women. He could feel sentimental over their memory but he remained defensively detached in their presence. He was, in short, the most pro-fessional of professional bachelors, self-contained as a sultan, following his own whims, his own tastes, his own strange hankerings for excitement and amusement in all he did.

If people bored him, he dropped them. If anything interested him, he pursued it enthusiastically until it, too, suddenly became boring. He played golf and bridge with almost perverse seriousness. There is something almost old-maidish about the ivory-tower existence which he now began to construct for himself. He decided that flowers gave him headaches, and flowers were therefore banned whenever he was around. He used to suffer from cracked lips in winter, and even today people remember the care with which he applied lip salve. One of the words he was always using was 'symmetry', and in the pursuit of symmetry in his own life everything was worked out—the restaurants he went to, the meals he ate, the friends he talked to, the women he slept with, and most of all the regular treats with which he rewarded himself. They were treats meticulously planned and anticipated with curious intensity.

The greatest treat of all in this life designed for treats was the two months he spent each year at Goldeneye. For this was to be more than a house where he spent his holidays: it was the place where his hidden self could come to life and where reality and fantasy could meet at last.

II

North Shore from Montego Bay to Oracabessa is still much the same today as it was on that January morning in 1946 when Fleming, stepping off the night plane from New York, sniffed again that sweet, faintly sickly smell of the tropics, picked up his hired Austin, and drove along the fifty-two miles of switchback corniche to take possession of his still unfinished house at Oracabessa.

It is an odd journey. Once the concrete villas and the sun umbrellas of Montego Bay are behind you it is like driving into the pages of *Treasure Island*. You wind through this lush, hot, tumbledown country with its wooden shanties and Baptist chapels, its black cattle grazing among coconut palms, its mangrove swamp, cane field, long stretches of blue-and-silver beach and forgotten stone villages where the wayside pulpit exhorts the passing motorist to prepare to meet his God. There is Falmouth, with its old stone church tower and Antonio's store, where Fleming used to buy cotton leftovers to be made up into brightly coloured shirts for the summer at $3 a time. Then Discovery Bay, where Columbus landed. And Runaway Bay where the escaping slaves made for.

The ads for Tropigaz and Red Stripe Brewery Fresh Beer flicker past, and when you reach the large blue notice-board of Drax Hall Estate (a name later to be commemorated in

Sir Hugo Drax of *Moonraker*) and the bizarre Marrakesh Hotel (site of Jamaica's first Bunny Club) you have arrived.

For here, hidden away in this tropical Frinton, with its bungalows, its new motel and its private driveways winding off behind the hedges of evergreen, lies the shingle-roofed, sea-girt centre of Fleming's private world.

From the start Goldeneye was his place of escape, the spot where he could indulge the irresponsible, fantastic, pleasure-loving, dream-bound side of his nature. On that first visit to his half-built house in 1946 he set the pattern which he was to follow every January for the remainder of his life. It was a routine he never really changed, and this corner of Jamaica entered his private mythology as a place of permanency and a place of dreams, the one spot in the world he could be sure would never let him down.

Goldeneye then was not a comfortable house, but he was not in search of comfort. The furniture made by the carpenter in Port Maria had the rough, do-it-yourself quality of furniture he had probably seen in some naval officers' mess on one of his wartime tours of the tropics. There was a canasta table presented by Lady Huggins, the Governor's wife. The chairs were covered in blue canvas which soon faded to a gentle shade of grey; possibly some dim nautical memory persuaded him to have the floor of the living-room navy blue, although the local builder's idea of blue concrete turned out to have a strange marbled effect, much admired by guests as the years went by.

According to his neighbour Noël Coward, who has his two houses (one for guests and one for himself) a mile along the coast in the direction of Port Maria, Fleming lost a great opportunity by building the house in the wrong place. 'If he'd built it slightly to one side at an angle to the beach he'd have had a view each evening of one of the most beautiful sunsets in the world. But even if he had it wouldn't have been any use, because Ian had been careful to set the window sills just that much too high.'

'Goldeneye, of course,' Coward goes on, continuing his vendetta against the unfortunate house which began when he named it Golden eye, nose and throat, 'is a perfectly ghastly house. I should know. Ian lent it me for three months the year after he'd built it (*and* charged me £50 a week for the privilege I might add), and as I told him, that was *too* much for bed and board in a barracks. There was no hot water in those days. Only cold showers. We were very manly and pretended to like it. But I did get tired of the iron bed-stead and the pictures of the snakes he had plastered all over the bedroom wall, and the *banquette* you sat on at the dining-table which was so narrow it bit into your bottom, and the cushions that felt as if they had been filled with chipped steel.'

But Goldeneye was really a great joke between them, and their close friendship, which started in Jamaica, lasted until Fleming's death.

'One of the things that still make me laugh whenever I read Ian's books,' says Coward, 'is the contrast between the standard of living of dear old Bond and the sort of thing Ian used to put up with at Goldeneye. When Bond drinks his wine it has to be properly *chambré,* the tournedos slightly underdone and so forth. But whenever I ate with Ian at Goldeneye the food was so abominable that I used to cross myself before I took a mouthful. Stewed guavas and coconut cream—salt fish and ackee fruit. I used to say, "Ian, it tastes like armpits". And all the time you were eating there was old Ian smacking his lips for more while his guests remembered all those delicious meals he had put into the books.'

Coward's theory is that the food and the discomfort of Goldeneye were exactly what Fleming wanted and secretly enjoyed. 'They're very strange people, the Flemings. There's old Peter without a taste bud in his head whizzing through Tibet before the war on a yak and feeding on cow dung. Ian was rather the same at heart.'

Maybe. But Goldeneye was the biggest treat of Fleming's year, and nothing as dull and ordinary as reality was to prevent him from enjoying it to the full.

Inevitably, with his later success, the whole idea of Jamaica became glamorized out of recognition: Goldeneye appeared a sort of Shangri-la at the heart of some Bond-inhabited, girl-girt, tropical lotus land, with Pussy Galore on the beach and Goldfinger sipping vodka martinis on the sun terrace. But for Fleming it wasn't like that at all. Harling has somewhere described him as behaving at Goldeneye like 'a sort of eccentric Jamaican squire', and Fleming's routine there was far closer to the life of some self-absorbed eighteenth-century original than to the glamour of the inter-national millionaire smart-set who build their summer houses along this coast.

To all the locals he was and still is quite simply 'The Commander', and it is for his quirks and extravagances—as well as his kindnesses—that they chiefly remember him. The great success of Violet, his devoted local cook and house-keeper, came from the way she unquestioningly accepted and then embodied all Fleming's ideas of how he wanted to live and eat at Goldeneye. She is a portly and impressive Jamaican matron now, with a house and family of her own up the road from Goldeneye, and as Graham Greene discovered when he fell foul of her during a stay at Goldeneye, she is utterly dedicated to Fleming's views of how the house was to be run.

'The Commander,' she says today, placing determined hands on ample hips and stating Fleming's Jamaican philosophy like an edict of God himself, 'just like all things easy here. He not fussy. He just like Jamaica food. He just *love* shrimp and fish and oxtail and liver . . . fish soup and black crab soup and calah soup—that Jamaica dish we make him with spinach. The Commander like it very much. He no like make-up pudding. He like guava and stew tamborine and fish and lobster every day at lunch and stew goat in the evening. The fish he like real special is kingfish and butter fish and snapper fish and goat fish . . . Real Jamaica fish, goat fish,' says Violet, rolling her eyes at the thought of it. 'Not many English people like him. But the Commander real crazy about goat fish.'

And as well as the goat fish there were all the other carefully prescribed ingredients of Fleming's routine at Goldeneye: the seven o'clock swim out to the reef, the shaving water brought by Violet on his return, the solitary breakfast of paw-paw, scrambled eggs and coffee beneath the sea walnut on the edge of the 'sinking garden', the humming birds he watched sipping from the hibiscus, the kling-klings that hopped around the breakfast table. Each had its place, its particular significance, and these small rituals could make Fleming appear an odd and sometimes a difficult host for those who did not understand him.

Peter Quennell stayed there three times and seems to have got used to the calah soup and the goat fish. 'Ian,' he says, 'was an excellent host provided you always remembered his peculiarities. Even there, you see, he tended to be a very restless, unrelaxed person, and he could be very prima-donna-ish, relapsing into tantrums if he felt you were intruding on any of the things he enjoyed about the place. For instance, in the morning, if you went for a swim, you had to make a great detour round the front of the house because the Commander's bedroom was on that side, and he had got into the habit of lying on his bed in the early morning, watching the view unmarred by mortal man.'

'Another peculiarity of the place,' says Quennell, 'was that it was always rather hard to get a drink when you wanted it. The Commander tended to drink in the American way. Vodka martinis or very brown whisky sodas would appear late in the day, and he would drink rather heavily then. But at dinner itself there was seldom anything to drink; and I had usually to ask Ian if I could have some beer; at which Ian would order "A bottle of beer for Mr Quennell, Violet!" in sepulchral and reproving tones, and Violet would throw up her hands and eyes, muttering "Lordie, Lordie!", and you would feel that you were upsetting the routine of the entire place.'

This routine included certain highlights Fleming seems to have devised rather as the headmasters of newly-established public schools devise traditions for the boys to observe. One was the routine of the sucking pig which he loved to arrange when he gave a party. Another was a special drink called 'Poor man's thing', which he invented as the finale to a Goldeneye evening with honoured guests.

Once again Violet is the expert. 'Well, you have a dish. You have skin of the orange, skin of the lemon. You pour a bottle of cheap Three Daggers rum on top. Put in sugar. Put on oven. Keep stirring. Set light to dish. Then turn out all lights in house when you carry the "Poor man's thing" into guests.'

During his bachelor days at Goldeneye Fleming was a conscientious if sometimes eccentric host. He did not come here to hide away all the time. He enjoyed the select band of artists, millionaires and misfits he was soon meeting, and he was far less difficult and defensive among them than he would have been in London. His looks, his charm, his eligibility made him a welcome addition to a society which was hardly likely to allow such qualities to pass unnoticed.

He knew the Vincent Astors, and Mr and Mrs Otis Q. Phelps, and Prince and Princess Liechtenstein. There was talk for several Jamaican seasons that he might become the next husband of the currently available oil heiress, Millicent Rogers. Then through Sir William Stephenson he met a second dynamic millionaire who was to have some importance in his own future. 'Lord Beaverbrook,' he wrote in a highly uncharacteristic gossip article on the island for the American *Vogue*, 'holds suave but impish sway over Montego, with that hectoring cajolery which has made him great in a larger pond even than the Caribbean.'

It was a peace-offering of a kind; for according to Stephenson there had been 'a spot of bother between Ian and Max' before Ian wrote this. It seems that one evening over at Beaverbrook's house Fleming had criticized an article in that day's *Daily Express* on the grounds of good taste. Later, when Stephenson mentioned Fleming's name to Beaverbrook, he drew the emery-voiced reply—'That's the young whippersnapper who tells me how to run my own newspapers at my own dinner-table.'

However, after a carefully prepared dinner at Hillowton, Jamaica's magic and Fleming's charm did their work, and Stephenson heard Beaverbrook saying, 'That's O.K. then, Ian. Now I have forgiven you your damned stupidity.'

Stephenson says, 'That put Ian in a very favoured position with Beaverbrook—Max was a complex man and he always had a particular affection for people who had defied him and he had subsequently forgiven.'

But there were others besides millionaires. In Jamaica Fleming got to know Cecil Beaton and other friends of Noël Coward. In time they too took their places on the Goldeneye *banquette* and wrestled with the conch gumbo and the fried octopus tentacles with the tartare sauce which Violet cooked in their honour. Truman Capote stayed for a fortnight. So did Rosamond Lehmann, who borrowed Goldeneye to work on a novel when Fleming was in New York.

But although Fleming hardly lived the self-denying life of an island solitary, he liked to maintain the idea of himself as something between Jean-Jacques Rousseau and Robinson Crusoe. He wrote:

If you burden yourself with the big-town malaises you came here to escape—the telephone, gin and canasta jitters, gossip and how to keep up with the procession—those will be the serpents in this Eden. But if you can leave this *triste* baggage behind, you will find Jamaica has everything you need for a holiday of twenty days or twenty years amidst a kindly and humorous people in the most beautiful large tropical island in the world.

Jamaica was a daydream he could always believe in, an island that seemed unlike anywhere else in the world. It was the one place where he was really free from Northern melancholy, free from the promptings of his solid Fleming ancestry.

It was also to be the one place where he felt free to write (if we except the journalism that came later on), and it is significant that the first real writing Fleming produced with his name to it should have been about Jamaica. This was an article done in 1947, for Cyril Connolly's magazine *Horizon*, as an escaper's guide to the island.

The style is polished, personal and completely recognizable. Indeed, for anyone who knew him in person the re-reading of this fragment of pre-Bond Fleming is slightly unnerving. For he wrote very much as he spoke, and some of the phrases seem to echo that curious voice of his, with its off-key drawl—'I can assure you that sun and calm blue seas and brassy heat can be more wearying and exasperating than the grey but ever-changing porridge in which you live and make sweet moan.'

The article also has that combination of odd imagination and hard practicality which was to provide one of the key ingredients of his books. It becomes apparent when he touches on a favourite fad—the Jamaican Blue Mountain coffee. For Fleming, Blue Mountain coffee had to be, like everything else he enjoyed, unique. It was, so he assured *Horizon*'s readers, 'the finest coffee in the world!' But like a schoolboy telling his astounded friends the full inside story, he had to go on to provide the hard details behind the mystique.

'You will drink this coffee cold-distilled,' he wrote in that peremptory style which at once ruled out any other way of drinking anything so precious. 'That is,' he went on, for the benefit of lesser mortals ill-acquainted with the intricacies of cold-distilling, 'the coffee, freshly ground, is percolated over and over again with cold water until a thin black treacle is produced. This is very strong and contains all the aroma which, by roasting, would otherwise be lost in the kitchen air. A third of a cup with hot milk or water added,' he concluded airily, 'will spoil you for all the more or less tortured brews you drink in England.'

All this is interesting, but anyone who takes the trouble to compare the original *Horizon* article with the later version which his friend Morris Cargill used as an introduction to his glossy guide book to Jamaica will find something very odd. The claims for Blue Mountain coffee are included as Fleming wrote them. So is the business about it spoiling you for those tortured English brews. But all the splendid particularization of the techniques of cold-distilling have been quietly suppressed. And of course the truth is that it is all quite preposterous nonsense. If you percolate cold water over Blue Mountain coffee the result is just as unsatisfactory as if you percolate cold water over any other coffee, freshly ground or otherwise.

He used his imagination in much the same way to enhance the trips he made to the surrounding Jamaican countryside. In this he was the true tourist-publicist's ideal. For he was so determined to enjoy his Jamaica that nothing was too insignificant, nothing too tawdry for him once his imagination was really ignited. And dream-dealing romantic that he was, he could become ignited by remarkably little.

It was typical of him to have picked up the old Jamaican names for off-shore and on-shore breezes—the Doctor's Wind and the Undertaker's Wind. These days you would need to go a long way over the island to hear anyone actually refer to them as such, but for Fleming the names were so evocative of the old romantic Jamaica that they immediately entered his private mythology.

'Every day,' he began another early article he wrote on Jamaica, 'the Doctor's Wind is pulling the sugar cane into the hills by its silver hair and every evening the Undertaker's Wind comes to the rescue. The fresh Trades blow every day and in the evening they pause at sundown and then the soft reverse breeze from the Blue Mountains clears the island during the night of its used airs.'

Another old Jamaican myth that he treated as if it were actuality is the story of the Cockpit Country, known, according to him, as the 'Land of Look Behind'. This was another part of his *Horizon* article which Morris Cargill discreetly omitted. Yet it is so typical of Fleming and the way he saw the island that it deserves to be rescued from the oblivion of inaccuracy. He wrote:

When taxes were introduced in 1790, the Maroons, the Spanish negro inhabitants of this province, would not pay. The Governor sent a company of redcoats up into their hills to enforce payment, but the Maroons repulsed them, set up their own government and refused allegiance to the Crown. They still refuse it, and are the only corner of the British Empire to do so. Their 'colonel' is a coloured man who, with all his 'government', wears a Sam Browne belt. He does very little governing, except to maintain the rights of his people vis-à-vis the Governor. His people work and mix with their neighbours, intermarry and go and come as they please. But since they pay no taxes, no roads have ever been built in the province and there are no public facilities such as post offices and social services. The terrain has never been surveyed and, if you look at the map, you will see a large white patch with the red veins of the roads coming to a full stop at the perimeter.

As Fleming could easily have found out for himself, you will look in vain on your map of modern Jamaica for that white patch where the red veins of the road come to a stop. The fact is that Jamaica fitted into that compartment of his mind where truth was not the primary concern. It was enough that he believed it, as he must have done to submit the story under his own name to a magazine like *Horizon*; and of course the whole theme is one which never ceased to fascinate Fleming and which he was to use several times in the books. This mythical coloured 'colonel' with his 'government' and his freedom from all official interference is a prototype Bond villain, and the position Fleming evidently believed he still held in Jamaica is almost identical with the sinister freedom enjoyed by the undercover 'government' of that other Negro leader, Mr Big in Harlem, and of the dreaded Dr No on Crab Key.

But not all of Fleming's Jamaican daydreams were founded on fantasy. When Princess Margaret visited Jamaica in January 1955, and it was announced that her programme would include a trip by bamboo raft down the Rio Grande river, Fleming wrote an anonymous piece in the *Sunday Times* describing the 'enchantingly languid voyage down between the great hills befeathered with bamboo and bright with the flowers of the giant Immortel. I hope,' he concluded, in what was a piece of lovingly remembered autobiography, 'that Princess Margaret will be piloted by Red Grant, a cheerful, voluble giant of villainous aspect and allow him to make for her his Strong Bak Soup—a ridiculous cauldron brew of langoustines and exotic roots which tastes of absolutely nothing at all but which somehow belongs to this elegant and delicately romantic adventure.'

For in fact the trip down the Rio Grande river was one of Fleming's own regular treats. Soon after his arrival in Jamaica every year he would send Red Grant a telegram saying: 'FLEMING COMING STOP PREPARE HOT BAK SOUP', and it is interesting that while he was recommending Red Grant and his soup to the Princess he was on the point of appropriating his name for the deadly killer from SMERSH in *From Russia, With Love*.

Another Goldeneye treat, which began early on and re-echoes in several of the books (most specifically in the offal

Suddenly, in the last year of the war, Fleming fell in love with Jamaica. The Goldeneye legend had begun

The last winter at Goldeneye: Anne and Ian Fleming with Violet, cook and housekeeper. He was then writing his last novel, *The Man with the Golden Gun*

harvest used by Mr Big to attract and enrage the sharks in *Live and Let Die*), was the shark hunting he used to enjoy with a local Jamaican called Aubyn Cousins. Owing his name and his light-grey eyes to the captain of a nineteenth-century schooner from Belfast, Aubyn Cousins seems to be Oracabessa's nearest to the original for James Bond's faithful Cayman islander, Quarrel. His father, Christie Cousins, formerly owned the fifteen acres of Goldeneye, and Aubyn used to go snorkelling with Fleming in the small bay at Goldeneye during the early days when Fleming came there on his own. But Aubyn's greatest speciality was to lasso sharks. He and Fleming would often go out by boat in the early morning with the carcase of a dead donkey as bait, and when they were well out beyond the reef they would heave it overboard and wait for the sharks to bite. Normally the sharks along this coast are a fairly placid, well-fed lot, but the effect of Fleming's dead donkey was usually as dramatic as the putrid offerings of Mr Big. When they were thoroughly enraged Cousins would slip a nylon noose over the side of the boat on the end of a long piece of bamboo. It was delicate work getting the noose over the head of a shark, but once it was in place the plunging of the great fish would pull it tight behind the gills and the chase would begin.

In a strong sea a fully grown shark, thrashing and plunging just after its capture, can easily upset a small boat with two men aboard. According to Cousins this was what Fleming most enjoyed—the sudden moment of excitement, *les sensations fortes*, when everything was at stake and one false move could spell disaster.

'Funny thing about the Commander though,' says Cousins. 'Once we got the shark tied up good and firm it seemed like he lost interest. And he never let me kill a shark. "Cousins," he'd say, "cut the damn thing loose—we've had our fun for today." If you'd not read his books you'd have thought the Commander was scared of death or something.'

There were other things to enjoy. Fleming's favourite place in the whole of Jamaica lay at the end of the garden, beyond the jacarandas, where the narrow path leads down the side of the cliff and the miniature bay of Goldeneye reveals itself like some Cornish smuggler's cove, a hidden, secret, silent place.

When he bought Goldeneye sight unseen through old Reggie Acquart, Fleming got a far better bargain than he realized. On most of Jamaica's North Shore the scenery tends to be better than the swimming: the reef is usually half a mile or so offshore and it is hard to find deep water free of rock and weed close in. But with Goldeneye he acquired one of the few places in Jamaica where the reef comes so close that there is white sand and deep clear water to swim in all the year round.

He explored the reef during those hot late January days of 1946, with his heavy black Pirelli mask pressing tight against his face and the twin plastic snorkel tubes leaving a trail of bubbles on the blue bay water. He floated out, face down, through the silent unbelievable underwater garden on the reef which he had suddenly found at his own back door. There he spent hours, swimming and floating and watching and exploring until his back was burned mahogany by the sun and he knew every rock and hole and cavern and every creature inhabiting them.

Sir William Stephenson believes it was this that killed him—'the strain on his heart of all that damned underwater nonsense. You'd have thought that Oshawa would have cured him of that.' In the end it may have added to the other strains that weakened his heart, but swimming at Goldeneye during these early years can hardly be blamed as a primary cause of his illness.

He didn't go deep. He rarely hunted anything more lethal than lobsters or the long-spined black sea-eggs which he would break open with his light three-pronged spear to feed the fish. He didn't come here for excitement, either. The shark and the barracuda lie farther out beyond the reef, and they were not what he was interested in.

The reef was simply a place of escape. By the mere act of donning his flippers and his mask he was back in the sort of world Captain Nemo inhabited in the Jules Verne books he read as a child; a world where nobody talks or makes demands or answers back; a world where boredom vanishes, where loneliness no longer matters, where the faintest stroke of a flipper would carry him over canyons, past great rocks, through the forests of tree coral, as he followed the rainbow fish and the blue parrot fish that went flashing between the niggerheads and the great clumps of brain coral in that cold underwater sunlight.

CHAPTER ELEVEN

FALLING MERCURY

To anyone returning to London in March after two months on the North Shore of Jamaica the Foreign Manager's office on the second floor of the old Kemsley building in Gray's Inn Road might have appeared depressing. But Fleming never seemed to object to it. Possibly there was even something about it that appealed to the puritan in him.

It was a room with a thinly sliced strip of bacon-coloured carpet on the floor, a lot of brown lino and cream paintwork, a few leather-backed chairs, and various frosted glass partitions protecting him from the sight but not the sound of the typists all round. He had another partition put up, sacrificing space to give himself the benefit of a tiny ante-room—a daring innovation which old hands at Kemsley House regarded with awe and distaste, as if this privileged newcomer were already halfway towards his own executive suite.

He hung a faded print of Montego Bay on one wall and furnished his desk with a silver cigarette box. He was in business. For fourteen years this matchboard hutch was the centre of his working life. It was by far the longest period he spent at a single desk doing a single job.

A great believer in routine now, he would arrive soon after ten, flinging the sinister black felt hat which he carried but never wore on the little table in the ante-room that displayed *Life, Time,* the *New Yorker,* the *Saturday Review, Fortune, Oggi* and many other examples of cosmopolitan journalism. Again the Kemsley House old pros found something offensively alien and smart-alec in the spectacle.

Barring accidents or a summons from Lord Kemsley to his office on the directors' floor above, he would hold a brief conference and spend the rest of the morning dictating cables to his correspondents and seeing a succession of people, the image already of the man the world had still to get to know—the black hair greying now above the ears, the umpteenth Morland's Special of the day already in the ebonite Dunhill holder, the lines of age just beginning to touch that sad, sensual, heavy-lidded face. By now, too, he had finally assumed the dress which was to be his working uniform for the rest of his life—the polka-dot blue bow tie, the black moccasin shoes (he had decided that shoe laces were obsolete), the blue shirts with the sleeves cut short just above the elbow, the dark-blue suit he would send back to the tailor so often that the man would talk about 'fixing some new cloth to Mr Fleming's original buttons'.

To those who worked closely with him Fleming's most endearing quality was the way he seemed able to dodge everything that was most boring, petty and tedious in the life of a journalist. He was a great invigorator and a great consoler. His sense of the ridiculous was always at the disposal of others.

'But my dear fellow, they can't have told you *that*.'

His head would go back, his eyes gleam delightedly, and his loud, long-toothed laughter dissolve explanations or justifications in a cloud of cigarette smoke.

Perhaps he was a man to be envied more than admired. For among all the anxious or ambitious men around him he seemed to have his life so much better worked out than anyone else. Where they were worried he was aloof, where they were involved he seemed somehow above the battle. He had no wife to interfere with his golf, no bank manager troubled his peace of mind, his exact position in the hierarchy was undefined yet he acknowledged no superior but Lord Kemsley.

He seemed to know everyone, and if he did not he could always make it clear that the heathen were not worth knowing. He had two months' holiday when even the highest of the other departmental chiefs had only one. He signed his own expenses. He was the one man in that entire drear building who called Lord Kemsley 'Gomer' and Lady Kemsley 'Edith'. Urbane and irreverent, invulnerable and unconcerned, he appeared as a sort of Crown Prince of Kemsley House. That is, until disillusion set in, and he lost his enthusiasm, and his lips turned down with dissatisfaction.

In the great battle that goes on in any big newspaper office between action and inertia, Fleming was all for action; so, in his own particular way, was Lord Kemsley himself. Though the arena for action was vast, Lord Kemsley's attention narrowed increasingly on his most important newspaper, the *Sunday Times*, and he personally directed the struggle it waged in the late 1940s and the 1950s with the *Observer*. Fleming played an important part and was full of ideas, some good, some crazy, to meet the sparkling competition put up by the rival newspaper. Out of all this developed his peculiar love-hate relationship with the *Sunday Times* and an association that he could never bring himself to relinquish.

Yet as Foreign Manager of the entire Kemsley group Fleming had a specific job and one that, in this difficult period for British newspapers, when the rationing of newsprint helped to choke enterprise, made his life nothing like as carefree and as uncomplicated as it might have seemed to the casual spectator. For all his dégagé air he was deeply involved in it, and it was the ups and downs at Kemsley House which helped to bring on the crisis of his early forties and changed the rest of his life. For this reason it is important to understand what he was trying to do as Foreign Manager and why he failed.

In theory the job was simple enough. In 1945 Lord Kemsley, with his wildly assorted bag of newspapers ranging from the *Sunday Times* to the barely literate Sunday *Empire News*, and taking in a network of provincial newspapers large and small, owned by far the biggest single newspaper empire in Britain. Fleming's idea was that a group of this size needed a proper foreign news service of its own. Good exclusive foreign news and features, so he argued, would enable some of the already threatened Kemsley provincial papers to resist being steamrollered into the ground by the regional editions of the national dailies.

Stimulated by an idea, Fleming could be a persuasive man. Now that some of the restrictions imposed by the war were being relaxed, Lord Kemsley was anxious to bring in young university graduates and ex-officers and train them for journalism and management. He loved bold moves yet had received little encouragement to execute them from some of the elderly and unsophisticated professionals who had been with him since he separated from his brother, the first Lord Camrose, in 1938 and set up on his own.

Moreover, he was fond of Fleming. Since the bridge-playing days at the Dorchester in the war he had got to know him well, and he invited him regularly to dinner-parties at his magisterial Adam home, Chandos House, just round the corner from the B.B.C. in Portland Place, and for week-ends at Dropmore, his country retreat near Taplow, an impressive Georgian-cum-Regency house with beautiful, gloomy grounds whose Douglas firs and rhododendrons and dark evergreens depressed Fleming whenever he deserted bridge or canasta for a breath of fresh air.

Beneath all his formality of manner and mind Lord Kemsley was probably the worthiest and least hard-boiled of the Press Lords of his generation, and the presence of this gifted and good-looking young man, with his ease of manner and knowledge of the world, his important City family, his wartime achievements and his influential friends, must have seemed as welcome an addition to his newspaper office as it was to his dinner-table at Chandos House. So Fleming got his job. For someone with so little experience of journalism it was one of the sleekest appointments of the year.

It was to be some time before he lived down the reputation of having entered Kemsley House as a sort of gilded outsider. He was attacked and he counter-attacked. 'I spend the first fortnight after I return from Goldeneye,' he told a friend, later on, 'plucking the assegais out of my back and sending them hurtling back along the corridors of Kemsley House.'

But whatever his enemies may have said of him he was anything but a dilettante holding down a sinecure. He was unquestionably excited by the challenge of his new job and seemed to see himself as another Sir Roderick Jones at the start of a great career as one of the impresarios of modern foreign journalism.

He began by bringing in several of his people from the Admiralty, including the travel expert William Todd, to whom he had been indebted for the Danish decoration. New correspondents were recruited for many of the big capitals of the world, and he engaged experienced journalists to work for him in Kemsley House. Soon he was building up a considerable organization—called the Mercury Service in the office after its telegraphic address.

The material that poured in from Mercury's correspondents was retransmitted to the *Daily Graphic*, to the Manchester *Daily Dispatch*, to the Aberdeen *Press and Journal*, to the rest of the Kemsley chain in various parts of the country. Not a remarkably high proportion of it appeared in print; paper rationing was still in force—it dragged on in some form or other until 1959—and even the *Sunday Times* was pegged down for a long time to issues of a mere eight or ten pages. In these most abnormal conditions Mercury became something of a luxury—an 'expensive toy' as one of the directors of the company sourly called it.

Outwardly Fleming showed no anxiety. Always a believer in telegrams of congratulation to correspondents or contributors who had done a good job, and no doubt spurred on by the electrifying effect of Lord Beaverbrook's messages to his staff, he quickly fell into the habit of sending long and not inexpensive cables to his far-flung correspondents, rejoicing in some scoop which had, or so he declared, reduced the opposition to a shambles. Later on these generously intentioned messages were to fall under the owlish scrutiny of managerial men trying to find out just where all the Mercury money was going; and they were considerably pained to discover on occasion that some story which Fleming had celebrated as a tremendous scoop in his congratulatory cable ended up as a modest ten lines on the back page of the *Daily Graphic*.

Soon he was in need of fantasy. Had he not permitted himself the schoolboy luxury of escape into his dreams one wonders whether his boredom-racked restlessness could have endured the tedium and the routine of his foreign news organization.

For the day-to-day running of Mercury and the grind of foreign politics never really caught his interest. Foreign politics bored him as profoundly as the politics of his own country. He never mastered the bizarre logistics of the agency business or travelled in search of new correspondents or made foreign sorties on his own account—apart from the occasional trip to Paris and his regular visits to New York en route for Goldeneye each January. He never wrote a leader or a straight foreign news report for Kemsley Newspapers in his life, and his contribution to serious thinking on foreign affairs must be accounted precisely nil.

But despite all such shortcomings it is impossible to write off Fleming's period as Foreign Manager of Kemsley Newspapers as a complete personal failure. When Mercury began to founder in the late 'forties the shipwreck had little to do with him. Newsprint controls went on and on, the expected expansion in the Kemsley newspaper interests failed to show up, and economies had to be enforced. The Foreign News Service, considerable as its prestige might be to the organization, was a natural and inevitable target. Yet all the time Fleming demonstrated certain qualities as an executive which were quite out of the ordinary. The first of these was that he knew the obscure secret of inciting loyalty among those who worked for him—he had learned something of this at the Admiralty. He knew how to handle subordinates, how to flatter them, look after them, make them feel wanted. He knew how to delegate. He backed up his own people with powerful, almost paternal, jealousy.

But there was more to the loyalty his people felt towards him than this. It was almost as if that offhand charm and panache which could captivate millionaires and girl friends and senior officers could beguile hard-headed journalists as well. For all his shortcomings (and he cheerfully admitted most of them) and his limited journalistic experience he was an immensely exciting man to work for.

There was one final asset Fleming possessed as Foreign Manager of Kemsley Newspapers: that bridge and Christian-name relationship with the Kemsleys which had caused some of the jealousy and suspicion when he first landed the job. He was a great favourite of Lady Kemsley's, and her husband too would allow him privileges accorded to no one else. 'Now don't be so ve-he-ment, I-arn,' the old viscount would say in a voice with the faintest trace of Welsh in it when Fleming had finished telling him why drastic action was needed on some Kemsley newspaper. And usually, like some favourite son, Fleming would end up by getting his own way.

During the first two or three years of its existence Mercury expanded impressively. It was not until the end of 1948 that the first cracks began to show. The trouble lay not in the way the service was being run but in the whole idea on which its existence rested. Where Fleming had erred, if erred he had, was in his original estimate of the power of specially written foreign news to attract fresh readers to the increasingly harassed papers of Lord Kemsley's chain. Competition was fierce; the price of newsprint was rising frighteningly; regional papers were being murdered by the regional editions of the big dailies. In this twilight of the Imperial Russia of the newspaper world it needed more than a revamped Foreign News Service to change things. And Fleming, for all his debonair charm and his zest for living and his friendship with the old Tsar himself, began to suffer the disillusion and sadness inherent in any declining regime.

Increasingly he found himself having to try to fight off economy drives which threatened the very existence of his department. Increasingly he had to cut back on staff and facilities abroad. Worst of all, he began to understand that the idea he had cherished when he first entered Kemsley House of becoming one of the great power figures of the place was increasingly irrelevant.

The least he had hoped for was a directorship. It never came. The editorship of the *Sunday Times* would have been acceptable. It was never offered—though it is difficult to see him holding down such a job. Gradually it dawned on him that there was a reason—a private reason—for this absence of recognition. In one respect, he was made to feel, he had failed to preserve the high moral tone of Kemsley House: it was the delicate matter of his friendship with a married woman. At any rate, by 1949 there were enough straws in the wind to tell him that his great hopes of an important career in newspapers were over.

From now on he was involved in an increasingly bitter struggle behind the scenes to save his News Service, and as it progressed he seems to have conceived the idea that certain directors of the company resented his having established something of a separate empire within the Kemsley empire and were determined to get rid of him. But even this hardly explains the state of gloom and defeat into which he fell.

The best evidence of his mood lies in a letter he drafted (but probably never sent) to Lord Kemsley in 1950. It began:

I have now been with you nearly four years and I confess that this summer I feel stale and disheartened.

Part of these conditions lie in myself and part lie, I believe, in Kemsley Newspapers, and I want to and I know I ought to tell you what is in my mind.

When I joined Kemsley Newspapers and was followed by many others of what is known as the 'officer class' you adopted a deliberate policy of putting new wine into old bottles with the fine ideal that the commercial properties which you had created should be turned from largely financial ends to properties embodying higher aims . . . intelligent journalism, the sanctity of the written word and other positive virtues.

It seemed to me, and I expect to others, that if we wished to be journalists your newspapers already, through your guidance, had the essential virtues. They were clean, honest and outspoken in their opinions. They had truth and courage. They also clearly had the necessary finance and apparently the will to take further steps towards being the best newspapers in England.

Now for four years I have been reading (more or less) our papers and those of the opposition. I have seen the business of our papers buttressed by fine Empire scholarships, the university candidates and so forth—but I have seen no signs of a scheme to improve the content of our papers . . .

All this was preliminary to an exceedingly frank examination of Lord Kemsley's chief newspapers. Even allowing for the tone of Old Testamentary reverence at the beginning, it was an outspoken letter for an employee, even so privileged an employee as Fleming, to write to a Press Lord like Lord Kemsley. He attacked not so much the treatment of Mercury as the whole system. Within Kemsley House, in the region of the sacred third floor, with its ramrod-straight, saluting commissionaires, such plain speaking was simply not done. Fleming must have been in a state to burn every journalistic boat he possessed to contemplate such a letter, let alone draft it.

Yet there may be exaggeration here. Lord Kemsley was not an entirely predictable man, and if he actually did see the letter his reactions to it could easily have been milder than the outsider would suppose. He could be indulgent to Fleming in his more vehement and apocalyptic moods, and the letter might have confirmed him in his belief—shared by the other top brass at Kemsley House—that Fleming was an irredeemable champion of other people's newspapers and a knocker of everything that came out of what he used to call ironically the 'Big House'. Probably Lord Kemsley, looking as grave as an old-fashioned headmaster in holy orders, would have called Fleming into his study at Dropmore, away from his entourage. On such occasions his formidable personality could mellow into something approaching avuncular, even paternal, affection. Ian, probably, would have been forgiven.

But the fact remains that Fleming must have been feeling that he was facing failure, and this was a sombre thought at his time of life—he was now past his fortieth birthday. At first he had seemed to be succeeding. Now things had gone wrong and he must have understood that he was being cast right back into the old pattern of disappointment and semi-success which had dogged him all his life until he entered the Admiralty. It was a crisis which reawakened his old uncertainty, his familiar lack of confidence in himself. It also marked the end of the period when the solid Fleming side of him had seemed so firmly and hopefully in control.

But as one side of his nature dipped, the other inevitably rose. It was to go on rising for a long time to come.

CHAPTER TWELVE

TOUGH MEN ARE VERY RARE

The patient admits to smoking seventy cigarettes a day and drinking at least a quarter of a bottle of gin. He is not seriously ill but during the last two months has complained of a constricting pain in the heart. He has slightly low blood pressure, the cardiograph shows an inverted T wave, but there are no important clinical symptoms of heart weakness. The above symptoms could all be the result of nicotine poisoning. I instructed the patient that the situation could not be improved by medication—only by will-power.

This was the verdict of a New York heart specialist whom Fleming, unbeknown to his friends, visited in the autumn of 1946. Presumably the knowledge that there was nothing organically wrong with his heart reassured him, and he seems to have ignored both the warning and the advice. Two years later, when he consulted his friend Dr Jack Beal, with whom he had played bridge during the days of the *Cercle*, he still admitted to sixty cigarettes a day and a high consumption of gin.

He liked large slugs of alcohol, usually in the evening—big martinis which were virtually iced gin. The liking for vodka was something he picked up a bit later on. And during this time the devoted Miss Cohen of Morlands in Grosvenor Street had a standing order to send Fleming 300 hand-made cigarettes a week. These were dispatched on Friday night, and he would often call at the shop during the week to replenish supplies.

'Ian had always been so strong and so full of life,' says one of his friends, 'that he took his health entirely for granted.' Yet he had always been highly strung and restless. Almost everyone who knew him in the Admiralty and in his early days at Kemsley House comments on the sense of tension that surrounded him. When he was on form it was part of his mystique.

'One of the reasons why richer, older men always found Ian so attractive,' says one of his more observant girl friends, 'was because of the energy which seemed to be bottled up in him. For ageing millionaires he seemed to have an aura of youth and unpredictability—a glamour—which must have made it very flattering for them to have him around.'

For a romantic melancholic like Fleming there must have been something particularly sad about being over forty. All his life he had been trying to cram unusual sensations and as much excitement and success as his energy could win him into the brief portmanteau of his days. Yet he had never managed to beat the feeling of failure, the sense of being deprived of the best life had to offer, the nagging suspicion that it was much more exciting somewhere else if only he could get there. And now his big career in newspapers had let him down, as had other things before, and his body was beginning to do the same.

He had already had trouble with stones in the kidney. Dr. Beal thought this was probably an inherited weakness. In 1948 he told Beal that the pain and tightness in his chest which he had felt in New York in 1946 had begun to recur. Beal sent him to Sir John Parkinson, doyen of Harley Street heart specialists, who repeated the New York expert's advice.

This time Fleming did take some notice, keeping off brandy, port and liqueurs after dinner and sticking, for a while at least, to cocktails and a little wine with the meal. But his standing order with Miss Cohen continued.

Then not long after his visit to Parkinson his kidney trouble began again, giving him the most painful attack so far. He joked about it later in a letter to Ivar Bryce, telling him that he had started a 'private diamond factory inside my kidneys'. But there was nothing funny about the actual attack. Fleming had been having dinner at the Étoile with a woman friend when the first excruciating pain caught him. He had to endure the ignominy as well as the anguish of being escorted back to his flat by her in a taxi, and by the time Dr Beal arrived he was in such pain that he had to be given an immediate intravenous injection of morphine.

It was bad enough, but for a man of his self-defensive vanity the cruellest blow of all came when another Harley Street specialist told him that he needed to have all his teeth out. Fleming seems to have spent some time thinking this over. Finally he wrote back: 'I am ashamed to say that I have decided to defer having my teeth removed. This does not mean, of course, that I am satisfied that your advice, supported by that of my dentist, is wrong, but I strongly dislike the idea of having so many teeth out at so early an age.'

With his characteristic reluctance to, as he put it, 'eviscerate myself' in public, he kept his troubles to himself. 'The only ultimate rule for an ageing man or woman, or for that matter dog, is not to become obscene,' he wrote. He did his best to follow his own advice. To acquaintances and all but his most perceptive friends he was as effusive and elusive as ever. The complexion was perhaps a shade more florid, the loping walk a little slower, but the façade was scrupulously maintained. He had a great sense of form.

Time after time his writing picks on the terrible fortieth year as the point where life's bitterness really begins. ' "Up to forty," says Bond to Tiffany Case in *Diamonds are Forever*, "girls cost nothing. After that you have to pay money or tell a story. Of the two it's the story that hurts most." He smiled into her eyes. "Anyway, I'm not forty yet!" '

But Fleming was; and he took the softening and decaying processes of his fifth decade as a direct affront to everything he had tried to stand for and believe in. 'Tough men,' he wrote in one of his notebooks, 'are very rare, particularly after forty, when nature and disease have dented them.' This was a sad thing to come from someone like Fleming, who had always made such a fetish of his own toughness.

An increasing amount of his energy seemed to go now into organizing people's lives for them. He could be surprisingly practical, and he took great trouble with his friends' little problems. Particularly he enjoyed giving advice about health, no matter if he had not the slightest intention of following it himself. To Lord Nuffield, near neighbour of the Peter Flemings at Nettlebed and owner of Huntercombe golf course, he sent an American book on how to give up smoking, of which he had imported half a dozen copies. It is possible that Fleming, with his practical eye for these things, had visions of a glossier future in the motor-car business, for it was a very flattering little note he included with the book, telling Lord Nuffield (who had resorted to desperate devices to reduce his own consumption of cigarettes) that it was 'a small return for the pleasure I have had during my life both from your motor-cars and your golf course. Incidentally,' he added, 'the book has had absolutely no effect on my own consumption of nicotine and tar.'

But whatever intention Fleming may have had, Lord Nuffield's reply was brisk and totally irrelevant:

Thanks very much for sending me the book on smoking, and the very kind sentiments you express in your letter are much appreciated. May I say that whoever professed to read this book cheated badly, as I had to use the paper knife six times to separate the pages.

It must have been merely coincidental that about this time Fleming wrote a disparaging article in the *Sunday Times* about the British motor industry.

Early in 1951 there was another misfire. His old friend Sidney Cotton was in Malta having his motor yacht refitted in the Naval Dockyard, and he wrote to Fleming to say that he needed someone to sail and navigate the boat and give a hand with his wartime memoirs. This was the sort of challenge Fleming enjoyed: he loved the sense of being able to find the right man at a moment's notice. A few days later he was writing enthusiastically to Cotton telling him that he had found him his 'Boswell', a young ex-Harrovian, whom he had met at his club, with a Cambridge history degree and 'almost unlimited experience with sailing boats, deep-sea trawlers and naval frigates, a distinguished writer and accomplished navigator'. At the same time he wrote to the young man advising him to 'treat the whole thing as a bit of an adventure and an experience! You would do well,' he added, 'to hastily brush up your typing and also to learn the elements of Speed Writing.'

On the strength of Fleming's recommendation Cotton sent the young man his air ticket and invited him out at once. The following day Fleming received a telegram from Malta:

THANKS FOR ASSISTANT WHO ARRIVED YESTERDAY ABSORBED FOUR BOTTLES RUM REPEAT BOTTLES TODAY AND RETURNS LONDON TOMORROW SIDNEY

Something of Fleming's essential naïvety over people shows in the letter of apology he wrote back to Cotton:

Ah, me, Ah me! The young man was introduced to me by General —— of the Royal Marines, and I wrote to you purely as a result of the introduction and after having taken him to lunch at my club where he consumed one pink gin and a pint of beer and spoke most intelligently of his life on the North Sea. I am horrified to hear of his behaviour and frankly cannot understand it.

Fleming was on safer ground when he began turning his organizing energies towards his mother. By now his relations with the redoubtable lady were much improved, particularly since she had gone to live in the Grand Hotel at Cannes. As far as her children were concerned she seemed satisfied at last that they were all something of a credit to her, as indeed they were. Peter had not allowed his success as a writer to interfere with his duties as a landowner, and the 2,000 acres of Fleming beech woods at Nettlebed were safely in his keeping. Since the war he had become more Fleming than the Flemings. In Oxfordshire he was known as Colonel Fleming, and in 1956 he was to follow his grandfather Robert Fleming and his Uncle Philip as High Sheriff of the county.

Richard Fleming, too, had more than justified himself at the bank in Crosby Square. A lean and likeable man, he was already a pillar of the City, director of many companies by his fortieth birthday, and as devoted to fishing and shooting as his brother Peter. Michael, the youngest brother, had died of wounds as a prisoner of war after Dunkirk.

Ian, of course, was still the odd man out in the eyes of his mother, but time had worked wonders on him. She felt he should be married, but his wartime success, his friendship with people like the Kemsleys and the Rothermeres, and his title of Foreign Manager of Kemsley Newspapers gave her the assurance that he, too, was making his mark in the world. She had helped him in certain ways. In the middle of 1948 she had let him move into a three-bedroomed flat she owned in Hay's Mews, Mayfair, and from time to time a contribution would arrive from the South of France towards his living expenses.

She was in her middle sixties now, still impressive and still a very rich woman. By the beginning of 1950 it was decided that the time had come to take steps to safeguard the Fleming money against death duties which guaranteed that when she died most of Major Val's bequest would pass to the Chancellor of the Exchequer instead of to the three surviving sons. The obvious way to avoid this would have been for her to have given the money to her sons: under the prevailing English law, gifts made more than five years before the giver died were not subject to death duties. Not unnaturally, Ian Fleming was in favour of this. Just as naturally, she was not, and hers was the decision that counted. *Faute de mieux* the accountants suggested that the only way of keeping a reasonable proportion of the money safely within the family was to make sure that when the *grande dame* died she was a resident of a country where the tax laws smiled more benevolently on the rights of property than in the England of the Attlee administration.

Somewhat reluctantly Mrs Val agreed, provided that the climate was suitable, the inhabitants polite, and the country the sort of place she would enjoy. The West Indies were suggested, and it was here that Ian, with his tact, his knowledge of the world, and his experience of Jamaica came in.

The letters he wrote around this time are a model of how a son should handle a rich and temperamental mamma starting off on a new life abroad at the age of sixty-five. In 1950, at the beginning of May, he was writing to her at Cannes—a reassuring, man-of-the-world letter recommending Nassau in the Bahamas and telling her that although July would be a hot month in which to arrive house prices would be lower then. He also informed her that he had found a new flat and thus she would be free to sell the one in Hay's Mews at any time.

I am returning to childhood surroundings in Cheyne Walk! Thanks to Hugo Pitman I have found a top-floor flat in Carlyle Mansions, an old-fashioned and gloomy Victorian block, but very solidly built and with nice rooms. It is on the right-hand corner of the building, so I have terrific views up and down the river and across London. The rent is £410 which is really extremely cheap nowadays, and I have taken a five years' lease. If anything happened I should have absolutely no difficulty in getting rid of it, though, of course, I shall have to spend a good deal on painting and decorating and there are an awful lot of windows to curtain.

After assuring her that she would have no difficulty in disposing of the flat in Hay's Mews he ends by mentioning one of his systems for roulette. 'Let me know if you try it out at the Casino. You don't have to stand up and, in fact, you need a chair at the table in order to work the system properly. It is simply a question of waiting a moment or two until one becomes vacant.'

Promptly, his mother began to wonder whether Barbados might not be more satisfactory for her than the Bahamas. Fleming replied that he was certain she would not like it. 'It is extremely small and provincial, and a very long way indeed from the rest of the world. There are only about half-a-dozen people whom you would be interested to talk to, and I think you would be bored stiff after a few weeks.'

It is clear that he knew his mother well enough by now to have the right technique for steering her on the way she ought to go.

The tax position is not so bad, I believe, but not so favourable as Nassau. If you had a house in Nassau, you could let it from time to time for dollars and then have a chance of doing some visits in the States if you got tired of sitting on the island. It will be very easy for you to come over to Europe whenever you like—only three hours to New York to catch a liner, which is a very different business from the problems of getting to and from Barbados.

The argument convinced her, for when he writes to her on June 2nd, 1950, he is saying how right she was to have chosen the Lyford Cay area of Nassau as the place to look for a house; and, admirable son that he could be now, he showed all the practical, helpful side of his nature.

I went over to Paris this week-end, and I was talking to a friend who has a house in Nassau—Josephine Douglas, an American millionairess who has just married Ivar Bryce who was at school with us—and she was saying that the end of the island which I thought you were going to near the Fort Montague Hotel was very windy, and she strongly recommended the Lyford Cay area.

He went on to say that he had rung up 'young Chester Beatty' (another millionaire school friend), whose father might be prepared to lease her a house for life. 'It would certainly be much better to deal direct with him than with these Nassau sharks, and since he is a comfort-loving and very rich man, I guess that his house is probably in first-class condition.'

So it was that in July, due in no small measure to the efforts of her son Ian, Mrs Valentine Fleming left the Grand Hotel at Cannes for a house called Emerald Wave on Cable Beach, Nassau, followed even now by his letters of advice. 'There is absolutely nothing to be done about the sand flies' —'don't forget that all labour costs are higher in the winter months'—'I should think it best to buy a second-hand car in Nassau after having it gone over by the best mechanic in the island.'

Even if one were cynical enough to detect an element of financial calculation in this filial solicitude, the care he showed for his mother remains altogether admirable, and it is hardly surprising that before long she was relying on him for an increasing number of those small favours which exiles always demand from relatives at home. While he was offering to send out wallpapers from Coles in London, she was requesting him to renew her subscription to *The Times* and the *Spectator* and to buy fresh ammunition for her Browning pistol. 'I have the cartridges I have had *since 1914* . . . the thing is to let the blacks know that I *have* a pistol.'

But apart from what they show of Fleming's increasingly friendly relations with this indomitable lady with the ·25 Browning under her pillow, the letters he wrote her also disclose how anxious he was about money; clearly, despite the £5,000 a year from Lord Kemsley and the care and acumen with which he managed his affairs, it was still a cause of concern. 'You are quite right about the expense of moving into Cheyne Walk,' he wrote. 'I have turned down out of hand the estimate put out by ——. They are far too expensive and I am going to go at it very slowly and certainly not spend anything like their figure if I can possibly help it.' He went on to thank her for her 'very handsome contribution. Without this help I should have had to have sold out some of my very meagre portfolio, and altogether your letter might have come from a fairy godmother.'

Within two months he was writing to her again asking for help with the £1,000 still owing on his flat, 'otherwise I shall be in the bankruptcy court'. It was presumably as something of a sweetener that he added, 'I will bear in mind your injunction that I should settle down and get married. Whom do you suggest and can they sew and cook?'

However serious he may or may not have been about the idea of marriage, over money he was in earnest. All his adult life it had been an unusually sensitive point for this millionaire's disinherited grandson, and it must have been more sensitive than ever now that he was in his early forties with his health and his career both beginning to slip. Two months after he moved into Carlyle Mansions (where he was able to gratify his love of looking out on to water) he was writing to his friend Margaret Case, the writer, in New York:

If you could be an angel do try and let the house [Goldeneye] for me for any period except those two months [January and February, when he was there himself] from now on. All the servants are there, and the price is between five hundred and six hundred dollars a month all-in or the equivalent in sterling according to the time of the year. This would indeed be a help, as the house runs away with money all through the year and it is really time I became something of a wise virgin.

The idea of Fleming as a wise virgin may be difficult to swallow, but he was making serious efforts to follow her uninviting example. He began to take a great deal of trouble to find among his own rich friends and acquaintances suitable tenants for Goldeneye, those who could and would fork out the requisite 500 to 600 dollars a month or its sterling equivalent. He was successful with Mr Olaf Hambro, the banker, who took Goldeneye in 1951. The carefully composed five-page letter Fleming sent him describing the amenities—everything is in it from Violet's limeade to advice about sunburn—is a tribute to his mastery of detail and an example that most professional house agents could emulate.

Another potential source of money that he turned to around this time was the Fleming Collection. It is clear that any idea of himself as a serious bibliophile was now long behind him. He had not bought an addition to the collection for more than ten years, and the books, despite occasional inquiries from Percy Muir, still lay in their crates in the London Pantechnicon, where they had been since the war.

By 1950 the rare-book boom in America was already reaching such proportions that inquiries about this cache of important first editions were inevitable, especially since a dealer as important as Percy Muir had had a hand in its formation. Mostly the inquiries came from America, and Muir asked Fleming whether he would be prepared to sell. Fleming's answer was guarded. Perhaps—if the price was right—but what was the price? Muir said he could not be sure but he knew from Dave Randall, then head of Scribner's rare book department in New York, that there would be no difficulty at all in selling the books for an extremely good price.

This seems to have been exactly the reply Fleming wanted. What he was really anxious to get out of Muir was not so much an offer for the books as the assurance that certain American collectors would give their right arm for the privilege of placing their left round the Fleming Collection.

For potential buyers Percy Muir took the trouble to prepare a detailed synopsis. "The Fleming Collection is an attempt to gather together, in first editions, the original contributions of the scientists and practical workers, the total body of whose work has been responsible for the modern (industrial) revolution.' But it was no use—Fleming was only flirting with the idea of selling. 'The way sterling is going at present,' he wrote to Muir on August 18th, 1950, 'it would be folly to sell this valuable asset except at an extremely fancy price . . . While I should be interested to hear of any offers, I am definitely not a willing seller and would not like to put you to trouble on any other basis.'

Fleming was so uncertain of himself and his career around this period that for the only time in his life he seems to have thought of trying politics—not very seriously, it must be admitted. Fortunately for him, for his future publishers, and possibly for the Conservative Party, he dismissed the idea entirely, and for the rest of his time he was able to maintain his attitude of bored disbelief in the antics of almost all political animals. It was in this mood that he mentioned in a letter to Sir William Stephenson, with noticeable absence of regret, how Mr Randolph Churchill's chances of becoming M.P. for Plymouth in the General Election of 1951 'were not improved by the descent of a number of beery members from White's Club, including Lord ——, who knocked on the doors of the fishwives of Plymouth and harangued them with the words: "Surely you don't want to go on paying taxes at 19s. 6d. in the pound for the rest of your lives!"'

But if politics were a sad case and Kemsley House could no longer be relied on, one unexpected diversion did present itself. It began with a meeting one evening between Fleming and Lady Rothermere's cousin, Major the Honourable Martin Charteris of the Life Guards, who was employed at the time as private secretary to Princess Elizabeth at Clarence House. It was a casual enough meeting, and Major Charteris happened to mention the visit the Princess was making to America later in the month. Fleming knew that one of the constant headaches of these visits was the writing of the royal speeches, and remarked, as many an honest Englishman before him, that the time had surely come for royalty to utter words of weight and wisdom on these occasions instead of the customary pious platitudes.

The Major knew that the Princess was scheduled to make a short speech to assembled American newsmen in Washington, and politely and conventionally asked Fleming, knowing him to be a journalist, what his ideas for such a speech would be.

With almost anyone else the matter would have ended

with a few words of advice, and that would have been that. It was different with Fleming. The idea of writing a speech for the heir-apparent to the Throne inevitably appealed to him, and a few days later a copy of the one and only royal speech written by Ian Fleming landed on the desk of Princess Elizabeth's private secretary.

According to the prescribed form it began:

My husband and I thank you for this very wonderful welcome to Washington and for this opportunity to meet the Press and also the representatives of Wireless and Television in the United States of America.

In my own lifetime I have seen the development of Wireless and Television and also the great technical advances in the publishing of the printed word, all contributing to a wide expansion of knowledge and a closer contact between the peoples of the world.

When one reflects on the power for good and evil released by these new methods of mass communication, we must be grateful that the men and women who wield this power are first and foremost servants of the Truth.

We, the public, depend on the integrity of these men and women, and upon their conscientious mastery of each technical advance in the science of communications. We have faith that, in your profession, it will never be a greater sin to be slow than wrong, for if the Truth should ever come second to efficiency, then the great Trust you hold for us will have been broken.

Today, this great Trust is most firmly in your hands.

Thank you all.

Along with this, Fleming, thorough as only he could be with anything that caught his imagination, included a small note.

I do think it is most important that when the Royal Family speaks in public a grain of one of the verities should be left in their listeners' minds. I feel it is wrong of the Embassy to think that the Press of America should be sent home with a few conventional phrases. Whether we like it or not, H.R.H. will be addressing the intelligentsia of America. These people are more powerful than the politicians and quite a different kettle of fish from the meagre scriveners of England.

Possibly with dim memories of his own days as a 'meagre scrivener' with Reuters, he went on to say that in the last paragraph of the speech he had included 'one or two combinations of words which will be eminently quotable, make good headlines and touch the tiny soul of the journalist, who knows that the battle between speed and truth is the one he shirks every day of his life.'

It took five days for a reply to come, typed under the solemn black letterhead of Clarence House, St James's, in that excessively large and sedate style that all royal establishments seem to use for their correspondence. Major Charteris was very grateful, yet he felt that the draft was rather too much directed at the Press as opposed to America herself. He felt also that the occasion was one on which something must be said about American reactions to the King's illness. But he thanked Fleming for his help and for his valuable hints.

Well there it was. Fleming blankly filed the letter away at Kemsley House and turned his mind to other prospects.

CHAPTER THIRTEEN

THE LITERARY CELL

ONE of the techniques of undercover activity that Fleming would have studied in Naval Intelligence is the technique of the cell—the carefully planted series of contacts, spies and surreptitious supporters built up in conditions of secrecy in preparation for the day, possibly years ahead, when their services are required.

It was a technique that would have appealed to his complicated temperament, and it was one that he had been practising for many years in his own private life. All those varied and meticulously insulated friendships of his—in the City, in the world of Intelligence, in journalism, in the Foreign Office—were there for use as well as for enjoyment; and in the classic manner of the best undercover apparatus, few of his friends seem to have been aware of the full extent of the network.

During the war one of the few complaints Admiral Godfrey made against him was that he never revealed the full range of these friendships—friendships which, so Godfrey says, he could have made good use of in the cause of Naval Intelligence. Fleming, however, stuck by the code of the undercover world. Once a network is revealed its usefulness is gone: the master-spy must never reveal his sources. It is amusing now to try to trace the outline of one of the cells he built up, the Fleming literary cell.

Even during his years as a stockbroker Fleming had never quite lost his interest in modern writing, although nothing these days excited him quite so much as Thomas Mann's *The Magic Mountain* when he was the smart young intellectual dabbling in culture in Munich and Geneva. In England just before the war he struck a candid friend as being slightly wistful about it all and 'rather like an intelligent stockbroker who adopts pet authors'. Cyril Connolly was one of these enthusiasms, and when they first met in Kitzbühel in 1937 Fleming introduced himself as a great admirer of Connolly's *New Statesman* articles. But while Fleming still read the *avant-garde* magazines and the literary journals and knew what was going on in the literary world, he was not of it. Nor had his threats to write 'the spy story to end all spy stories' ever come to anything.

Then at the beginning of 1948 he began to enrol and cultivate a number of carefully selected literary contacts. He had never bothered to do this systematically before, and the start of this cell is the first sign he gave that he was in earnest about writing. As it turned out, each true member (as distinct from the fringe personalities) was to play a part in the curious birth of James Bond.

It was an odd way of grooming oneself to become a writer, but then he was an odd man. He had little self-confidence and great fear of ridicule. He liked to have influential supporters whatever he was doing, and by now had got into the habit of beginning any new project in this way— obliquely, tenuously sniffing around like the nervous animal he was to find out who were his friends and who would bite.

One friend, who was virtually the founder member of the Fleming literary cell, was there already. This was William Plomer, the poet and novelist who had worked with Fleming in Naval Intelligence during the war and who, both before and after it, had acted as literary adviser to the publisher Jonathan Cape. Plomer's fiction, particularly his first novel *Turbott Wolfe*, a South African story which was published in 1926, held a particular appeal for Fleming, and it was as a result of a fan letter which Fleming had sent the novelist that the two men got to know each other in the early 'thirties. Their friendship began when Fleming invited Plomer to parties at his mother's house in Cheyne Walk and it lasted until Fleming's death.

As Plomer is the first to admit, in the beginning it seemed an unlikely friendship, one between an unassuming high-brow and a restless and ambitious young man-about-town. Plomer, however, possessed qualities notably rare among the few intellectuals whom Fleming knew. A profoundly unaggressive personality with beautiful manners who has lived since the war in a small house in a village near Little-hampton, he has generally avoided the cliques and the malice of literary London; and as something of a student of the oddities of the English character he appreciated from the start the singularity of Fleming's most singular nature.

Fleming, for his part, enjoyed knowing a distinguished poet, and after the war this was one of the friendships that he took particular pains to keep in good repair. But it was not until early in 1948 that he began to look to Plomer to extend his contacts in the literary world and in publishing. It was through Plomer, in fact, that Fleming got to know his future publisher, Jonathan Cape, who had also published Peter Fleming's early books.

Once again it was an unlikely combination, for Cape, the self-made son of a Cumberland carpenter, was a craggy giant of a man, supremely self-confident, complacent almost at his success in finding writers of the quality of Hemingway and T. E. Lawrence, and not at all disposed to smile benevolently on charming if vaguely ambitious amateurs. All the same, Cape took to Fleming and, believing him to be the literary grey eminence of Gray's Inn Road, began to send him proof copies of his books. Soon he was inviting Fleming to a private dinner at the Savoy to meet Popski, the Pole who ran one of the best-known private armies of the war and whose book was just about to appear. 'Get busy,' Cape wrote to Fleming after the dinner, 'and see that Popski has a good show.'

With letters like this arriving from a distinguished publisher and with his acceptance of an increasing number of invitations to cocktail parties to launch new books (though he never did more than 'look in'), Fleming seems to have appreciated some of the pleasures of becoming a literary power-figure. Increasingly at the *Sunday Times* editorial conferences he brought forward laundry lists of forthcoming books which might make desirable serials. He also suggested that Cape should reprint one of his own favourite books—Hugh Edwards's *All Night at Mr Stanyhurst's*.

This curious baroque tale of eighteenth-century England, with its cruelty, its melancholy, its over-ripe flavour of underlying corruption and romantic hopelessness, was the sort of book Fleming might have written himself had he been an historical novelist instead of a writer of thrillers. As it was, eighteen months before he died he did finally persuade Cape's to reprint it, and he wrote an introduction for it. But in 1950 the name of Ian Fleming would have meant little. *All Night at Mr Stanyhurst's* had to wait for James Bond to rescue it from oblivion.

At any rate, long before he sent William Plomer the manuscript of his first novel *Casino Royale*, Fleming seems to have regarded Jonathan Cape as 'his' publisher, just as Morlands were 'his' tobacconist and Benson, Perry and

Whitlow 'his' tailors. So now the Fleming literary cell possessed a publisher and his literary adviser. Other members were needed.

There were a number of possible candidates, but Fleming was wary of trying to enlist them. Intellectuals, except rather special ones like William Plomer, were suspect. He saw Cyril Connolly every so often and had written the Jamaica article for *Horizon*, but he didn't let him know what was in his mind; later on he would be able to accept Connolly's jests about Bond, but not now. Similarly with Rosamond Lehmann. When she read his *Horizon* article she told him he could and should write more. However flattered he was, he merely shrugged and smiled and told her life was too short.

One writer he did take into his confidence at this time was the novelist Paul Gallico. He had originally chosen Gallico to write some articles on America for the Kemsley papers, and when they met they immediately took to each other. Gallico was the sort of writer Fleming could get on with—genial, amused and ready to enter at once into that 'joking relationship' which Fleming liked to maintain with his close friends.

Then while he was getting to know Gallico he was also wooing his most unexpected and impressive literary ally of all—Dame Edith Sitwell. The origins of this curious friendship date back to the Christmas of 1947, when William Plomer received the following letter from his great friend Edith Sitwell, who wrote from Renishaw:

I went to London for two days to see Osbert given the 'Sunday Times' [literary] prize—but two days was quite enough for me. The luncheon party at the prize-giving was delightful, however. There was a man there who began talking to me by saying he knew you. I think I have got his name wrong, but it was either Frazer or Fleming, I think the latter. I thought at first, from his manner with her, that he was Lady Cunard's social secretary, but realized afterwards that she would scarcely have employed him in that capacity. He told me he was 'very amused' to see that you had put my 'Shadow of Cain' on your 'Horizon' list. He ran no immediate risk by saying this as we were both guests at a luncheon party given in honour of Osbert. He then, until I was at last released from him, expatiated on the other 'amusing' and 'surprising' choices.*

The incident was a good example of the sort of unconscious offence Fleming was always liable to cause on polite occasions

*© 1966 by the executors for the estate of the late Dame Edith Sitwell.

186

such as this, and Plomer wrote back to her promising to talk to him about it.

Dame Edith must still have been quivering with rage, for back by return of post came a note thanking Plomer 'for so kindly saying you will reprove Mr Fleming. As I say, he was very lucky to have been rude to me under those particular circumstances.'

The idea of a battle royal between Ian Fleming and Edith Sitwell is one of the more piquant might-have-beens of literature, but thanks to Plomer's discretion it never occurred. Plomer told his friend of the perturbation he had caused, and Fleming, until then quite unconscious of the effect of his airy remarks, promised to write an immediate apology to the sensitive poet. So it was that Plomer received a third letter from her, as full of forgiveness as the other two had been of indignation:

How nice you are! I have had one of the most charming letters I have ever received from Mr Fleming as a result of your 'speaking' to him. Really his letter could not have been nicer. So all is now well, and I have written back . . . and have said I hope he'll come, with you, to lunch with me when I am in London.*

For the next two years there continued an extraordinary literary flirtation between the man who was to invent James Bond and the poet who dressed like Henry VII. She was at pains to prove that her forgiveness could be as wholehearted as her anger. He seems to have relished having a private line to the *grande dame* of English literature. Both of them took considerable trouble over each other.

To start with, Plomer tactfully attempted to give them a quiet lunch. Dame Edith was not to be diverted, however, and Fleming was duly summoned to meet her and some of her lions for lunch at the Sesame Club in Grosvenor Street. Besides William Plomer they were to include T. S. Eliot, Maurice Bowra, John Lehmann, 'and one or two others'. Fleming must have been flattered, but it was hardly his sort of gathering, and there is a touch of real apprehension in his reply: 'I would love to lunch with you on Thursday although I am horrified by the array of talent you have asked. Please let me sit in the shadow of William, so that I am not drawn into any discussion on your use of the semi-colon or the degree of emphasis inherent in italics. I just don't carry the guns for such abstrocities.'

*© 1966 by the executors for the estate of the late Dame Edith Sitwell.

187

It was all very diffident and rather coy, but behind the coyness Fleming was out to make as good an impression as possible. From the way things developed it is clear that he was by no means as naive as he sounded. For in the very letter he wrote to Edith Sitwell accepting her invitation he promised to make her a gift of 'a ham-fisted translation from the German which I made many years ago of a speech by the psychologist Jung at Paracelsus's birthplace in Switzerland. My English translation is almost as Germanic as Jung's original German, but there are one or two interesting points in the speech and it has never been published over here.' He knew that Paracelsus, the sixteenth-century physician, mystic and alchemist, and the subject of Browning's poem, was catnip to Dame Edith.

After this things began moving. The lunch at the Sesame Club took place. Fleming was even more charming in his neat blue suit with the narrow cuffs than he had been in his letters. A fortnight later he succeeded in getting 'The Shadow of Cain'—Dame Edith's poem that all the trouble had been about originally—published in the *Sunday Times*. And by the autumn they were discussing writing a joint book on Paracelsus, with a revised version of Fleming's translation of Jung's lecture and a long introduction by Dame Edith.

In the end the project came to nothing, but while the idea lasted Fleming and Dame Edith were able to enjoy a lot of fairly high-flown correspondence on the subject of their new-found mutual hero. It was the high-water mark of Fleming's aspirations as a highbrow.

Certainly this friendship with Edith Sitwell had brought him nearer to writing a book of his own than he had ever been before in his life. However apprehensive he might still have been, it is possible he might just have risked it, shielded by her formidable petticoat.

As it was, the possibility of putting his name to a book clearly stirred his literary ambitions, and it is around this time that Fleming seems to have started to plan a future for himself as some sort of accepted highbrow literary figure by writing book reviews and short articles for the *Sunday Times*.

Fleming's attitude to intellectuals was always to be ambiguous. He was not an intellectual himself and was later to suffer at the hands of some who were or thought they were. But he wanted the respectability, the sense of acceptance, which the intellectual establishment in England

188

still manages to carry with it. He seems to have struggled rather hard to get it. Certainly the first articles and reviews that appeared under his name in the *Sunday Times* are quite unlike his later writing. Laboured, larded with quotations, they might almost be college parodies of the higher journalism at its mandarin worst.

Gradually he gave up, although his friendship with Edith Sitwell continued. Clearly any ambitions he may still have had as an author had switched from the sort of book he might have written with her, back to the thriller spy story he had always hankered after.

In March 1950, on his return from Goldeneye via New York, he described himself in the *Sunday Times* as 'fortifying' himself 'for the stratocruiser flight home with *My Gun is Quick* by Mickey Spillane, which the *New York Times* has just reviewed with horrified awe.' But Spillane he found a great disappointment, and he went on to lament the softening-up and sentimentalizing of the American thriller.

As he wrote, Fleming was undoubtedly reflecting on how much better he could do this sort of thing himself. For by now he was beginning to think of those games of make-believe he had always amused himself with as possible sources of plots for books. Soon, with luck, there might be work to do for the Fleming literary cell.

CHAPTER FOURTEEN

MARRIAGE

I

PORT MARIA, in the parish of St Mary, is a colourful crumbling slice of old Jamaica smelling of fish, bananas, hibiscus, rum, bad drains and diesel fumes. The Mizpeh Furniture Establishment offers 'windows, coffins and caskets of every description—Call Now and Be Satisfied'. The optician visits at 13½ Banana Street every first Thursday of the month, 10 a.m. to 2 p.m. And up on Hodgson Street, past the Bluebell Hairdressing Parlour and the clapboard premises of Eddie's Lay-away Plan, stands Port Maria's gently decaying white town hall.

It was here on March 24th, 1952, that Ian Fleming's carefully maintained bachelor's life went for good. Shortly after three p.m., in the magistrate's office with the apple-green walls, he married Lady Rothermere, formerly Lady O'Neill, née Anne Charteris. Noël Coward was one of the witnesses, Cole Leslie, Coward's secretary, the other.

The bride wore an eau-de-nil dress run up at short notice by Port Maria's top lady dressmaker; and according to Coward the couple were surprisingly timorous. 'The first thing we saw as we came into the office was an enormous oleograph of Churchill scowling down on us with bulldog hatred, and an official had such terrible breath that when he asked them whether they took each other for man and wife they both turned their heads away and said meekly, "I do. I do."'

After this everyone began to see the funny side of things, and by the time the ceremony was over the groom and the principal witnesses were beginning to lose control of the situation. 'We were so desperate with laughter,' says Coward, 'that I tied the wedding shoe on the rear of my own car and drove back to Goldeneye with it trailing behind all the way.'

In Jamaica the wedding breakfast is called a brekinge. Fleming had arranged it at Goldeneye and the sense of anti-climax continued. 'We all crouched round that horrid table,' says Coward, 'on that excruciating *banquette*, and Violet brought in an enormous wedding cake gleaming with green icing while dusky heads peered round the door to make sure we all ate it. Then as a special treat for the Commander there was black crab. It can be wonderful, but that month can't have been a good time for crabs and it was like eating cigarette ash out of a pink tin. I think the black crab finished the lot of us, and we sat there speechless with laughter and with tears running down our faces.'

To add to the hilarity Noël Coward had written a special Goldeneye Calypso in honour of the occasion.

> Mongoose dig about sunken garden
> Mongoose murmur, 'Oh my—Oh my!
> No more frig about—beg your pardon,
> Things are changing at Goldeneye!'
>
> Mongoose say to Annee,
> Mongoose say to Annee,
> Your man shady as mango tree,
> Sweet as honey from bee.
>
> Hey for the Alka-Seltzer,
> Ho for the aspirin,
> Hey for the saltfish, ackee, canja, booby's
>   eggs, Gordon's gin.
>
> Mongoose listen to white folks wailin'
> Mongoose giggle, say, 'Me no deaf!
> No more waffle and Daily Mailin'
> Annee Rothermere's Madame F.'
>
> Mongoose say to Annee,
> Carlyle Mansions N.G.,
> Goldeneye a catastrophee,
> White Cliffs too near the sea.
>
> Hey for the blowfish, blowfish,
> Ho for the wedding ring,
> Hey for the Dry Martinis, old goat
>   fricassée, Poor Man's thing.
>
> Mongoose love human sacrifices,
> Mongoose snigger at Human Race,
> Can't have wedding without the Bryces,
> Both the Stephensons, Margaret Case.
>
> Mongoose say to Annee,
> Now you get your decree,
> Once you lady of high degree,
> Now you common as me.
>
> Hey for the piggly wiggly,
> Ho for the wedding dress,
> Hey for the Earl of Dudley, Loelia
>   Westminster, Kemsley Press.

When it was all over Fleming gathered together the remains of the green wedding cake and buried them carefully in the garden.

The following morning Mr and Mrs Ian Fleming flew to New York en route for London. Included in his luggage was the rough manuscript of a book entitled provisionally *Casino Royale*. The hero was a man called James Bond.

In later years, whenever Fleming was asked how he came to start writing novels, he would invariably say that it had been quite simply to take his mind off 'the shock of getting married at the age of forty-three'. It was the sort of flip, faintly cynical remark he enjoyed making. It embodied the Old Etonian myth of the effortless amateur able to turn a casual hand to anything with equally spectacular success. It effectively stopped any further speculation on the origins of Bond and how the books really came to be written. For what had happened was far more complicated than he liked to admit. To understand it properly we have to set down the story of his own life during 1951 and how he came to marry the woman he did.

II

In the early morning, at about 7.30, the stringy whimperings of the piped radio brought visions of a million homes waking up all over Britain . . . of him, or perhaps her, getting up to make the early morning tea, to put the dog out, to stoke the boiler. And then will this shirt do for another day? The socks, the pants? The Ever-ready, the Gillette shave, the Brylcreem on the hair, the bowler hat or the homburg, the umbrella and the briefcase or the sample case? Then 'Dodo', the family saloon out on the concrete arterial, probably with her driving. The red-brick station, the other husbands, the other wives, the clickety-click of the 8.15 round the curve by the golf course. Hullo Sidney! Hullo Arthur! After you Mr Shacker . . . and the drab life picking up speed and flicking on up the rails between the conifers and the damp evergreens.

Bond switched on his electric blanket and waited for his hot water with a slice of lemon and contemplated the world with horror and disgust.

Into this opening of a short story he never finished Fleming managed to cram his horror of the idea of marrying and settling down. It was a typical piece of Flemingesque black fantasy—he must be one of the few men it is totally impossible to imagine stoking an early morning boiler before driving off in a family saloon with a bowler hat and a caseful of samples. It gives some idea of the passion with which he clung to his independence during the long years of the romance before 'Annee Rothermere' became 'Madame F'.

For when the marriage did take place not even its bitterest opponents could say that the couple needed more time to get to know each other or that they failed to realize what they were in for; rarely can two people in love have had quite such a gruelling prelude to a wedding.

She had first seen him one week-end, just before the war, at Le Touquet, where he had arrived aboard a yacht. She had thought him 'godlike but unapproachable'. She was already married to Lord O'Neill (who had played golf and bridge with Fleming for a few years) and had two children: a beauty with unforgettably striking eyes, very young, and used to getting what she wanted. He was moody, interested in some other woman at the time, and quite unprepared to indulge in the sort of intelligent conversation which this great-niece of the brilliant and audacious Margot Asquith seemed to regard as one of the necessities of life. The meeting was not a success. Nor were their other chance encounters. It was not until the early days of the war, when Fleming was invited by his friend Shane O'Neill to play bridge at the Dorchester Hotel, that they began to get to know each other at all well.

'I thought Ian original and entertaining,' says Anne Fleming. 'He was immensely attractive and had enormous charm. But it was as a character that he really interested me. He was totally unlike anyone else I had ever met. There was something defensive and untamed about him, like a wild animal. He would never do anything out of mere politeness or because it was expected of him, and he never wanted to talk about himself. Of course, I found it a great challenge to get through this barrier and find out what lay behind.'

Apart from seeing each other at the Dorchester and the bridge-table, their usual routine when they met during the war was to go to the cinema together and follow it with a modest meal at Bertorelli's Italian restaurant in Charlotte Street. As total opposites they were attracted to each other, but this was the wariest of romances. For it was not only Anne O'Neill who recognized that she was dealing with someone quite out of the ordinary. Fleming, too, with that sure instinct he had for such things, sensed from the start that this was a different sort of person from the women he was used to, and that with her there could be no question of his behaving in his usual manner, culminating in the abrupt dismissiveness with which he treated all the rest. Fleming had met his match, and he knew it.

She was widowed by the death of Lord O'Neill in action in Italy and married Lord Rothermere. Fleming continued to pursue his familiar routine, with its careful allocation of work, treats and love-affairs. They continued nevertheless to meet and confide in each other as they always had done.

In 1946 Anne Rothermere's holiday in Jamaica coincided with Fleming's first visit to his partly-built house at Goldeneye, and when she visited him, accompanied by Loelia, Duchess of Westminster, she saw a part of his life which she had ever suspected. The place had everything to appeal to her love of nature and animals, and Fleming showed her Goldeneye's secrets with all the excitement and delight of which he was capable.

'The beach,' she wrote, 'is a semi-circle of white coral sand with arms of rock on each side and a cave on the left full of sand-martins. Water—warm, transparent, shallow; then rocks emerge here and there and far beyond a white line of waves where the reef ends and the depths begin.' She saw the orange and lemon and grapefruit trees and the wild palms at the back of the house. She saw Felix the gardener planting roses and hibiscus round the 'sinking garden' to attract the humming birds, and she noted, like Blake before her, that 'each rose has a large black beetle eating its heart out'. She went swimming with Fleming out to the reef, seeing the underwater world of Goldeneye for the first time and trying to spear the small local lobsters that peered nervously from under the rocks. 'If they emerge far enough,' she wrote, 'one can thrust the spear into the horny head. So far I have failed, but Ian has shot one or two and they are delicious to eat.'

'Ian has devised a halcyon way of life,' she went on, 'and only he could have done it.'

'My first day in Goldeneye,' she says, 'was a wonderful day of birds and flowers and fish.' And in the evening, before dinner, she waited in the big, still unfinished living-room watching the moths and beetles circling the lamps in each corner of the room and hoping for a praying mantis or some particularly beautiful moth which she could capture and paint.

For dinner there was lobster and curried goat served with a lot of rice, and after it Fleming insisted on taking his guests out for what was to become one of the rituals of Goldeneye. All of them had to stand leaning against the railing, just erected at the edge of the cliff, gazing into the warm Caribbean night.

'As our eyes grew accustomed to the dark,' wrote Anne, 'we watched the spray of the reef and the high bright large stars of that region. The air was so clear of dirt and dust that there was an illusion of vast universe and the sea horizon was very round. Ian remained longer than us, smoking and wallowing in the melancholy.'

After this first visit to Goldeneye they both acknowledged in their own way that they were indispensable to each other, but the situation seemed to be one that could never change. She had her highly organized life and duties, he the precious symmetry he had so carefully constructed, and he knew that however deep their feelings for each other the fragile bird-cage of his existence would never stand up to the strains of a permanent relationship. There was little either of them could do to alter things.

'I think Ian liked me because I amused him and because I made no real demands on him,' she says. 'He always said that I was the one person who could "kill the day" during his bouts of melancholy,' and one of her self-appointed tasks was simply to make him laugh. This was something she never failed to do. Her wit and outrageousness had always appealed to him.

One of the strengths of their relationship now was that they had few illusions about each other. 'It is astonishing,' she wrote in a pencilled postscript to a letter she sent him from New York, 'that I cannot be in any capital in the world for more than a day without meeting some woman with whom you have had carnal relations.'

Sometimes she complained about the shortage of news from him. 'You're a *damned idle beast* to stuff my letters with lumps of "Time" and "Life" magazine instead of your thoughts (if you have any) and your actions (if you do anything).' This was a standing grievance she had against him. 'Kindly *cease* to make "tristeness" and colds in the head and the whole gamut of your vast range of Freudian moods an excuse to write me three unsatisfactory lines and stuff up the rest of the envelope with fragments of the "Evening Standard".'

But Fleming did not rely entirely on newspaper cuttings. Tenderness as well as humour began to show in his letters. One of them, which he sent to her from Lord Kemsley's house Dropmore and was marked 'midnight', began:

This afternoon I walked in the woods which are high and wet and full of jays and I saw you dressed up as a golden pheasant. You were nervous and preoccupied and you really hadn't got time for me, so you scurried back into the rotting rhododendron manure where you live. You thought (or rather hoped) no one was watching you, but you were such a bright light on the damp pine needles that this was silly of you and you might just as well have stayed and talked.

There is an eclipse of the moon tonight and I suppose that is why I am writing to you. My love, I think you are sitting in your small room with your tiny life gathered round you like the folds of a warm and pretty skirt. I think you are a consumptive dragonfly in Hackney Marshes and, as an obstinate water-lily among the prevailing moss, I hope you will stay on my leaf and keep the flies off—even though you may munch holes in me until I wither.

From now on this picture of the dragonfly and the waterlily symbolizes something of his attitude towards her. The difficulties and ramifications of her marriage apart, he felt that she presented him with the sort of dilemma which a melancholy romantic like himself could savour. She was all in life that he longed for yet feared. She had the force of the unexpected, the exciting, the unbargained for; but she spelled chaos and disorder within the tidy loneliness of his existence.

She was his 'darling banshee'—'You certainly do upset the décor when you come down the chimney,' he wrote. 'Already I feel rather filleted like those other poor souls whose bones you took out to make a daisy chain.'

But filleted or not, he was lonely again when she went. 'Certainly the house feels rather empty now that you have left it for a little and I am going round smoothing out the dents in the chair covers and sheets, sweeping the cigarette ash off the carpets, and cleaning the lipstick off the antimacassars. It's nice to have everything tidy again, or is it?'

And alone once more he answers his own question. 'I wish I wish you were still whirling around inside the house. I don't really mind the mess you make. It was time someone made it and brought a smell of *Je Reviens* into the musty manse. I miss you just as much as I knew I would—neither more nor less but just as much as I can.'

Once he had acknowledged this their relationship changed. The longing to escape together was still there. 'I wish wish wish you and I could sit on your Jamaican beach for a month without having to bother about scandals and chaperones,' she wrote.

They began to talk now of 'the hope that one day we may be together without too much hurt to others'. They met in Paris, in Oxford and again in Jamaica. The rumours started, and the American gossip writer Cholly Knickerbocker reported, 'The real romance of Captain (*sic*) Ian Fleming, writer, traveller and Beau Brummel of Montego Bay, Jamaica, is not the Duchess of Westminster, but another British lady—who is married. Captain Fleming, at one time, was considered Standard Oil heiress Millicent Huddleston Rogers's hottest romance.'

At the same time a new disquiet appeared. 'Listen, my darling,' said Anne. 'Please be honest with me about your chest pains. I am glad you are going to a specialist next week and I hope you will be sensible about what he says.' And as part of her anxiety she complained that his work was taking up too much of his time and energy, for one of the periodic crises which afflicted the last tortured days of the *Sunday Graphic* made it imperative for him to cut short his holiday. '*Please* let that horrible "Daily Graphic" flounder a few days longer. And anyway the "Daily Graphic" has been floundering for *years* and one more crack in its old bottom won't hurt anyone . . . If,' she added, 'I express myself more coarsely than Edith Sitwell, you must attribute it to returning vitality and the literature you provide me with, which is not suitable for a gently nurtured aristocrat.'

She had been ill, and her illness had taught him how much he depended on her; and his concern showed someone very different from the coolly uninvolved amorist of his past. 'I shall get impatient soon if you don't grow up and care for yourself,' he had told her. 'If you don't there won't be anything except *espièglerie* left for me, and the light touch day in day out is thin fare for forty years of the same bed and toothbrush and griefs and pains. Please say NO a bit from now on. Fleming's theory of the Imperative Negative is still the best cure for stomach ulcers and galloping fatigue.'

Not long after this she was in hospital in Edinburgh and he was complaining wretchedly of feeling 'further away than before and quite useless'. 'But anyway,' he went on, 'they seem a bit happier about you and I feel I can breathe a little and not feel desperate the whole time and deep in deep gloom.'

While he was waiting for news of her he stayed at Gleneagles and had nothing to do except

beat round the golf course morning and afternoon and exhaust myself. Various vague acquaintances have appeared—no one of interest—and I play with them. It is all completely unreal and I hope it never happens again. Pain is a completely selfish thing. I can't feel any part of yours and you can't know my aches at being away from you and fears for you. Human beings are really precious things and we don't treat them as treasures until we fear for them. But although I shall kick and bite you as much as before when you are well, I shall never forget what I have felt for you these days. Ah me!—I suppose we are growing up in spite of ourselves.

He was confronted now with the reality of human suffering. He wrote to her the following night:

Everyone is pushing your dear body about and being bad to it and I'm not there to protect it or even hold your hand.

These things shouldn't be done to you. You have many privacies and little closed corners where you won't let anyone in, and now you are at the mercy of anyone who happens to be in Edinburgh and has a medical certificate, while I sit home full of health and living a great full life and all I can do is bite my nails and scratch my soul and wonder if anyone listens to my wishes and prayers for you.

But it's no good protecting people or even looking after them past a certain point. One can't grasp more than a piece of any-one. Most of the rest can only be protected by themselves and the remainder by hired specialists and doctors and dentists and professional protectors.

You can beat a person for leading away from the King of Trumps or for spitting on the floor, but no amount of beating will stop the spot growing on their nose. One's health and one's life is only one's own in the end, and love has no impact on it whatso-ever. If you sit in a draught or have a baby the consequences are fixed and written down and sweet words and heart things are no use.

But I go on writing to you while you are in another room with the door locked because at the end of the day I must talk to someone about you and I feel so urgently that you must get well quickly that I feel if I do something it will help.

Dear baby, don't hurry. Be patient. Don't fuss. Everything will be all right. Don't be wilful and superhuman. The second thirty-five years will be better than the first, but give yourself a bit more chance this time my sweet.

By the end of her illness Fleming knew that the one thing he had tried to avoid all his life had happened. He was involved totally with another human being and there was no going back. But it was hard to see how there could be any going forward either.

Early in 1951 they were able to be together for a while in Jamaica. But although they were talking now of marrying and trying to sort out the conflicting strands of their existence, the impasse was still there.

With careful common sense Fleming attempted to work out what he called 'a sensible balance sheet' for the two of them. It stated what they knew already and settled as much as such balance sheets usually do.

My headache is nagging at me and making me say a lot of things which I expect I only half mean. But they are things which have been in my head all along and which you know about and which I suppose are decisive now. I can't write you a love letter about them because the way we love each other is a simple and stupid and selfish way which doesn't lend itself to phrases and about which we have never pretended.

The point is that a lot of people depend on you. No one depends on me. I have nothing except my cherished freedom. My love for you is entirely selfish and if I married you I shouldn't give a hoot for what you had left behind. None of it means a thing to me and, for your own *happiness*, I think you would be well quit of nine-tenths of the weight on your shoulders.

So what is left? A warm but very prickly nest with shame for the present and uncertainty for the future and a lot of squalling obligations on your conscience. I would be worrying at what I had taken from you (I suppose) and with no new stability to offer in exchange for the old.

You know it just as well as I do and it doesn't need anyone's advice. We know enough to be good about it, and don't let's cheat. Something may make it easier. The world's in a funny state. Perhaps one day we may get married. I hope so with all my heart. I know we would be happy so long as it comes about the right way. Otherwise we wouldn't. We both know it and that's the final argument.

Then in a hurriedly scrawled P.S. he added, 'I haven't said all the nice things because you know they are in my heart. I love you so much more than any other woman and we have had so much happiness that I am brimming over with you.'

Soon he was writing:

We have now had a week more or less together and I love you as

199

much as ever. But I feel the fog encroaching more and more and the odds lengthening and I know it's no good unless the atom bomb falls. We shouldn't be happy unless it did.

We behave together in an uncivilized way and we love in the same way. We would be happy beside the blue lagoon but not in Kensington Gore. I would not have the patience or the tolerance and you would hate me for my harshness and lack of sympathy and you would hate me for putting the simple things first.

You are surprised that I wish to spend all my evenings alone, and I am surprised that you prefer 'company'—not the people that you would choose but just any people rather than none. You hate silence and I prefer it. You are natural and I am unnatural.

But once he had told her of his doubts the tenderness and optimism returned:

My darling, last night I looked round my room and saw all the bits of you. I have often looked at them before and almost counted the strings that bind my heart to yours. All the warmth in me comes from you. All the love I have for you has grown out of me because you made it grow. Without you I would still be hard and dead and cold and quite unable to write this childish letter, full of love and jealousies and adolescence.

He went on:

Hell, this is a stupid letter and I am stupid to write it. I believe in my heart that we shall still live our lives together because we shall both come back to a love which is the true love which not many people have known. But now, or tonight, I feel that I must say what I have said and make us both unhappy. I feel the weight of your public life upon me and I know I shan't shake it off and so I had better tell you about it and help you out of this dear blind life we have been living together.

When I have given you this letter let's try and grow up and if we fail please my darling let's come together again and make each other happy. I believe we would, but I'm not certain enough now to want to go on tearing each other to tatters—and that's what the undertones in our voices say we are going to start doing soon.

It was an indecisive if understandable end to such a letter, and once again he wrote a hurried postscript in blue Biro: 'My darling, darling, there are so many years left us both. Please let's have some of them together.'

The simple truth was that whereas by now she was whole-heartedly in love with him and had made up her mind that she was ready to sacrifice her entire position by marrying him, he was still in a dilemma.

He was plagued by familiar anxieties. He was worried about money. He was worried about the clash between his solitariness and her love of friends. He was worried by all the apprehended boredoms of marriage which he had been avoiding for so long. Then during the summer of 1951, when it was clear that there was no going back, all these long-held doubts about marriage came to the surface, so that for him the crisis over marriage became part of a much larger crisis—over money, over health, over age, over everything he stood for and believed in.

'He entered marriage,' says Anne Fleming, 'with characteristic gloom and foreboding. He told me, "I can promise you nothing. I have not an admirable character. I have no money. I have no title. Marriage will be entirely what you can make it." '

She replied that none of this mattered; and plans for the divorce and for their subsequent marriage went forward. In London, until they could find a suitable house, they would live in Fleming's flat at Carlyle Mansions. Provided they could both get away for week-ends they would be happy, and it was to provide for this that just before Christmas 1951 he bought White Cliffs, Noël Coward's house at St Margaret's Bay.

Fleming and Anne Rothermere had often stayed there as guests in the past. Now its purchase was the first sign of their new status together, and shortly after the deeds were signed they left together for New York, flying on to Jamaica two days later for Fleming's 'statutory two months' at Goldeneye.

On March 22nd the *Daily Express* carried news of the divorce. It was hardly unexpected, but it produced a discreet sigh of relief from all their friends who had been keeping their secret for so long, and it was Noël Coward who put these feelings into yet another of his poems. He called it Don'ts for my Darlings'.

> The quivering days of waiting,
> Of wondering and suspense,
> Without regret
> Can at last be set
> In the Past Imperfect tense.
>
> The agonies and frustrations,
> The blowing now cold, now hot,
> Are put to rout
> For there's no more doubt
> As to whether you will or not.

The over-publicized secret
That thousands have known so well,
Lo and behold,
Can at last be told
To the peal of a marriage bell.

Ah! The stories that could be written,
Ah! The legends the world could spin,
Of those turbulent years
You've lived my dears
In excessively open sin.

Permit me, as one who adores you,
An eminent 'Eminence Grise',
To help you in finding
Some method of minding
Your marital Qs and your Ps.

DON'T, Ian, if Annie should cook you
A dish that you haven't enjoyed,
Use that as excuse
For a storm of abuse
Of Cecil or Lucien Freud.

DON'T, Annie, when playing Canasta,
Produce a lipstick from your sac,
And do up your face
With a roguish grimace
While giving dear Loelia the pack.

DON'T, Ian, when friends are arriving,
By aeroplane, motor and train,
Retire to bed
With a cold in the head
And that famous redundant migraine.

DON'T be too exultant, dear Annie,
Restrain each ebullient 'bon mot',
The one thing that vexes
The old boy's old Ex-s
Is knowing the Status is Quo

DON'T, either of you, I implore you
Forget that one truth must be faced.
However you measure
Repentance at leisure
You HAVEN'T been married in haste!

CHAPTER FIFTEEN

THE BEGINNINGS OF BOND

JAMES BOND was born at Goldeneye on the morning of the third Tuesday of January 1952, when Ian Fleming had just finished breakfast and had ten more weeks of his forty-three years as a bachelor still to run. He had already had his swim out to the reef, and he was wearing white shorts, a coloured beach shirt from Antonio's in Falmouth, and black hide sandals. He came up the steps from the garden while Violet was clearing away the remains of breakfast, shut the door of the big living-room, closed the jalousies, and settled himself down at the brown roll-top desk with his oxidized gold cigarette case, his twenty-year-old Imperial portable, and a ream of best quality folio typing paper he had bought at a shop on Madison Avenue ten days earlier.

He had already appropriated the name of his hero: James Bond's handbook, *Birds of the West Indies*, was one of the books he liked to keep on his breakfast-table. 'I wanted the simplest, dullest, plainest-sounding name I could find,' he said later. 'James Bond seemed perfect.'

Apart from this he had no notes, had made no preparations. He simply began to type in his cool, big, shaded room, and for the next seven weeks he kept at it steadily. Every morning between nine and twelve, while Anne was in the garden in a large straw hat painting flowers, the sound of the machine echoed through the still house. There were no distractions.

Around midday the noise of typing would cease and Fleming would come out of the house and sit yawning and blinking in the strong sunlight by the cliff. He liked to sun himself, usually with his shirt off, before lunch. After he had eaten he slept for an hour or so. At five he returned to his desk to read through what he had written before putting the pages into the blue manilla folder in the bottom left-hand drawer of the desk. By six thirty he was ready for his first real drink of the day.

On March 18th, six days before the marriage at Port

Maria, the manilla folder was full. Le Chiffre was destroyed and Vesper Lynd, 'the bitch', was dead as well. Bond had scored his first recorded triumph, and the 62,000 words of one of the strangest thrillers ever written were finished. Probably never before has a book that has sold so well been produced quite so effortlessly.

The apparent ease with which *Casino Royale* was written is only one of the several curious things about this whole curious episode in Fleming's life. It is odd enough for any novelist to produce his first book at forty-three and find it a ready-made formula for success. It is odder still for it to happen after half a lifetime of literary repression and unfulfilled daydreams about writing a best-seller.

There were corrections and additions still to be made to the typescript—more with *Casino Royale* than with any of the subsequent books he wrote—and the changes are observable in the first manuscript, which Fleming, bibliophile that he was, lovingly preserved and had bound in blue morocco and embossed with his initials in gold. There is not a page without its maze of corrections in his strong, forward-sloping handwriting. Many paragraphs have been re-written and pages re-typed and pasted in.

Yet it is clear that the whole story was there from the beginning—Bond and his world, the heroine, casino, the torture scene, the death of the two Bulgars—all came complete as he rattled the story down with such swift assurance at about 2,000 words a day.

Of course it was absolutely in character for Fleming to produce a book in this way. Ever since the time when he startled his friends and enemies by becoming an athlete at Eton with a burst of furious adolescent energy, he had enjoyed accomplishing the unexpected in a sudden spasm of activity. It was part of his old dream of himself as Renaissance Man. It fitted in with the Etonian ideal of effortless effectiveness. And, easily bored and discouraged as he could become, it is doubtful if he could ever have finished writing a book under any other conditions.

But why did he write it at this particular moment of his life and why should something he had been thinking about for so long have been finally achieved so casually? Fleming himself never gave any real answer to this beyond his endlessly repeated remark about writing *Casino Royale* to 'take my mind off the shock of getting married at the age of forty-three'. There was just one letter, however, in which he did elaborate slightly on this. It was to a wartime friend, and he told him that writing the book had been 'roughly the equivalent of digging a very large hole in the garden for the sake of the exercise', a remark which agrees closely with Anne Fleming's account of what happened.

'There were,' she says, 'just the two of us at Goldeneye that year. It was rather a tense period of our lives, and I had started painting again and found I enjoyed it enormously. But my painting bored Ian. He said he had no intention of sitting out in the sun watching me at my easel, and I suggested he should write something just to amuse myself. He wasn't very anxious to start, but once he'd begun, of course, he found himself enjoying it, and he finished the book in a great burst of enthusiasm. I think he was very surprised by what he had produced. We never discussed what he was writing, he didn't show it me and, of course, I didn't ask to see it. I had my painting and he had his writing. It was as simple as that.'

What is ironic is that although he had been waiting for so long to get started as a writer he should have stumbled on the ideal conditions for it by the merest chance. With the divorce in the air, there were no guests that year at Goldeneye to distract him. Thanks to his anxieties about marriage and the future, he had just enough immediate worries on his mind to make him welcome a distraction. He was not thinking of money or success. He was not fretted either by self-doubt or possible ridicule. Throughout his life, in times of crisis or boredom, he had found it diverting to turn to fantasy, and he did this now. The only difference was that this time he lived his fantasy by writing it down.

According to Anne, Fleming wrote so effortlessly and with such zest that he came to look on the eight weeks he spent writing at Goldeneye as the greatest treat of his year. Yet nothing can have quite equalled his excitement at writing *Casino Royale*. Unlike the books which he researched and thought about beforehand, this one came straight from his memory and imagination.

He always insisted that when he got to the end of *Casino Royale* he had very little idea of exactly what he had produced, and the speed and unselfconsciousness with which he wrote this first book are strangely reminiscent of Henry Miller's description of the way another natural adventure-story writer, Rider Haggard, used to work. 'His method of writing these romances—at full speed, hardly stopping to think, so to speak—enabled him to tap his unconscious with freedom and depth.'

Certainly with Ian Fleming it was the freedom and depth with which he succeeded in tapping his own unconscious which puts *Casino Royale* in a class by itself among thrillers and adventure stories.

It was typical of him that he would usually shrug off *Casino Royale* along with the rest of his books as something of a joke between himself and his public, a mere entertainment he had knocked off with his tongue in his cheek. 'To Paul, who has always seen the joke', was how he inscribed one of his later books to Paul Gallico.

But as the film-makers discovered when they first tried turning James Bond into a screen property, there is no joke. The one quality the books lack entirely is humour. Each is written in deadly seriousness, and nowhere is this more so than in *Casino Royale*. Fleming is absorbed in arranging scenes from his dream world into the pattern of a more or less conventional espionage thriller.

But the pattern of *Casino Royale* is almost all that is conventional about a most original, unusual and curious novel. With the later books Fleming inevitably became more aware of what he was doing, and they rapidly gained in polish and construction. But they were never quite able to repeat the odd achievement of the first; and it is interesting that Raymond Chandler, himself a friend and admirer of Fleming, should always have insisted, often to Fleming's mild annoyance, that *Casino Royale* was the best book he wrote.

What is so rare about it is that here, encased within the flimsy bodywork of a cheap production-line espionage story, is the essence of this odd man's weird obsession with himself. It starts with that very first paragraph:

The scent and smoke and sweat of a casino are nauseating at three in the morning. Then the soul-erosion produced by high gambling—a compost of greed and fear and nervous tension —becomes unbearable and the senses awake and revolt from it.

From here the obsession builds up and the odd, airless landscape of the dream world of Ian Fleming unfolds. All the emotions are Fleming's emotions, the fads and beliefs are his fads and beliefs, and even when he bases his action on a genuine incident from real life it has a habit of becoming so overlaid by the fantasies with which he enhanced ordinary existence that it too becomes indelibly his own.

The background of Royale-les-Eaux, for instance, is drawn from his own visits to Le Touquet and Deauville before the war. Yet this is not the Deauville and Le Touquet other people saw, with the prosaic casinos set against the hum-drum life of the French seaside and the English Channel. This is casino life as Fleming always felt it to be—a life romantically enhanced by financial risk and physical danger, a symbolic battleground, a focal point for human greed and hope and despair. For Fleming a casino had always been something very special.

When he visited Deauville before the war with Ivar Bryce, it was Bryce who really gambled: for Fleming the fascination lay beyond the immediate losses and rewards of the table. It lay in the whole idea of the casino—the subdued lighting with the sharp yellow glare above the green of the tables, the smell of human stress, the glitter of risk, the impassive voices, the hush as the cards were turned or the wheel came to rest.

The casino was the only theatre Ian Fleming ever enjoyed, and the carefully repressed passion of the gaming table found a response in his own nature which in *Casino Royale* was to bring out some of his best writing:

The long game was launched and the sequence of these gestures and the reiteration of this subdued litany would continue until the end came and the players dispersed. Then the enigmatic cards would be burnt or defaced, a shroud would be draped over the table and the grass-green baize battlefield would soak up the blood of its victims and refresh itself.

But for Fleming the excitement of the casino lay beyond even the romantic thrill of his 'grass-green baize battlefield', and it was at Deauville in 1938 that he found what he had been looking for. This was an organization—it still exists —known as the Greek Syndicate, a partnership of wealthy Greek financiers and shipowners who as an investment buy from the casino the right or concession to run a baccarat game. During the winter, when the real wealth of the world was still to be found on the Riviera, the Greek Syndicate operated at Monte Carlo; and in the summer, as money migrated north, they came shuffling their cards after it. And wherever the Greek Syndicate operated in those days its best and most famous 'dealer' at baccarat was an ex-shipping clerk with a gentle manner and an infallible memory for cards and faces. His name was Zographos. He was one of Fleming's earliest heroes. Through him Fleming felt that he had finally begun to understand the real mystique of the casino.

Not long before he died, Fleming actually began a short story in which James Bond met Zographos. It never got beyond the first page and a half, but it managed to convey something of the excitement its author felt for the really great ice-cold gambler.

. . . 'It was like this, Mr Bond.' Zographos had a precise way of speaking with the thin tips of his lips while his half-hard, half-soft Greek eyes measured the reactions of his words on the listener . . . 'The Russians are chess players. They are mathematicians. Cold machines. But they are also mad. The mad ones forsake the chess and the mathematics and become gamblers. Now, Mr Bond.' Zographos laid a hand on Bond's sleeve and quickly withdrew it because he knew Englishmen, just as he knew the characteristics of every race, every race with money, in the world. 'There are two gamblers . . . the man who lays the odds and the man who accepts them. The bookmaker and the punter. The casino and, if you like'—Mr Zographos's smile was sly with the 'shared secret' and proud with the right word—'the suckers.'

What seems to have excited Fleming most of all was the thought that the Greek Syndicate and Zographos were the bankers and in the long run had the odds in their favour. It made him think that somehow, whether through skill or crime or self-control or knowledge of human nature, a really determined man could beat the system, establish his final ascendancy, his uniqueness as a human being, over Mr Zographos's 'suckers' and all the other dull worthy people who gambled without appreciating what they were up to.

This was what Fleming always wanted to do. But since he was a careful man with a profound appreciation of money and a gambler only in the imagination, he never did. It was left to James Bond to risk everything on that single throw and clean out the bank.

Instead, the sort of problem Fleming tried to solve at Deauville (as Gerald Coke recalls) was the exact nature of the odds in favour of the banker—0·8 per cent—although baccarat was not a game he played very often. He was obsessed, too, with the hunt for the perfect system and would spend hours trying to work out the mathematical risks involved.

Ivar Bryce, too, remembers that on several occasions

Fleming, instead of gambling, spent his time in the casino at Le Touquet carefully studying the security arrangements surrounding the *caisse* and mentally working out a perfect crime—how to rob the bank. It was then that he hit on the idea which Le Chiffre's gunman used on Bond, of pretending to be a cripple and bringing the pistol with its silencer into the casino hidden inside the stock of a heavy walking-stick —the deadly tube which Bond claimed to have tested in the war. And it was then, too, that he made the careful estimate, which Bond was to repeat, that it would need a minimum of ten professional gunmen to carry out an armed robbery on the casino.

It was all the purest daydream, but Fleming seems to have thought it out with deadly seriousness, and it was this highly coloured, romantic, danger-charged attitude to gambling and casinos which formed the emotional basis of *Casino Royale*. The incident from which he adapted the plot was that dismal night out with Admiral Godfrey at the Estoril Casino. Fantasy situations like this, once started, had a habit of building up in his mind. By a strange coincidence Ralph Izzard, who had worked for British Naval Intelligence in South America during the war, actually did find himself playing against genuine Nazi agents in the casino at Pernambuco, and he happened to mention it in a report which found its way to Fleming at the Admiralty. Immediately Fleming's interest was aroused, and when Izzard came back Fleming invited him out to dinner and spent most of the time going over the incident, asking the most precise details about the run of the cards, the characteristics and appearance of the Germans, their voices, everything. It was all to be turned to good account in Fleming's first novel.

Another minor but important event from the past which Fleming adapted for the book was the brief description of the killing of the Japanese cipher expert in New York. This again was a dramatic elaboration on that far tamer incident from his own life. According to Sir William Stephenson, Fleming was immensely excited by the affair, savouring it as something very special to recount to Admiral Godfrey. But that was not the end of it. The details lodged in his memory and became coloured by his imagination, until the occasion becomes one of the crucial events of James Bond's career as a member of the British Secret Service—one of the two justified killings which earned Bond his double-O classification, his official licence to kill.

'The first was in New York—a Japanese cipher expert cracking our codes on the thirty-sixth floor of the R.C.A. building in the Rockefeller Center, where the Japs had their consulate. I took a room on the fortieth floor of the next-door skyscraper and I could look across the street into his room and see him working. Then I got a colleague from our organization in New York and a couple of Remington thirty-thirtys with telescopic sights and silencers. We smuggled them up to my room and sat for days waiting for our chance. He shot at the man a second before me. His job was only to blast a hole through the window so that I could shoot the Jap through it. They have tough windows at the Rockefeller Center to keep the noise out. It worked very well. As I expected, his bullet got deflected by the glass and went God knows where. But I shot immediately after him, through the hole he had made. I got the Jap in the mouth as he turned to gape at the broken window.'

Bond smoked for a minute.

'It was a pretty sound job. Nice and clean too. Three hundred yards away. No personal contact.'

With almost any other thriller-writer it could be argued that a passage like this was a straightforward invention. Fleming, however, was no ordinary writer of thrillers, and as he sat at his typewriter on a February morning at Goldeneye the episode from the Rockefeller Center finally emerged as another of the lethal fantasies of the self he might have been.

For one of the slightly disconcerting things about Fleming in real life was that he liked to imagine that he had killed someone in the line of duty. Very few of his friends were taken into the secret, but to those who were he took elaborate precautions to suggest, subtly, and with a great show of reluctance, that he had once been compelled to perform this terrible deed which marked him off so cruelly from other men. To one friend he confided the bare fact that the killing had been done with a sandbag; he had never realized, he said, how really hard you needed to hit a grown man with a sandbag to kill him. To another he hinted that he had performed the deed by firing a small automatic which he had concealed in his old brown leather briefcase —that was how the hole in the corner had got there. Another close friend believed that Fleming's black hat from Lock's had somehow played its part in a carefully planned assassination. Yet another is still firmly convinced that Fleming slugged an agent of the Vichy Government and tipped him over the waterfront at Marseilles.

Because he was fundamentally isolated from people Fleming never succeeded in introducing a single really credible outside character into the dream world disclosed in his novels. He was never a man to get really close to other human beings, and he had none of the real novelist's interest in human character—his curiosity was reserved for material objects and practical techniques, and he no more invited profound confidences from people than he bestowed them. The result of this isolation was that everything had to come from within himself. While this provides much of the uniqueness of the James Bond books, it also limits them drastically. It accounts for their oddly claustrophobic atmosphere.

When he came to construct his characters Fleming dredged up some essential figures from his own past. He would usually paint a new face on them for each story, but the shapes beneath never altered very much. One was the villain-figure, who made his bow in *Casino Royale* in the fat, white, slug-like Le Chiffre, with his sadistic impulses, his benzedrine inhaler and his insatiable appetite for women. It is likely that Fleming borrowed some of his external characteristics from Aleister Crowley. Not only does the general figure of Le Chiffre, with his size, ugliness and all the overtones of unmentionable vice match the impression Crowley usually created, but minor parallels exist between them. Both called people 'dear boy', and both, like Mussolini, had the whites of their eyes completely visible around the iris.

But if Fleming did use his recollections of Crowley to embellish his first villain, Le Chiffre had undoubtedly existed in his imagination before he met Crowley. (Perhaps the Hairless Mexican in Somerset Maugham's *Ashenden* had done something to install Le Chiffre there, just as R, the Intelligence Colonel who recruits Ashenden, brings M. to mind. Lady Mary Clive remembers seeing Fleming at Ebury Street and telling him how sinister he looked when he used a benzedrine inhaler. 'When I write my book,' he replied, 'I'm going to have a villain who sits alone in a room just like me, and he'll live on a diet of benzedrine and women and be hairless and quite horrible to look at.'

Yet Le Chiffre never becomes a genuine character, no matter if Fleming did brood on him for years. He remains a sort of Identikit figure assembled out of a number of physical characteristics which Fleming seems to have found repellent or terrifying in people he had known. Some of these, like the eyes and the repellent fat face, were superficial enough. Others were not, and as they have a habit of recurring in almost all Fleming's subsequent villains, they are worth looking at. What is so interesting about these particular characteristics is that they all seem to share a strong element of overwhelming infantilistic terror. All the deep qualities of evil which Fleming ascribed to Le Chiffre and to his later villains are precisely the qualities which children most fear in adults. All demonstrate the threat of extreme physical power which an adult presents to a child, and their sadism contains that element of fearful irrationality which a child detects in the cruelty of an adult.

It is significant also that Fleming's collective villain-figure tends to base his evil on a number of strictly limited sources of adult superiority. One is extreme wealth, wealth as a source of power, as a licence for the exercise of unrestrained wickedness. Another is overwhelming male sexual potency, which for some reason Bond, who after all is not lacking in virility himself, always encounters as something faintly threatening and obscene. This is more so with Le Chiffre than with any of the later villains, for in the celebrated torture scene with the carpet beater and the carving-knife Le Chiffre actually threatens Bond with castration. As he does so, to quote Fleming's own words, 'Le Chiffre spoke like a father' to Bond.

If this villain and his successors have deeper roots in Fleming's subconscious than appears at first glance, much the same would seem to apply to the character of James Bond's director, the old Admiral M., who is head of the Secret Service. Once again, as with Le Chiffre, it is perfectly possible to pick on a superficial resemblance between M. and a real-life character on whom Fleming might seem to have modelled him, namely, Admiral Godfrey. Apart from their both being admirals, Godfrey in his heyday in Room 38 was an impressive man with something of M.'s toughness and omniscience. In reality, however, the relationship between Commander I. L. Fleming and Rear-Admiral J. H. Godfrey was nothing like the shepherd-and-sheepdog situation between M. and Bond. While they were together at the Admiralty they were close friends and on Christian name terms; moreover, Fleming had considerable power of his own, and in some ways he was more of an M. figure himself than a loyal Bond being ordered around by that icy old paragon with the shell-case tobacco jar on his desk.

But if Admiral Godfrey was not M., who was? One theory

is that M. stood for Menzies, Sir Stewart Menzies, formerly head of M.I.6. Yet once again there is little—apart from the initial and the position in the intelligence service—which really corresponds. For Menzies, an Old Etonian, was a soldier, and although while at the Admiralty Fleming knew him and had some contact with him he never seems to have been particularly deeply impressed by him.

There is reason for thinking that a more telling lead to the real identity of M. lies in the fact that as a boy Fleming often called his mother M. There seem to be distinct parallels between the demanding old autocrat in Universal Export bestowing on James Bond his grudging praise, his terrifying blame, and the way Mrs Val Fleming tended to treat her son Ian during various crises in his life. While Fleming was young, his mother was certainly one of the few people he was frightened of, and her sternness towards him, her unexplained demands, and her remorseless insistence on success finds a curious and constant echo in the way M. handles that hard-ridden, hard-killing agent, 007. Never has a man who slaughtered so mercilessly taken orders so meekly. Never has such cool ingratitude produced such utter loyalty.

The third of Fleming's basic characters who make their entrance in *Casino Royale* is Vesper Lynd, the first of that long line of James Bond's nubile, eager and ultimately disposable bed-mates. She has little interest beyond the way she seems to embody most of Fleming's own somewhat grudging view of female dignity formed during those hit-and-run affairs of his early thirties. Unlike Anne Fleming, who changed Fleming's own existence by providing the elements of chaos and the unexpected, Vesper Lynd is essentially a passive girl who like all these heroines (and the dispatch rider) never answers back and has the decency to die before she can really complicate James Bond's neat bachelor's existence.

Apart from Le Chiffre, M. and Vesper Lynd, the minor characters in *Casino Royale* are the merest shadows with names attached. The only other character who matters is Ian Fleming himself. For James Bond is not really a character in this book. He is a mouthpiece for the man who inhabits him, a dummy for him to hang his clothes on, a zombie to perform the dreams of violence and daring which fascinate his creator. It is only because Fleming holds so little of himself back, because he talks and dreams so freely through the device of James Bond, that the book has such readability. *Casino Royale* is really an experiment in the autobiography of dreams. From the very first page Fleming seems bent on exploiting material drawn from his own mind and memory, and often he uses it with a minimum of alteration. Bond's feelings, for example, during the late-night session at the casino: 'The bad harsh taste in his mouth and the slight sweat under his arms . . . The front of his face, his nose and antrum were congested.' Fleming himself, the seventy-cigarettes-a-day man, was always complaining of the 'bad harsh taste' in his mouth, and ever since his nose was pushed in by Henry Douglas-Home at Eton it had a tendency, like Bond's, to become congested in the close atmosphere of a crowded room.

There are plenty of other similarities. Bond is made to smoke the same number of the same cigarettes a day as Fleming did. He wears the same clothes—the black moccasins, dark-blue Sea Island cotton shirts, lightweight blue suits—is the same height, has the same love of scrambled eggs, *sauce béarnaise* and gunmetal cigarette cases, the same spoiled child's love of 'double portions' of coffee and orange juice for breakfast.

Bond's *rationale* of gambling is entirely Fleming's—'above all he liked it that everything was one's own fault. There was only oneself to praise or blame.' So is his patriotism, his attitude to Americans—'good Americans were fine people and most of them seemed to come from Texas' —and above all his attitude to women: 'Women were for recreation. On a job they got in the way and fogged things up with sex and hurt feelings and all the emotional baggage they carried around. One had to look out for them and take care of them.' Bond's combination of ruthlessness and sentimentality towards women—'his first reaction was one of scorn. Damn fool girl getting herself trussed up like a chicken . . . But then he felt sorry for her'—is also very like Fleming's own, while those brief and spartan love-feasts with which Bond sparingly rewards himself when victorious sound very like the briskly therapeutic affairs with which Fleming had once kept boredom at bay during the long nights at Ebury Street and Carlyle Mansions.

But despite all these similarities James Bond is not Ian Fleming, nor is he an Ian Fleming that ever was. He is Fleming's dream of a self that might have been—a tougher, stronger, more effective, duller, far less admirable character than the real Fleming.

The more superficial resemblances Fleming could establish between Bond and himself the more credible his daydream would become: hence the items of self-portraiture so carefully written into the books, the similarities of clothing, philosophy and speech between James Bond and his creator. They were what carried the fantasy along for that lonely man typing his 2,000 words a day in the silence of Goldeneye.

Yet once Bond was established as a genuine dream-self Fleming was free to send him into action as he had sent people into action during the war, performing all the deeds he longed for but of which he had been cheated. As he once said, Bond really was 'a blunt instrument'—blunt in sensibilities, blunt in everything that could impede his efficiency as a man of action: an uncomplicated character who compensated his creator for his own tortuous temperament.

As a gambler Fleming had always been hamstrung by his curiously complex attitude to money, his deep fear of poverty, his innate puritanism, and had never in his life managed to make the great gesture of an all-or-nothing throw at the casino. Bond does so without turning a single immaculate black hair and walks off with the biggest single coup ever made at Royale-les-Eaux.

In his contact with the Secret Service world during the war, Fleming had been the man behind the desk. In Bond he got his own back, slipped his Beretta with the skeleton grip into his chamois leather shoulder-holster and went off to face death on his own account.

For Bond is the man who would always succeed where Fleming failed. He was not a spy—he was a man of action; and although he suffered from almost all the weaknesses Fleming pretended to despise in himself—his fear, his materialism, his drinking and womanizing—he could always turn these weaknesses to good account and always win: the ideal Mitty figure for Fleming and for all of us who watch and want but do not do.

CHAPTER SIXTEEN

THE GOLDEN TYPEWRITER

BRYCE'S new Thunderbird, with Fleming as passenger, took the road north from Albany at a steady seventy-five, turned right towards Mechanicsville, and scarcely seemed to slacken speed as it purred its way up the backroads of New York State. For a few miles the smooth-flowing Hudson River was visible. Then the road climbed higher still into the clear, green, New England countryside with its small, red-painted farmhouses, low-angled hills, undulating lush valleys, and the car surged forward on each stretch of straight black asphalt.

This was Fleming's first visit to New England, and he enjoyed the drive as he always enjoyed long journeys in fast cars. He was glad of the chance to see his friend Ivar Bryce and spend these few days at the farm in Vermont he had heard so much about.

Eighteen months before Ivar Bryce had married one of the richest women in the world—Josephine Douglas, sister of Huntington Hartford, joint-heiress of the fortune her family had built up in the A. & P. supermarket chain throughout America.

Since the marriage the Bryces had bought two very large luxurious houses on Bay Street in Nassau. They also owned the house on 74th Street where Fleming always stayed now when he was in New York, and they were soon to buy Moyns Park, the Elizabethan place not very far from Newmarket where Ivar Bryce was born.

For the Bryces collect beautiful houses. Each in its way is perfect with the slightly unnerving perfection bestowed by great wealth. Nowhere was this more so than at Black Hole Hollow Farm, their country house near Saratoga on the State line between New York State and Vermont. By millionaire standards the place is not big: the old stone farmhouse with its low ceilings and heavy wooden floor is still its centre, and the guest bedrooms, the music-room, the dining-room and bar and sun lounge have all been added without destroying the scale or character of the house.

From the moment the Thunderbird drove up through the avenue of maples that afternoon and he caught his first sight of the farm with its low-pitched slate roof through the trees, Fleming loved it. He was given the room on the right of the front door—a luxuriously simple, old-style New England room with pine floor and brightly coloured rugs and a turned maple four-poster with white chintz curtains. Just before dusk he and Bryce strolled out on to the terrace and down to the lake and on through the woods of fir and spruce that surround the farm on three sides, giving it a stillness and melancholy that went straight to Fleming's heart.

During the next few years the Bryces and Black Hole Hollow Farm were to play their part in the story of James Bond and the life of his creator. Fleming was to get material for some of his books here, and he set one of his stories—the hideaway of von Hammerstein in 'For Your Eyes Only'—against the background of the farm.

Bryce had bought himself an oil well in Texas which had just started to produce, and out of the proceeds he had decided to acquire a controlling interest in the North American Newspaper Alliance. N.A.N.A. had represented a consortium of big newspapers working together to acquire important serial rights, but by the time Bryce bought it its prestige was not what it was. He and his associate, Ernest Cuneo, were planning to rejuvenate N.A.N.A., and Fleming was drawn into the project.

Cuneo, who was staying at his own summer house just a couple of miles down the road from the Bryces, was already an old friend of Fleming's. Formerly one of Roosevelt's legal aides, and a man of overwhelming energy, Cuneo had been an important figure behind the scenes in wartime Washington. He was one of the group around General Donovan and Sir William Stephenson, and he had first met Fleming in Stephenson's office in 1942.

They became great friends, for Fleming, like Bond, warmed to 'cheerful expansive people with a zest for life'. Every subsequent trip he made to New York would include lunch at Sardi's or dinner at '21' with this eloquent, argumentative, broad-shouldered little man with the bald head and piercing black eyes.

The purchase of N.A.N.A. had been largely his idea. For Bryce it was never much more than a rich man's hobby, something which, as he says himself, 'I thought it would be rather fun to get involved with'. Cuneo was more serious, and Fleming was invited to help and become European Vice-President. It was the sort of invitation he could never resist. He became excited by the prospect of a new and richer life, and his elation lasted all the way back to England.

Carlyle Mansions is an ugly, comfortable, solidly built and entirely respectable block of late-Victorian flats in Cheyne Walk. T. S. Eliot lived in the flat below, sharing it with Fleming's friend John Hayward, who was to become the editor, in association with Fleming, of the magazine the *Book Collector*. As the black animal-cage of a lift bore him sedately aloft to the third floor Fleming, returning from his exciting week-end in Vermont, admitted that all his fore-bodings about giving up his freedom had been proved baseless; and many of his old friends were soon to observe how well the confirmed middle-aged bachelor seemed to be taking to marriage.

Not that there was really any reason why he shouldn't: he was married to one of the very few women he had ever loved, and it was not as if he had exchanged all the freedom of his bachelor days for the tedium of a middle-class marriage. His wife had the most stimulating circle of friends of any woman in London. Many of them were already his friends. He still had his bridge and his clubs when he felt domesticity oppressing him, and every week-end he and Anne would drive off eagerly to their house at St Margaret's Bay, which they had now taken over from Noël Coward.

The last stages of the negotiation for the house had produced a splendid exchange of letters between the two men, with a glimpse not only of Fleming's sardonic humour but of his instinctive carefulness about money. In January 1952 he had written to Coward explaining that he had recently had a chance of looking at 'my new mansion and quite honestly it is in a pretty poor way with your pictures taken down and the book-shelves removed, etc. There are yellow patches on most of the walls and battens up in your workroom which will have to come down and be made good. I gather that as the outgoing tenant the cost of putting this straight should fall on your slim shoulders.'

By May 9th Fleming was writing to tell Coward that the repairs had been done and that the bill came to £100 10s. 2d. 'May I assume that a cheque will reach me in due course?' he asked, 'or would you rather work this off in writing an article for the "Sunday Chronicle" entitled "The most scandalous things I know about my most intimate friends"?'

To this Coward replied that he intended to use 'the good old British plan of compromise and enclose a cheque for fifty pounds. If you do not want it I can give you a few suggestions what to do with it when you come to lunch on Sunday.'

This produced the following retort from Fleming by return of post:

Dear Messrs Noël Coward Incorporated,

The mixture of Scottish and Jewish blood which runs in my veins has been brought to the boil by your insolent niggardliness.

Only Anne's dainty hand has restrained me from slapping a mandamus on your meagre assets and flinging the charge of bottomry, or at least barratry, in your alleged face.

Pending the final advices of Mann, Rogers and Greaves, my solicitors, I shall expend your insulting pourboire on a hunting crop and a Mills bomb and present myself at one o'clock exactly on Sunday morning.

I shall see what Beaverbrook has to say about your behaviour at lunch today.

Tremble.

IAN

In fact, Fleming was delighted with his house by the cliffs near Dover, with its view across the Channel (he erected a telescope on the terrace to watch the shipping) and its blessed proximity to the 'best seaside golf course in the world' at Sandwich. Meanwhile, in one of his letters he gives an idea of the sort of life he and Anne were enjoying in London during the week. 'Lord Kemsley came to dinner at Carlyle Mansions last night and paid rather heavily at Canasta for the privilege. The *clou* of the evening was when Lord Beaverbrook rang us up to ask us to dinner next week, leaving the pleasing impression on the evening air of rival proprietors bidding for our talents.'

Fleming's new life must have been exciting during those months of the early summer of 1952. All within a matter of a few months he had got himself a wife, a new house, a new 2½-litre Riley, and the possibility of two new careers, one rather doubtfully as a novelist and the other as European controller of the North American Newspaper Alliance. He was carried along by an unaccustomed mood of optimism. Even money was not a matter of serious concern. There was always the Fleming Collection to fall back on if the worst came to the worst, and on May 6th he was writing to Sir

William Stephenson saying that once again he had been bid 'many thousands of pounds for it. But I have turned the offer down,' he added blithely, 'as I can see Anne and I living on it when the currency system fails.'

He had high hopes of making a success of his work for the North American Newspaper Alliance—work which he was doing with Lord Kemsley's permission. During May and June he took a lot of trouble on their behalf. At one moment he was having to tell Bryce that Randolph Churchill might not be the best person to do a series of articles which N.A.N.A. hoped to sell to Kemsley House, 'since he is not in great favour in this stable'. The next he was advising him to communicate direct with newspaper proprietors rather than with their editors—'they always like receiving personal cables. It makes them feel like editors themselves instead of financiers.'

As a Press Lord *manqué* this was the sort of advice Fleming loved giving. All his old energy and optimism seemed to be rising to the surface again. It carried him through the anxious period of putting the final touches to the first draft of *Casino Royale* and actually getting it to a publisher.

For Fleming this was inevitably a tortured and tortuous process, for he was still dogged by the lack of confidence which had followed him from Eton. Worse still, he was as terrified as ever of making a fool of himself in public.

Some years later when he described how *Casino Royale* got into print Fleming made it sound almost a matter of accident, with himself dragged in as an unwilling participant. 'When I got back to London I did nothing with the manuscript. I was too ashamed of it. No publisher would want it and if one did I would not have the face to see it in print.' It so happened, however, that on May 12th he was having lunch with William Plomer at the Ivy Restaurant and suddenly he asked his friend 'how you got cigarette smoke out of a woman once you've got it in'.

'Always, I hope,' says Plomer, 'alert to the caprices of the human race, and generally expectant that they are likely to be grotesque, I must have speculated rapidly on this intimate-sounding injection.' Fleming went on to explain that one couldn't use a word like 'exhales' while 'puffs it out' he thought 'sounded silly'. It was at this point that Plomer looked up sharply and said, 'You've written a book,' adding predictably that he would like a chance to see it. With some show of reluctance Fleming agreed.

Such, at any rate, was his version of how Plomer came to be interested. In fact, the incident was typical of his approach to something he was deeply concerned with, and the difficulties of getting the cigarette smoke out of Vesper Lynd were more apparent than real. In *Casino Royale* the phrase reads quite effortlessly—'and then exhaling it casually through her lips and nostrils'. For Fleming had almost certainly worked out the approach to Plomer very carefully beforehand, so as to inform him of the existence of the book without seeming to and without actually asking him to look at it. His self-respect could remain intact: responsibility for reading *Casino Royale* would rest with William Plomer.

One can feel for Fleming, poised as he was between the desire for success and the fear of failure. For at last, after all those years, he had actually done what he said he would do: he had written his 'spy story to end all spy stories'. Yet a painful dilemma remained: as he must have realized by now he had put far more of himself into *Casino Royale* than most authors put into their novels. He of all people, the man who had gone through life switching from personality to personality, and always attempting to avoid 'eviscerating myself in public', had finally made his great act of self-revelation.

Even so, the process of getting the book to the publisher was painfully slow. It was nearly two months before he let Plomer have his dog-eared and heavily corrected manuscript, and when he did so he accompanied it with a note of eager self-depreciation. After telling Plomer that he had not sent him the book before because 'I am really thoroughly ashamed of it', he went on:

I had the idea that one could write a thriller with half one's mind, and I simply wrote 2,000 words a day to show myself that I could. I didn't read it through as I wrote it, and when I got back to England and did so I really was appalled.

The dialogue, a lot of the description and the main characters are dreadfully banal and three-quarters of the writing is informed with what I can only describe as vulgarity. Such good action moments as there are in the story have been more or less thrown away and so far as I can see the element of suspense is completely absent.

Having dissociated himself from the story almost as if he had never written it, he went on to say that the only reason he was letting Plomer see 'this miserable piece of work' was

221

that he wanted to know whether any of it was worth saving. 'Then when I go back to Jamaica next year, I might try to sweat it out again and this time take a bit more trouble.'

'After riffling through this muck,' he concluded, 'you will probably never speak to me again, but I have got to take that chance. For God's sake don't mention this dreadful oafish opus to anyone else, and for heaven's sake believe, as I am sure you will after you have read a few pages, that this is not mock humility.'

Then, once more, in the very last sentence, he tried to cover himself by placing the responsibility on Plomer. 'If you had not again asked for it on that postcard, you would certainly never have seen it, so it is all your fault anyway.'

With this last abject warning the book which launched the most popular fiction character of its decade lumbered on its way to its future publisher.

Fortunately Plomer knew Fleming too well to pay over-much attention to the twistings of his serpentine ego. He read the manuscript quickly and, ignoring Fleming's veto on showing it to another soul, passed it to Daniel George, Cape's other reader, before giving his own considered verdict.

The life of a publisher's reader is a curious one. The financial rewards are not great. Success brings with it no great measure of fame, and there are occasional moments when an error of judgment can rob the publisher of a fortune and ruin the reputation of the reader. But William Plomer and Daniel George did not miss, and on July 14th, 1952, the first fan letter about James Bond was written. Daniel George wrote to Plomer:

My dear William,
I sat up till 1.20 last night. 'Casino Royale' made me sit up. It was so exciting that I could persuade myself that I was back at the old baccarat, and the vodka and caviare were so delicious that I tolerated the abominable condition of the typescript.

He went on to say that the author had 'evidently had great fun in a genre of which he is a connoisseur' and that the details were original and interesting, although he also felt that the book, though publishable, needed extensive revision.

I couldn't reconcile some of the details and I was bothered by some abrupt transitions. How the carpet-beater worked was not very clear to me; and I doubted whether castration could be carried out with a pair of garden shears, rusty at that [the shears became a carving-knife in the final manuscript]. Anyhow it has given me very great pleasure and I hope to be given more by the author's next excursion into fiction. He knows all the tricks.

Despite Fleming's elaborate show of caution, things did begin to move now. The manuscript was passed to Jonathan Cape himself with a note from Plomer strongly recommending publication. Daniel George's letter was sent to Fleming, and Plomer told him that while it was up to Jonathan Cape to make up his own mind about the book, 'it certainly looks as if Jamaica may again resound with the diligent clatter of your typewriter this winter if you feel in a revisionary frame of mind.'

But by now Fleming was in no mood to wait that long. Almost by return of post he was promising Plomer that he would see whether 'another two months with my road drill could get the book into publishable shape . . . It remains to be seen whether I can get a bit closer to Eric Ambler and exorcise the blabbering ghost of [Peter] Cheyney.'

What Fleming didn't confess to Plomer was that even before disclosing the manuscript he had chosen a symbol to remind himself where, with luck, his future lay. It was a new typewriter to replace his old Imperial: a gold typewriter.

He had ordered it in New York, and on May 17th, some weeks before first sending Plomer the manuscript, he wrote to Bryce: 'Here is one vital request. I am having constructed for me by the Royal Typewriter Company a golden typewriter which is to cost one hundred and seventy-four dollars. I will not tell you why I am acquiring this machine,' he added, but simply asked Bryce to bring it over on his next trip to England.

The golden typewriter duly arrived. Fleming hid himself away when he had the chance in his bedroom at Carlyle Mansions, working over his battered manuscript with his gold-plated 'road drill' and not telling Anne or anyone else what he was doing.

By the end of August he was finished, and the revised manuscript was sent off to William Plomer at Bedford Square. This time Fleming was confident—all his cautious anxiety had been blown away. The man with the golden typewriter was on his way to the top.

There were no reservations now, no anxious disclaimers,

no more talk of keeping the book back until he had the chance to revise it thoroughly the following year at Golden-eye. At last he was allowing himself to be in love with the idea of authorship and all the possibilities the book could offer. It was now that the painstaking, highly practical side of his nature joined forces with his fantasy self to make certain that those possibilities were realized.

For just as no one but Fleming would have thought of using a gold-plated typewriter for his first thriller, so no one but Fleming would have taken quite so much hard-headed trouble to whip up outside support for it either.

In the note to Plomer which accompanied the revised manuscript he said:

By now I would like to see it take wing . . . Lord Kemsley who has been in on the fringe of the grisly secret has asked who I would like to have review it in the 'Sunday Times'. And since I have Lord Beaverbrook and W. H. Smith [one of his friends was a managing director of the big bookselling firm] in two other pockets, I think I could cold-bloodedly complete the operation of selling the vile body to the public.

His hope was that the book would be a big enough success to ensure his escape from journalism for ever. 'As you see, I am treating my muse with small respect and largely as a means to move from one scaly profession to another.'

It was not only outside support which called for his attention. There were still numerous small points in the book that needed vetting or expanding, and it was now that he began the process, which became almost a matter of routine with his later books, of drawing on his various contacts to check his facts.

It is interesting that his method never really changed; from the very beginning he relied on writing the entire book at full speed and then going over it later to fill in the details. It is also interesting to see just how shaky the expertise of this apparent master of certain kinds of expertise really is. For example, despite James Bond's apparent familiarity with all the byways of ballistics, Fleming's own knowledge of firearms was really very slight. He was a good shot and could admire guns for their workmanship and for what they symbolized, but he could never take the trouble to become an expert.

There is surprising proof of this in a letter he wrote to Robert Churchill the gunsmith at the end of August, asking him to check over the names of the four different firearms

Anne Fleming, eldest daughter of the Hon. Guy Charteris, son of the 11th Earl of Wemyss. She married Ian Fleming in March, 1952 at Port Maria, Jamaica

A beach photographer gets a vivid picture of the Flemings on holiday in Venice. (*Below*) On the set: Sean Connery, James Bond to millions, talks to Bond's creator

mentioned in *Casino Royale*. Only one of them, the ·38 Colt Police Positive (the gun that General Donovan gave him during the war for 'special services'), did he succeed in naming correctly. The other three were incorrect, and the personal weapon he had given to Bond was not only spelt wrongly but had the calibre wrong as well. He admitted his doubt quite cheerfully in his letter to Mr Churchill:

The gun I have most serious doubts over is the ·28 Biretta. In the book this is supposed to be a very light and flat automatic pistol. If you do not know the weapon I mean, or if, as is quite possible, it does not exist, it would be very kind if you would pencil in the most exotic-sounding weapon of about this calibre to be carried unobtrusively in a shoulder holster.

Churchill the expert soon put him right, briskly informing him that the gun was a Beretta, not a Biretta, and that its calibre was ·25, not ·28.

Although later on Fleming was to appear to make something of a cult about the arcane information he introduced into his books, he knew perfectly well that it was little more than a device for conveying credibility and carrying his readers with him. In essence he used facts like these in his books in exactly the same way as he used them time and again in conversation with his friends. Thus he always showed a predilection for quoting a line of Rilke in the original or for describing the mechanism of a blow-fish's reproductive system or an Hispano-Suiza gearbox. But when it comes to it, it is hard to think of a single subject on which he was a genuine expert. His knowledge of food was erratic, of wine almost non-existent. He was a sound driver, but he relied on the advice of experts like Aubrey Forshaw, head of Pan Books, for the really detailed facts of automobile technology in his books. It was the same with weaponry, the same with high finance, the same with gambling, the same even with the Secret Service. Only on matters of sex did he rely entirely on his own carefully guarded expertise.

The truth is, as he had shown years before when he first engaged Percy Muir to start building his library for him, Fleming had neither the inclination nor the staying power of the expert. He was something different: he was a born journalist, and true to his calling he knew how to mobilize and exploit the knowledge of others. Few men were ever more adroit with the knowing phrase, the exotic-sounding fact, the lightly brushed-on dust of expertise.

As a writer his originality lay in the way he searched for

his scraps of information, selecting them with a true connoisseur's eye, becoming excited over them, giving them significance and sparkle, and checking them with as much care as he and his friends could manage.

During the fine days of early autumn, 1952, as he went over his manuscript putting the final details into place, there must have been times when he felt that he was on one of life's winning runs at last. Now that he had plunged none of his old fears seemed to matter.

That August Anne had a son, and to his surprise Fleming found himself thrilled at becoming a father for the first time at forty-four. She left the registration of the birth entirely to him, and the two names he chose reveal something of the pride he felt in his son. Caspar was the name which his mother's old admirer, Augustus John, had given to the son of his who became Admiral of the Fleet Sir Caspar John—and all his life Fleming admired, almost idolized, Augustus John. Robert was the name of his grandfather, the Fleming who had brought the family out of Scotland and obscurity.

'The compost of Fleming and Charteris essences who is to be called Caspar,' he wrote to his brother-in-law Hugo Charteris, 'weighed 9 lbs 2 ozs, and is up to Fleming and far beyond Charteris standards. Anne is very pleased with him and he is the darling of the wards.'

It was not just fatherhood which began to thaw this lonely man out of his emotional ice age. 'Caspar Robert progresses well,' he wrote to a friend a few weeks later. 'If it were possible to make a better man out of me he is certainly assisting the process. I am having a good deal of trouble from my wife now that she has regained her health, and after forty-four years of avoiding society I am finding its increasing incursion into my life a grievous burden. But this also,' he adds, 'is being very good for my character.'

Certainly he seemed to be bearing his 'grievous burden' quite cheerfully. He wrote to Hugo Charteris at the beginning of September:

Anne is looking very thin and lovely and already brewing mischiefs for the autumn. She is coming up on Thursday in order to go to Noël Coward's first night on Friday, leaving me to worry about her health during the performance and dry her exhausted tears afterwards. As the privileged keeper of the only dodo outside a museum, I am bearing the burden with crotchety fortitude and working doubly hard to keep Lucien Freud, Peter Quennell,

Freddie Ashton *et al* in champagne during the coming months and years.

And a few weeks later he wrote to a friend:

> We went over to Le Touquet the week-end before last and gave the *Syndicat des Bains de Mer* a sharp lesson and ate some wonderful meals. Then Anne went on to Paris with a heavy cold and the object of buying 'one simple black frock which will do for afternoon and evening', but which as usual turned out to be a majestic affair suitable only for the Congress of Vienna. There will be no room for it in Carlyle Mansions and we will have to hang it out of the window.

Apart from marriage, fatherhood and this new social whirl which he was bearing with 'crotchety fortitude', he was living a fuller and busier life now than he had done for years, occupying himself among other things with a variety of literary matters: it might be sending Hugo Charteris's new, unpublished novel to Rosamond Lehmann for her opinion, or negotiating with John Betjeman for an article he had written on O.K. words to be published in de-luxe form by Lord Kemsley's Queen Anne Press, the literary policy of which Fleming himself was directing, or showing Evelyn Waugh his books after dinner and writing to Percy Muir to tell him that Waugh had suggested that the Fleming Collection ought surely to include something on religion. And most week-ends he and Anne would rush off in the 2½-litre Riley to St Margaret's Bay, where they played host to guests like Somerset Maugham, Noël Coward, Evelyn Waugh, the Duff Coopers and Patrick Leigh Fermor. 'I have only survived,' he wrote to a friend, 'by giving extremely short hostmanship weight and playing a lot of golf with a man who once got second prize in the Calcutta Sweep—£25,000—of which I have so far relieved him of only one.'

At the end of October Caspar Robert was christened at Chelsea Old Church, with Noël Coward and Anthony Eden's wife Clarissa among the godparents. 'It was a great success,' Fleming told Bryce, 'and all the fairy godfathers and godmothers performed well. Afterwards we had an extremely unchristian rout in Carlyle Mansions consisting of the sweepings of Mayfair.'

In the midst of all this unaccustomed sociability *Casino Royale* is typed out for the last time and accepted by Jonathan Cape for publication the following April. Fleming is finally free to indulge in the delicious preliminaries of successful authorship. Gone now is the embarrassed novice of the weeks before, painfully daring himself to show his 'deplorable story' to William Plomer. Fleming has a new part to play—the cool professional, drumming up supporters, dictating terms, excited and confident and taking the success of his book almost entirely for granted. He sent a copy of the manuscript to Paul Gallico, who wrote back:

The book is a knock-out. I thought I had written a couple of pretty fair torture scenes in my day, but yours beats everything I have ever read. Wow! It goes in for frankness and detail far beyond any American-type thriller and could have a big sale . . . Get out of that office kid and write, because you can.

Fleming thought so, too, and all the hereditary instincts of the Scots banker in him came to the surface as he planned the operation to make *Casino Royale* a best-seller.

On September 17th he met Jonathan Cape to settle terms for the book. The following day this most business-like of novice authors sent Cape a four-page letter of recapitulation. It is a fascinating document. In the margin Cape wrote his replies to some of Fleming's points, and apart from what it shows of the personalities of the two men the letter makes quite clear the scale on which Fleming was planning the James Bond books.

Most authors, particularly when they begin, leave details of publication to their agents or to the goodwill of the publisher. Not so Fleming. After setting down the royalty agreement—ten per cent on the first 10,000 copies rising to twenty per cent when 20,000 had been reached—he wrote, 'If you are feeling in a more generous mood today, for symmetry's sake you might care to include 12½ per cent on the 5,000 to 10,000, but I will not be exigent.'

Besides this Jonathan Cape scribbled simply 'No'.

Fleming's second point was that the first printing should be 10,000 copies, but Cape refused to go beyond 7,000. Under the heading 'Advertisement and Promotion' Fleming wrote, 'I hope you would agree to consulting with me on the text of anything you publish regarding the book.' Under 'Design' he said that he would 'submit some designs for a jacket and for the binding of the book (conforming with your own very high standards) to which I hope you would give sympathetic consideration.' 'Yes, but NO MORE,' wrote Cape.

Fleming then made a suggestion that only he would have

thought of: 'For the fun of it and to make useful copy for gossip paragraphs, etc., I would like to suggest that I toss your secretary double or quits on the trade price for any additional personal copies I may require. (The odds will be exactly even on either side!)' To this Cape says, 'O.K. up to 24.' When Fleming did toss for the copies the following April Cape's secretary, Jean Mossop, beat him.

'I hope you won't find any of these suggestions unreasonable,' he concluded the letter, 'since I am only activated by motives of (a) making as much money for myself and my publishers as possible out of the book; and (b) getting as much fun as I personally can out of the project.'

As old Jonathan Cape probably realized, Fleming's 'fun' had started already. For behind all this show of hard practicality Fleming was playing out the various moves in his splendid new game of preparing to be a best-selling author. Everything was minutely worked out in that precise yet dreamlike way which he had perfected for all his fantasies.

He wrote to Ivar Bryce at the beginning of October, asking him to spy out the land for a potential American publisher. 'What I want is not a publisher but a "factory" which will shift this opus of mine like "Gone with the Naked and the Dead". I am not being vain about this book but simply trying to squeeze the last dirty cent out of it.' In the same week, again playing the part of best-selling author, he bought up a defunct company called Glidrose Productions to ease the tax burden on a book which had not even been published. Earlier—on September 15th—he had written to J. M. Ruddy, Kemsley Newspapers' correspondent in Hollywood, asking him, 'What sort of sums do the big studios pay for a novel by a writer who is not yet established?'

It was ironic but perhaps inevitable that when Fleming finally achieved the runaway success of his last years it never brought him anything like the pleasure with which he dreamed of it all during these delicious months of the autumn of 1952.

Finally, during the last months of the year the excitement of *Casino Royale* became part of the promise of a new and exhilarating life which seemed just around the corner: he and Anne were escaping from Carlyle Mansions. He wrote to Bryce, 'Have bought a beautiful Regency house in Victoria Square—between the Queen and the Goring Hotel. Whatever Anne says it is the same size as the flat, only vertical instead of horizontal. An expensive shift of posture!'

Before this Bryce happened to have mentioned that he was thinking of buying himself a Continental Bentley, and he suggested, in that easy way of his, that his good friend Ian might look into this for him; he was not quite sure how one went about buying such a car and what was available in the way of upholstery, paintwork, and accessories. But, as he knew, there was no one in London who would get more pleasure from finding out than Fleming.

At the beginning of December Fleming wrote to his friend enclosing a brochure on the latest Continental Bentley. 'I have examined one,' he added, 'and thoroughly applaud the whole scheme!' With as much devotion as if he were planning a car for James Bond himself, he had absorbed all the details.

The car is certainly a dream, and the only snag I can perceive is that the luggage space is restricted and you would need to use the back seats for surplus. So far as colours are concerned they have a new and very attractive one called Lugano Blue which I like very much, and I can only describe it as a darkish blue with a lot of grey in it. I rather like the idea of having this with black wings and elephants' breath grey upholstery.

He also suggested 'painting a good deal of the chrome black, perhaps just leaving the bonnet'.

Bryce agreed to everything, even to Fleming's last private fad—the removal of all the maker's insignia from the car. 'When you've paid all that amount, why go on giving Rolls-Royce free advertisement as well?'

Just now Fleming was in a curious frame of mind. Seven years later, when he came to write about Geneva in his series of articles, *Thrilling Cities*, he was to describe how 'the thwarted or affronted Swiss readily goes, as the psychologists say, "into paroxysms"'. He added, 'These states of paroxysm—the reaction of the symmetrist to chaos—are signs of the deep psychosis that results from restraint. They are the lid blowing off the pressure cooker.'

At the end of 1952 Fleming was neither thwarted nor affronted like his Swiss, but there was more than enough activity in his life to blow the lid right off the pressure cooker of his own symmetrist's existence. One career was crumbling, several new ones beckoning. The pace and variety of his life had never been so extraordinary. And in the middle of all this, just before Christmas, he received the final proofs of *Casino Royale* from his publisher and began to prepare for the next move. With barely suppressed excitement he told Bryce:

You should clear a wide space round January 16th–20th and write the dates in toothpaste on your shaving mirror. We shall be flying over and then taking the Silver Meteor on the night of the 20th to St Petersburg, Florida, where I want to inspect a live worm factory. We then fly on the 21st from Tampa to Jamaica.

CHAPTER SEVENTEEN

THE BEST-SELLER STAKES

I

THE Oyster Bar at Grand Central Station in New York is a sombre, no-nonsense, crypt of a place on the station's suburban level where men in hats tend to eat alone. It has ochre-coloured tile arches, a large oil painting of the sea-bed and very old Croat waiters. For Fleming it provided the best meal in America.

The oyster stew he liked so much is made separately for each customer in small, steam-heated steel crucibles; part of the charm of the place is to observe the off-hand expertise of the silent chefs as they slurp the oysters, the cream, the Worcester sauce, the salt, the paprika, stir them solemnly together, bring them to the boil, and allow them to simmer before decanting the rich, white-foamed, sea-scented stew into your own private bowl.

Fleming usually came here on his own for a solitary treat, as he did at the beginning of March 1953, just after he had written his second novel at Goldeneye. He had a title for it already—*Live and Let Die*—and he was particularly pleased because it had taken him twelve days fewer to write than *Casino Royale* and was already 12,000 words longer.

As usual, there were parts of chapters still to be filled in and rewritten and details to be checked, but they could wait until later. The point was that he was working now to make his dream of being a best-selling writer come true. He was following the advice Michael Arlen had given him the year before: write another book quickly before the critics have had a chance to savage the first. It was still five weeks before *Casino Royale* was due to be published in London, and here in New York he already had its successor—a book he had taken much more trouble with, planning various episodes beforehand, taking notes for certain scenes as he went along, working out the plot so that this time the real climax came right at the end instead of two-thirds of the way through.

As he sat alone under Grand Central finishing his stew and sipping his Miller's High Life beer, he had his first chance since he had left Jamaica to read through the last few chapters. He felt pleased and still slightly surprised at what he had done.

For in this new book he had gone one vital step beyond *Casino Royale*. There he had written so hurriedly, so excitedly, drawing on the past; it was a nostalgic book, and he knew that he had no chance of repeating it. But now in *Live and Let Die* he had discovered a way of making life itself fit into his dream, of seeing the present through the eyes of James Bond and then working it back into the plot in any shape he wanted.

Suddenly in this book James Bond becomes for Fleming a means of observing the world around him and of making it more glamorous, more exciting, more truly his than ever it had been before. In *Casino Royale* he had taken an event from the past, say the cipher-stealing episode in Rockefeller Center, and turned it into a more exciting might-have-been. In the new book he performed the same trick of the imagination with a succession of events from the present.

For instance, there had been his arrival with Anne at Idlewild on his way down to Jamaica aboard the big leisurely B.O.A.C. Stratocruiser. Unlike his wife he loved air travel, and he got enormous pleasure from suddenly arriving in a city in the early morning after a night's journey of 4,000 miles. He was important yet anonymous, purposeful yet free, and the most exciting moment of all came as he cleared customs, collected his luggage and stepped out towards whatever the city had to offer.

This was one of the moments he looked forward to like a schoolboy savouring the highlights of a Christmas treat in advance, and that year he had made special preparations for it. A fortnight before he left London he had cabled instructions to Clare Blanshard, the Kemsley representative in New York, and included a request for her to make sure that the Bryces sent their Rolls-Royce to Idlewild to meet the Flemings.

For once Clare Blanshard misinterpreted the mood of the master. She thought he was making a joke. He was not.

All the way across the Atlantic he had been anticipating that delicious moment of emerging from the Idlewild customs hall and finding an immaculate Rolls-Royce waiting outside to purr him and Anne off like royalty travelling incognito to the Bryce house on 74th Street. But instead of a Rolls there was only a Lincoln. True, it was that year's model, but a Rolls and a Lincoln aren't quite the same thing.

The Flemings stayed only one night in New York instead of the four days Fleming had originally planned. As they left next day and took the Silver Meteor down to St Petersburg 'to inspect a live worm factory', the mistake over the Rolls still rankled with him. He was unusually sharp to Miss Blanshard about it when he spoke to her on the telephone that morning.

But once he reached Goldeneye and entrenched himself safely behind his roll-top desk he put the whole mistake right by beginning *Live and Let Die* with that splendid arrival scene of James Bond's at Idlewild aboard the same Stratocruiser that he and Anne had flown on. He did Bond proud:

There are moments of great luxury in the life of a secret agent. There are assignments on which he is required to act the part of a very rich man; occasions when he takes refuge in good living to efface the memory of danger and the shadow of death; and times when, as was now the case, he is a guest in the territory of an allied Secret Service.

From the moment the B.O.A.C. Stratocruiser taxied up to the International Air Terminal at Idlewild, James Bond was treated like royalty.

The unmistakable relish of this opening scene sets the tone of zest and enjoyment with which Fleming wrote every subsequent chapter and makes *Live and Let Die* the most engaging of all his novels. For the dream is suddenly unfolding, and in the middle of it Fleming finds himself able to transmute his own journey out to New York and down through St Petersburg to Jamaica into an allegory of everything he found exciting. James Bond becomes a device for redeeming the past and enhancing the present, and Fleming, that uneasy, apprehensive man behind the smiling mask, finally sees a way of discovering a world that will never let him down again.

Even his own arrival in New York during the war alongside the director of Britain's Naval Intelligence had not been quite as memorable as the welcome he arranged the Central Intelligence Agency to give James Bond, with that official from the U.S. Department of Justice waiting to greet him in person, sidestepping customs and immigration, offering him a thousand dollars' spending money—'It's Communist money we took in the Schmidt-Kinanski haul'—then chauffeuring him away in an immaculate black Buick with

Dynaflow transmission to the 'best hotel in New York, the St Regis at the corner of Fifth Avenue and 55th Street'.

As a fictional character Bond remains as shadowy and unreal as he had been in *Casino Royale*. It is still almost impossible to visualize him from anything Fleming says. In both books the only time we catch a glimpse of the physical Bond is when he looks at himself in a mirror, and then we see just how closely Fleming identifies himself with his hero. The face the author describes staring back, with its 'black hair and high cheekbones' and its 'grey-blue eyes', is unmistakable. James Bond is simply Ian Fleming daydreaming in the third person.

The dream grows amusing as Fleming realizes its potentialities, and Bond is whirled up into one of Fleming's oldest and most joyous boyhood fantasies, a hunt for the buried treasure of Bloody Morgan. Fleming took trouble to get the details correct: he used to go to Spink's of St James's, the dealers in medals and rare coins, to buy silver pieces of eight as christening presents for his friends' children, and he spent an afternoon there with one of the firm's experts making notes about seventeenth-century gold coins—the coins M. tells Bond about when he is explaining just how the villainous Mr Big, the first 'great Negro criminal' in history, is financing his black underworld on behalf of the Russians. And the whole episode of Mr Big with the table that descends through the floor of the Boneyard Strip Club, the supernatural awfulness of his presence and his reliance on voodoo and black magic to keep his followers in order, is a skilful re-creation of the world of Sax Rohmer and Fu Manchu which Fleming enjoyed as a boy at Eton.

Always he had trouble with his villains, just as he did with his heroines, for the obsessive nature of his dreams meant that he had to return to the same basic characters with each book. He would try to give them new faces and different accents and surroundings, but Mr Big remains the same lumbering and obscene father-figure as Le Chiffre, and Solitaire the same insufferable bedfellow as the unfortunate Vesper Lynd.

The element of sadism continues too as strongly as ever in *Live and Let Die*, despite the objections of Anne Fleming when she read through the typescript of *Casino Royale*. Indeed, *Live and Let Die* is Fleming's nearest approach to the sadism of writers like Spillane and James Hadley Chase. Whenever Fleming was questioned about the violence in his books he would usually shrug and say that he was merely providing his fans with what they expected. In his later novels he toned down the cruelties, but here, in *Live and Let Die*, the sadism is so much part of Fleming's entire day-dream that it would be naive to see it merely as something he added for the sake of sales. On the contrary, like every-thing else in his books, the elements of cruelty seem to have been set down in total seriousness, and it is their very authenticity within this dream-world of their author's that makes them so disturbing.

In themselves the incidents of torture and sudden death in both *Casino Royale* and *Live and Let Die* would hardly attract attention when considered against the whole of our current literature of violence. Bond nearly loses his man-hood at the end of Le Chiffre's carpet-beater, the Robber is eaten alive by a shark in one of the fish tanks of the Ourobouros Worm and Bait Company (an invention based on his visit to St Petersburg), incidental gunmen are shot, strangled and blown to pieces—surely, it could be argued, such deaths and departures are part of the stock-in-trade of every writer of thrillers worth his royalties? The point is that even the Flemingesque cruelty has a flavour and a purpose of its own. It may be part of a fantasy, but it is not a fantasy suddenly dreamt up for the sake of the books.

One short scream came up out of the depths. There was a splash and then a great commotion in the water . . . Bond heard one terrible snuffling grunt as if a great pig was getting its mouth full. He knew it for the grunt that a shark makes as its hideous flat nose comes up out of the water and its sickle-shaped mouth closes on a floating carcase. He shuddered, and kicked the bolt home with his foot.

That snuffling grunt is not invented. It is the real thing. Fleming had heard it many times when he had been out baiting for shark with Cousins off the reef of Goldeneye and the big fish came in fast and made a sudden bite at the floating carcase of the dead donkey which they trailed behind them in the water.

Nor was James Bond's agony at the hands of Le Chiffre entire invention either. Fleming had recently suffered the sudden torture of an attack of kidney trouble so severe that his doctor had had to dull the pain with morphine, and in the torture scene of *Casino Royale* he is clearly embroider-ing his own agony. The clenching of the muscles, the 'in-voluntary spasm', the taut sinews and violent sweating which Bond felt at the first touch of the carpet-beater are what Fleming himself felt at the first real attack of his kidney stones. He even described the effect that Dr Beal's injection of morphine had had on him: it is when James Bond feels himself approaching a 'wonderful period of warmth and languor leading into a sort of sexual twilight where pain turned to pleasure and where hatred and fear of the torturers turned to a masochistic infatuation'.

Perhaps 'masochistic infatuation' is putting it too high, but Fleming was clearly obsessed by pain, as he was by sex and by danger. Those opponents of Bond's in each book who get shot in the mouth, those fingers which are always getting broken in the line of duty, are not there by chance. What Fleming inflicts, he feels.

And what he enjoys he feels too. The quality that makes *Live and Let Die* stand out from all the other books Fleming wrote was the zest with which he reacted to the American scene. It was as if James Bond had given him new eyes. From those earliest days when he had first begun to hear of the legendary exploits of his grandfather in the re-organization and re-financing of big American railroads, trains and particularly the great American trains had held a deep fascination for him. He loved their size, their smell, their power, their comfort as well as the sense that once you had embarked on a long journey in one you were in a private world and in a way immune from the laws of the states and cities through which you passed.

It is true to say that *Live and Let Die* is notably free from the gloom, the fears of fleshly decay and imminent disaster which creep into the later books. Here Fleming seems to have few doubts about himself or James Bond.

II

When he reached London at the end of March 1953, he brought with him a door-knocker in the shape of a brass anchor. It was for his new house in Victoria Square. Anne was already in residence; she had been back in London for nearly a fortnight, getting things straight.

Number 16 is a house with a Regency air in one of the smallest squares in London. Round the corner is the high, savagely spiked brick wall of the backside of Buckingham Palace. Victoria Station is two minutes' walk away, St James's Park and Whitehall are very near. Yet Victoria

Square still manages to remain one of those backwaters of London where the traffic and the office blocks have been kept at bay and the houses suggest the Regency elegance of Brighton. The older Fleming got the less he really liked houses—his particular talent was to turn a hotel bedroom into a casual male home from home. But he took warmly to this handsome house with its cream stucco façade and long first-floor window looking primly across the square. Built around 1837, with four floors and a basement and a lot of stairs, it gives the impression of one of those big town houses of Bloomsbury or Belgravia in microcosm. Inside, it is elegantly itself. Anne Fleming has an eye for beautiful things and curious trifles, and Fleming shared her enjoyment in them. 'I like the smell of this house,' he used to say sometimes when visiting friends. He felt the same way about his London home. The walls of the two rooms which form the drawing-room are thick with portraits, among them an Augustus John drawing of Ian Fleming done in 1942 and a portrait of Anne by Lucien Freud. This part of the house is Anne Fleming's territory. Two floors above Ian's began—up the narrow white staircase where he had his crow's-nest bedroom with his favourite dark-green striped Regency wallpaper. He crammed it with a hoard of schoolboy possessions, among them a miniature of Nelson and a silver crucifix which he had brought back from his second trip to Russia. There was a portrait of his father in the uniform of the Oxfordshire Yeomanry and another of his friend Hugo Pitman. There were, in identical thin black frames, *The Times* appreciation of his father written by Winston Churchill and the cyclostyled Order of the Day issued by the Admiralty on V.E. Day: '8.5.45. IMMEDIATE. Splice the main brace.'

The books were a strange mixture. On a shelf above his pillow the *Gesammelte Werke* of Rilke rubbed its spine against the Obelisk edition of Chester Himes's *Pinktoes*. Oswald Jacoby on *Gambling* was neighbour to a first edition of Einstein. *The Waste Land* cohabited with *Firearms Through the Ages*.

When he arrived at his new home in March there was a new book waiting for him in his bedroom—or rather six copies of it, in a brown paper parcel. They were advance copies of *Casino Royale*. Publication day had been set for April 13th. There was work to be done.

At this last-minute stage most authors are content to lean

back and allow fate and the reviewers to take charge. Fleming was more active. With engaging relish he devised a special letter to the editors of all of Lord Kemsley's provincial newspapers, and with it he sent a personally inscribed copy of the book:

Dr Jekyll has written this blatant thriller in his spare time, and it may amuse you. If you don't think it too puerile for Sheffield [or Stockport, Macclesfield, Middlesbrough, Blackburn, etc.] it would be wonderful if you would hand a copy with a pair of tongs to your reviewer.

He also took good care to make sure that Lord Kemsley had an early copy. To an outsider this might have seemed an injudicious move, for Lord Kemsley had very strict notions of propriety. But then and later he was amused by Fleming's fictions, though very properly he left the choice of a reviewer for them to the discretion of his editors or literary editors. Anyway, on April 13th, a Tuesday, James Bond made his bow, to be greeted with a round of critical applause. For Cyril Ray (writing in the *Sunday Times* under his then penname of Christopher Pym) Fleming would certainly become the best new English thriller writer since Eric Ambler, if he could give a shade more probability to his work. For the *Listener* he was a 'supersonic John Buchan'. Even the *Observer* conceded that this first thriller by their rival's Foreign Manager was a 'sort of Peter Cheyney de luxe'. The columnist Whitefriar, who writes for booksellers and publishers and journalists in W. H. Smith's *Trade News*, went one better and called him the 'Peter Cheyney of the carriage trade'. It was a compliment that gave Fleming particular glee, and thereafter Whitefriar—a strictly anonymous but very skilled newshawk of the book trade whose nutcracker chin is to be seen at all literary parties worth the name—received inscribed copies of all the Fleming books; and Fleming wasn't one of those authors who hand round complimentary copies freely.

There were private tributes as well. The one which thrilled Fleming most of all arrived at St Margaret's Bay on April 15th from the Villa Mauresque, Cap Ferrat. Somerset Maugham, using every cliché he could lay hands on, wrote:

My dear Ian,
Thank you very kindly for sending me the first of what I trust will be truly the first of a great many books. I started it last night

in bed and at half past one, when I was about half way through, I said to myself: I really must get to sleep; though what I really wanted to do was to read on till the end. I finished it an hour ago. It goes with a swing from the first page to the last and is really thrilling all through. I particularly enjoyed the battle at the casino between your hero and M. Chiffre. You really managed to get the tension to the highest possible pitch.

I'm sorry Annie hasn't arrived here. I suppose you just didn't dare to let her out of your sight.

Fleming was away in France with Anne when the letter reached Victoria Square, and it was not until the end of April (the Flemings had stayed for a few days with Somerset Maugham in the meantime) that he replied:

Dear Willie,

I have just got your letter. When I am 79 shall I waste my time reading such a book and taking the trouble to write to the author in my own hand? I pray so, but I doubt it. I am even more flattered and impressed after catching a glimpse of the empestered life you lead at Cap Ferrat, deluged with fan mail, besieged by the press, inundated with bumpf of one sort or another.

Anyway I am indeed grateful—and for the kind things you say about these leaves from a Cosh-boys Own Paper. The main thing is that you read it instead of going to sleep. That is all that some books are for and—no Balzac I, as 'Time Magazine' would say—that is all I hoped for from mine.

Is it bad literary manners to ask if my publishers may quote from your letter? Please advise me—as a *parrain*, not as a favour to me and my publishers.

The reviewers—particularly 'T.L.S.'. 'Manchester Guardian', 'Listener' and 'Telegraph' have been very kind and the book goes well. But God knows what even successful authors live on unless the films take a book. My royalties will barely keep Annie in asparagus over the Coronation.

After several pages of highly disrespectful comment on a number of distinguished writers he had recently met with Anne, Fleming ended up by asking whether Maugham's secretary Alan Searle would be very kind 'and send me an introduction to the people in New York who will get me into the *Cinéma Bleu* in N.Y. It is part of the plot of my next book but one and only he holds the platinum key.'

Maugham was on his travels by now, and his reply came from the Park Hotel on Avaz-Pasa in Istanbul. It was very much to the point. After telling Fleming graciously that he wrote nearly as good a letter as Anne, 'whom I regard as the Madame de Sévigné of our day,' he went on:

No, please don't use what I said about your book to advertise it. Not that I didn't mean what I said, but that I am asked all the time to write something that can be used in such a way to help some book or other and have always refused it. It is obviously difficult to do that kind of thing for one person and not for another. I would not do it even for the author of the Book of Genesis.

After this cool refusal the only consolation Maugham could offer Fleming was to say that Alan Searle had promised to get in touch with his friends in New York who knew all about *cinéma bleu*. Searle said it would have a bad effect on Fleming's morals—Maugham didn't really know what it was—and Searle added that he had never been the same man since. And in a postscript Maugham referred unkindly to the announcement Fleming had just put in *The Times* about his change of address. 'I saw the "ad" in the "Times" about 16 Victoria Square. Do you take in P.G.s?'

Maugham's refusal was a relatively minor setback. A more serious disappointment was that despite the critical success scored by *Casino Royale* it showed no sign of bringing in even a fraction of that best-seller income which Fleming had dreamed of.

The first printing of 4,750 copies had sold out by late May, earning him £218 19s. 7d. From the publisher's standpoint it was—for a first novel—highly encouraging. From Fleming's it was almost an insult, and on May 15th he was writing a note to Jonathan Cape himself asking for higher royalties on his next book.

To add to his discontent, the first reactions of American publishers to *Casino Royale* were decidedly dim. He had shown an advance copy to his devoted admirer Elsa Maxwell, and she had wondered whether the story really had sufficient pace and action for the U.S.—'Quicken up the beginning for America,' she advised him.

He sent it as it was, and three leading U.S. publishers (unlike William Plomer and Daniel George) promptly turned down one of the biggest best-sellers of our time in swift succession. Doubleday, who had first refusal, didn't like it and returned it to Fleming's agent without any particular explanation. It was passed on to Norton. Back it came, this time with the objection that this first James Bond book was a 'very English cross between early Ambler and Mickey Spillane, which would be all right except that parts of the story don't seem to us to hold together and the result

241

is a lack of belief throughout'. Knopf had next crack at it. Again it bounced back, this time on the grounds that 'its excesses outweigh its readability' and that it had too much 'melodrama and blood and gore'.

All this was disappointing, but Fleming continued to feed his dream of making a fortune out of his books, no matter if the receipts so far wouldn't keep Anne in Coronation asparagus. He was immensely excited by the reviews, and even in his dealings with his lantern-jawed publisher nothing could really stifle his exuberance:

This thriller business is a fly-by-night affair—a light-weight read with a probable ceiling of around ten thousand copies. Whether this can be done with your servant's works remains to be seen, but these astonishingly handsome reviews do, I think, weigh the odds sufficiently in our favour to have a go for the best-seller stakes.

The first reward in the best-seller stakes came fairly quickly. By July Fleming was writing gleefully to his friend Philip Brownrigg that he had 'just got a contract for a second book with royalties as good as Hemingway's, which should make Hemingway blush with pleasure'. But a more important effect of the best-seller stakes was the pressure they now began to exert on Fleming himself; for this point marks a stage in the strange story of how James Bond gained ascendancy over the man who created him.

Until now Fleming's world of fantasies had been a secret world—private, undercover, faintly reprehensible; in those few weeks of self-revelation at Goldeneye the year before it had amused him to put some of them down on paper; in a mood of longing for success he had made what he had written public; and instead of being laughed at, instead of being publicly reprimanded, he found himself being compared with John Buchan and Eric Ambler and Peter Cheyney. Everyone seemed to enjoy his inventions. Nobody sniggered. Nobody who mattered complained. With the publication of *Casino Royale* the secret life of Ian Fleming received the stamp of public approval.

But for Fleming, exciting though all this was, there was one small catch. The fantasies behind James Bond were *his* fantasies. They were part of him. If the books were to continue, his own fantasy life would have to continue; not merely continue either, but expand, proliferate, become ever more extreme if it was to feed the novels and satisfy that public which he now had reason to believe was hungry for his novels.

It was only a very small catch, and probably for Fleming in that early successful summer just after his forty-fifth birthday it didn't seem a catch at all.

It is now that he consciously begins to observe himself to find out how his hero would react, and starts to plan his life to provide the material and the sensations James Bond requires; the small blue notebooks for Fleming's own observations and reactions make their appearance; and Fleming begins to understand that if James Bond is to keep going Ian Fleming must somehow keep up with him. On one side was Victoria Square, with its dinner-parties and its devoted court of writers and politicians and its clever conversation sparkling along into the small hours. On the other lay the life of the man of action he never really was, with the speed, the physical exertion, the emotional unconcern, everything which James Bond from now on would demand of him. The character did not make his creator any the easier to live with; it is clear that the tempo of Fleming's life was changing.

The first signs of this came with a series of articles Fleming undertook during 1953 on behalf of the *Sunday Times*. Undoubtedly he embarked on them partly to rebuild as a journalist the prestige he had lost as Foreign Manager. Yet the ideas behind the three big stories he did for the newspaper in this year were all his own, and it is fascinating to watch how each in its own way turned into a quest for the world of James Bond. The first began in April. Just as *Casino Royale* was being published and Fleming was putting the finishing touches to his account of the underwater hunt for the treasure of Bloody Morgan in *Live and Let Die*, he and Anne and the 2½-litre Riley drove off to the South of France to watch an underwater treasure hunt for an even older ship than Sir Henry Morgan's. Just off the harbour of Marseilles, preserved in a thick layer of mud, lay the wreck of a Graeco-Roman galley which foundered in a storm in 250 B.C. Commandant Cousteau, doyen of underwater explorers and archaeologists, had just started salvage work with his boat the *Calypso*, and Fleming, on behalf of Kemsley Newspapers, had secured exclusive rights to describe the discoveries.

Jacques Cousteau, that lean, vital, ex-gunnery officer of the French Navy, with his cool efficiency and panda-ringed

Dear Sir / or Madam,
Thank you very much for your
communications. I plead guilty to making mistakes
in all my books & I regret them. In extenuation
I can only say that William Shakespeare made gross
errors in all his (C) works. & Jane Austen, in
——, had cherry trees flowering in September, ...

Waving away complaints. In Scott's Restaurant Fleming seized a
menu-card and on the back of it wrote out for Admiral Godfrey
an outline of what to say if readers accused him of making
mistakes in his naval memoirs

eyes, had a very special appeal for Ian Fleming. Cousteau
was his sort of hero—'this man,' he wrote, 'who has so much
of the quality of wonder in him and so little concern for
the public glare'. And like all Fleming's real-life heroes
Cousteau possessed several of those vital qualities which
Fleming lacked but desired. He was a man of action devoted
to a cause with a whole-heartedness which Fleming had
never really succeeded in bringing to anything. He was an
expert and something of a scholar. He was self-sufficient.

When Fleming joined Cousteau aboard the *Calypso* he
seems to have been overcome by one of those fits of sudden
enthusiasm to which he was always engagingly prone. The
danger, the beauty, the unexpectedness, the constant sur-
prises of this treasure hunt with history appealed to just
those romantic schoolboy instincts which he had been
putting into *Live and Let Die*; in one letter he wrote he
said that he was 'aiming to become *the* journalist of the
underwater world'.

Certainly, in one way and another, he did a great deal to
popularize in Britain the sport of underwater exploration
and skin diving. Yet he never became the specialist of the
silent world. A fortnight on the *Calypso* probably gave him
enough experience of the rough end of underwater exploration to last him a lifetime.

The facts and bread-and-butter details of Cousteau's
adventure seemed to bore him. He needed to be able to see
these things as part of one of his own dreams, as he
succeeded in doing when he described the winching-up from

the sea-bed of the big net enmeshing the latest finds from the wreck.

We all hurled to the dripping muddy pile of gifts like children unleashed on a Christmas tree, carrying anything strange or new in triumph to the archaeologists, sorting, cleaning, panting under the weight of the objects that under the sea the divers had lifted so easily, quickly clearing the container so that it could go down again to this wonderful bargain basement whose doors had been thrown open to us by Cousteau.

'I cannot describe the romance and excitement of the scene better,' said Fleming, laying all his enthusiasms firmly on the table, 'than to say that it contained at the same time elements from "King Solomon's Mines", "Treasure Island" and "The Swiss Family Robinson".'

It was later, in his extended pieces of reportage for *The Diamond Smugglers* or *Thrilling Cities*, that Fleming discovered that his real gift as a reporter lay in his ability to see certain dangerous or exotic or exciting situations through the eyes of James Bond. Much the most revealing as well as the most readable part of his three articles on the Cousteau expedition is the brief description of how he attempted to dive down to the wreck on his own:

I put on 30 lb of equipment and went over the side, and looked down into limitless grey depths and tried to remember to breathe quietly through the aqualung. I swam slowly down and drifted with my arms round the broad tubes of the suction pump. It rattled and shook against me with the upward jet of stones and broken pottery. I looked up at the distant hull of the ship and at the idle screw. The surface of the sea was a sheet of mercury, illuminated in one spot, like a star sapphire, by the sun.

Here Fleming was doing what he could do best—describing his own sensations, isolated in a world of novelty and beauty and potential danger. He was alone now, just as the hero of his books is always alone, and if he had later changed the 'I' to 'Bond' this passage could have fitted quite naturally into any of the novels.

But normally he could write like this only when he had James Bond to hide behind, for Bond was a mask which this anxious romantic would slip on when he wanted to elaborate one of his private fantasies or put his delinquent schoolboy's view of the world into a form which was immune both to ridicule and criticism.

As he almost certainly intended when he first planned this assignment with Cousteau, it was not only the *Sunday Times* which benefited. Fleming's experience with the expedition, and particularly the underwater swimming, gave him a chance to add to the description of Bond's underwater swim to Mr Big's ship, the *Secatur*, in the manuscript of *Live and Let Die* which was awaiting his final corrections when he got back to Victoria Square. When he left the *Calypso* and Marseilles he and Anne drove along the coast road to the big aquarium at Monte Carlo, where he noted some of the final details for his description of the aquarium in the same novel along with the names of the rare fish which Mr Big's organization used as a front for their gold smuggling.

By the end of April Ian and Anne Fleming and the Riley were back home, and during the following months he finished the final draft of his second novel and Cape accepted it, giving him his new contract with its royalties (but not, of course, its advance on royalties) equal to Hemingway's. At the same time he heard that Macmillan, the fourth American firm to see *Casino Royale*, had bought the novel for publication early in the following year. He was pleased but distracted: the Coronation of Queen Elizabeth II was near and Anne was preparing to enjoy the occasion.

III

At the beginning of June he wrote to Elsa Maxwell, who was staying at the Ritz in Paris, describing his wife's latest social adventures with that amused irony he always adopted when writing about her to this devoted mutual friend:

I have only just managed to stop Anne turning our house into a sort of vespasian for all our friends, but she has devised other tortures for me, including a boating expedition in the evening and then the French Embassy from midnight until breakfast the next day. Anne likes her parties to be in the St Petersburg tradition—come for lunch and stay for a month.

He rather enjoyed presenting himself as a sort of simple-minded martyr on the pyre of his wife's burning sociability. It was a joke, an act, with a central grain of truth. But many of Anne's friends were his friends, and his life was never seriously disorganized by the social fireworks at their London home. In any case he had his bridge and his golf and his precious week-ends with Anne at their other home at St Margaret's Bay.

Yet James Bond was waiting for him now with insistent demands on his time and energy. No sooner was he back from the Cousteau expedition than he was planning his next venture—another search for hidden treasure, this time on land.

The *Sunday Times* published an appeal which Fleming had written asking readers to send in tales of buried treasure; nothing would be considered too far-fetched, and the newspaper promised to investigate the most likely tale it received. As a labour of love Fleming gave himself the task of reading through all the replies and working out really up-to-date methods of treasure detection. Once again he was back on the beach at St Ives, a boy looking for untold riches.

Fleming set about discovering the technical hazards of treasure hunting. He went along to the Royal School of Mines to inquire about the latest methods of metal detection; Siebe Gorman, the diving experts, demonstrated some of the problems of finding underwater treasure; he spent an afternoon with an inspector of the Special Branch at Scotland Yard making notes on the places where people hide their valuables. All this ingenious information-tapping was characteristic of him. As his books show, he had a supreme instinct for knowing where to find the facts along with a remarkable talent for making experts reveal them. On this occasion his most practical support came from the Royal Engineers. They were testing out various new mine-detectors at the time, and one or two highly placed contacts from his wartime days told him that the Sappers would be delighted to help if it gave them a chance to experiment in an enclosed area.

He went on wading about in the hundreds of letters received by the *Sunday Times*, and some of his colleagues still recall his uproarious enjoyment of the more crackpot suggestions. In the end, rejecting sunken Armada galleons and Viking hoards in the Fens, he picked on Creke Abbey in Norfolk, where tradition maintained that the monks had buried a great cache of gold and silver to keep it from the hands of Henry VIII's assessors. The reasons he advanced for choosing the Abbey were interesting: it was partly 'because of its spectral name' and partly because Creke Abbey was near Burnham Thorpe, birthplace of his great hero, Nelson.

There was a pause before he could embark on the hunt: he had to make one of his periodic visits to the *Sunday Times* office in New York. While he was there he had a meeting with Ivar Bryce and Ernest Cuneo about the future of the

North American Newspaper Alliance. He still set great hopes on N.A.N.A. He had persuaded Lord Kemsley to give it office space in Kemsley House in return for first call on its services, and he was bringing all his considerable flair to building it up.

All his New York friends were there, and he found they showed their excitement at the success of *Casino Royale* without the reservations which he detected among his friends in London. It was this spontaneity which made him feel more at ease here than in any other city. Sir William Stephenson, as influential as ever, had arranged for copies of *Casino Royale* to be introduced into the library of the Senate, and already he was carrying on a discreet promotion campaign of his own for the book before its appearance in the following January. Iva Patcevitch, President of Condé Nast, publishers of *Vogue*, was delighted with his copy of the book, which was inscribed—to commemorate long discussions at Goldeneye on spies and spying—'To Pat, who was the model, Ian'. Then at Macmillan's, his newly found American publishers, Fleming met Al Hart, who was to act as editor for his first six books in the United States and become his crony, confidant, and drinking companion on all his subsequent visits to New York. Once again he stayed at the Bryces' house on 74th Street, and at dinner there and afterwards at bridge he found that he was already what he could never hope to be in his own home—a celebrity.

'There was', said Roald Dahl, the short-story writer, who met him there several times, 'a great red glow when Ian came into the room.' Many very different people felt this sense of singular attraction about Fleming long before he became well known, and here in Bryce's house he was always at the top of his form.

It was the end of June before he was back in London again, ready to pursue the treasure of Creke Abbey with a three-man team from the Royal Engineers. It was the sort of half-serious schoolboy expedition he was always game for, and he was thrilled by the Army's latest electronic mine-detector. For the next three days the four of them went methodically over the site of the old Chapter House, the Abbot's Lodging, the Cloister and the old Abbey itself. Every time the mine-detector buzzed they marked the spot with a large piece of paper, returning to dig when they had covered the whole area.

'In two days,' wrote Fleming, 'we dug up about thirty nails

of different sizes, one frying pan, one mole-trap, one oil drum and about a hundredweight of miscellaneous scrap iron. Our jokes about twelfth-century sardine tins ceased at an early stage.'

Finally, they gave it all up as a bad job and left Creke Abbey as secure in its secrets as it had been for the past four hundred years.

He was light-hearted enough about it all in the *Sunday Times*, yet far from light-hearted about his future in Kemsley House. Cold winds were blowing along its dun-coloured corridors, and Fleming's Foreign Department was feeling the draught. The Editorial Director of the group and Lord Kemsley's star protégé, Denis Hamilton (today editor of the *Sunday Times*), had been one of the first to recognize the brilliance of Fleming as a special reporter and was anxious for him to do more writing. But Fleming had Bond to think of and wasn't willing to take on indiscriminate assignments. Besides, he was not prepared to see the Mercury Service sink without his putting up a fight for it—his pride was understandably involved. Just after the treasure hunt he was telling Bryce about 'swingeing economies being made throughout Kemsley House from which the Foreign Department has not been spared . . . the place has been whistling with positively icy winds.'

It was partly to take himself out of the cold and partly to transport himself into the warm, real-life world of James Bond that he rapidly set about organizing his next trip for the *Sunday Times*. One can only admire the coolness with which he did it. All the talk at Kemsley House was of economy and retrenchment. His Foreign Service was being practically washed away from under him. He knew that his two months' annual holiday and his recent jaunt to New York had been under fire, and Lord Kemsley had told him that he would like to see more of him in the office during the next few months. Fleming calmly went his own way.

This time he wanted to descend not into the depths of the sea but into the bowels of the earth. The 1940s and 1950s were one of the great periods of cave exploration in France, and the excitement generated by the accidental discovery of the wonders of Lascaux had produced a new breed of French speleologists. In their way they were not unlike the young men who worked with Cousteau and who had such an appeal for Fleming, with their dedication, their toughness, their scientific curiosity, and their willingness to expose themselves to the extremest hazards of nature.

They were a natural quarry for Fleming in his new quest for action, and as a representative of the *Sunday Times* he had no difficulty in getting himself accredited to the current exploration led by the doyen of French speleologists, Norbert Casteret, who by now has spent fifty years in subterranean research and investigated more than 1,200 caverns, potholes and rivers. In the early 1950s France, still tottering towards normality after the defeat and frustration of the war, felt a desperate need for heroes. Cousteau was an authentic specimen, and so was Casteret, the good-looking archaeologist whose narrowed eyes had peered at such unbelievable caverns of limestone and crystal. Now he had returned to the Gouffre Pierre Saint-Martin, on the Franco-Spanish frontier, where his companion Marcel Loubens had been killed when his safety harness broke more than a thousand feet underground.

Fleming was excited at the prospect of meeting Casteret and his wife Maude, yet there were other things to do on this trip to France:

We shall press on through the Massif Central which I have never yet been able to find on a map, to the painted caves of Lascaux, stopping perhaps to buy an Aubusson at Aubusson, and then on to the foot of the Pyrenees. When I get to a place called Pierre St Martin I get lowered on a rope through a small hole just about 4,000 feet down to the foundations of the Pyrenees just about opposite where Anne will be sitting sobbing into her *eau de vie de framboise* outside some foothill inn . . . I shall spend the next ten days or so going up and down on the rope.

After this, just to make the most of a good thing, the Flemings planned to visit Somerset Maugham at Cap Ferrat. On August 10th the Riley was flown by air ferry from Lydd to Le Touquet and the new adventure began.

Ever since he was nineteen and owned the old Standard that met its doom on the light railway, Fleming had loved long rapid drives across the continent of Europe. 'It was,' says Anne, 'always a great moment when we had got the car through customs at Le Touquet, lunched at the airport restaurant, and were free to go. I think Ian was probably happier then than at any other moment of his life.'

He loved the kilometres 'clicking past like the leaves of a book', the 'delicious, always new sights and smells of abroad' and, above all, as he wrote in *Thrilling Cities*, the 'sense of achievement, of a task completed when each target is reached without accident, on time and with the car still running sweetly. There is the sensation that one has done a hard and meritorious day's work'—and he added, with a sly, retrospective dig at Anne, 'Few women understand this —perhaps, poor beasts, because they have been only passengers.' But there was more even than the sense of accomplishment to account for his passion for these long journeys across Europe: by driving well and fast and reaching his destination safely his precious symmetry was maintained, his passion for order reasserted over the disorder and antagonism of inanimate things, over nature and chaos and boredom.

The Riley took the Flemings sweetly to the Pyrenees, to the icy black river and the claustrophobic underground world of the great cave of St Martin, now known to be the second deepest cave in the world. Even more than with the Cousteau expedition or the treasure hunt at Creke Abbey, the exploration had all the elements of excitement and danger that appealed to Fleming—the small entry to the cave, high in the mountains, leading immediately to a dangerous vertical shaft of more than a thousand feet, the vast underground river, the gruesome and all too easily imagined manner of death if anything went wrong, as it had with Marcel Loubens in 1951.

Yet he was to be severely disappointed in one respect. He had seen himself 'going up and down on the rope'. No such risk was permitted him. There was nothing for him to do but wait at the cave's entrance while the explorers descended with infinite slowness. Once again he was the man who watched and waited and experienced vicariously. After a few hurried conversations with Casteret and Georges Lépineux, who discovered the great pothole, Fleming described the hazards and splendour of this underground world with an intensity all the greater because he knew he would never see it for himself.

The chief recent discovery—the bottom was not reached until 1962—was the vast Verna cave, and Fleming made it sound like something from the pages of Jules Verne:

It is domed. The walls and floors are straight and smooth but the floor is encumbered here and there by uneasily balanced towers of stone blocks, each as big as a cottage, which soar up into the darkness. Through the floor runs the great black river, swift and deep and silent. The air is pure and damp with a temperature of four degrees centigrade. The water temperature is three degrees centigrade and it runs at half a cubic metre a second.

There was also the macabre circumstance that the body of the dead Loubens was still inside the mountain. This, too, fascinated Fleming:

It may not be buried or cremated. It must remain under its pile of boulders perfectly preserved in this frigid air, surmounted by the disintegrating cross of phosphorescent paper that has long since ceased to shine and the epitaph cut into the rock face: *Ici Marcel Loubens a vécu les jours derniers de sa vie courageuse*—a perpetual warning to the explorers who go down the jagged shaft that rock is stronger than man.

By August 21st the last of Casteret's party had come safely to the surface and Fleming was free to leave 'this gloomy antechamber of Hell'. Soon he and Anne were driving, for the second year running, to the Villa Mauresque.

To the Flemings Somerset Maugham was the perfect host. Maugham adored Anne and unlike some of her other admirers valued the husband, too. (The refused testimonial to *Casino Royale* was never mentioned between them.) No one else was staying in the house apart from Alan Searle. They swam in the pool, they wandered about the gardens, they enjoyed Maugham's food and his conversation and his pictures. It was a peaceful interlude. Then London again, early in September 1953, with James Bond and his creator drawing closer than ever before.

The ordered background to Fleming's life remained much the same: bridge at Boodle's or the Portland Club, Anne's St Petersburg entertaining at Victoria Square, the lunches— generally with a male friend—at the Etoile or the window table on the first floor of Scott's, the sad war of attrition at Kemsley House, the long golfing week-ends at Sandwich. It was a background which Fleming decided to draw on here and there for James Bond's next adventure; and the blue Biro went to work in the notebook. *Moonraker* was in the making.

Fleming's favourite corner of England, 'where Caesar had first landed two thousand years before', was ransacked for the book—Kingsdown, where Drax builds his rocket on the cliffs near Deal, 'the two-mile stretch of shingle that runs at low tide beneath the towering cliffs to St Margaret's Bay', and the Café Royal in Dover, which was one of Fleming's own favourite haunts and where Bond went to eat the inevitable plate of 'scrambled eggs and bacon and plenty of coffee with it'.

That autumn, as he began preparation for the book he was to write the following January at Goldeneye, Fleming began to share his London life with Bond too. Blades Club bears traces not only of White's Club, of which Fleming was a member from 1936 to 1940, but of Boodle's and the Portland as well. He also shared with his hero the same favourite restaurant table in London, 'the right-hand corner table for two on the first floor' of Scott's, where Bond sits at the beginning of Chapter 19 of *Moonraker*, gazing at the traffic down the Haymarket, drinking his second vodka dry martini brought by Baker the head waiter, and awaiting the arrival of the overdue Gala Brand. Baker, who called in Scotland Yard when Fleming took the German submarine officers to Scott's, is retired now and lives with his daughter near Tunbridge Wells. He remembers how particular the Commander always was about that large twist of lemon peel in the vodka martini and how he would always call the window table on the first floor the 'honeymoon table'. It was a honeymoon of a sort. That autumn, as Fleming sat there with his character walking about in his head, or drove with his spirit down the A20 towards Dover and St Margaret's Bay, or strolled with him to Kingsdown, the final stage of his mortal involvement with James Bond really began.

In the first novel they had discovered each other almost by accident. In the second Fleming still had certain reservations about how much he could rely on him. But with *Moonraker* the conscious self-identification is almost complete, and for the first time he uses Bond as a deliberate way of escaping from everyday life. Bond is 'saturnine', a word which many women had used of Fleming before the war, and Bond feels, as Fleming always did of himself, 'that there was something alien and un-English about him'. More important, the creator loads the character with his own mental and physical discomforts, and Bond is sent off like some bellicose scapegoat to do symbolic battle on behalf of Fleming. For the defeat of Sir Hugo Drax is also a vicarious defeat of the depressing facts of Fleming's own middle age.

It was only two or three times a year that an assignment came along requiring his particular abilities. For the rest of the year he had the duties of an easy-going senior civil servant—elastic office hours from around ten to six; lunch, generally in the canteen; evenings spent playing cards in the company of a few close friends, or at Crockford's: or making love, with rather cold passion, to one of three similarly disposed married women; week-ends playing golf for high stakes at one of the clubs near London.

Fleming never risked lunch at the Kemsley House canteen. He used Boodle's and the Portland Club, not Crockford's, for bridge. Since his marriage he seems to have had little time for the wives of other men. Otherwise the description of Bond's daily life could be a description of his own. In 1953, just like Bond, he had been able to dodge the daily tedium with three assignments—to Marseilles, to Creke Abbey, and to the great cave of St Martin.

Moonraker was the most serious novel Fleming had written so far. Here the James Bond books begin to reveal themselves as the undercover autobiography of Ian Fleming.

IV

Then in the late autumn of 1953 Fleming confided to a few of his intimate friends that his life as peripatetic adventure writer for the *Sunday Times* was over: those three annual assignments which James Bond relied on to brighten the tedium of office routine were not to be repeated. Fleming had just been offered—and felt bound to accept—the position of Atticus on the *Sunday Times*.

It might have been worse. Atticus was an insufferable old bore, a pseudonymous weekly column for peddling the stale left-overs of smoking-room gossip and high-table reminiscence. But it *was* an honour of a sort to be offered it. In its day it had been written by genuine writers like John Buchan, and inside the office—and out of it for that matter— it still trailed wisps and tatters of prestige. Undeniably, too, it carried more guns than the column which Peter Fleming wrote in the *Spectator* under the pen-name of Strix. Perhaps something could be done with it.

So Fleming accepted the job—with conditions. From the beginning of his association with the *Sunday Times* he had insisted, very properly, on anything he wrote for it being immune from editing or interference; it was a matter on which he had strong feelings and which brought him for once, somewhat to his discomfort, into agreement with Randolph Churchill, who occasionally dined at Victoria Square and with whom Fleming sometimes had a bellowing match. Allied to this was his advocacy of more candour in the paper, more controversy, more vigorous praise or blame —and he usually wanted blame—of public figures. Since those days the *Sunday Times* has gone far and soared high, as Fleming acknowledged to Denis Hamilton before he died. But in the early 1950s the pall of genteel discretion which hung over certain areas of it, allied to the invincible predictability and 'soundness' of its political opinions, gave Fleming exquisite discomfort. He therefore stipulated for freedom in the Atticus column, even to the extent of being allowed to mention Mr Cecil King of the *Daily Mirror* or any other person about whom Lord Kemsley, as editor-in-chief, happened to be less than enthusiastic. And, as vehement and obstinate as ever in conveying his views to the old autocrat, he won his point.

The idea of writing behind a veil of transparent anonymity appealed to Fleming here just as it did in his books, and he planned to make the most of it. As with his books he wrote his own blurb, and it bore his own stamp of efficiency and amusing effrontery:

ATTICUS: Many distinguished men—politicians, authors, journalists—have worn the secret mantle of Atticus, and over the years many other famous names have, mistakenly, been linked with his.

Today the cloak of anonymity has fallen upon another distinguished pair of shoulders, and beneath a title of his own choosing the new Atticus makes his debut on page 3 in PEOPLE AND THINGS.

In many ways Fleming was almost totally unfitted to become a successful gossip columnist. He hated parties, he loathed Society, he was not really interested in people, as a general thing he despised gossip. All the same, his period as a columnist on the *Sunday Times* was curiously successful. The stories from the smoking-rooms and the high tables died overnight. The phrase 'my young friend tells me' took a dive and never reappeared. At last old Atticus, his secret mantle flapping in the wind, jumped feet first into the twentieth century.

Fleming's success as a columnist derived in a way from one of the sources of his success as a writer of thrillers. He was one of those naturally autobiographical writers who are unable to type a paragraph without colouring it with their own personality; and as with James Bond, the by-line Atticus left him free to reveal himself without his having to worry about ridicule or direct personal criticism.

In the week following the appearance of his first piece he told Bryce: 'All the intelligentsia seem to have detected my scaly hand in Atticus, and the enemies among them have privately suggested to Anne that I should call myself "Attila" which I assume to be some sort of a joke. Only one communication was received as a result of my first effort: a postcard from Porthcawl saying, "A change for the worse".'

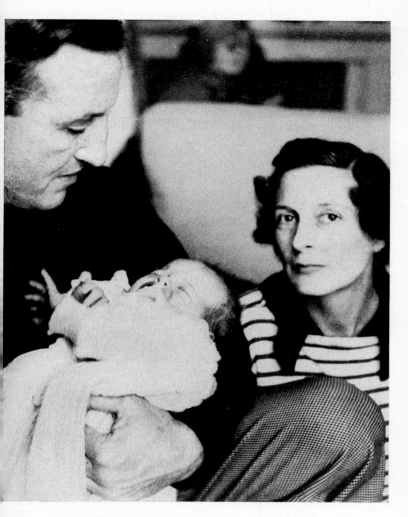

The baby is the Flemings' son Caspar

Fleming's last country home: Sevenhampton Place, Highworth.
(*Below*) His bedroom at his London home at 16 Victoria Square.
The design on the bedspread is of Victoria Regina

CHAPTER EIGHTEEN

THE TEN BEST NOVELS IN THE WORLD

I

ELSA MAXWELL wrote on March 15th, 1954, to the readers of her syndicated newspaper column 'Elsa's Log':

And speaking of books, Ian and Anne Fleming arrived for two days from Jamaica on their way to London and dined with me the other night. Anne was married to Esmond Rothermere. She is a beautiful woman and very happy with Ian, who is one of Lord Kemsley's editors on the London *Sunday Times* etc. Ian's book, coming out over here on March 23rd, is called *Casino Royale* and is one of the most breath-taking thrillers I have ever read. Don't miss it.

Fleming must have been at his best at dinner that night with Elsa Maxwell at the Waldorf Astoria—bronzed with nearly two months of Jamaican sun, happy at being back in New York again, relaxed with the rare sense of accomplishment which he allowed himself on the completion of another book. He was relieved to find that the writing had been as effortless as ever; and now that yet another novel was behind him he was free from Bond for a bit.

There were other things to think of now, other things to savour. There was Miss Maxwell, for instance, as full of goodwill and good stories as ever, insisting so emphatically over dinner how much she had enjoyed *Casino Royale* and prophesying great success for it. This public and private praise of the novel gratified him: many of the Flemings' influential American friends still thought of him as little more than the good-looking, very English ex-naval officer who happened to have married Anne Rothermere.

Once *Casino Royale* was securely in Scribner's window and on the American best-seller lists there would be no more of that, and he brazenly set about making sure that it received attention. Cuneo was asked 'to blackmail Winchell into sounding a tucket about it on the radio or in his column'. Roald Dahl was told, 'If you get a chance of putting in a word with the TV tycoons for "Casino" I shall be very grateful. Money is despicable stuff but it buys Renoirs.'

And to Iva Patcevitch he promised, 'If you can possibly give it a shove in "Vogue" or elsewhere, Anne and I will allow you to play Canasta against us, which should be ample reward.'

With most authors this sort of backstage blackmail is the surest way to lose friends. Fleming was so open and unabashed, however, that his influential friends would have had to be profoundly humourless to have taken real offence. 'You will soon be fed up with this book as I have sent copies round to all our friends asking them to give it a hand in America, which is a very bare-faced way to go on,' he blithely informed Margaret Case. 'I know Harry Luce won't be bothered with it, or Clare, but if you could somehow prevail upon "Time" to give it a review you would be an angel.'

The Flemings arrived home from New York on March 15th. Upstairs Fleming found early copies of *Live and Let Die* awaiting him—publication day was April 8th. Because of the books and the way he chose to write them, the shape of his life seemed now to be more firmly established than ever. Spring and summer were for the *Sunday Times*, and in early autumn it was time for James Bond: the small notebooks appeared, plots were fashioned or discarded then finally adopted. Everything was made ready for the impending eight weeks at Goldeneye. This annual and enjoyable routine was to rule his life from now on, and he followed it until his death.

Moonraker, though, might easily have been his last book, and the ten James Bond novels that followed really owe their existence to the remarkable way his life and his career as a writer happened to interlock at this point. For he was not one of those natural writers who can produce their books regardless of time or place or circumstance. Just as he had needed the freak conditions of Goldeneye in 1952 to get him started at all, so his writing was dependent now on the tightly patterned routine which he had grown used to, with all its pressures and discontents, its odd sources of excitement and fresh material.

If the North American Newspaper Alliance and *Casino Royale* had brought him the immediate financial success he had banked on, it seems unlikely that he would have gone on writing a book a year regularly for the rest of his life, even if he was doing it for enjoyment and reputation as well as for money; and if, as seemed not impossible nine months earlier, his career with Lord Kemsley had come to an abrupt halt, it is hard to think that any other employer would have been tolerant enough to continue that vital salary of £5,000 a year along with that still more vital two months' holiday at Goldeneye. Fleming's readers, not to speak of his film audience, owe more than they know to the unconscious backing of Viscount Kemsley.

The year 1954 was to be a key one for Fleming, for during it his routine passed out of jeopardy. He seems to have accepted once and for all that Bryce and N.A.N.A. were never going to offer him a viable alternative to Lord Kemsley and Kemsley Newspapers. Indeed, the end of March saw him writing Ivar Bryce an untypically sharp note on the subject. 'It seems to me that I have put forward a lot of excellent ideas and a constant stream of offerings, none of which have been favoured on the grounds that they cost a few dollars. Even the accreditation of all my correspondents to N.A.N.A. has been fraught for me with nothing but brickbats.'

Bryce replied at once with a cooling letter. Fleming wrote back that it 'has greatly cheered me and straightened out a number of wrinkles in the prune that I use for a heart. I take everything back,' he added, 'and am perfectly happy with the *status quo* so long as you are.'

But it was the meagre *status quo* and not the land of opportunity he had hoped for when he first became N.A.N.A.'s European Vice-President. Nevertheless, he had one great compensation. The horizon was clearing in Gray's Inn Road, and soon he was to recapture his old influence; there were more important things for him to do in Kemsley House than lament the shrunken state of the Mercury Service.

There are times when the ebb and flow of fortune within a great newspaper seems to follow the veiled but perpetually exciting theory of Buddhist theology. As the wheel of Karma turns, anything is possible; he who dies a dung beetle is reincarnated a king, the harlot becomes a hook-worm, the cockatoo a cabinet minister. So at Kemsley House as Fleming's prestige as Foreign Manager waned he took on a new influence as one of the key figures of the *Sunday Times*. It was a period when the paper, hard-pressed by the *Observer,* was experimenting and beginning to tap the possibilities of a wider, younger readership. Fleming was the sort of ideas man it needed at such a moment, and the sort of writer too.

He returned from Jamaica to two resounding successes. The first occurred in April, when *Live and Let Die* received reviews which showed that in the eyes of the critics at least Fleming had more than lived up to the promise of *Casino Royale*. He had cleared the dangerous hurdle of his second book, and already he could sense that if only he could keep going, writing novel after novel, James Bond might become as famous a character as Maigret or Sherlock Holmes or Poirot or Bulldog Drummond. As he wrote to Bryce, a few days after the book was published, ' "Live and Let Die" has the wind under its tail here, and Annie is horrified that I may be becoming famous.' His second success dramatically reinforced his position on the *Sunday Times*—it was the sort of coup anxious newspaper executives dream of and one he stumbled on almost by chance.

It began when Somerset Maugham wrote to Anne, soon after the Flemings had returned from Goldeneye, explaining that he was unlikely to be in London for several months because he was finally getting down to a book he had been intending to write for years—a critical and biographical account of the ten best novels of the world and their authors. Fleming was interested at once. As he wrote later:

From the moment on one Sunday night in April that the secret of Mr Maugham's new book was revealed to me, I was convinced that it contained a wonderful new series for the 'Sunday Times'. This was a personal view. I am an avid reader of all that Mr Maugham writes, and I longed to see the extremely sharp edge of his mind applied to the arguments for and against the first ten novelists in the history of literature and to learn his choice.

My first step on Monday morning was to telephone the Literary Editor, Mr Leonard Russell, and I was encouraged by the words of sceptical interest which I knew were his way of expressing professional enthusiasm.

Lord Kemsley, the Editor-in-Chief, was emphatic: 'We'll simply have to find space for it,' he said. 'See if you can persuade him.'

I telephoned Mr Maugham: 'I wouldn't think of it,' came back the dry, amused voice. 'But come down by all means and I'll put you up.'

Fleming arrived at the Villa Mauresque just before lunch. His host came out of the house to greet him, and instead of going indoors they sat in the sunlight beneath the cypresses at the end of the terrace. Maugham was at his most courteous but detached, pretending to be amused by all the fuss. He insisted that he had spoken his last word about the book on the telephone and that he had invited Fleming only for the pleasure of hearing the latest London gossip and because it would give him a short holiday at Lord Kemsley's expense. Fleming laughed but said that he had never been more serious about anything in his life.

They were a strange pair of negotiators—Maugham with his stammer, his hanging-judge mask, his judicial attitude to a career which had been one of the most profitable in literary history: and Fleming, with his drawl, his sudden laughter, his sardonic diffidence, on the brink of a success more spectacular than anything even Maugham himself had known.

'I have never been published in a newspaper,' said the old man, and smiled acidly. 'When I began I would have given anything to earn a guinea or two from the *Morning Post*. But they always turned me down. Now I don't care. I have been offered a pound a word to write for serialization in America. I have refused.'

'We could buy you a Renoir,' replied Fleming. 'A small one.'

'I don't want a Renoir. Anyhow, it would be illegal.'

The old man seemed to lose interest in the conversation. There was a long silence. They went into lunch. It was served in the famous dining-room downstairs, where Maugham, Fleming reflected naïvely, had entertained Churchill, Beaverbrook, Noël Coward, Aristotle Onassis and the Duke of Windsor. When he was back in London he described it all in an article which he intended for the *Sunday Times*, but which was never published. In it Fleming was wafted away into a haze of veneration and self-promotion, but he can be excused for that, for he got what he came for. When he flew back to London next day he carried with him a message of love for Anne, a box of avocados from the Villa Mauresque, and the reluctant permission of Somerset Maugham for the *Sunday Times* to publish instalments from his book on ten great novelists of the world as soon as it was finished. Fleming rang Lord Kemsley from London Airport to tell him the news.

The whole operation was an example of Fleming at his most energetic and effective. He was one of the very few people who could have persuaded the genuinely reluctant Maugham to forget his suspicion of newspapers and agree to publication, and even when he had done this he still took great pains to make sure that nothing went wrong. The fee was fixed—and it was ridiculously moderate even by the standards of 1954—at £3,000 for from four to six articles. On May 6th Fleming wrote to tell Maugham that 'the transaction will not be complete until our literary advisers have seen enough of the book to make up their minds. But', he added cheerfully, 'Lord K. has the bit between his teeth and unless the book contains lengthy extracts from "Fanny Hill", it is unlikely that he will have second thoughts. Even in this grim building', he went on, 'we are all exhilarated and everything will be done to see that the series is a success'. The transaction was agreed almost immediately; and when the proof of the first article was ready Fleming importantly boarded the Blue Train with it in order to discuss any last-minute changes with Maugham over another lunch.

The solitary, cynical octogenarian of the Villa Mauresque actually seemed excited now at the prospect of being serialized in the *Sunday Times;* and on June 3rd he wrote Fleming a note from the Gritti Palace Hotel in Venice beginning, 'My dear Ian and Revered Employer'. He said that he was 'much pleased' with Fleming's advance notice published in the paper on the previous Sunday and that he had (the perennial author's objection) only one complaint: 'What an unflattering photograph you published! It will cost me half my fans.'

But thanks to Fleming the wizened and wicked old face of Maugham was to become public property that summer. All the hoardings in the country seemed to be carrying it to herald the series, and a note of distinction was added to the furore when it was announced in the Birthday Honours that the Queen had appointed William Somerset Maugham a Companion of Honour.

Fleming's letter of congratulation is a fascinating document, for apart from what it shows of the sort of brutal charm he could exercise on an old gentleman like Maugham it contains the germ of one of the best touches of invention he ever used in one of his own books—the trap-door in the film-poster face of Marilyn Monroe in *From Russia, With Love.*

This is a great day for 'les amis de Somerset Maugham'. In honour of the Queen's birthday the town is being plastered with your face and the massed bands are playing for you both.

The Hallowe'en turnip being reproduced on the front page of

the 'Sunday Times' is nothing to the giant scraper board mask which, on the top floor of this building, is gazing angrily up Gray's Inn Road towards Lincolns Inn. It reminds me of the 'Black Widow' poster designed to 'Keep Death off the Roads', but in fact the whole campaign is having an electric effect on England and people can be seen in restaurants with scrubby bits of paper and pencil jotting down their team of novelists.*

Incidentally, our twenty-foot-square posters would just about paper the outside walls of your villa and I like the idea of you and Alan emerging from between your lips. It would be a good scene in a Cocteau or Dali film, and I may steal it for my fourth thriller. (The third is with Cape's and they say it is the best, but it doesn't amuse me as much as the others.)

Annie is in wonderful form and is delighted with the announcement in the 'Times' this morning although she says it isn't enough and hopes that you have at least precedence over Dame Sitwell. She is spinning like a top through the season and I am looking forward to enjoying her company again when she comes to rest at the end of July.

Soon he had good news for the Master. The serial was proving a really substantial success and the circulation was running at a remarkable increase of about 50,000 copies a week. The jubilation infected Maugham, who entered into the fun of the thing and generously—and without extra fee—allowed the serialization to be extended to fifteen weeks—an unprecedented span. For the first time in the history of the paper the back-dates department ran out of copies.

From the beginning Fleming treated the episode as a minor historical event or a major journalistic one, keeping careful note of all its various stages; and in a sense he was right. Out of its success arose the first magazine section in British journalism, devised by the *Sunday Times* as a vehicle for the memoirs of Lord Montgomery, a serial which ran, again with spectacular effect on the circulation figures, for fourteen weeks—but still one fewer than Maugham. Sunday journalism in Britain has never been quite the same since.

Characteristically, Fleming made no plea to Lord Kemsley on behalf of his rejected article about the whole affair, even

---

* Somerset Maugham selected the following as the ten best novels in the world: Henry Fielding's *Tom Jones*; Jane Austen's *Pride and Prejudice*, Stendhal's *Le Rouge et Le Noir*; Emily Brontë's *Wuthering Heights*; Balzac's *Le Père Goriot*; Charles Dickens's *David Copperfield*; Flaubert's *Madame Bovary*; Dostoevsky's *The Brothers Karamazov*; Herman Melville's *Moby Dick*; and Tolstoy's *War and Peace*.

though Maugham praised it warmly. In some respects he was a careful, canny man, and he had long since learned to disguise his deepest feelings or convictions at the *Sunday Times* editorial conferences without becoming completely cynical.

II

It might have seemed out of character for him, with his contempt for what he called 'gabfests' and committees in general, to have been so tense about the impression he made at these Tuesday morning meetings between, on the one side, Lord Kemsley as editor-in-chief, three of his sons, and two or three other directors of the company, and opposite them the editor of the *Sunday Times* and six or seven of his senior staff. But he took it all very seriously. The room became depressingly familiar to him: Lord Kemsley's own mahogany panelled office, with the Shotter Boys lithographs of London on the walls, the portrait of Lady Kemsley over the fireplace, the bronze bust of Lord Kemsley himself by Reid Dick, the charming little Tissot of a top-hatted, bewhiskered Victorian gentleman in a hansom going to the City, the nondescript collection of leather-bound books, the big undistinguished desk, the view from the window of the squalor of back streets, with King's Cross in the far distance, and a clutter of blank brick walls and vacant lots surmounted by the unprepossessing rump of the General Post Office building at Mount Pleasant. The editor-in-chief, magisterial for all his Edwardian pearl tie-pin and red carnation, would sit with his back to Clerkenwell's grimness, flanked by his sons and other directors, with Fleming in the outside-left position. Gravely, the executives of the paper would form themselves into a half-circle round the big desk, their papers on their knees.

Fleming's conduct at this conference, like his role in the hierarchy itself, was always slightly equivocal. Urbane, fluent, full of ideas, he nevertheless gave very little of himself away. At first sight he was the most attractive and least prejudiced personality in the room, yet men who sat with him there year in and year out agree that ultimately he was the one in that room they knew least about. When he was questioned or opposed he would evade discussion, sometimes with an exasperated little laugh which he reserved for occasions when he was particularly ill at ease; if a genuine issue of principle was raised he would usually look out of the window; and though he reserved a special distaste for people who had 'sold out' to Lord Kemsley, and though he never really sold out himself, it was not his habit directly to oppose anything the editor-in-chief sponsored at these meetings. He was still Foreign Manager of Kemsley Newspapers (though the position held little glory now) and still Atticus. It was not enough: he wanted, particularly for America, some title with a more impressive sound. So he took to referring to himself as a member of the *Sunday Times* Editorial Board. Pleased with his invention, rather as if he had attained Cabinet rank, he romanticized the Tuesday morning proceedings until they came to have something of the flavour of an executive committee meeting of SPECTRE itself. It was in 1962 that he put on record his private impressions of these conferences. He had suggested a memorable series of articles for the *Sunday Times* on the Seven Deadly Sins, and when these essays by various hands were published as a book in Britain, with singular lack of success, he tried to do his best for the American publisher by writing an introduction specially for his edition. This was after Mr Roy Thomson had bought the paper, but what Fleming had to say applied even more strongly to Lord Kemsley's regime:

It is quite a small Board of seven or eight heads of departments—I was Foreign Manager at the time—together with the Editor and the Proprietor, Mr Roy Thomson, and we were all good friends, though at this weekly meeting, beneath the surface of our friendliness, lurk all the deadly sins with the exception of gluttony and lust. Each one of us has pride in our department of the paper; many of us are covetous of the editorial chair; most are envious of the bright ideas put forward by others; anger comes to the surface at what we regard as unmerited criticism, and sloth, certainly in my case, lurks in the wings.

After his resignation from Thomson Newspapers at the end of 1959 he was delighted to accept Roy Thomson's suggestion that he should continue to attend on Tuesdays. And it was in that same room, under the eyes of half a dozen people with whom he had worked for fifteen years, that he had his first heart attack.

Meanwhile, in the late spring and early summer of 1954 everything was going his way. There was the *Sunday Times* for the exercise of the kind of power he loved and Bond for dreams. Anne and Victoria Square were for living,

St Margaret's Bay for leisure. He had his innumerable cronies for bridge and golf and other male occasions and his growing success as a novelist. In the early summer of this year, when the pressure of James Bond was not so insistent, it must have seemed as if all the elements in his life could live happily together for ever after.

The letters he wrote now were confident in tone. When he corresponded with Elsa Maxwell he had the assurance to advise her about a social chronicle she was writing and suggested that she 'expand considerably' her pages on the Duke and Duchess of Windsor.

For instance, I should have thought you could have put in many more personal details of what they like to eat, how they treat the servants, her wardrobe and jewels, the physical health of both of them, autograph letters from them, a description of their apartment and life in New York, security precautions, threatening letters etc. (your friends in the Police Department should help you over this) and so forth.

Miss Maxwell replied that she had doubts about the wisdom or good taste of this sort of treatment of her friends, and added, for good measure, that Noël Coward felt the same. Unabashed, Fleming wrote back: 'I quite see your point and Noël's about the Windsor passages, and, of course, it is up to you how you treat them. But Noël is exceptionally sensitive, which I am not, about allusions to any members of the Royal Family, and I should not take his warnings too much to heart.'

Another writer Fleming was attempting to organize at this time was Rose Macaulay, whom he had got to know in the first place through Anne. On his return from Jamaica he learned that Miss Macaulay had been attacked in her flat when she disturbed a pair of burglars:

I heard yesterday of the really monstrous misfortune you have suffered. I am afraid until we get the cat back in England solitary ladies will continue to be attacked in this brutal fashion.

Do you think you oughtn't to write a short piece on your experiences so that the general public can realize just what dreadful things are going on every day? The police cannot be everywhere but if the punishment were made to fit the crime perhaps these brutes would be deterred.

To take your mind off your misfortunes—though I hope not to give you more nightmares—here's the first copy I have sent out of my new thriller. It will not be published until April 5th, but I am so horrified by what I have heard that it occurred to me that the book might be a distraction—particularly as you were so kind about my first story for delinquent children of all ages.

Slightly horrified, poor Miss Macaulay begged Fleming to save her from any publicity, pointing out that she was just knocked over, not coshed, strangled, gagged or anything that people usually are, and observing spiritedly that although the 'cat' might be a deterrent 'so were the rack and the thumbscrew'. Fleming wrote back: 'Of course your secret life is safe with me and I dare say you are right about the cat. But personally I would rather have it myself than a long prison sentence.'

As Atticus he was as idiosyncratic, as unpredictable and as readable as ever. He had been quick to organize the column. Both before and after him it was often a headache for the printers: copy tended to be late and there were too many last-minute changes of mind, punctuation and material. Under Fleming copy was never late and changes were rare. In his engaging drawl he would dictate the whole thing to his secretary through a great cloud of cigarette smoke between three o'clock and four thirty every Thursday afternoon. It all seemed quite effortless. On the following morning he would correct the long ribbons of galley proofs, scrawl in a few additions, check the illustrations, have the whole thing assembled in page form, and be ready for lunch by twelve thirty at the latest.

It was always a joyful moment for the printers. They knew perfectly well that this present Atticus aimed to enjoy his Friday afernoon game of golf at Sandwich, and as it is seventy miles from Scott's Restaurant in Piccadilly to the clubhouse of the Royal St George's, he dare not be a moment behind schedule. There was never, said the printers wonderingly, an Atticus quite like him.

Early in June Fleming finished his corrections to the manuscript of *Moonraker* and delivered it to William Plomer, who was enthusiastic. Fleming was not so sure. As he wrote to Curtis Brown in New York, 'In my opinion it isn't much of a book, but it should make a good film.'

For all the enthusiasm of the critics and his publishers he was still a long way from the fortune he had dreamed James Bond was going to make him. *Casino Royale,* which had been out just over a year in England, had reprinted twice and sold just over 8,000 copies; its earnings were £325 8s. 5d. The prospects in America were less satisfactory, for

Macmillan's had sold fewer than 4,000 copies. All the same, this was not bad for a first thriller by an unknown British author, and Al Hart's letters to Fleming were full of hope as well as of humour. Yet to the author figures like these must have seemed a disappointing return for all the private log-rolling he had undertaken. So far the British sales of *Live and Let Die*—it was to come out in America in the following January—were respectable but by no means phenomenal: a first printing of 7,500 copies and a reprint of 2,000. At this stage in the game Fleming's earnings from his books were still under £2,000, and the only bonus which had so far come his way was a cheque—just arrived—for $2,625 from the American Popular Library for the right to publish *Casino Royale* in paperback under the title 'You Asked for It'. As Al Hart had said in the letter announcing the sale, 'the Great Unwashed won't know how to pronounce "Royale".' He added a P.S.: 'If "You Asked for It" turns your stomach bright green, it might be a good idea to suggest an alternative title or titles.' Fleming did so, but with a certain lack of enthusiasm. 'How about "The Double-O Agent" or "The Deadly Gamble"?' he asked. Then: 'But please don't worry about it either way.'

III

The fact was that Fleming had more important things to think about than paperback titles. Quite suddenly the big money had begun sniffing around James Bond.

It started with Sir Alexander Korda, the film producer, who according to Fleming 'had particularly asked to see' an advance copy of *Live and Let Die*. A little later Fleming was writing to his agent Naomi Burton in New York informing her with just a touch of self-satisfaction that Bennett Cerf had been trying to tempt him over to Random House for his next book—'but I see no particular reason to transfer to Random House unless their offer is outrageously lush'. The Columbia Broadcasting System suddenly offered $1,000 for the right to do a single one-hour television production of *Casino Royale*. And Fleming wrote to Naomi Burton again to tell her, 'We now have three offers for the film rights of "Casino", two by American companies and one by Ealing Studios, and we are keeping the balls precariously in the air.'

So it had come at last as he had always imagined it—film

bids, sales of paperback rights, publishers pursuing him with offers. It was about time and he had worked hard for it. Already he was suffering from insomnia and attacks of lethargy, and in April he had had excruciating pains in his back. At first he thought he must have strained it at golf, but when he saw Dr Beal it was diagnosed as yet one more sign of that old age he feared and resented. It was sciatica; and it was very much worse than he had thought sciatica ever could be. He would sit down and suddenly find that he could not get up. He developed a limp. For the first time in his life he felt like an old man—and suspected that he was beginning to look like one, too. 'Effort is desirable for its own sake,' he wrote grimly in one of his notebooks, echoing what Cyril Connolly called that 'rugger-scrum philosophy of life' which he had carried with him from Eton. 'Everyone must try. Those who succeed through their own endeavours are heroes.'

Now that he was so near to getting what he wanted there could be no letting up. By June of 1954, with the Maugham articles safe and settled, the time had come for his next encounter with James Bond. He had the basic idea ready for his new book and he knew where to get the facts he would need; he also had a title, which was half the battle. He had noticed it in the American *Vogue* when he was in New York in March—a very simple, very expensive advertisement containing just four words—'A Diamond is Forever'. There was something about those four words, the way they formed a promise which was also a threat, which made them stick in his mind.

Fleming was lucky. His Old Etonian friend Philip Brownrigg, who was one of the regiment of editors which the *Sunday Graphic* had enjoyed during the last three years of its existence, had recently left that newspaper's quavering decks for the dry land of de Beer's, the biggest and the richest diamond merchants the world has ever known. He was a success; he had an office near Hatton Garden and as a senior executive of de Beer's enjoyed the entrée to that curiously closed society of the London diamond market. When Fleming told him that he planned to write his next book on diamonds and diamond smuggling, it was not difficult for Brownrigg to arrange for his friend to have an insider's view of what went on. (Three years later, when Fleming wrote a series of articles called 'The Diamond Smugglers', he was to call on Brownrigg again.)

The older Fleming got the more seriously he treated his wide variety of friendships. In return they sometimes helped by providing him with a knowledgeable inside view of the different closed worlds where James Bond's licence to kill would operate. With diamonds, as usual, Fleming showed much more than the ordinary reporter's ability to pick a friend's brains, and here there was the additional consideration that as soon as he entered the offices of the Diamond Corporation in Charterhouse Street he found a world that could have been made for Bond. The international diamond trade has all the ingredients of one of his own richest fantasies, and like the world of Le Chiffre or of Mr Big it is a society within a society, with its own mystique and a particularly subtle expertise.

Brownrigg arranged for him to visit the neat, homely premises of the London Diamond Club, where most of the trading takes place, to see the Diamond Corporation's stones being graded and cut and sorted, and to discuss with Sir Percy Sillitoe, formerly head of M.I.5, the measures he was taking in his new post as head of the Corporation's security organization in its international battle with illicit diamond buying—later on Fleming was to meet Sillitoe again and write the story of the organization. But the most useful contact he now made through Brownrigg was a diamond-broker named Harry Abrahams, who had been in the business all his life. Warm-hearted, voluble, full of stories and unexpected information, he was the sort of expert Fleming always relished.

'You must understand the passion for diamonds,' M. tells Bond at the beginning of *Diamonds Are Forever*, and this passion was what Fleming sensed in Abrahams. At lunch at the offices of the Diamond Corporation, as the broker talked and answered his questions and produced stones from a small chamois leather bag, Fleming finally understood the absolute nature of the wealth which diamonds represented. All his life his own passion for money had been the insatiable passion of the financial romantic, and here in these stones Abrahams was spreading out so casually on the table lay the ultimate symbol of that elusive material he had been pursuing since boyhood. Here, indestructible, unshakeable, was wealth that would never let you down.

Something of Fleming's emotion must have come across to the diamond-broker, for when they parted he did something utterly exceptional—he gave Fleming a diamond. And the following day, full of schoolboy glee, Fleming wrote to thank him:

I can't describe to you the chagrin expressed by Brownrigg, Baring and company, when I rang up and said that on getting back to my office I had found a diamond in my pocket and what could I do about it without embarrassing them too much.

It was fun having them on the hook for a moment or two and then to enjoy the effect of saying that in fact you had presented me with a diamond. That caused almost as much consternation.

Anyway it was a very kind gesture of yours and I am very proud to be, with Queen Mary, one of the few people who can ever have left the Diamond Corporation with an actual diamond in their pocket . . .

IV

There were now only a few more days of London to endure. On July 23rd Fleming, like Bond, was again packing his 'battered but once expensive pigskin Revelation', and the inventory was identical with his hero's—'evening clothes; light-weight black-and-white dog-tooth suit for the country and for golf; Saxone golf shoes; a companion to the dark-blue tropical worsted suit he was wearing, and some white silk and dark-blue Sea Island cotton shirts with collars attached and short sleeves'. He also packed—like Bond—Tommy Armour on *How to Play Your Best Golf all the Time*. The only differences were that Fleming had no Q branch to build him a secret compartment for ammunition at the bottom of his suitcase and the ·25 Beretta with the taped butt and sawn-off foresight was not under his armpit but in his imagination.

That evening when B.O.A.C.'s Monarch flight for New York 'hurtled down the two miles of stressed concrete and rose into the West' with Ian Fleming aboard, James Bond travelled with him. Partly as a tacit reward for good work done with Somerset Maugham, Fleming was off on one of his trips to the United States. This time he was planning to be away longer than usual. James Bond had some calls to make.

In New York, with *Sunday Times* business disposed of, there was Ernest Cuneo to see. It turned out that their plans for the next few days were identical with the plans James Bond made with 'the boiled sweet', Miss Tiffany Case, when he was in hot pursuit of Shady Tree and the Spangled Mob.

First, a trip to Saratoga 'to back a horse that's to make me some money'. Saratoga is not far from Black Hole Hollow Farm in Vermont; Mrs Jo Bryce had several horses running at Saratoga, and her husband was anxious for Fleming to be present during the few days in early August when the place puts on 'the smartest race meeting in America and the place crawls with Vanderbilts and Whitneys'.

After Saratoga Cuneo had to go to Chicago and Los Angeles. For a long time now he had been telling Fleming that for his next book he ought to learn some of the facts of life about American big-city crime and gambling. They decided that when Fleming had had his fill of horses and Vanderbilts the two of them would go off together for ten days, 'taking the 20th Century to Chicago and then the Superchief to Los Angeles'. From Los Angeles they would drive to Las Vegas, the biggest gambling city in the world.

For the next three carefree weeks Fleming lived out the world he was soon to describe in *Diamonds Are Forever*. There was no danger, of course, no action, but all that, like the ·25 Beretta, could be left to his imagination. Otherwise it was all there for him—the rich, the horses, the sulphur-smelling mud-baths of Saratoga, the bourbon and branch water, even the 'Studillac' car, that mongrel Studebaker with the Cadillac engine, 'special transmission and brakes and rear axle', in which Felix Leiter touched 110 up the Taconic Parkway. In reality it belonged to William Woodward Jr, millionaire playboy, racehorse owner and friend of the Bryces who was accidentally shot dead a few months later when his wife mistook him for a burglar. Fleming dedicated the novel to his memory.

All this was the genuine world of James Bond. As Fleming drove Woodward's car and bet on the tote and took the mud baths at Saratoga he and Bond were one. They remained so in Los Angeles and Las Vegas and for the rest of the stay in America.

CHAPTER NINETEEN

ENTER CHANDLER

I

THE exterior of 16 Victoria Square had just been repainted. Fleming's lease from the Westminster Estate stipulated this at least once every two years, and now that the painters had moved on the trim cream face of the house gleamed in the sun of early June 1955. So did the car which backed carefully into an empty space in front of it just after midday. It was long, low and black, and its arrival signified something special; for the day was a Wednesday, and it was almost unheard-of for Ian Fleming, man of strict habit that he was, to come home for lunch in the middle of the week.

Luncheon was normally the time Anne Fleming chose to entertain her friends, and he preferred plaice or halibut and a glass of Guinness in the window seat at Scott's with a solitary male friend. Indeed, like some Austrian or Italian husband, he made rather a point of keeping his professional life and his home life hygienically apart. But today was an exception. Today he and not Anne was the host.

The first guest to arrive was Rupert Hart-Davis, the publisher, a large, affable blond man who had known Fleming since they were at Eton together. He was a great friend of Peter Fleming's too, and he had a cottage on the Fleming estate at Nettlebed. For some reason Ian Fleming always called him 'Old Rupe'. No one else did.

After him came Stephen Spender and his wife, the pianist Natasha Litvin. Fleming admired Spender more as one of the editors of a successful magazine, *Encounter,* than as a poet; it was through him and his wife that the host had first met the man in whose honour the luncheon was really being held.

It was an easy gathering so far—Anne knew these three guests well. But not the man who had still to arrive. Fleming had been talking about him a lot lately, and she had made a point of asking her husband to invite him to lunch to meet her. For she had never met Raymond Chandler, now in his middle sixties.

He arrived rather late and already a little drunk, an uncomfortable, shy man with a pug-dog face, peering with vague bafflement through large spectacles, an English-born American who had shed all traces of his origin and who now looked rather like a senator broken by an inquiry into some oil scandal. Fleming treated him with the deference he reserved for very few. Chandler had arrived in England a month before and was just emerging from a long spell of drinking which had followed the death of his beloved wife Cissie at La Jolla in California the previous year. He was still in a state of emotional shock when Fleming had met him, on this same visit, for the first time. Later Fleming described him as being 'puffy and unkempt with drink', although he added that he must have been a good-looking man in his prime:

In talking he never ceased making ugly Hapsburg lip grimaces while his head stretched away from you, looking along his right or left shoulder as if you had bad breath. When he did look at you he saw everything and remembered days later to criticize the tie or the shirt you had been wearing. Everything he wrote had authority and a strongly individual slant based on what one might describe as a Socialistic humanitarian view of the world.

The first meeting between the two men had taken place at dinner at Spender's house in St John's Wood—Natasha Spender and one or two other women had made it their business to look after Chandler and try to ease him off the bottle. Fleming's account of this first meeting, written some time later, is curiously revealing about Fleming himself as well as about Chandler:

He was very nice to me and said he had liked my first book, 'Casino Royale', but he didn't really want to talk about anything much except the loss of his wife, about which he expressed himself with a nakedness that embarrassed me while endearing him to me. He showed me a photograph of her—a good-looking woman sitting in the sun somewhere. The only other snapshot in his notecase was of a cat which he had adored. The cat had died within weeks of his wife's death and this had been the final blow.

Two more different characters than the creators of Philip Marlowe and James Bond it would be hard to find, but since that dinner at the Spenders they had met on several occasions and got on well together. Fleming knew his man well enough to understand that he detested polite literary conversation. 'It will be a very small informal gathering,' he had taken the precaution of telling Chandler when inviting him to lunch.

'They are all great admirers of your books, but no one will ask you how you think up all those marvellous plots.'

Nobody did. But tact and admiration are a dubious recipe for a successful little luncheon party, and Chandler was very different from the writers Anne had grown used to at Victoria Square. 'The luncheon,' Fleming admitted later, 'was not a success . . . Chandler was a man who was shy of houses and entertaining and our conversation was noisy and about people he did not know. His own diffident and rather halting manner of speech made no impact. He was not made a fuss of and I am pretty sure he hated the whole thing.'

'It was,' says Anne, 'a total disaster. Chandler was quite incoherent, and afterwards Ian said he was never going to bring anyone home again.' In his decline poor generous Ray Chandler was foggily suspicious of English manners and customs and seemed to think that hostesses were always high-hatting him.

The following week he sailed back to New York. But although the lunch had been a catastrophe the friendship between the two men survived and was to prove of importance to Fleming and also to James Bond. Indeed, but for Chandler it is more than likely that Fleming would have finished off his hero for good at the big desk at Goldeneye the following year.

For when he came back to London from Jamaica with the manuscript of *Diamonds Are Forever* in March 1955, Fleming had had enough of his creation. It was not the writing of the book which had exhausted him—those steady 2,000 words a day had come as easily as ever, and when he had reached New York and read the manuscript right through for the first time he liked what he had written. But all the effort which led up to the book had left him in a bad state. It was all right to play at James Bond in Las Vegas if you really were James Bond. But if you were Ian Fleming, aged forty-seven, with a wife and a child and three houses and a job and imperfect health the game could not go on for ever. When it stopped, when you returned to face nine months in Gray's Inn Road, the withdrawal symptoms could be acute. Fleming found that they remained acute for the remainder of that spring.

This feeling of let-down and exhaustion was not just physical. However good the reviews of *Moonraker* had been when it was published that April, and however much better still he privately believed *Diamonds Are Forever* to be, he seems to have convinced himself that he had gone as far with writing about James Bond as he ever would or could. 'My talents are extended to their absolute limit writing books like *Diamonds Are Forever*,' he told Chandler. 'I am not shortweighting anybody and I have absolutely nothing more up my sleeve.'

It was this feeling of having nothing more up his sleeve that seems to have convinced Fleming now that he had gone as far as it was ever worth going with James Bond. If the previous year's hopes of a great American success had materialized Bond might have been worth saving, but the dreams of best-seller lists and of a big sale to a film company had evaporated. Korda had politely returned the script of *Live and Let Die*. The waves of the American paperback market closed silently over *Casino Royale*, finally called *Too Hot to Handle*. C.B.S.'s one-hour production of the same book had been screened and mercifully forgotten. The newly published American edition of *Live and Let Die* had sold barely 5,000 copies. Even Al Hart of the Macmillan Company, the loyalest admirer Fleming's books possessed in the New World, wrote, 'Mr Bond will have to do better than this.'

But Fleming felt that Mr Bond had now done as well as he ever would and that there was nothing else to be done with him.. He wrote to his friend Hilary Bray just after his return:

I baked a fresh cake in Jamaica this year which I think has finally exhausted my inventiveness as it contains every single method of escape and every variety of suspenseful action that I had omitted from my previous books—in fact everything except the kitchen sink, and if you can think up a good plot involving kitchen sinks, please send it along speedily.

Certainly, judged by the hopes of fame and fortune Fleming had had of his hero, James Bond was a great disappointment. For all the favourable reviews, not a single one of his hard-cover books had so far sold more than twelve thousand copies. That spring he began to wonder how much longer he could afford Goldeneye. To one potential tenant at this time he replied that he was raising the rent to £50 a week—'I find that the property is costing so much to keep up that unless I get my rent in line with rather less than what is charged all along the North Shore, I shall not be able to afford to keep it up.'

Claudette Colbert and her husband had spent part of the previous January as guests of Noël Coward and were thinking of renting Goldeneye for a while at Christmas, but they finally decided against it. A letter to her from Fleming, dated April 28th, 1955, shows that he was not seriously thinking of giving up Goldeneye but that he was far more concerned about money than appeared on the surface:

. . . I am very sad that you will not be in Goldeneye next winter, but you may change your mind and it is always there if you want it.

I hear there were great dramas after I left, with David Niven catching chicken-pox and so on, and I fancy the general atmosphere was considerably disturbed. I shall hear all about it this week-end as Noël is coming over to have dinner with us before going back to America.

I have little hope of getting out to Los Angeles this year. I was there last November and I have absolutely no excuse for a holiday unless Hollywood suddenly decides to film one of my books. You would be the perfect heroine for any of them, so if you see my literary Agent on the Coast, Swanee Swanson, get him to tell you what you are missing.

For Fleming to have suggested Claudette Colbert of all people as a potential Tiffany Case shows how much hope he really had now of making a fortune out of Hollywood.

Since James Bond had failed to earn his keep Fleming practically made up his mind that the time had come for him to free himself of 'that cardboard booby', as he was to call Bond in a letter to William Plomer, and discover a more lucrative and less demanding subject for his writing talents. At last, in a letter to Al Hart, Fleming explained what he was going to do. 'I have a fifth book more or less in mind, but after that the vacuum is complete.' The intention was to free Ian Fleming for ever from his involvement with James Bond. It would be done in the grandest possible manner: SMERSH would arrange his execution in detail—step by step the plans would be drawn up and the agents of death assembled; Bond would be lured into a terrifying trap and the bait would be the most beautiful girl in his whole career. This time, though, there would be a final twist which no one would expect: James Bond would *not* escape, and thus Fleming would be free of him. The vacuum would really exist at last.

Indeed, during these weeks of early spring the vacuum was almost acknowledged, and for the first time since *Casino*

Royale Fleming seems to have dismissed Bond completely from his mind. As a last gesture he decided to off-load the screen rights of *Casino Royale* for the best price they would fetch. Gregory Ratoff had already paid $600 for an option on them, and when he offered $6,000 for an outright sale Fleming clinched the deal. With the money he bought himself something he had wanted for a very long time. It had a four-barrel down-draught carburettor, Fordomatic transmission, and a power output of 190 h.p. It was called a Thunderbird and it cost him £3,000. For Fleming it was a considerable extravagance.

Anne took against the Thunderbird on sight, complaining with infuriating feminine logic that it was 'above our price bracket and below our age range'. She also, according to Fleming, thought the car hideous:

There was no room for taking people to the station (a point I found greatly in its favour) and, anyway, why hadn't I bought her a mink coat? To this day she hasn't relented. She has invented a disease called 'Thunderbird neck' which she complains she gets in the passenger seat. The truth is that she has a prejudice against all American artifacts and, indeed, against artifacts of any kind.

Predictably, Fleming was a cautious, extremely tidy driver with a marked dislike of unnecessary risk. He always treated his cars with great respect, and whilst he much enjoyed the sensation when the 'two extra barrels of the four-barrel carburettor come in, at around 3,000 revs, with a real thump in the back', he was never a man who went speeding for the fun of it; and he always maintained that the brakes on his Thunderbird were not good enough for what he called 'dangerous' driving.

This subject of cars and driving in general was a constant source of raillery between Anne and himself. On one occasion she vented her dislike of the Thunderbird by putting sugar in its petrol tank, which for some reason improved its performance considerably. Fleming got his own back by describing her driving in an article in the *Spectator*:

She herself drives like Evelyn Waugh's Lady Metroland,* using the pavement as if it were part of the road. Like many women she prides herself on her 'quick reactions' and is constantly twitting me with my sluggish consideration for others in traffic. She is unmoved when I reminded her that in her previous car, a grey

* Fleming got it wrong. It was Mrs Stitch, not Lady Metroland, who drove along pavements.

and heavily built Sunbeam Talbot whose interior always looked as if it had been used as the dustcart for the circus at Olympia, she had been guilty of misdemeanours which would have landed any man in gaol. She once hit an old man in a motorized bath chair so hard in the rear that he was propelled right across Oxford Street against the traffic lights. Turning into Dover Street she had cut a milk cart so fine that she had left her outside door handle embedded in the rump of the horse.

But now Fleming found other things besides the Thunderbird and his wife's driving to keep his mind off James Bond. There was, for example, his friendship with Lord Beaverbrook, which was to have such important consequences both for him and his books. Ever since the reconciliation between them engineered by Sir William Stephenson in Jamaica, Beaverbrook had enjoyed Fleming's company. Like so many older, wealthy men before him who had more or less come to terms with success and respectability, Beaverbrook enjoyed the zest, the wit, the air of casual outrage which Fleming could still adopt when he was at his best and the audience was worth it.

He always took good care to send Beaverbrook an advance copy of his books, and in April the old man had sent a staccato acknowledgment and review of *Moonraker* from his villa at Cap d'Ail, La Capponcina.

A month later, on May 25th, Lord Beaverbrook, his family, his staff and his newspapers celebrated his seventy-sixth birthday. Fleming tried to persuade Lord Kemsley to make Beaverbrook the subject of the *Sunday Times* Portrait Gallery that week but Kemsley, even though Beaverbrook flattered him outrageously in paragraphs in the *Evening Standard*, somewhat resembled his brother Lord Camrose in his aversion to mentioning other newspaper proprietors in his own newspapers. Fleming kept pegging away at Lord Kemsley, and in the end Atticus was allowed to join in the celebratory chorus. Fleming wrote, a shade fulsomely:

History will have to decide whether he or Northcliffe was the greatest newspaperman of this half century. In the sense that he combines rare journalistic flair, the rare quality of wonder and a consuming interest in people and life with courage and vitality, and a point of view about absolutely everything, the verdict may quite possibly go to Lord Beaverbrook.

Fleming went on to speculate on who would be found worthy to write the true story of Beaverbrook—'who will be the literary Graham Sutherland who will do for him in words what has been so supremely well done in paint?'* Perhaps Churchill should be asked to write about Beaverbrook the politician while there was still time, 'and there would surely have to be one enemy,' he concluded, 'to write the chapter Lord Beaverbrook himself would most enjoy'.

One of Lord Beaverbrook's well-known traits was an engaging appetite for flattery, and the following Wednesday morning a special messenger brought a note to Victoria Square addressed in his lordship's own strong handwriting. The note inside was also handwritten. He told Fleming that the exhilarating piece about him in the *Sunday Times* would ensure his fame. He knew that Ian had praised him more than he deserved, but it was to Beaverbrook just like the permanent effect of champagne.

While Fleming was furthering his friendship with Lord Beaverbrook, who in his seventy-seventh year was sitting on the high pinnacle of success, he was also admiring Raymond Chandler, lonely, burnt-out, not even bothering to make sense of a life which had become meaningless to him after the death of his homely and elderly Cissie. Chandler had taken a flat in Eaton Square, a bare five minutes' walk from Victoria Square, and after their meeting at the Spenders' house Fleming had sent round a copy of *Live and Let Die* for him to read. A few days later, apparently, Chandler rang Fleming to say how much he had enjoyed it, and went on to ask the author—vaguely perhaps—if he would care for him to endorse the book for the benefit of his publishers—the kind of thing he was always refusing to do in the United States and a subject on which, in his published letters, he displays such ferocious cynicism. 'Rather unattractively,' wrote Fleming later, 'I took him up on this suggestion,' and he told Chandler: 'I wouldn't think of asking you to write to me about *Moonraker,* but if you feel in a mood of Quixotic generosity, a word from you which I could pass on to my publishers would make me the fortune which has so far eluded me.'

Chandler was as good as his word, although it sounds as if it was rather a struggle. On May 25th he wrote pathetically to Fleming apologizing for taking so long—'in fact lately I have had a very difficult time reading at all'. But finally on June 4th Chandler wrote the few words about *Live and*

---

*The choice has fallen on A. J. P. Taylor, whom Beaverbrook called, in an essay written before his death, 'The Man Who Stirs Things Up'. That was the role Ian Fleming played at Kemsley House.

Let Die which he had promised. They were worth waiting for:

Ian Fleming is probably the most forceful and driving writer of what I suppose still must be called thrillers in England. Peter Cheyney wrote one good book, I thought, called 'Dark Duet' and another fairly good one, but his pseudo-American tough guy stories always bored me. There was also James Hadley Chase, and I think the less said of him the better. Also, in spite of the fact that you have been everywhere and seen everything, I cannot help admiring your courage in tackling the American scene.

If this is any good to you, would you like me to have it engraved on a slab of gold?

Fleming knew it was not necessary. He answered:

These are words of such gold that no supporting slab is needed and I am passing them on to Macmillan's in New York and Cape's here, and will write my appreciation in caviare when the extra royalties come in. Seriously, it was extraordinarily kind of you to have written as you did, and you have managed to make me feel thoroughly ashamed of my next book which is also set in America, but in an America of much more fantasy than I allowed myself in 'Live and Let Die'.

And the same day Fleming sent a copy of the letter by express airmail to Al Hart in New York. It was an effective reply to Hart's 'Mr Bond will have to do better than this' letter. 'Will this help you sell any books?' wrote Fleming in a sharp little covering note. 'If not, if I were you I should move out of the fiction department before it folds on you.'

The interest and support of Raymond Chandler had come at a crucial moment for Ian Fleming, and the brief meetings between them in May and early June, even before the testimonial was written, had an electric effect on the attitude of Fleming to his writing and his hero. It was undoubtedly Raymond Chandler's interest which restored Fleming's enthusiasm for both.

At any rate, from the middle of May there was no more talk from Fleming of his being played out. On May 12th something that Chandler had said to him was already firing him to send off a spirited if somewhat petulant defence of his craftsmanship to Naomi Burton at Curtis Brown in New York:

By the way and sucks to you, I had a drink with Raymond Chandler last night and he said that the best bit of 'Live and Let Die' was the conversation between the two Negroes in Harlem, which he said was dead accurate. Perhaps you remember that you nearly sneered me into cutting it out on the grounds that 'Negroes don't talk like that'.

And by June 14th, little more than a week after receiving the golden testimonial from Chandler, Fleming's faith in Bond seems to have been entirely restored. It was then that he heard from Curtis Brown in New York that Ian Hunter, the actor, was interested in buying a six-months' option on the film rights of *Moonraker*, and his reply was very cool. He would give his assent only if the price was right: he insisted on a minimum of £1,000 for the six-months' option and £10,000 for the full film rights, despite his having just sold *Casino Royale* to Gregory Ratoff for only $6,000. He gave his reasons in a prophetic last paragraph: 'I have an idea that one of these days the film and television rights of James Bond and his adventures may be worth quite a lot of money and I hope you agree that there's no point in throwing them away.'

All this arose out of Chandler's aproval, yet the real importance of the friendship went beyond the mere restoration of Fleming's confidence in James Bond. It quickly seems to have changed the whole attitude of Fleming to his hero and his work and to have made him decide that his next book, instead of finishing off Bond for good, would go to the opposite extreme. It would be different from any other book he had written, it would have depth and seriousness. Bond would become a 'rounded character' like Chandler's hero, Philip Marlowe. Fleming would have done with him not by killing him but by transforming him into a genuine character at last.

With Chandler back in the States it was to be nearly a year before the two men met once more, but neither distance nor the memory of the unhappy lunch at Victoria Square seems to have affected their friendship, and at the end of June 1955 Fleming was to receive an all but undecipherable letter from Chandler, the core of which was that he had just re-read *Live and Let Die*, that parts of it were 'pretty wonderful and he'd have been proud to have written the book himself, and 'Could you lend me Solitaire for a week?'

But as well as the affection one lonely writer on the way down felt for another lonely writer on the way up there was the fact that Chandler recognized, or thought he recognized, in Fleming a far greater talent than anything he had used so far on behalf of James Bond. This Fleming denied vigorously when he wrote to Chandler. 'I am not,' he insisted, 'in the Shakespeare stakes.' Understandably, he was flattered, and not only flattered—he was tremendously encouraged. Indeed, the real significance of this brief incursion of poor drunken Ray Chandler into the life of Ian Fleming is that he managed to revive Fleming's morale and his sagging ambitions as a writer by reminding him that James Bond, like Philip Marlowe, could still become a source of genuine acclaim for his creator.

II

Of all the disappointments and frustrations which seemed to converge on Fleming in the spring of 1955, possibly the worst was the growing suspicion that he was making a fool of himself over James Bond. Previously he had not felt this: the excellent reviews, the enthusiasm of important friends like Maugham and Plomer had seemed sufficient safeguard against ridicule—no one laughs at success. But after *Moonraker* was published and America showed such resounding indifference to the exploits of James Bond his creator was bitten by the conviction that, apart from a very few loyal friends, no one—or at any rate no one who mattered, and this included Anne and her circle—took his writing very seriously. On one occasion he had arrived back at Victoria Square to find Cyril Connolly giving an extempore reading from the latest exploits of James Bond to a full-scale gathering of Anne's friends. It was very funny; and Fleming was the only one who did not laugh. (He overcame this sensitiveness later on and encouraged Connolly to publish a parody of Bond in a very limited edition.)

The truth was that although he had long pretended to despise intellectuals, and although James Bond was a projection of the hard, tough man of action he dreamed of being, Fleming had never really overcome his longing for a resounding intellectual success. He was really an unfrocked intellectual himself—this former translator of Jung and admirer of Rilke and Thomas Mann—and like all renegades he longed for those he had rejected to accept him one day on his own terms. Fleming saw how this could still be achieved. Chandler had done it, just as Hemingway and Simenon had done it. Chandler had ignored the intellectuals (though he made no secret of his gratification when Desmond MacCarthy 'discovered' him in the *Sunday Times*), he had played his own solitary, tough, unselfconscious line and he had managed it so well that the man who had written so much for *Black Mask* and other pulp magazines found himself the pet of the intellectuals when he came to England. Perhaps there was a chance for James Bond after all.

If Fleming was anxious to be taken a shade more seriously he managed to acquire at least one source of legitimate intellectual esteem that summer. He finally became the proprietor of a distinguished learned journal. This was a quarterly called the *Book Collector*. Lord Kemsley had originally acquired its predecessor, the *Book Handbook*, and then in 1951, through the efforts mainly of Percy Muir and John Hayward, the *Book Handbook* was re-named the *Book Collector* and transformed into something that became the leading bibliographical journal of our times. As a 'gentleman' collector and a director and the inspirer of Kemsley's small Queen Anne Press, which published the *Book Collector*, Fleming was very involved in all this. But by the beginning of 1955 the magazine, despite its growing prestige, was still not covering its expenses, and Lord Kemsley decided that it would have to go. Rather than allow this to happen Fleming offered to buy it from Lord Kemsley for whatever he thought it worth. Kemsley mentioned a figure of £50. Fleming sent him his cheque the same day. But, typically, he left the work to others—chiefly to Percy Muir and to its unpaid editor, John Hayward, who joined in persuading several American bodies—including the Mellon Foundation—to provide a fund which was to ensure the future of the *Book Collector*. Fleming never wrote for it or really directed its policy. All the same, the magazine was 'his'. He was very proud of it. After all these years he was a publisher.

In his role as guardian of Fleming's literary conscience William Plomer had been quick to realize how anxious his friend also was for a genuine *succès d'estime* with at least one of his books and of how seriously he was considering the plot of what was to become *From Russia, With Love*. When he wrote on July 3rd, 1955, to give his first reactions to the manuscript of *Diamonds Are Forever*, Plomer was careful to stress the novel's literary merits along with its other qualities. He singled out Fleming's description of the racing stables at Saratoga in the early morning—'This,' he said, in a phrase that must have been music to Fleming's ears, 'is the work of a serious writer.'

So it was that with Chandler's example before him and

Plomer's encouragement behind him Fleming now began, in thinking about *From Russia, With Love*, the difficult task of attempting to elevate James Bond to a higher literary level. He wrote to Chandler:

Probably the fault about my books is that I don't take them seriously enough and meekly accept having my head ragged off about them in the family circle . . . You, after all, write 'novels of suspense'—if not sociological studies—whereas my books are straight pillow fantasies of the bang-bang, kiss-kiss variety.

He concluded by telling Chandler that he had taken his advice to heart 'and will see if I can't order my life so as to put more feeling into my typewriter'.

He knew Russia, or thought he did. He had reported there, made love there, done intelligence work there. Ever since he had learned Russian from old Maslov in Geneva he had been fascinated by these gloomy, terrible, tragic people. The rough plot of the book had been inhabiting his head since the spring of 1954. He said to Simenon the year before he died: 'I invent the most hopeless sounding plots; very often they are based on something I have read in a newspaper. And people say, "Oh, this is all nonsense"—and then the Russians come along in Germany and shoot people with potassium cyanide pistols. Last year a Russian got a heavy sentence for killing three West Germans in this way—so I find constantly that things I've read about in some obscure magazine or somewhere are always coming true in real life.'

It was the disclosures made by the Russian diplomat Vladimir Petrov (who had organized espionage in Australia for the Russians and defected in April 1954) which had given him a start. He had written in Atticus, just after Petrov talked, about the 'messengers of death' sent by the M.G.B. to liquidate, during the aftermath of Beria's rule, certain renegades and traitors, and he had also dwelt on a Russian colonel, the enigmatic Madame Rybkin, whom he believed to be possibly the most powerful woman in the world of espionage. From the first she seems to have appealed to his sense of the macabre as a sort of potential female Le Chiffre. In the book she became Rosa Klebb, and he named the courier of death, SMERSH's chief executioner, after Donovan Grant, the gentle giant who had punted Princess Margaret down the Rio Grande in Jamaica. SMERSH, however, was not his own invention; he had first come across the name in a magazine soon after the war, and he embroidered on what little information he had about the organization and introduced it melodramatically into *Casino Royale*. Russian experts were quick to point out to him that SMERSH was really a body which worked very largely with the Red Army during the war, rounding up German spies and saboteurs and Russian traitors, that it was a mistake to think that it had operated outside the borders of the U.S.S.R., that it was never a counter-intelligence unit in the sense that it worked against enemy secret services, and that in any case it had changed its name at the end of the war. Fleming, who always knew a good thing when he met one, took no notice and continued to base himself on his outdated conception of SMERSH.

It was when he was brooding over Rosa Klebb and Red Grant that a mysterious Russian in a frayed blue suit turned up one day at Kemsley House. He said that he knew all about SMERSH at first hand—he had even been in its headquarters. In the end, writing away in his bed-sitting-room, he produced a dossier of 20,000 words on SMERSH, and some of this information, suitably embellished, went into *From Russia, With Love*. The dossier is curiously convincing but, it seems, unauthentic. Perhaps its author has gone on to a writing career of his own, where his imaginative powers can be given full scope.

But before taking the dossier with him to Goldeneye Fleming had to decide where to set the action of his new novel once Bond appeared on the scene. New York was a possibility, but he felt that he had written enough about New York—and the same went for London. There was Paris, but Paris was a city that held no real mystery for him: it was not James Bond's sort of city. Fleming went on wondering, particularly about the Middle East—Cairo perhaps; and then the answer suddenly presented itself through the agreeable personality of Assistant Commissioner Sir Ronald Howe of Scotland Yard.

Fleming had known Sir Ronald for some time. He was an acquaintance more than a close friend whom he had met on several occasions at Lord Kemsley's bridge-table. He knew that Howe had once been tutor to one of Lord Kemsley's sons and, more important, was a very old friend of Somerset Maugham's. Clearly the head of the Criminal Investigation Department at Scotland Yard was a valuable contact and Fleming took trouble to keep in touch with him.

Back on the last day of 1953 Fleming had written to the

Assistant Commissioner asking a small favour. He owned three guns and had suddenly realized that none of them was properly licensed. They were a twelve-bore shotgun which was kept permanently with Holland and Holland the gunsmiths, the Colt ·38 given to him by General Donovan 'for certain services I rendered his Office of Strategic Studies [*sic*] during the war', and a Browning ·25 issued during the war to protect John Godfrey's life and my own. I take it with me each year to Jamaica'. Fleming added, echoing his mother, 'for defence against the Blackamoors'. He told his correspondent that he knew that theoretically he had been breaking the law by failing to get his guns properly licensed, but honestly it had always slipped his memory—could Ronnie Howe 'tidy up the situation, please?' Obligingly the Assistant Commissioner did so, and as a slight return and modest investment Fleming put Howe into his next book as Superintendent Ronnie Vallance.

In the New Year's Honours List of 1955 it was announced that Howe had received a knighthood. 'I hope,' wrote Fleming, in a letter of congratulation, 'that Interpol is proud of you!'

The remark referred to the fact that for several years Howe had been chief United Kingdom delegate to the International Police Organization, and when the two met again later that year Fleming asked how Interpol was getting on. Howe replied that it was now represented in fifty-two countries and that in the autumn, for a change, it had decided to hold its annual conference in Istanbul. Fleming was interested. Were reporters, he asked, ever allowed into these affairs? Howe replied that while normally the Press was not encouraged the attendance of a journalist who could be trusted might be a different matter.

'Of course,' said Fleming. It was as good as settled, and on July 25th he dictated a letter to Sir Ronald Howe, K.B.E., C.V.O., M.C., Criminal Investigation Department, Scotland Yard, SW1:

I am delighted that our trip is to come off and Lord Kemsley is most enthusiastic. I have to go off to New York for three weeks, but let us get in touch when I get back.

Do you think it will be possible to get some sort of accreditation to the Interpol Conference? Perhaps I could come as your press adviser or something of the sort to make our union appear respectable.

The problem of where to send James Bond for his encounter

with the chief executioner of SMERSH, Donovan Grant, had been solved. Fleming left for New York full of new zest, first to visit the *Sunday Times* office and then, taking once more the road James Bond had followed in *Diamonds Are Forever*, driving up the Taconic Highway to mingle with the millionaires at Black Hole Hollow Farm during the Saratoga races.

Fleming was never a predictable man. Inwardly, and sometimes outwardly, he was actuated by a spirit of contradiction, and his inconsistencies were lifelong and numerous. This year, for example, Vermont lost some of its attraction for him. He was easily disgusted or bored with women, especially rich café-society women, and he took particular offence when a friend of the Bryces told him that since breakfast she had taken two pep pills, two indigestion tablets and three tranquillizers; his puritan disgust after too rich a meal of worldliness and wealth could sometimes be as strong as his other puritan reactions. He was glad to return to England at the end of August and then fly on to Istanbul.

CHAPTER TWENTY

THE IRON CRAB

I

ISTANBUL is a city in decay, the grim wreck of what was once, unbelievably, the greatest city in the world—Byzantium. It is a shambling, grey, half-forgotten place, neither Europe nor Asia; and by the end of summer, as the hot winds, the *lodos*, from the Sea of Marmara, carry the dust from the back streets of Istanbul into the heart of Taxim Square, the temper of this sullen city is as raw as the back of one of those Turkish mules which will suddenly lash out against the discomfort and indignity of life in this terrible country.

At the beginning of September 1955, the mood of the inheritors of New Rome was worse than usual. There was hardly a subject which had not become a cause for frustration—the government, the standard of living, the new currency regulations, the corruption in high places which everyone discussed but which no one remedied. And as usual when Turks reach the manic phase, their frustrations were just about to be released through the one safety valve every patriotic Turk is born with—his hatred of the Greeks.

Not that any of this showed on the surface to the delegates attending the 23rd Interpol Conference who in the first week of that dangerous month suddenly filled up the rooms of Conrad Hilton's newly-built Istanbul Hilton. Solid, serious men from fifty-two nations, with their black homburgs and their black brief-cases, they crammed themselves into Mr Hilton's air-conditioned American palace like satisfied patients in a luxury sanatorium on Manhattan Island. They jostled the wives of the colonels from the American Aid programme who had previously had the Brunch Bar to themselves. They gazed from their picture windows, as even policemen will, at the golden mesh of Istanbul at night. And by September 6th they were ready to discuss calmly among themselves the world battle against lawlessness and violence, unaware that this very city was about to stage its own special demonstration of lawlessness and violence.

Fleming's own journey to Istanbul had been as uneventful

as the journey taken by James Bond in the same Viscount aircraft when he came the same way in *From Russia, With Love*. Again like Bond, Fleming read Eric Ambler's classic thriller about Istanbul, *The Mask of Dimitrios*, during the seven-and-a-half-hour journey.

Yet, typically, Fleming was not anxious to undergo all the hardships he had in store for his hero. True, he had always shared Bond's 'perverse liking for the sleazy romance that clings to old-fashioned Continental hotels', but he drew the line at the fly-blown palms and the bed-bugs of the Istanbul hotel where Bond was to spend his memorable night in the honeymoon suite with Tatiana Romanova and was duly grateful for Mr Conrad Hilton and his hotel.

The idea of an Interpol Conference sounds like a thriller-writer's private gold-mine. The reality must have given Fleming one more reminder that fiction is stranger and infinitely more satisfactory than truth. For the truth about the Interpol Conference was that it was a very serious, very unspectacular convention of dedicated professional men, and it needed all Fleming's ingenuity to discover sufficient news for an article on the conference agenda for that week's *Sunday Times*. There was a guarded paper about the international smuggling of gold and dangerous drugs, and Sir Ronald Howe was to plead for a tightening-up in the policing of air traffic. There were discussions on such subjects as 'Crime and Disease' and 'The General Relationship between Policing and Banking'.

All this left Fleming rather stunned, and he gave his private verdict on the Interpol Conference in a letter to Admiral Godfrey. It sums up the curious contempt which the man who dreams about crime must always feel when he meets the men who merely deal with it. 'The trouble with these policemen,' he wrote, 'is that they have no idea what is really interesting in their jobs and regard criminal matters as really a great bore.'

However, if the Interpol Conference seemed to have so little to do with the world of James Bond, Istanbul was all set to make up for it. September 6th, a Tuesday, was the first official day of the conference. That morning, just as the delegates were settling themselves, a trifle incongruously, amidst the ornate décor of the conference hall in the former Chalet Palace of the Sultan, the newspaper offices of Istanbul began vibrating with the news that the birthplace of Kemal Ataturk at Salonika had been bombed by Greek terrorists during the night. Before lunchtime the first editions of the evening papers were on the streets with joyfully exaggerated accounts of the damage done to the shrine of the father of modern Turkey. And that night, 'by the peaceful light of a three-quarter moon,' as Fleming wrote on the following Sunday, 'the Turkish Common Man broke out from behind Turkey's smile of welcome and reduced Istanbul to a shambles.'

'It was,' reported Fleming in the *Sunday Times*, with a touch of pride, 'the worst insurrection in the history of modern Turkey. On both sides of the Bosphorus in every noisome alley and smart boulevard hatred erupted and ran through the streets like lava.' He was deeply fascinated by what was going on around him, and he gave this Bond's-eye view of his behaviour during what he called 'The Great Riot of Istanbul':

Several times during the night curiosity sucked me out of the safety of the Hilton Hotel and down into the city, where mobs went howling through the streets, each under its streaming red flag with the white star and the sickle moon. Occasional bursts of shouting rose out of the angry murmur of the crowds, then would come the crash of plate glass and perhaps part of a scream.

A car went out of control and charged the yelling crowd, and the yells changed to screams and gesticulating hands showed briefly as the bodies went down before it. And over all there was the trill of the ambulances and the whistling howl of the new police cars, imported from America.

Here at last then, in Istanbul, we have Fleming confronted with that face of violence which had haunted and fascinated him since boyhood. Here in reality was what he had written about so many times from his imagination—the smell of death and the tumult of danger—bloodshed, chaos and carnage. And how did he react? He was, he wrote, 'nauseated' by what he had seen. He was relieved to find that a 'muddy, tough-looking squadron of cavalry were guarding the approaches' to his hotel and that a formation of American Sherman tanks were there to restore order before dawn and 'get a grip on the town'. His chief worry was that millions of pounds' worth of damage was done that night. 'Countless businessmen,' he went on, 'are wiped out, including several British merchants, and the Consulate and the rest of the British community are rallying to their help.'

Fleming the symmetrist had seen real violence at last. Fascinated yet appalled by it, he had retreated gratefully to the side of order and tranquillity. For the riot brought out in him the strange quality which was at the root of all his fantasies and all his books—that 'threat of doom', that 'atmosphere of suspense married to horrible acts'—which he had thrilled to at Eton in the stories of Robert Louis Stevenson and Edgar Allan Poe and which was really the thrill and horror with which the obsessively ordered mind reacts to apprehensions of chaos.

There is in fact a touch of supreme irony about these few days of his in Istanbul. He had come prepared to gather material for an imaginary act of violence and cruelty. Instead he found the real thing; and his reaction was that it was all 'a reminder that Great Britain is very fortunate in being an island nation' and consequently had avoided 'those hatreds that fester between neighbours . . . and that sometimes end in murder'. He was glad, when the riot was over, to contemplate more serious if less disturbing business, namely, the details of SMERSH's plot to murder James Bond.

There was time to do this as he attended the long sessions of the Interpol Conference during the rest of the week. The elaborately embossed blue pads which the Turks had distributed were ideal for a thriller-writer's notes and queries, and he brought several pages of these back with him. And then Istanbul itself began to offer some of the material and characters he needed. He had introductions to a number of the leading merchants and businessmen of the city. among them an Oxford-educated shipowner named Nazim Kalkavan. Kalkavan, cultivated, voluble, highly pro-British and extremely upset at the impression the riot must have made on these distinguished visitors to his country, called at the Hilton the morning after all the excitement to invite Fleming and any of the Interpol delegates who cared to come for a day at his villa on the Bosphorus. From the moment they met Fleming and Kalkavan took to each other. It was the sort of instant friendship Fleming could always inspire in certain people.

'I have rarely met anyone in my life,' Kalkavan said later of Fleming, 'with so much warmth and with a personality so full of life, an alertness encompassing all.' Kalkavan in turn had all the qualities in a man that appealed to Fleming —'a warm dry handclasp', immense liveliness and love of life, a great fund of stories, a resounding enthusiasm for food and women, and a total lack of that English reserve which

K. I have always smoked & drunk far too much. In fact I have lived not too long but too much. One day the iron Crab will get me. Then I shall have died of living too much.

Like all people who have known poverty my chief pleasures are the best food, the best servants & changing my underclothes every day.

The Iron Crab. Fleming makes a note of the words of the Turk on whom he based Darko Kerim in *From Russia, With Love.* He was never to forget the phrase the 'iron crab'

Fleming suffered from but from which he was always so grateful to escape when he had the chance. Another of Fleming's real-life heroes was in the making.

During those few days, as he roamed Istanbul with his friend, Fleming could enjoy once again his secret pleasure of experiencing new sights through the eyes of James Bond. 'He was always inquiring,' says Kalkavan. 'We used to have endless talks mooching about the city. Always disdainful of appearing to be an intellectual, Ian was living Istanbul.'

He was also observing Kalkavan himself as the model for a new type of character who was to make his appearance in *From Russia, With Love.* For Darko Kerim, with his 'curling black hair, his crooked nose' and the face of 'a vagabond soldier of fortune' is one of those rare characters whom Fleming's hero respects and admires as a fellow spirit. 'Bond thought he had never seen such vitality and warmth in a human face. It was like being close to the sun, and Bond let go the strong dry hand and stared back at Kerim with a friendliness he rarely felt for a stranger.'

As well as the spontaneity and love of life which Fleming warmed to in Kalkavan there was something else—the attitude they shared to living and dying. One morning after they had dined together, Fleming made a note of his friend's words while they were still fresh in his mind. In Fleming's handwriting and on the official paper of the Turkish Criminal Police Commission they have a defiant air, like the words of an accused man which change from a confession into a boast even as the police are writing them down:

K. I have always smoked and drunk and loved too much. In fact I have lived not too long but too much. One day the Iron Crab will get me. Then I shall have died of living too much.
Like all people who have known poverty, my chief pleasures are the best food, the best servants and changing my under-clothes every day.

Fleming, who had his own anxieties about heart disease, had never before heard it called 'the iron crab'. The phrase haunted him.

When the Interpol Conference was over and the foreign delegates had left by air he stayed on and took the Simplon-Orient Express. It was worth it. When James Bond caught sight of the flat iron sign on the train announcing 'Istanbul —Thessaloniki—Beograd—Venezia—Milan—Lausanne—Paris' he thought it 'one of the most romantic signs in the world'. So did Fleming on that warm September evening as he left Istanbul. Indeed, his romantic view of the train was almost his undoing. For the Simplon-Orient Express was great no longer. Its spies and its style had departed. So had its restaurant car. Luckily Kalkavan, who had come to the station to see his eccentric friend off, had remembered this and gave Fleming a large woven-mat basket full of Turkish cheese, sausage and fruit. For most of the three-day journey through the Iron Curtain countries the gift provided Fleming with his staple diet.

Nevertheless, all the way up the Sea of Marmara, through northern Greece and across the rich spy-lands of the Balkans, Fleming was happy. What did it matter if the dining-car had disappeared or if he mistook the train's pneumatic brakes for hydraulic ones (and so launched one of James Bond's howlers that the critics were later to pick on)? Bond was aboard one of the celebrated trains of Europe and life was very sweet.

II

It was not until he was back in London and normal life began again that he realized quite how much he had enjoyed his summer interlude with James Bond. 'Life,' he wrote, 'is mud and cream,' a rather futile and desperate business. Yet if it was futile that was all the more reason for repeating to himself the words from Scott Fitzgerald's *The Crack-up* which he was later to place, almost verbatim, into the mouth of James Bond. It was necessary 'to marry the futility of the effort with the urge to strive'. Smoking as much as ever, drinking rather more than before, he did his best to do so himself.

There were still compensations, of course, particularly the long week-ends away from London with Anne and his son Caspar at the house at St Margaret's Bay. They were happy here, and life was simple. He was the most permissive of fathers; Anne cooked; he loved the sea; and once he was playing golf at the Royal St George's he soon recovered his old energy.

But for the rest of the week his routine never changed. Every morning from Tuesday to Friday, just as Big Ben was striking ten on the other side of St James's Park, his Thunderbird would perform a neat right-hand turn round the marble skirts of the Queen Victoria monument at Buckingham Palace, with the old Queen staring blankly at him, and glide off along the Mall. He enjoyed this drive to the office. He also enjoyed the attention the car drew when it was parked under the windows of Kemsley House. Provided he was careful how he swung his body round, he could still pull himself out of the car's low, youthful front seat without too much discomfort.

But although he still appeared as regularly as ever at the office the place depressed him increasingly. He was particularly bored with writing Atticus now and had taken on two assistants, who provided him with most of the copy. The column still worked efficiently, but the personal touch had begun to fade. When he looked about him in the 'Big House' he could see little future for Lord Kemsley's empire. He was one of the few members of the staff who were on close enough terms with the proprietor to realize what might happen, and in any case stories had been openly circulating that the chain might be vulnerable to a take-over bid. Yet if Kemsley House was leaving him increasingly 'exhausted and frustrated' there were other things to claim his attention that autumn. To his surprise Robin Darwin, of the Royal College of Art, proposed him as one of the governors of the college. He was suitably flattered, rather liked the idea and accepted promptly. He also tried to pick up with Percy Muir the threads of his pre-war book-collecting interest, deciding that it would be sensible to collect first editions of John Betjeman and Dylan Thomas. Muir went to work on Dylan Thomas and was soon able to offer Fleming a remarkable collection of letters, ephemera and first editions which were duly added to the works on syphilis, Marxism and fire-damp in the Fleming Collection—still crated-up as it was in the vaults of the London Pantechnicon.

Muir had just returned from Austria when Fleming wrote accepting his offer of the Thomas material. The last sentence of Fleming's brief letter strikes a sad little note of sentimentality for the past: 'Hope you had a fine time in Austria and I was thrilled to get the postcard which reminded me of those wonderful days in which the sun always shone.' All the same, it was the future he was really concerned with now—and particularly the future of his hero. That autumn Pan Books published *Casino Royale*, the first James Bond book to appear here in paperback, and its success in the mass market revived his old hopes about the potential of Bond. If he was to succeed in converting him from a 'cardboard booby' into the sort of 'rounded character' Chandler might approve of, Bond would have to develop. Fleming found the answer, as he had always done, in himself and in his immediate reactions to the life he was leading. There were minor details like the black leather sandals, the strong de Bry coffee, the insistence on a boiled *brown* egg for breakfast which Fleming copied straight from his own early-morning routine. And while he was noting more of these details than ever for his book he was also observing less material aspects of himself with the same intention. In the attempt to make his hero a living character Fleming was offering him his own spiritual malaise as well as his taste in shirts:

The blubbery arms of the soft life had Bond round the neck and they were slowly strangling him . . . At 7.30 Bond awoke . . . and was disgusted to find that he was thoroughly bored with the prospect of the day ahead. Just as, in at least one religion, *accidie* is the first of the cardinal sins, so boredom, and particularly the incredible circumstance of waking up bored, was the only vice Bond utterly condemned.

Fleming condemned it too but suffered from it just the same, particularly that autumn. He would try the same cure for it that Bond employed—'kick oneself out of it' by exercises, cold showers and long walks—but it wasn't much use. For Fleming, as for his hero, life seemed more than ever to be dividing itself into 'mud and cream'. The mud was everyday life with its boredom and broken health. The cream began once he could get away on a plane from London Airport—to New York or Las Vegas or Istanbul or anywhere where Bond might find himself and the fantasies of the Bond-world could restore wonder and excitement to life. It was a desperate expedient; for as his brush with violence during the Istanbul riots had shown, the fantasies made no contact with reality, and behind all lay the efforts of a man attempting to escape from himself. And in the end all his attempts to 'round out' the character of Bond simply ended by his identifying himself with his hero more completely than ever before.

He considered again those few words of Kalkavan's about the 'iron crab' which he had carefully copied down in Istanbul. In their simple way they gave him what he needed —a description of heart trouble of which James Bond would approve. Even the phrase itself, 'the iron crab', gave the malady a sort of dignity; the idea of regarding it as the price which a man ultimately paid for a full life made it seem almost worth achieving. This theory of illness as the just price for past pleasure appealed strongly to Fleming, and when he put the words about the iron crab into the mouth of Darko Kerim in *From Russia, With Love* they offered a manlier and more romantic attitude to heart disease than mere worry or medicine or self-denial.

'Death,' he wrote in his notebook, copying out a phrase of Aloysius Horn, 'is like any untamed animal. He respects a scornful eye.' The iron crab, by the same token, would scarcely respect a man who cut down on his Morland Specials.

CHAPTER TWENTY-ONE

NOT SAYING NO

I

ESSENTIAL YOU ACCOMPANY FIRST SCIENTIFIC VISIT SINCE
1916 TO FLAMINGO COLONY INAGUA MARCH FIFTEEN STOP
PARTY CONSISTS ARTHUR VERNAY BAHAMAS FLAMINGO
PROTECTION SOCIETY COMMA ROBERT MURPHY OF
AMERICAN NATURAL HISTORY MUSEUM AND SELF STOP
FAIL NOT BRYCE

The invitation arrived at Goldeneye just as Fleming was
finishing off the manuscript of *From Russia, With Love*.
There was only one more week left before he must face the
cold March winds of Gray's Inn Road, and he felt inclined
to spend it where he was, lying in the sun and snorkelling
on the reef.

Despite the book, it had been a self-indulgent two months.
At Goldeneye that year he and Anne had enjoyed many of
the old pleasures of this 'green and generous island'. They
had also gone back to the wonderful forgotten beach at
Negril—which she had first discovered—on the east coast of
the island and which they thought the most beautiful in the
world.

It was here that Fleming used to come to swim, naked
except for his black Pirelli mask and flippers, and it was
here that he was so delighted when a remora, the parasite
fish that normally lives attached to the belly of a shark,
clamped itself on to his own stomach; and when he brushed
the thing off he reflected on how 'extremely smart it would
have been to carry for ever the marks of a remora's sucker
on one's stomach—so much more *chic* than the claw marks
of a tiger'. Jamaica was full of adventure and surprise that
year: even the humming-birds in his own back garden must
have seemed preferable to the idea of flamingoes on an
unknown island between Jamaica and Haiti. But Anne had
already decided to leave Jamaica early by ship to avoid the
air journey home, as it always upset her. So on the day he
received the telegram from Bryce he cabled back that he
was on his way.

There was another reason why he decided to spend the last few days of that year's holiday among the flamingoes. He mentioned it when writing about the expedition in the *Sunday Times*—it was a revealing fragment of autobiography to come from the creator of James Bond:

After the age of forty, time begins to be important and one is inclined to say 'Yes' to every experience. One should of course be taught to say 'Yes' from childhood, but Wet Feet, Catching Cold, Getting a Temperature and Breaking something add up to a permanent 'No' that is apt to become a permanent ball and chain.

Here for once he was acknowledging the caution, the wariness of danger and reality, which had always made him (like his grandfather) say 'no'. He used to tell Anne to practise saying 'no' in front of a looking-glass every morning, and in one of his notebooks he was still more specific. 'I've always been inclined to say "No",' he wrote. 'It's a shorter word than "Yes", and it commits you less. But it's wrong and a bad way of life. What people call the "full life" is commitment up to the hilt.' So on this occasion Fleming followed his own advice, and a few days later was sitting with Bryce, Arthur Vernay and Dr Murphy

crushed together in a tiny Cessna plane flying the 400 miles down the beautiful necklace of the Bahama group to Inagua, where there is the largest flamingo colony in the world. The object of the expedition was to make an approximate count of the colony and to see that the Society's protective measures were working well on the eve of the mating season.

As soon as Fleming saw Inagua he loved it for its strangeness. He was wrong about its having the largest flamingo colony in the world—in African colonies flamingoes number millions to Inagua's thousands. But the silence and the unearthly desolation of the place must have appealed to the romantic melancholic in him. He also realized that he had found the ideal setting for his next book, and the few descriptions of Inagua and its 'dreadful lake', only a couple of feet deep and the 'colour of a corpse', which he gave in the *Sunday Times* already resound with the eerie overtones of the fearsome island of Dr Julius No.

While the expedition was on Inagua the party lived in tents, and Fleming took to camping with a sudden schoolboy zest. He enjoyed listening to the reminiscences of Dr Murphy and formed with this distinguished naturalist another of his instant friendships. One of the birds on which Dr Murphy was a great expert was the fertilizer-producing guano bird of South America, and Fleming made mental notes about it for his next book. He was also to remember the marsh buggy in which he made several journeys across the shallow lake—a jeep fitted with enormous balloon tyres—and his imagination finally turned it into the mechanical marsh dragon which Dr No employed to keep unwanted guests away from his headquarters.

For the few days he was there Fleming was in his element. He felt well and free. He was living the sort of adventure he had enjoyed since boyhood, and Inagua soon became Crab Key, the scene of one more of James Bond's exploits. But time was short. He was due back in London on March 22nd, and less than three days after watching the flamingoes and making scrambled eggs outside his tent in the hot dry sunlight of Inagua he was home again. Almost at once he caught cold, and the sciatica and bouts of lethargy which had ceased to plague him in Jamaica returned. While he was away Anne had been to Enton Hall, a health cure clinic near Godalming, in Surrey. He decided that he would have to try it too.

But first there was the publication of *Diamonds Are Forever* to attend to—it was to appear on April 4th, and to his joy the *Daily Express* had bought the serial rights. As usual he enjoyed the publicity and the reviews, although he felt that a first edition of 12,500 copies wasn't good enough—he was still nowhere near the best-seller stakes. He was pondering the situation when he found that his little habit of amusing himself by bestowing the names of friends or relatives on characters in his novels had this time involved him in a difficulty. He had begun in *Casino Royale* by appropriating the surname of John Leiter the millionaire. In *Live and Let Die* Bond and Solitaire travel south on the Silver Meteor under the pseudonym of Mr and Mrs Bryce; May Maxwell, housekeeper at the Bryces' home in New York, became Bond's own treasured housekeeper; the taxi-driver in *Diamonds Are Forever* is called Ernest Cureo; Loelia Ponsonby, Bond's secretary, bears the maiden name of Loelia, Duchess of Westminster—the books are littered with such borrowings. But when *Diamonds Are Forever* was published one of the victims objected strenuously to Fleming's private joke. This was Anne's cousin, the present Lord Arran, the columnist, who in those days was known to a large circle of friends as 'Boofy' Gore. As a surprise for him Fleming borrowed the nickname and attached it to a particularly unsavoury character in the book. Great displeasure resulted, and this was the only occasion when Fleming is known to have apologized and changed the name of one of his characters in subsequent editions.

He had not meant to be unkind. Although he was the most selfish and egocentric of men in the way he planned his life and pursued its objectives, he could take much trouble over people he cared for. He went to some pains to help Raymond Chandler sort out his English tax position and patiently made arrangements for him to go to Rome to meet Lucky Luciano, the gangster who had been deported to Italy in 1946 by the U.S. authorities, in the hope that the encounter would revive Chandler's waning interest in living and writing (the *Sunday Times* found the resultant article unusable). He was assiduous in 'inserting' his friends into suitable clubs—Cyril Connolly into White's, Sefton Delmer into the Garrick, and quite a clutch of them into Boodle's. He was a great careers adviser and procurer of jobs for his friends and their children. He was particularly good at commiserating—by letter—with people in ill health and at encouraging them by relating surprising cures he had discovered for their own particular malady.

And now, encouraged by Anne, he himself was going to the health clinic known as Enton Hall, a large, well-maintained Victorian mansion in the heart of the Surrey stockbroker belt. When he visited it for ten days at the end of April it was his first experience of such a place, and he began by wondering if he was going to be able to stand this 'Orange-juice Land', as he called it. He was allocated one of the chalets in the grounds and became entitled to his statutory glass of orange juice for breakfast, his plate of tomato soup for lunch, his Sitz baths and his massage. He was also given treatment for his sciatica on a traction machine, designed to stretch and loosen the spine.

For the novice the first few days are traditionally difficult. This is the purgative period when, like some physical religion, the cure draws out the impurities of the body. Fleming suffered and felt himself in a perpetual hangover. But when this began to lift he found to his surprise that the atmosphere and the regime of Orange-juice Land suited him very well. Never before had he known a place more attuned to the conflicting demands of his highly contradictory nature. Here he could punish himself in agreeable company, suffer in an atmosphere of comfort, be as solitary as he liked yet always have an audience on hand, be hedged in by rules which he could break if he felt like it.

It might almost have been the world of Bond himself, and he started making notes for the health clinic setting in which he was to immure James Bond at the beginning of *Thunderball*. For the treatment at Shrublands, that exclusive hydro to which Bond is banished by M. in order to work out the poisons left in his system by his dangerous way of life, is based on the treatment Fleming cheerfully endured during these April days of 1956 at Enton Hall. It was there, too, that he picked up much of the special knowledge which was to go into *Goldfinger*. It seems almost too considerable a coincidence even for Fleming that the first man he met in the steam bath at Enton Hall turned out to be a goldsmith from Garrick Street. He was an urbane, forthcoming man in his middle fifties named Guy Wellby; his family had been in the business since the Regency, and the firm had held Royal Warrants. For the next ten days Fleming listened assiduously to everything that Wellby the enthusiast had to tell him about gold.

'I had a Bentley,' explains Wellby, 'a large comfortable old car, and for some reason Ian seemed to love being driven in it. So in the afternoon, after we'd had our treatment in the steam rooms, we'd drive off, and as we drove we'd talk about gold. He wanted to know how the accounting was done, how gold was tested for carat, how it was transported and stored and smuggled. There was something in this magical substance that seemed to appeal to the romantic in him.'

But if the regime was good for his books it made little impression on his sciatica; and a few weeks after the cure Fleming was back in Dr Beal's consulting-room complaining of palpitations and an accelerating heart beat. In his file the doctor noted, 'He complains of greater exhaustion than is natural in a man of his age' and adds in retrospect, 'By now Ian's arteries were clearly beginning to go.'

Beal prescribed a stricter diet and advised against cigarettes and alcohol. Fleming cut down to fifty Morlands a day and turned from vodka martinis to bourbon. At golf he kept to his handicap of nine and in the *Sunday Times* office he seemed as much his old blue-suited, sardonic self as ever. But he was chronically restless. Vitality was changing to tension.

Bridge at Boodle's bored him now—the stakes were too low. He could afford to risk the Portland Club regularly: play was higher there and he had his cronies. New faces had no interest for him now—he wanted just his own friends and then on his own terms.

'I think Ian's capacity for human beings was extremely limited,' says Anne, 'and it became more limited as he got older, whereas I enjoy meeting strangers. He always described dinner-parties as me sitting next to two interesting men while he sat next to their terribly boring wives, and that was why he didn't want to be there. So when he began going regularly to the Portland Club I invented a night life and gave occasional dinner-parties.'

When he married Anne she had symbolized excitement, chaos, the unexpected for him—all the forms of vitality which lay outside his ordered bachelor's existence. She remained the most precious and stimulating influence in his life, but although very few people were aware of it he was beginning to turn back into himself, and his familiar non-chalance was assumed now rather than felt. 'There are few things more disturbing,' he wrote in his notebook, 'than seeing your face in the window of a train or plane at night, riding beside you in the dark outside.' His own face, his own appearance, obsessed him as much as ever, except that he was now disturbed by what he saw.

The most important human quality of eyes is that they should express interest in the outer world. The inward-looking eyes are dead or dying. They do not renew themselves and nourish the spirit by contact with other eyes, other people. Focused inwardly, they become sterile with constant examination of the same landscape, the same personality, the same ego.

Gratefully he turned his attention to a buoyant letter from Ivar Bryce, who had formed a new holding company in Nassau for his different business enterprises. More impor-tant, he had finally sold his interest in the North American Newspaper Alliance and with the money realized he and Cuneo were launching themselves into commercial tele-vision. Fleming's role and income with N.A.N.A. had ceased, but he was naturally to be included in the new bonanza. 'Please start by refurbishing your contacts with all buyers of programmes in the B.B.C. and commercial television. I foresee a busy and intoxicating summer.'

'No one,' as Anatole France sagely remarked, 'offers so much as he who offers hope,' and Fleming adopted the role of Bryce's financial adviser almost by return of post:

Independent Television over here is getting pretty short of capital and anyone with a hundred thousand pounds to spare would be warmly welcome.

At present I.T.V. is not being very successful in selling cheese and brassières, but seeing what the medium has done in America there is obviously a profit in it here one day, and it is just a question of choosing the right day. If your American T.V. operation wanted to link up over here, they can get in on the ground floor after the press lords and others have mulched the ground with their millions.

This last piece of advice was extremely shrewd, and if Bryce had taken it he might have made the financial killing of a lifetime. Instead, by a strange irony, someone who was to become Fleming's boss at the *Sunday Times* had already seized the opportunity. He was a Canadian newspaper millionaire—and proprietor of the *Scotsman*—called Roy Thomson, and he was to buy out Lord Kemsley in 1959 from the profits of Scottish Television. It was the greatest irony of all that Lord Kemsley himself was originally offered the pick of commercial television franchises by the Independent Television Authority, but like Bryce later on he had failed to grab his chance.

II

It was about this time that Fleming began to have doubts about the now completed *From Russia, With Love*. Through Anne he had recently met a young artist named Richard Chopping, a master of *trompe-l'œil* painting who had the brainwave of suggesting that he should do a wrapper for the book. Chopping's painting of a rose and a sawn-off Smith & Wesson that Fleming borrowed from Geoffrey Boothroyd, the Edinburgh firearms expert who was later to become James Bond's 'Armourer', was a great success. Indeed, Chopping's wrappers were to provide the British editions of Fleming's later novels with a trademark of their own. But however good the jacket and ingenious the story, Fleming realized that Bond was still as resolutely his old, humourless, two dimensional self as ever and was seriously concerned whether the book had sufficient pace and excitement. To William Plomer he wrote:

. . . My greatest fear is staleness. It is so difficult to communicate zest if it isn't there, and though I still enjoy writing about Bond,

I constantly find myself piling on adjectives (as you sapiently note) to fill the vacuum created by my waning enthusiasm for this cardboard booby . . . and of course by waning years.

Plomer's reply was reassuring. So was the verdict of Daniel George. Both of them hastened to assure him that *From Russia, With Love* was both original and exciting. Almost from the start, however, other people seemed worried about the book, and someone told Fleming that Chandler did not like it. These unfavourable reactions all added to his anxieties. Perhaps he *had* made a terrible mistake and over-reached himself this time by trying to be too clever, and a petulant letter in which he replied to the criticisms of Michael Howard, one of Cape's directors, showed just how edgy about his writing he was becoming.

But Howard might have been less disconcerted had he known of a short letter Fleming had dictated six days earlier. It was to a wartime friend in Naval Intelligence whom he had been meaning to meet in London; he apologized for failing to fix a day and repeated his rueful joke: 'Sorry for taking so long to answer, but I suddenly started a small private diamond factory in my kidneys and had to retire to the London Clinic for a few days . . .'

Kidney trouble was the most painful of his afflictions, worse even than his sciatica, yet even in its clutch this romantic pessimist seems to have felt that there was an inevitability and a certain justice in what was happening to him. 'All my malaises,' he wrote self-accusingly to a former girl friend, 'come from youthful over-indulgences,' and an aphorism of Raymond Chandler's which had stuck in his mind seemed to him very apt—'lust ages men but keeps women young'. In all, with that careful introverted logic which he brought to life's problems, Fleming was on the way to convincing himself that life was going to cheat him yet again, that the success of the last few years was too good to last and retribution was waiting at the end of his bed.

A period of bad health would always bring out his latent pessimism and exaggerate his old feelings of hopelessness. But a week-end at St Margaret's Bay or the promise of travel and his troubles would soon evaporate, and even now he saw no reason for meekly submitting to his fate. Though his kidney stones were still giving him pain he refused to linger between the expensive sheets of the London Clinic. Already that year he had received serious offers from film and television companies eager to exploit the money-making potential of Bond, but he had been playing hard to get. Then at the beginning of July an inquiry had arrived which really interested him. Quite recently the select group in New York whom he never failed to contact on his brief excursions there had been joined by Lord Beaverbrook's grand-daughter, the future bride of Norman Mailer, Lady Jean Campbell. Fleming had a standing date to see Cinerama with her when he reached Idlewild, and it was she who mentioned him to Henry Morgenthau III. Morgenthau, who was very rich, was working at the time as a television producer for the National Broadcasting Company, and a project on which he was engaged was a half-hour adventure series provisionally entitled 'Commander Jamaica', to be filmed in Jamaica. He wondered if Fleming would be interested in collaborating.

Somewhat surprisingly Fleming was, and within a few days of leaving the London Clinic he was writing Morgenthau a long and enthusiastic letter. He said that he expected to be in the United States within a matter of days, and in Vermont he worked on a plot for the series. The name of the chief character may have been Commander James Gunn, but Fleming was strictly a one-hero man and he was really the same old James Bond. The twenty-eight page pilot script Fleming sent off to Morgenthau at the end of August told a swashbuckling tale of a tall, dark-haired, fast-moving R.N. commander who receives his clipped orders from an endlessly demanding admiral through a hidden loudspeaker in the cabin of his thirty-foot yacht moored at Morgan's Harbour in Jamaica. The commander, while pretending to be on a treasure hunt, is really investigating the activities on an uninhabited Caribbean island of a gang thought to be behind a plot to deflect the course of American missiles from Cape Canaveral. As Fleming sent it to Morgenthau the script was unfinished and the villain had still to make his appearance. But the commander had already tangled with a gang of Chinese-Negro cut-throats and saved his Man Friday, Joe Montego, from a sudden end between the crushers of one of Jamaica's bauxite plants.

Fleming himself does not seem to have been unduly surprised when the project collapsed. As he wrote to Morgenthau in a consoling letter, 'The film and television world in America is a hell of a jungle and I know how long is the road between specious promises and the actual signing of the contract.' In the circumstances he could afford to be philosophical; for if he had lost a television programme he had at any rate gained his next book. James Bond could throw off the false whiskers of James Gunn and be himself again, and Fleming already had the background of swamp and desolation at Inagua to draw on for his villains' hide-away. *Dr No* in fact was in the bag.

After the dangerous experiment of trying something new in *From Russia, With Love* Fleming seems to have made up his mind that he would play *Dr No* very safe indeed. And that autumn the formula for James Bond was finally established. From now on, quite consciously, as he told Al Hart, Fleming would write 'the same book over and over again', with only the settings changing: from now on it was the best-seller stakes and an abandonment of Raymond Chandler's belief in him as a writer capable of higher things.

All the same, the one feature which made all the Fleming stories unique was to remain—the grim obsession with James Bond. Fleming still had no other source but himself for information about his hero, and because of this *Dr No* was to become more than ever a part of his own autobiography for that painful autumn of his forty-ninth year. He was preparing his final notes for his new novel, and as he did so he carefully transferred his woes to the uncomplaining body of James Bond. Twelve months earlier all that Bond had had to endure was boredom and twenty press-ups every morning to fight off the demoralizing effects of the 'soft life'. Now he had to suffer not only his creator's physical pains but their spiritual aftermath as well. In a way he even had to share the same specialist. This was Mr J. A. Molony, the Harley Street dental surgeon, whom Fleming had recently consulted.

Fleming gave Mr Molony a knighthood, turned him into a 'famous neurologist', and brought him in to deliver his specialist's report on Bond, who was only just recovering from that near-lethal kick from the barbed toe of Rosa Klebb which is described on the last page of *From Russia, With Love*. In the end, reluctantly, M. agreed with Sir James Molony that Bond deserved a break. And weighed down with Fleming's afflictions the long-suffering Bond was sent off to the same spot where his creator was shortly to go to find relief in the sun from *his* troubles. But before Fleming reached Jamaica that winter Goldeneye was to enjoy a strange interlude of its own.

CHAPTER TWENTY-TWO

EDEN AT GOLDENEYE

Towards the end of November the North Shore of Jamaica becomes one of the best places in the world for a man of philosophic disposition with time on his hands, and Anthony Lahoud, who had both, always enjoyed this moment, when the damp heat of summer was over, the rains were forgotten, and the visitors had still to arrive.

With his close-cropped white hair and his strong Marseilles accent, Lahoud was an unusual man to find in a forgotten little village like Oracabessa. He had come here years before from Martinique and had built up a considerable standing in the local community, with intricate business interests and a rambling bungalow off the main road to Port Maria. He called himself an attorney, but in Jamaica 'attorney' is a flexible term and Anthony Lahoud was many things—an agent, a manager, a man of affairs; and since Goldeneye was less than half a mile up the road he had managed it on behalf of the Commander ever since it was built, paying the bills, sending him the accounts, dealing with any repairs, and working with Violet the cook whenever there were guests to take care of.

The morning the telegram came he was sitting outside his bungalow, and he watched the telegraph boy, who had pedalled the seven miles from Port Maria, with misgiving. For Lahoud was a realist. As a realist he knew that in Oracabessa telegrams invariably mean work or trouble or both. But not even his shrewd old Southerner's nose can have told him just how much of an upheaval this innocent-looking message in its pink envelope with the heavy-fisted date stamp was to bring to Oracabessa, to Goldeneye and to Anthony Lahoud.

Like most of the telegrams Lahoud received at this time of the year, it was from the Commander, and as usual with the Commander's telegrams it was brief almost to the point of obscurity:

ANTHONY LAHOUD ORACABESSA JAMAICA
THREE IMPORTANT FRIENDS ARRIVE NOVEMBER TWENTY-
SECOND FOR THREE WEEKS VISIT STOP PLEASE TELL
VIOLET GET EXTRA STAFF PREPARE HOUSE STOP CLEAN
YARD AND DRIVE STOP CABLE CONFIRMATION REGARDS
FLEMING

Lahoud scratched his head and wondered what Violet
would say. No one had been expected at Goldeneye before
the Commander and his lady arrived in January, and two
days was short notice to get the place ready; there was still
no hot water in the Commander's shower, and the garden
wasn't all it might be. But for her part Violet was unper-
turbed by the news. The Commander's guests were always
easy people and would make allowances. The bed-making
and the sweeping could be left until the following day and
she would catch the afternoon bus into Port Maria to order
the extra food they would be needing. After ten years with
the Commander Violet was used to taking things like this
in her stride, and it was not until the evening, on her
return from Port Maria, that she got her first inkling that
this visit might be something out of the ordinary. A second
telegram had just arrived:

SORRY PARTY NOW ARRIVES FRIDAY TWENTY-THIRD
POSSIBLY LUNCHTIME STOP ONE MARRIED COUPLE TWO
MEN STOP ENDEAVOUR FIX UNIFORMS FOR COOK AND
EXTRA GIRL STOP BE PREPARED FOR CONSIDERABLE
PUBLICITY REGARDS FLEMING

And as Violet and Lahoud puzzled over which of the Commander's friends could possibly want the staff in uniform
and bring 'considerable publicity' in their wake, events in
London were moving fast. The word 'Goldeneye' was
already being whispered by a knowing few in Whitehall, and
certainly Violet and Lahoud might have had a surer idea
of the identity of their mysterious guests if they had seen
the London newspapers of that day. For the front-page
headlines summarized a communiqué issued from Downing
Street at ten minutes before midnight on November 19th:

The Prime Minister is suffering from the effects of severe over-
strain. On the advice of his doctors he has cancelled his
immediate public engagements.

Sir Horace Evans, Sir Anthony Eden's personal physician,
had gone to Downing Street during the evening, and
according to the *Daily Telegraph* he had been for some

time 'urging on the Prime Minister the absolute necessity of seeking some rest and relief from his duties as soon as possible. The point has now evidently been reached where the advice can no longer be disregarded'. It was not known how long the Prime Minister's 'rest' was to last or whether he would go into hospital. He would, however, be leaving Downing Street, and Mr Butler, Lord Privy Seal, would preside at Cabinet meetings in the absence of the Prime Minister. Thus twelve days after the British cease-fire at Port Said the Anglo-French adventure at Suez seemed to have claimed its most impressive victim, and Oracabessa was on the eve of the most exalted and bizarre moment in its history.

Though it had become important that the Prime Minister should rest it was not easy to find a suitable spot for his recuperation, and secrecy was necessary at the outset to protect the Administration from the speculations of both the Press and the Opposition. Mr Alan Lennox-Boyd, who was then Secretary of State for the Colonies, was a friend of the Flemings; and to avoid premature gossip the Edens decided to approach Ian Fleming through him. As a first step it seemed reasonable that Mr Lennox-Boyd (who is now Viscount Boyd) should ask his friend Ian if he might borrow Goldeneye for himself for a few weeks' holiday. Fleming said he would be delighted—it was no trouble at all.

This explains the strange veil of Bond-like secrecy which surrounded the entire affair until the very moment when the Prime Minister's destination was made public on the morning of November 22nd. It also helps explain why it was that, out of all the places which might have been made available for a Prime Minister to escape to, the honour ultimately fell upon Goldeneye.

During those last few anxious days before Eden took Sir Horace Evans's advice the only person in the Government who had given the matter any real thought was Mr Lennox-Boyd. This was far-sighted of him: he realized that if the Prime Minister was to go on convalescence outside England he would almost inevitably become the responsibility of the Colonial Office. But what Mr Lennox-Boyd achieved by foresight he almost undid by discretion. It was his anxiety to arrange the whole thing with a maximum of secrecy and a minimum of outside advice that caused events to take the singular course they did.

The actual choice of Goldeneye seems to have been Lady Eden's. She was one of Anne Fleming's oldest friends and had heard enthusiastic reports about Oracabessa in the last few years. But all the arrangements were left to Lennox-Boyd, and for some reason Lady Eden had no chance of discussing the idea with Anne Fleming in person.

But on the face of it Goldeneye was a brainwave, and of all the places which the Prime Minister might wish to go to it seemed almost ideal. The weather would be perfect, the populace loyal, the visit could be arranged at a moment's notice with a minimum of fuss and protocol; nor would the Prime Minister and Lady Eden be going to the home of strangers—Lady Eden was godmother to the Flemings' son Caspar.

As he sat at his large desk in his large office behind Westminster Abbey making his discreet preparations, the Colonial Secretary overlooked only one small fact. It was that neither he nor the Edens nor the Governor of Jamaica, Sir Hugh Foot, had ever been to Goldeneye. He knew nothing about the iron bedsteads or the cold water in the shower or the absence of a bathroom or the bush rats in the roof or Violet's curried goat or the fact that the nearest telephone was nearly a mile up the road. Graham Greene could have told him, or Noël Coward, or even Truman Capote. But the Colonial Secretary never asked them. Instead he asked Ian Fleming, and consequently the reality of Goldeneye eluded him.

At any rate, Fleming can have had no reason to be surprised when on November 19th the Colonial Secretary telephoned to ask whether he could spare the time for a chat at the Colonial Office the following day—he wanted some journalistic advice and fancied that Ian might have the answer. The fact was that the Colonial Office was sponsoring a series of books—known as the Corona Library —on the various colonies; Hong Kong and Nyasaland had already been written about and he was wondering if Ian could suggest some likely authors for a few of the territories remaining.

That night the communiqué about the Prime Minister's illness was published from 10 Downing Street. Next morning Ian Fleming called at the Colonial Office to talk about the Corona Library.

When the discussion was over and the visitor was preparing to leave the Colonial Secretary asked whether

Fleming would mind if not he but the Prime Minister stayed at Goldeneye for a few weeks. Fleming, of course, was enthusiastic. Nothing could be easier. The house was always ready, the staff were used to his friends arriving at short notice, elaborate preparations would be entirely unnecessary. Of course, it was no luxury place, but Anthony and Clarissa could stay as his guests for just as long as they liked—he was sure they would love it as much as he did.

The two men understood the need for absolute discretion at this stage, and when later that afternoon Lennox-Boyd sent a copy of one of the Corona series to Kemsley House— it was *Sierra Leone* by Roy Lewis—he made no mention of Goldeneye. All he said in the short note which arrived with the book was that he was *so* grateful for all Fleming's help and understanding. That same afternoon Fleming sent off his first telegram to Lahoud.

At first Fleming was as mysterious about the whole business as he had once been with Admiralty secrets during the war; all that he would tell Anne was that Lennox-Boyd had asked whether he could borrow Goldeneye for a short holiday before Christmas. But beneath all the secrecy he was obviously thrilled. Perhaps he should have told Lennox-Boyd that Goldeneye was simply not the place for a sick Prime Minister—that it was not big enough or comfortable enough or secluded enough—and suggested someone else, Noël Coward or Sir William Stephenson, who would have been delighted to have lent Eden the sort of house in Jamaica that he needed. Yet it is doubtful if Fleming would have accepted all this, and now that the myth of Goldeneye was about to enter history it was too much to expect its creator to upset it.

On November 22nd the news broke that the Prime Minister and Lady Eden were going off for three weeks to Goldeneye —'a white house with no phone—but a garden leading to the sea', as the *Daily Express* romantically described it. The *Express* also carried a short interview with Anne. 'The villa,' she said, 'is whitewashed and easy to run. We will not be there. The idea is that the Edens will have complete privacy.' And Fleming, still scrupulously maintaining N.I.D.-style secrecy, sent off a third telegram to Lahoud, giving the final date of arrival:

PARTY NOW ARRIVES SATURDAY TWENTY-FOURTH STOP TELL VIOLET RELAX AND TREAT GUESTS EXACTLY AS US REGARDS TO ALL FLEMING

On the evening of Friday the 23rd the Prime Minister, over-coated and shawled against the night air, boarded a special B.O.A.C. D.C.7C at London Airport. It was very new, very empty; and B.O.A.C. announced that 'The aircraft in which the Prime Minister will travel will be making a crew-familiarization flight from London to Bermuda, New York and Gander, preparatory to its introduction into regular service between London and the United States in the New Year.' While the great aircraft roared on through the night the Prime Minister tried to sleep, the crew familiarized among themselves, and Oracabessa made ready for its great day.

Violet was all for following the Commander's instructions, 'relax and treat guests exactly as us', but events were against her. So was the Governor of Jamaica, Sir Hugh Foot, later to become Lord Caradon. Now that the Prime Minister's visit was official he had had a chance to take a look at Goldeneye. It was not exactly what he had expected, but it was too late now to find the Prime Minister anywhere more suitable. So the Governor and the wife of the Governor, with that energy and practicality for which they were re-nowned, set to work to make the best of a distinctly odd job.

The first essential was to correct the idea that the Prime Minister of Great Britain was coming to Jamaica as the private guest of Mr Ian Fleming. Protocol, if nothing else, demanded that he should be the guest of the Government of Jamaica, and this was hurriedly arranged. Next, there was the question of Goldeneye itself. It was all very well for the newspapers to get excited about white-washed walls and the absence of telephones—Sir Hugh Foot had been in the Colonial Service long enough to know that romanticism is dangerous where Prime Ministers are concerned. There would *have* to be telephones. There would have to be secretaries. There would have to be police protection, servants in uniform, a couple of cooks who knew what Prime Ministers liked to eat; in short, Government House would have to take over. But when the Governor of Jamaica decided this he had reckoned without Violet, and Violet stood by her Commander's orders.

'No, Lady,' she replied to Lady Foot, who had undertaken the delicate task of asking her to make way for the staff from Government House, 'I obey my Commander.'

'But, Violet, your Queen would like you to do this for the sake of her Prime Minister.'

'I still don't care, Lady. I respect the Queen but I obey the Commander.'

Obey the Commander she did, and Government House, with time running out, could only do its best to make the Prime Minister's stay a comfortable one. A squad of gardeners was drafted in to tackle the lawn and the weeds behind the house. Several ladies came over from Kingston with the Governor's wife in a last-minute attempt to give Goldeneye what it notably lacked—comfort and the womanly touch. An office was set up in the summer house with a couple of emergency telephones and a typewriter on a trestle table. Dispatch riders on motor-cycles were organized to make the journey between Goldeneye and Government House several times a day. And just down the road, at his house Blue Harbour, Noël Coward, with notable common sense, drove off to Kingston to buy the Edens a very large basket of caviare, pâté de foie gras and champagne— 'Anything I could see in fact that might mitigate the horrors I knew the poor dears were in for.'

While all this was going on Fleming had retreated for the week-end to St Margaret's Bay, and from the Kent coast he was watching events with an excited if slightly cynical eye. He wrote to Al Hart:

I hope that the Edens' visit to Goldeneye has done something to my American sales. Here there have been full-page spreads of the property, including Violet emptying ashtrays and Heaven-knows-what-all. It has really been a splendid week and was greatly increasing the value of the property until Anne started talking to reporters about barracuda, the hardness of the beds and curried goat. Now some papers treat the place as if it was a hovel and others as if it was the millionaire home of some particularly disgusting millionaire tax dodger.

This morning the cables flashed the news that the Prime Minister and Lady Eden had their first lunch of roast beef and Yorkshire pudding, and I learn that the Governor sent over six gardeners and a posse of Kingston gracious ladies to 'tidy up' the place before the august visitors arrived. I can just see them punching up my faded cushions and putting cut glass vases of flowers beside the detectives' beds in the room you two had. Four policemen are stationed in the grounds, helicopters are flying overhead and half the fishermen's canoes conceal television cameras.

What Oracabessa must be saying to all this I can't imagine The whole area couldn't have been more devastated by a hurricane. Anyway it's a hilarious affair and you should hurry off and sell your memoirs of the place to the magazines.

The truth, of course, was that Fleming was very much in two minds about his distinguished visitors. On the one hand he was thrilled and delighted that out of all the great houses, all the luxurious millionaires' establishments on the island, it should have been his own house, built for £2,000 in 1946, which had been chosen; he had won ascendancy again, and it was all a tribute to his dreams, proof-positive of his skill in making his myths come true. As he wrote to Ivar Bryce:

I am reminded that Reggie Acquart, when I told him the name I had chosen, said with the sapient shake of that head of his, 'Commander, it doesn't matter what you call the house. Everyone will always call it Rock Edge.' Little did he know that not only Oracabessa, but the whole of Jamaica, has now been made famous by the name.

That was one aspect of it. But there was another more serious side. He wrote to Sir William Stephenson:

In the whole of modern history I can't think of a comparable shambles created by any single country. But leaving countries and sentiments out of account, two months ago the Middle East was an angry boil about to burst. It has now burst and the wound is open to the air, which can only be a good thing. I am sure, however asinine our action was, it has upset a great number of secret plans which would have done much more harm to the world than Eden.

Meanwhile it seemed that the Edens were enjoying the amenities of Goldeneye; and within a few days the Prime Minister was reported to be rising at six a.m. and having a glass of green tea before going off for a short swim. The *Daily Express* correspondent claimed, without disclosing his sources, that Sir Anthony had gained a full four pounds in weight.

As a place of escape from everything, Goldeneye may have been ideal, but Eden was still concerned with affairs of State and as the centre of the Commonwealth it left much to be desired. The first problem was that of security. The reporters were held off and it was decided that police passes were to be issued to 'authorized' visitors only. When policemen manned the pineapple-topped gates of Goldeneye the reporters felt their professional pride challenged, and photographers trained their long-range lenses on the Prime Minister's breakfast-table. The siege of Goldeneye began.

Before long there was scarcely a bush around the perimeter of Fleming's fourteen tropical acres without a white-capped policeman sitting beside it. Two officers from Scotland Yard were doing their unobtrusive best to make sure that the Prime Minister was never beyond their sight a moment longer than delicacy demanded. Several dozen reporters, keeping boredom and News Editors at bay, informed the world of every imaginable and unimaginable detail in the daily round of the inaccessible occupant of Goldeneye. Watched by reporters, shot by photographers, guarded by detectives, Sir Anthony did his best to run the Commonwealth and recover his health. The Edens dared not expose themselves still further to the inquisitiveness of the reporters and decided to forgo excursions and visits. They stayed put in Goldeneye, virtual prisoners of the Press.

Yet Sir Anthony Eden was not the only one to find the siege of Goldeneye uncomfortable. Anthony Lahoud, still nominally responsible to the Commander for the whole establishment, had become increasingly irked by all these outsiders usurping his authority. He was issued with a police pass, but then, as Fleming explained to Al Hart on December 12th, it was revoked:

Officiously the Governor has removed Anthony's pass to Goldeneye on the grounds that he is gossiping to reporters and I have just been on to Downing Street asking them to cable the Prime Minister to get this put right. Otherwise his standing in the community will collapse and I will be without an attorney.

The trouble involved a report which had reached the London newspapers about a doctor being summoned during the night to the Prime Minister at Goldeneye soon after he arrived there.

This visit was firmly denied by the Prime Minister's party and Lahoud equally firmly denied that he had been the source of the report. The outcome was that his pass to Goldeneye was cancelled.

At the Admiralty Fleming had never been the man to allow a slight on one of his own people to pass unchallenged, and the immediate action he took to save Lahoud's feelings explains something of the devotion he could always inspire in those who worked for him. The Prime Minister's office at 10 Downing Street was called on to take action on behalf of Anthony Lahoud and a priority signal sent to Anthony Eden in person. Happily the Governor relented. Despite all the fuss, therefore, Lahoud was among the notables of Oracabessa who were allowed to line up and shake the Prime

Minister by the hand on the day he left. Honour was saved and Fleming kept his attorney.

The other incident in the Edens' stay which caused Fleming some concern was the business of the bush rats in the roof. It was and still is almost as mysterious as Sherlock Holmes's Giant Rat of Sumatra. Like the reports of the doctor summoned to the Prime Minister by night, the origins of the story are obscure. What is clear is that during the second week of the Edens' stay the *Evening Standard* reported that Sir Anthony was being troubled by rats and that after several disturbed nights he had gallantly organized a rat hunt with his two detectives. Seven rats were reported missing.

The paper spoke to Fleming about the rats. He expressed surprise and tried to make it clear that the affair had been much exaggerated. 'They are not really bad rats at Golden-eye,' he said. 'They are field rats, not house rats, and they have never given trouble before. They wake one up in the night, knocking coral and crockery off the shelves. But I cannot believe they seriously frighten anyone.' What was Commander Fleming's reaction to the success of Sir Anthony's campaign? 'Violet,' he replied diplomatically, 'will be delighted that they have been removed.'

For distinctly practical reasons of his own Fleming was not really quite so unconcerned as he tried to appear. As he wrote to Ivar Bryce:

The greatly increased rental value was brought down sharply by a completely dreamt-up report to the effect that Goldeneye was over-run by rats and that the Edens and the detectives had spent the whole night chasing them . . . Clarissa now says this was a complete fiction . . . All this has confused the general public greatly and they are even less decided whether I am a millionaire or a garbage collector—or possibly a millionaire garbage collector.

The whole thing remains one of the unsolved mysteries of Jamaica.

Fleming had become news: the Prime Minister's visit to Goldeneye had brought him to the attention of a much wider public than his books had ever done so far. And at this point also he was given a great shove up the ladder of popularity by the *Daily Express*, who bought the serial rights of *From Russia, With Love* for £3,000.

It was now that his public began to change. Up to then he had really been 'the Peter Cheyney of the carriage trade', admired by a small and sophisticated audience. After Eden's visit to Goldeneye many people were suddenly interested in this 'millionaire garbage collector', and since his books were being serialized and put into paperbacks they began to read him. After five long years the 'Best-Seller Stakes' had begun in earnest.

Yet it would be misleading to over-emphasize the part Goldeneye played in all this. At most Eden's visit brought Fleming's name before an audience who would never otherwise have heard of him. But it so happened that this was precisely the kind of publicity he needed at this particular moment, and if Fleming with his flair for self-promotion had planned the whole thing himself it could hardly have been better done.

For the Prime Minister, too, the visit to Goldeneye must finally be counted a success. It achieved its main object. Unscathed by the hazards of his stay, he landed at London Airport on a regular B.O.A.C. scheduled flight on December 14th. Several of his Cabinet were waiting loyally in the icy wind to welcome him home. He looked bronzed and well, and when he faced the television cameras in the Nissen hut on the edge of the airport he began with the words, 'As you know, I went away to get fit, and I now am absolutely fit to resume my duties.' Three weeks later his health broke down again and he resigned the Premiership.

Today the souvenirs of Goldeneye's brief moment of glory are a tree behind the house, planted by the Prime Minister, and the inscriptions which the security guards carved on the bark of several of the big trees in the garden. One is still legible. It reads 'God Save Sir Anthony Eden.'

CHAPTER TWENTY-THREE

GOLF AND GOLD

To the right lie the dunes of Sandwich Bay, with Deal in the distance and the splendid Guilford Hotel looking like a big Victorian tea caddy dumped and forgotten by the edge of the sea. To the left are the toy cliffs of Ramsgate and the shallows of Pegwell Bay, where they once gathered oysters which were shipped to Rome. The turf is firm and green and the Channel breeze starts the players off with an instant bonus of ozone and energy. For Fleming it was quite simply 'the best seaside golf course in the world'.

The Royal St George's is a rich club and an exclusive one. The Duke of Windsor was captain when he was Prince of Wales and is still a member; Churchill was an honorary member and so is ex-King Leopold of the Belgians. Fleming had been playing here since the days of the *Cercle*, and he always looked forward to his first game here in the early spring when he returned from Jamaica. He loved golf and at this time made the Royal St George's the focal point of the 'Fleming Four-Day Week'. For he was now allocating a bare four days to Lord Kemsley and Gray's Inn Road—from Friday afternoon until Monday night he could relax and enjoy himself with Anne and Caspar and golf and the house at St Margaret's Bay. On Friday afternoon his Thunderbird usually screeched up the drive of the St. George's in time for him to squeeze in nine or eighteen holes before tea. Normally tea was a drink he never touched—Bond considered it 'liquid mud'—but the clubhouse tea had become a ritual, and Fleming was now in the habit of always sitting in the same leather-backed wing chair on the left of the big bay window: alone at first, for he could still not bring himself to make expansive gestures, and then holding court as his cronies gathered round until it was time for martinis at six.

He was a good talker in this relaxed male society, and in March 1957 he was in infinitely better spirits than the previous year when he returned from Jamaica after writing

From Russia, With Love. Life seemed once again on an upward curve. Now that he had completed *Dr No* and James Bond had triumphed over *his* malaise of the previous year it was almost as if Fleming himself had written his various afflictions out of his system. The sciatica had miraculously eased, there were no more private diamond factories in his kidneys, and when he began a course of lessons with Whiting, the Royal St George's professional, fondly imagining that there was still a chance of correcting his flat, fast swing that resembled 'a housemaid sweeping under a bed', he appeared to have recovered all his old zest.

But this was bound up with something else, something for which he had been waiting almost all his life. The paper-back sales of the books had helped; the *Daily Express* serialization of *From Russia, With Love* had added to it. After all the false starts and recurrent disappointments Fleming knew for certain that spring that he had really succeeded and the Bond boom was about to begin. 'Ian's public,' said old Maugham, 'will never let him go again.'

It was now that Fleming recognized two key factors which were to play their part in the overwhelming phenomenon of the Bond boom in the years ahead. One was that the books, although in interest apparently confined to a very small class of a very small country, were beginning to have an appeal far beyond the people they were written for. As he wrote to the Columbia Broadcasting System when they were considering Bond for a television series:

In hard covers my books are written for and appeal principally to an 'A' readership, but they have all been reprinted in paper-backs, both in England and in America and it appears that the 'B' and 'C' classes find them equally readable, although one might have thought that the sophistication of the background and detail would be outside their experience and in part incomprehensible.

The other point he had learned from the rash of personal publicity during and following Eden's Goldeneye visit, and it was that by simply being himself he could become Bond's best publicist. The conundrum of Fleming-Bond had suddenly become news: the moment had arrived when Ian Fleming and James Bond could become a cult. Guardedly, but with considerable foresight, Fleming wrote about it to Wren Howard at Cape:

If I were a bit more hard-boiled it would be easy to guy the whole

Bond operation in a great splurge of promotion and sales, but somehow it all goes against the grain a bit and I daresay much the same problem faces authors whose books are made into a lot of films. Perhaps I have an abnormal affection for privacy and antipathy for display.

True, in a deeper sense he had, but as he must have realized, it was precisely this that had always made his acquaintances feel curious about him. Nothing is more inviting than a closed garden.

He might have his doubts, but he knew quite well that he had to make up his mind or have it made up for him. Already he had received an offer which might become the first step towards 'guying the whole Bond operation'. To Wren Howard he wrote in the same letter:

You will be interested to know that the *Express* are desperately anxious to turn James Bond into a strip cartoon. I have grave doubts about the desirability of this. A certain cachet attaches to the present operation, and there is a danger that if stripped we shall descend into the Peter Cheyney class . . . Unless the standard of these books is maintained they will lose their point and I think there is a grave danger that inflation will spoil not only the readership but also become something of a death-watch beetle inside the author. A tendency to write still further down might result. The author would see this happening, and disgust with the operation might creep in.

It was an important decision, for he knew that once he gave in to a 'great splurge' there would be no going back. As it was he was in two minds, and finally he told Howard that he would consult William Plomer and abide by his advice.

Plomer was quite definite. It would be a grave error to accept the *Express* offer.

In the end this was the one occasion when Fleming rejected his friend's advice. There was the money (the *Express* was offering a minimum of £1,500 a book, with the possibility of a share in the syndication rights); Edward Pickering, the editor, guaranteed that the newspaper would make a 'Rolls-Royce job' of turning Bond into a strip character; and Fleming must have asked himself whether he really could refuse the chance of a lifetime. For all his doubts, he could not.

As the *Daily Express* put it when they finally announced that he had agreed to the strip, 'James Bond, the sardonic secret agent who stormed into popularity as THE post-war fiction hero, now begins a new career.' So, it seemed, had

Fleming. For by then Bond and his creator were being swept up in a popular cult which finally promised the fortune he had just been missing all his life. The treasure was there at last; and for all his doubts about 'a death-watch beetle inside the author' it was immensely exciting.

As usual, Fleming put all this into the book he was working on at the time—'the next volume of my auto-biography', as he called it. In that summer of 1957 he was preparing the ground for *Goldfinger*, and in *Goldfinger* the emphasis was to be very different from that of the books he had written latterly. Gone was the obsessive concern with suffering, softening-up and heart disease which had dogged poor Bond since *Diamonds Are Forever*. There was none of the nostalgia which had crept into his musings in *From Russia, With Love*. Instead Fleming was now expressing his pent-up excitement about great wealth, treasure and tycoons. Like Goldfinger he felt the time had come to storm his own Fort Knox.

How differently the world appeared to him now—it seemed that what he needed to restore his health and vitality was not Harley Street and Orange-juice Land but success, financial success to match the golden dreams he was already conjuring up for *Goldfinger*. And suddenly success began to attract success. He wrote to Ivar Bryce at the beginning of April:

The most startling and exciting assignment of my career has just swung into my ken, and means that I have to fly off to Tangier immediately, there to settle down for two or three weeks in a hotel with a famous spy—male alas. The results of this union are going to be most startling but the whole project is so 'Hush' that I can't tell you more about it now.

As usual, Fleming loved to mystify his friends, but his excitement was genuine. Ever since *Diamonds Are Forever* he had been keeping an interested eye on one particular affliction of the international diamond market. He thought that the whole story of the battle against diamond smuggling and illicit diamond buying might have formed a plot for one of his own books, but he saw no chance of writing it because the necessary basis of fact would never be revealed to him or anyone else. He had, however, reckoned without Sir Percy Sillitoe, formerly of M.I.5 and now winding up his private organization known as I.D.S.O. (International Diamond Security Organization), which had been set up by the Diamond Corporation to investigate the great leakages which had been threatening the stability of the world diamond market.

Sillitoe, seldom averse to publicity, conceived the idea of having a book written about the success story of his small security organization; and in the closing days of I.D.S.O., somewhat disgruntled that it was being disbanded, he commissioned one of its senior members, an English solicitor named John Collard, later known as 'John Blaize', to put down the story before returning to his legal desk. The solicitor duly wrote a sober and balanced narrative which Sillitoe took to his friend Denis Hamilton of the *Sunday Times*. Hamilton, who knew his *Diamonds Are Forever*, realized that it was a remarkable story but one which would be all the better for a professional hand. Ian Fleming must meet Collard—who would have been astonished and derisive had he known that Fleming had described him as 'a famous spy'.

At any rate, the two of them spent a week together in Tangier, and Fleming came back with sufficient material for the big series the *Sunday Times* carried that autumn under his name—'The Diamond Smugglers'. Although he had been working regularly as a journalist since 1945 this was his first major success as a reporter, and it seemed to offer him a new reputation almost overnight: the role of reporter could complement his role as the best-selling author of James Bond. If necessary it might even provide an alternative, as he saw when he found how effortlessly he could turn the articles into the book of *The Diamond Smugglers*—his first book without Bond. Provided he picked subjects that really excited him there were great possibilities here for the future. He was grateful to Denis Hamilton, who had become his close friend and confidant after they found themselves colleagues in the late 1940s.

But the trip to Tangier was not the only unexpected excitement which cropped up that summer. One of the signs of his growing fame was an invitation to compete in the Bowmaker professional-amateur golf tournament at the Berkshire golf club. 'They have film stars and suchlike to amuse the crowds,' he was told; flattered, he accepted, and when the draw was announced he saw that he was partnering Peter Thomson, 'three times Open Champion and certainly the greatest golfer after Ben Hogan'. He expressed horror but was obviously thrilled. He wrote joyfully to Bryce:

There is no way out with honour from this nightmarish situation, and it's just a question of whether I fill myself with benzedrine or oblivion. The whirring cameras, the closely lined fairways, with the handkerchiefs of greens closely encircled by the expert crowds and Fleming ambling up to play his second shot out of a rabbit scrape. The crowd holds its breath. Will Fleming be putting for a three? Boing! Fleming's head has lifted like a frightened stag's and his ball, socketed sideways, is now rattling among the spectators' shins a few yards away to his direct right.

Then the two-foot putt jabbed two inches outside the hole. What's the matter with the man? He shouldn't be allowed on a golf course. There is a low and threatening growl from the crowd.

And so on.

Well, there it is. My friends are agog with the prospect. I have looked to my equipment and bought two pairs of socks with which to walk this hideous plank. Please, on Sunday and Monday summon the staff and the guests to the hall for prayers before breakfast . . . prayers for the heaviest two days' thunderstorm that has ever deluged the Home Counties. There is no other way.

The thunderstorm was not necessary. Fleming, whose handicap was nine, and Alec Shepperson, the Walker Cup player, were playing with Thomson, who in this threesome against bogey went round in seventy-two on the first day and sixty-nine on the second. Fleming did a net sixty-six on both days and 'assisted' Thomson to win five holes. Secretly, and rightly, he was proud of his performance in partnership with a world champion over a course black with crowds. He had succumbed completely now to golf—it was a very important thing in his life and his passion for it intensified as other pleasures staled. Soon he was to write a golfing classic: the battle between Bond and Auric Goldfinger at Sandwich.

By now he fully understood that what his rapidly growing public expected was the mixture very much as before. *Dr No* had provided the formula, and from now on he was to follow it, with the fantasies becoming wilder and his identification with Bond closer. There was no more talk now about that 'cardboard booby'. Instead, that summer saw Fleming exercising as much care with the details of James Bond's existence as he did with his own: 'In connection with James Bond's new car, I would like it to be a cross between a Continental Bentley and a Ford Thunderbird—i.e. a smallish cockpit with a long bonnet line and a large boot behind.' So he wrote to his friend Whitney Straight, the chairman of Rolls-Royce, going on to inquire if one of the Rolls-Royce designers could tell him who were 'the best people to have designed such a body, which should be a press button convertible'.

Now that Fleming had decided to write the whole novel around the subject of gold the research for it became a labour of love. His old friend from the Reuters days, Rickatson-Hatt, who was now at the Bank of England, introduced him to one of the Bank's experts for light on the latest gold-smuggling rackets. Guy Wellby showed him how gold could be oxidized, and a City gold merchant allowed him to spend an afternoon in his smelting rooms. In Jamaica that winter Fleming found *Goldfinger* one of the easiest of all his books to write. Life was continuing to smile upon him.

He returned to England to discover that with the publication of his sixth book, *Dr No*, the world had suddenly awoken to his existence. He had even become important enough to be controversial. It is interesting that when he wrote *Casino Royale* for what was thought to be a minority audience almost all the critics politely applauded the 'civilized' qualities of this 'Peter Cheyney of the carriage trade'. But nothing disturbs like success, and now *Dr No* was subjected to two cannonades—one by Bernard Bergonzi in the *Twentieth Century* magazine, the other by Paul Johnson in the *New Statesman*: both strongly objected to the 'sex, snobbery and sadism' of the books even if it had taken them five years to notice the phenomena.

Fleming was shaken by the suddenness of the attacks—he felt the allegation of snobbery to be particularly unfair; but he also understood the value of the publicity.

But if the left-wing *New Statesman* was against James Bond, the leader of the Labour Party was not. 'Thank you very, very much for sending me your latest,' wrote Hugh Gaitskell. 'As you know I am a confirmed Fleming fan—or should it be addict? The combination of sex, violence, alcohol and—at intervals—good food and nice clothes is, to one who lives such a circumscribed life as I do, irresistible.' And there were certain critics Fleming always enjoyed. One was Noël Coward, who wrote to him about a blunder which was certainly a strange one to come from the Foreign Manager of the *Sunday Times*:

Your descriptive passages, as usual, are really very good indeed, but, as the gentleman in 'Oklahoma' sings about Kansas City, 'You've gone about as fur as you ken go.' I am willing to accept the centipede, the tarantulas, the land crabs, the giant squid (except on that beastly table at Goldeneye). I am even willing to forgive your reckless use of invented verbs—'I inch, Thou inches, He snakes, I snake, We palp, They palp,' etc., but what I will neither accept nor forgive is the highly inaccurate statement that when it is eleven a.m. in Jamaica, it is six a.m. in dear old England. This, dear boy, to put not too fine a point on it, is a f—— lie. When it is eleven a.m. in Jamaica, it is *four p.m.* in dear old England and it is carelessness of this kind that makes my eyes steel slits of blue. I was also slightly shocked by the lascivious announcement that Honeychile's bottom was like a boy's. I know that we are all becoming progressively more broadminded nowadays but really old chap what *could* you have been thinking of?

Fleming's reply was delayed but to the point:

I can't be bothered to argue with you about what time it is in Jamaica. I have my views and you have yours and if the twain meet I shall be very surprised.

As for criticizing my English, you may be interested to know that a lengthy extract from my writings has recently been included in 'Interpretation and Precis with Language Exercises' by Clara C. Harris, M.A., of the James Guillespie High School for Girls, Edinburgh. This is a textbook on the use of the English language for advanced students and if you wish one day to promote yourself into that category you would do well to study this excellent primer.

I have a slight confession to make. While in Bombay I met a very beautiful girl who has intellectual pretensions as well as a 38-inch bust. She reviews for the top Bombay weekly, which is read by all the top gurus, and proudly showed me her book collection which contained one of your opuscula. She was so excited when I confessed to knowing you that I at once autographed the book for her, more or less in your hand-writing and certainly on the correct note of fatuity. I was drunk on Coca-Cola at the time (Bombay is dry) and it was only afterwards that I realized I was guilty of forgery. If you wish to get together with Stephen Spender, William Plomer and W. H. Auden, you might scrape up enough money to bring a case and get some damages, for I regret to say that I also autographed their books together with appropriate messages to the Indian people.

The reason for Fleming's visit to Bombay that spring of 1958 lay in yet another of his treasure hunts. Since the success of 'The Diamond Smugglers' the *Sunday Times* had been asking for a further series on virtually any subject that interested him, and he took the slow boat from Bombay to the islands of the Seychelles, drawn by the fact that treasure worth £120 million was supposedly hidden there by the French pirate Levasseur.

But the Seychelles, 'that ramshackle paradise' in the Indian Ocean, were a disappointment, as he confessed in the articles he was to write. The treasure seemed no closer than when Levasseur originally buried it and the islands themselves inferior to the West Indies. Despite the excitement with which he had set out, he had no sooner arrived at Mahé than he was already looking forward to getting on to Rome. He had arranged to meet Anne there: he had promised her a holiday in Venice as some recompense for the weeks he had been away.

When he arrived she found him very sick from coral poisoning with an open sore on his thigh—he had cut it when swimming—and she had to look after him for two days in Rome before his temperature came down and they could leave for Venice. Once there he was soon back on form. It was a perfect holiday: Anne had never seen Venice before and he was thrilled with this chance of introducing her to one of his favourite cities. He had specially booked the Princess Margaret suite at the Gritti Palace Hotel, with a sitting-room, marble bathroom, several bedrooms and one of the finest views in all Venice; but when they found out how much it was costing he agreed, sheepishly, to move into a smaller room at the back.

Venice was a city where they were both happy. She loved sight-seeing, he enjoyed walking and sitting in the sun. Each morning they would stroll off together, and when they found a church or a picture gallery Anne liked the look of he would settle himself with a newspaper and a cigarette at a table outside the nearest café and wait for her there. Once she persuaded him inside the Accademia for a few minutes, but he muttered that there was 'far too much of everything' and returned gratefully to his café table in the sun.

Another of their favourite trips was to take the boat to the Lido and then the bus, to get away from the smart hotels and the holidaymakers to the long deserted stretch of beach where Byron used to come to ride. The sea, the silence, the pearly light of the Adriatic appealed to them both—he was soon to use this place and its atmosphere for the scene where James Bond is chased by the Italian gangsters in his short story 'Risico'—and they would walk on, talking and looking for shells, until they were both hungry and finally found somewhere to eat.

It was towards the end of their stay that he gave Thomas Mann's *Death in Venice* to Anne. 'Once I had read it I understood for the first time the sad nostalgic beauty of Venice and I realized that this was how Ian saw the city and why he loved it.'

Yet his own mood now was anything but nostalgic. He suggested as a motto for a friend, 'The possible is not what you can do but what you want to do'; for him it was to be a dangerous motto, but that summer he lived up to it. Rather than spend the entire holiday in Venice, he suggested driving back and stopping a few days in Monte Carlo, where he was arranging with Aristotle Onassis to write some articles on the Casino. It was a subject after his own heart, but there was better still to come. Just a week after his return to London he was writing excitedly to William Plomer with news of his latest good fortune:

Since seeing you I have been quite gigantically propositioned by the Columbia Broadcasting System. In exchange for a huge weekly sum of gold over the next two years they want me to write a series of thirty-two Bond episodes for television. I have agreed and if I don't run out of puff, which at this stage seems very possible, fame and fortune are now at my feet.

The treasure he had been seeking seemed to be on his own doorstep at last, but he was still as fascinated as ever by hidden treasure, and when Enid Bagnold wrote to congratulate him on his *Sunday Times* articles on the Seychelles he suggested she should write a play about hidden gold:

A psycho-analyst once pontificated to me at length on the subject. He said that treasure hunting is a perfect example of that weakness of character which makes one hunt for the short cut to happiness and away from the realities of living. One will find the pot of gold and, at a fell swoop, you can say 'No' to authority and discipline and hard work. You can cock a snoot at authority and, with the gold you have found, have everything your own way.

He even wrote an outline of the play for Miss Bagnold: its point was that the treasure which all the trouble was about turned out to be no treasure at all.

And that autumn of 1958 Ivar Bryce introduced Ian Fleming to Kevin McClory.

CHAPTER TWENTY-FOUR

THUNDERBALL BACKFIRES

I

KEVIN MCCLORY was a young Irishman of ambition. He had worked in Hollywood for Mike Todd, on *Round the World in Eighty Days*, and by the autumn of 1958 he appeared to be on the threshold of a great career as a film-maker. He enjoyed life and lived it in his own style. There was a house in Belgrave Place where he kept a black butler, a pet monkey, and a green macaw; and celebrities like John Huston and Elizabeth Taylor believed in his talent. So did Ivar Bryce. They had met in New York, and Bryce, languidly anxious to find yet a new field for his money and attention, decided that the moment had come for him to enter the film business.

McClory had all the fabled persuasiveness of the Irish. He was also the co-author of a script, *The Boy and the Bridge*, that he wanted to turn into a film. It was a simple little tale, with opportunities for pathos, about a small boy living near London Bridge, and Bryce, suddenly enjoying the idea of himself as a power in the film world, decided to back it. As usual, he told Ian Fleming of his plans, and Fleming, a little wary by now of the entertainment industry, advised caution. But the film went ahead, and by the late autumn of 1958 Kevin McClory and his camera team had shot most of the sequences.

It was now Fleming's turn to become involved. McClory was assembling the film and Bryce, who was back in the States, asked his friend Ian to see how things were progressing and privately to give him his candid advice. Fleming agreed, and one morning in mid-November 1958 he joined Kevin McClory and the heiress Miss Bobo Sigrist, who later became McClory's wife, in a private viewing theatre at 146 Piccadilly to see the first rough version of *The Boy and the Bridge*.

If Fleming could have known where all this was to end he would have left it at that. Instead, he took the first of the steps that were to lead to a catastrophic case.

A few days later he was writing to Bryce to say that on the whole he had been most impressed by the film. 'The photography and the direction are splendid and the whole thing stands up excellently.' But he went on to criticize what he considered its excessive sentimentality. 'Please don't think I'm being James Bondish about all this. Nobody loves a good hunk of sentiment better than me, but nobody likes to have sentiment stuffed down his throat.' However, he promised to see what he could do to persuade McClory to tone it down. He would even 'try and get Dilys Powell to come along with me. Her judgment on just this sort of point would be admirable.'

This last idea never came off, but from now on Fleming seems to have cast himself in the role of unofficial adviser in the final stages of the film. He saw more of McClory. Soon he was telling Bryce that he had 'considerable respect' for McClory's abilities and for the energy which he had put into the film.

He visited McClory at Belgrave Place and, confronted by one of McClory's celebrated film parties, seems to have felt distinctly out of place. There was a 'bevy of more or less attractive girls dressed to look like Anna Magnani or Greco or some other famous star. I rather liked their pale matt make-up and puce lipstick,' he told Bryce. 'But once they discovered I was nothing to do with show-biz they started looking furtively over my shoulder.'

But if the girls in the pale matt make-up failed to see the importance of the man who had invented James Bond, Kevin McClory did not; and long before *The Boy and the Bridge* was finished the eager Irishman was suggesting a joint production of the first film of 'James Bond, Secret Agent'. McClory had the talent and Bryce the money and Fleming had Bond—what could be easier?

As Fleming was quick to point out, this whole idea really hinged on one point. Who was to play James Bond? It was a question to which they both gave much thought for the rest of 1958. Fleming was in favour of his friend David Niven. McClory had other ideas and suggested a number of equally famous names who might suit. Fleming wrote to Bryce about one well-known star he had met:

Apart from the fact that his face is blotchy with alcohol and he has about five hairs left on his head and must be over fifty, I initially saw no objection, but he then harangued me in such compulsive terms for half-an-hour about not having had a job

for a year that suddenly the whole idea seemed to me a dreadful
bore and . . . I left with perspiration pouring down my brow.
I must say there is something very grisly about show-biz and
its denizens.

Bored, and suddenly uneasy about this film world in which
he had become momentarily involved, Fleming seemed to
lose interest. He had a number of other things on his mind.
One of them was the strange and highly embarrassing
behaviour of his mother. At seventy-four Mrs Val, as
obstinate, as high-handed, and as original as ever, was in the
middle of a bizarre legal struggle with a Parsee lady over
the affections of the oldest peer in Britain.

In a sense Fleming might even have felt himself slightly
responsible, for it had been partly on his advice that his
mother had bought a house and settled in the Bahamas, and
it was here in 1951 that the elderly widow met and became
attached to the sixteenth Marquess of Winchester, a harmless
but indigent old aristocrat who had been mixed up in the
collapse of several of Clarence Hatry's companies and had
chosen to live abroad since his bankruptcy in 1929. For a
while they were even engaged. Perhaps, as Mrs Val claimed,
it was on her doctor's advice that the engagement was broken
off. Perhaps the terms of Major Val's will, which would have
reduced her income to a meagre £3,000 a year, also played
some part in the decision.

The engagement ended in June 1952. In July—with a
haste possibly excused by the fact that he was now nearing
ninety—the Marquess married Miss Bapsy Pavry, daughter
of a Parsee high priest. When Mrs Val heard the news she
told him that he was letting down the House of Lords: it
was the first shot in a hard-fought battle. Lord Winchester
and his bride were soon apart. In 1954 an action in the
Bahamas by Lady Winchester against Mrs Val for alleged
enticement of her husband ended with an agreement
between the two ladies to steer clear of each other. But the
following year the battle began again, this time in the High
Court in London.

By now Mrs Val had sold her house on Cable Beach,
Nassau, and together with Lord Winchester and three full-
scale oil paintings of herself by Augustus John had turned
up in Monte Carlo. The couple lived successively but
separately ('Our association,' she said, 'was pure as an Easter
lily') in three hotels, and Lady Winchester claimed that, in
direct contravention of the Bahamas agreement, Mrs Val

had incited and financed her husband in an action to have his marriage annulled.

The new action was before Mr Justice Devlin, and the ladies were well matched. 'Hate, jealousy and venom' were alleged against Mrs Val. Finally the Court found against Mrs Val, but even then the fight was not over. Spirited as ever, she carried the case to appeal, and in the autumn of 1958, while Ian Fleming was trying to make up his mind about who was to play James Bond, three Appeal Court judges tried to make up theirs over his mother and the aged Marquess.

With admirable loyalty the Flemings rallied round. Peter, Ian and Richard sat in court with their mother throughout the case, and they were there when the judges upheld her plea that Mr Justice Devlin's judgment should be set aside. Like a good Fleming, she had finally succeeded, and as she left the court several people noticed the remarkable resemblance between this frail and distinguished-looking old lady and her son Ian.

Another problem taking Fleming's mind away from the plans of Kevin McClory was the question of the next book. Fleming had already announced to William Plomer that, as he had 'really run out of puff', *Goldfinger* would have to be 'the last full-length folio on Bond . . . Though I may be able to think up some episodes for him in the future, I shall never be able to give him 70,000 words again.' The full-length James Bond books which had once been such a treat to write were by now becoming a chore. The fears Fleming had expressed to Wren Howard about the 'death-watch beetle' of disgust once he started writing for a mass public seemed to be coming true.

But in a sense it hardly mattered. For even if he was running out of puff, he still had James Bond, and now that he knew Bond was in demand the real question was how to make the most of him. As he realized, the big James Bond television deal with the Columbia Broadcasting System offered an easy way out. It was James Bond he was selling to the Americans, not the books. He could have his sack of gold in return for a series of outlines for half-hour James Bond episodes on television. He found that writing these was child's play. He had finished six already, and these television episodes had another advantage. Without too much effort they could be turned into short stories, which was what he did that winter at Goldeneye, adapting 'Risico', 'From a

View to a Kill' and 'For Your Eyes Only' directly from the television outlines he had already prepared for C.B.S. He enjoyed short-story writing and found the length suited him now. He added a story he had written on the way back from the Seychelles the summer before, 'Quantum of Solace', and another, 'The Hildebrand Rarity'. Together they formed a respectable collection under the title *For Your Eyes Only* which Cape accepted in lieu of that year's full-length Bond.

But the facility with which he could turn a plot for one medium into a story for another was to set a hazardous precedent for the future. Not that it seemed to matter at the time. William Plomer thought 'Quantum of Solace' 'very Willie Maughamesque', as indeed it was, and suddenly the idea of concentrating on short stories and becoming 'the Willie Maugham of our generation' began to appeal to Fleming. In one letter to Maugham he even laid down what he thought was the secret of the popular Bond success:

> If authors were half as professional as I am they would know that it is far more important to tap the non-literary public than the followers of, say, Cyril Connolly. I'm sure that half my own modest success has been due to writing knowledgeably about subjects like cards and gold which have their own huge public. I really must start a correspondence course for authors.

But none of this was quite enough for him: *Goldfinger* was a success, the C.B.S. deal was all but settled, the *Sunday Times* was begging him to get started on a global adventure and the James Bond strip and annual serialization of each Bond book had become regular features of the *Daily Express*. Things had never been better, but his impatience was beginning to outstrip his success. 'The possible is not what you can do, but what you want to do,' and he would settle for nothing less than overwhelming success.

It was now that McClory re-entered the scene. During the spring of 1959 *The Boy and the Bridge* was completed and looked like being a minor triumph. McClory was already being spoken of as the *Wunderkind* of British films; Bryce arrived from America and was hopefully seeing *The Boy and the Bridge* as the start of an important future for himself as an independent film producer; it was confirmed that Princess Margaret was to attend the première of the film, and it had the honour of being chosen as the official British entry for that year's Venice film festival. Anything seemed possible now, and it was against this background of high hope and euphoria that Ivar Bryce, Kevin McClory and Ian Fleming resumed discussions in earnest about filming James Bond.

One of the things about McClory which appealed to Fleming was his enthusiasm for James Bond. Unlike some of the film-makers Fleming had tried to deal with in the past, McClory was more impressed by the possibilities and potentialities of filming Bond than by the difficulties. The Rank Organization, for instance, who had originally bought the film rights of *Moonraker*, had done nothing with the book and Fleming was soon to buy it back.

But while McClory was excited by the idea of making a film around James Bond, he was not satisfied with any of Fleming's existing plots; he wished to make an underwater film and during a week-end at Moyns Park, Bryce's house in Essex, Fleming, McClory, Ernest Cuneo and Ivar Bryce began discussing the sort of story James Bond really needed. At this stage it was all rather light-hearted. In one way or another a plot was roughed out which included a girl agent called Fatima Blush and the arrival of a plane-load of show-business celebrities, to appear briefly and thus give Bond the benefit of a star-studded cast. Fleming agreed to develop the idea into a rough script to form the basis of a film.

At the beginning of July 1959, a couple of weeks before the première of *The Boy and the Bridge*, it was generally agreed that Kevin McClory would make the first James Bond film, that Bryce would find the capital, and that Fleming would work closely with McClory on the script. In the whole subsequent history of this uncomfortable partnership nothing was ever to be quite so clear again.

Immediately the situation began to change. Fleming reported to Bryce that he was 'ploughing on dutifully but painfully with a rough James Bond script' which he hoped to have in draft form by the end of July. 'Meanwhile, conflicting bids for and interests in part or whole of the James Bond sausage have been coming thick and fast and, in desperation, I have had to appoint the Music Corporation of America as my agents for all film, television and dramatic rights.'

C.B.S. were still trying to tie up the big television deal, especially now that several American operators were beginning to bid for joint film and television rights. Nothing was settled, but the time had come when Fleming understandably felt compelled to ask Bryce for a legal agreement—'since

James Bond is my entire stock-in-trade and I have not got the energy to create a new character'.

As a friend he offered Bryce some advice:

You have made one successful film perhaps too expensively; you should now make a second successful film perhaps watching the costs a bit more carefully. This film should be a James Bond film and thus be likely of success under Kevin's brilliant direction. You should pay the copyright owner and author of the story such an authorship fee as you would have to pay any other writer for good material and you would give him a percentage of the gross profits.

Bryce agreed and the following week came to an arrangement with Fleming for 'the right to make the first James Bond feature film'.

Then something quite unforeseen occurred. *The Boy and the Bridge* had its Press show and got a disappointing reception from the critics. Somehow the profit and reputation both Bryce and McClory had hoped to gain from it melted away, and the discussions during August and September about the first Bond film were sadder and warier than in June and July.

But there was no going back. The mounting success of the James Bond books provided an unanswerable incentive. Everyone knew that they had a success on their hands if only they could make the most of it. But after *The Boy and the Bridge* were they really sure they could?

Fleming certainly had his doubts. At the beginning of August he wrote as tactfully as possible to Bryce saying that it had crossed his mind 'that you and Kevin might consider having Anthony Asquith as a co-producer. If you thought well of the idea it would have to be put very delicately of course to Kevin, but it does seem to me that there might be something in it, as Asquith is immensely experienced ... and has a great sense of style.' Next day Fleming wrote again. He had just lunched with his new agent, Laurence Evans of M.C.A., who had told him plainly that really big stars might not be too anxious 'to be produced and directed by a young man with only one film to his name, and that a film that has not found favour with the critics'.

As Fleming had been thinking in terms of either James Stewart or Richard Burton for Bond, with James Mason a third choice, this was all very worrying. Evans seemed to agree with Fleming that one solution might be to make McClory 'number two to a bigger man; say Asquith or

Hitchcock for instance', and said that as he was soon flying to Hollywood he would make inquiries while he was there to see if any major company was anxious to make a Bond film. If one was, it would seem good sense for Bryce's company Xanadu Productions to join forces with it.

More than a month was to elapse before Fleming put any of this before McClory, and work went ahead on the outline of the plot, with McClory making various suggestions which Fleming accepted. The idea of the plane-load of celebrities was dropped and so was Fatima Blush.

McClory came up with the theme which was to prove basic to the plot: an R.A.F. Valiant bomber with an atomic bomb aboard would be stolen and flown to the Bahamas and crash landed in the sea.

Although they were working together, relations between Fleming and McClory were cooling fast. As Fleming told Bryce, 'the final straw' came when he arrived back at 16 Victoria Square from Le Touquet where he had had lengthy story discussions with McClory to discover that Bobo Sigrist had taken the house opposite 'and that Kevin's Thunderbird was parked alongside my own'.

At the end of September, Fleming lunched with McClory and finally made his suggestion about bringing in a major director and letting McClory work with him as producer. He thought that Alfred Hitchcock was interested in the Bond books and suggested an approach to him through Eric Ambler. It was a relief when McClory agreed, and Fleming told Bryce:

Personally I feel this would be by far the best solution for all of us. It would mean perhaps smaller profits, but we would have a solid company of experts behind us and the prestige value would be colossal. To be allied with a friendly if very business-like group like Hitchcock's would, I believe, be healthier for all of us.

It certainly would have been, but Hitchcock declined and events rolled on.

At the beginning of October, at McClory's house in Belgrave Place, McClory introduced Fleming to Jack Whittingham, one of the most experienced British screenplay writers in the business, and suggested him as the writer for the screenplay. Fleming was clearly becoming bored with the whole affair by now and looking forward to getting off round the world in a few weeks' time to write about 'thrilling cities' like Hong Kong, Tokyo, and Las Vegas for the *Sunday Times*. Whittingham was an expert. Fleming was soon reporting to Bryce that he seemed to have 'some excellent ideas which cut out a lot of the muck at the beginning of my story', and it was agreed that Whittingham should write the full-scale film script of 'James Bond, Secret Agent'. 'At this stage,' says Whittingham, 'I naturally expected to collaborate fairly closely with Fleming.' Instead, on a soft, grey October morning the creator of James Bond grabbed a portable typewriter, visas, and a 'round-the-world suit with concealed money pockets' and gratefully boarded B.O.A.C. Comet G/ADOJ for Hong Kong. Whilst he was away Jack Whittingham, as writer, and McClory, as producer, worked closely to evolve a storyline and script which Fleming would approve.

At first he had been reluctant to undertake this five-week trip round the world. As he recorded in the book, *Thrilling Cities*, which reprints the articles, he told Leonard Russell, the *Sunday Times* Literary and Features Editor, that he was the world's worst sightseer and that he had 'often advocated the provision of roller-skates at the doors of museums and art galleries'. But Russell had been firm. 'We don't want that sort of thing from you,' he told him. 'In your James Bond books, even if people can't put up with James Bond and those fancy heroines of yours, they seem to like the exotic background. Surely you want to pick up some material for your stories? It's a wonderful opportunity.'

At the outset of his career as a novelist Fleming had told William Plomer that success would enable him to say goodbye to the 'prison walls' of 200 Gray's Inn Road. Now something happened which shook those 'prison walls' to their foundations. Lord Kemsley rang Roy Thomson at the *Scotsman* office in Edinburgh and asked him to come to London immediately. There were secret negotiations. Three weeks later Thomson lunched at Kemsley House with Lord Kemsley, his sons, and his directors. For the first time the directors positively understood that the outfit had been sold, Lord Kemsley's beloved *Sunday Times* and all, to the Canadian, who was rumoured to run his properties on a shoestring. It is safe to say that everyone of any importance in Kemsley House, including Ian Fleming, began to think that nothing would ever be the same again and he must start looking for another job.

It was premature pessimism. Within a few weeks the whole place was feeling reassured, and Fleming and Thomson took to each other from their very first meeting. Partly to please Thomson and Denis Hamilton, who disclosed some of their plans for the *Sunday Times* to him, Fleming showed himself eager to take part in them and agreed to undertake the round-the-world trip and, if it came off, to do a companion series of articles on European cities in the spring of the following year, 1960.

It was this first tour which originated Ian Fleming's enthusiasm for Japan and which was to lead to his last book but one, *You Only Live Twice*. As the Comet flew over Zurich and Venice for Bahrain, New Delhi and the China Sea, the trip must have seemed the ideal solution to the profoundly boring business of the James Bond film. He would be away for five weeks—time enough to let everything sort itself out and for Whittingham to complete the script. He had arranged to come back through America, and then, with a clear mind, he could meet Bryce and McClory in New York, read the script and, as he proposed to Bryce just before he left London, make a swift visit to Nassau. 'A week of concentrated work there should get everything more or less set.' He was always a great optimist when it suited him.

The first 'Thrilling Cities' series was a great success. Russell's hunch was confirmed. 'What an extraordinary personality emerges from them'—wrote Russell with some truth when sending proofs of the articles to 'dear old Ian'— 'part sensational journalist, part diehard old clubman, part ruthless revolutionary, the whole adding up to a unique and endearing eccentric.' These superficial, jet-travel glimpses of the world exactly echoed the quirky, restless temperament of the reporter, disclosing his ability to skim the exotic and the odd from the unlikeliest as well as the likeliest places. He had never been to Hong Kong before and thought it 'the most vivid and exciting city I have ever seen'.

He also struck up an immediate friendship with Richard Hughes, the mountainous Australian ex-heavyweight who had represented the *Sunday Times* in the Far East since the Korean war. Tough, sentimental, immensely knowledgeable, Hughes was exactly the man Fleming needed for the success of this first brief introduction to the Far East. Hughes is like the best sort of Hemingway hero, living life to the full, a repository of the inside stories of all the biggest rackets and the finest restaurants in the East. He was the genuine man of action Fleming had always admired and always longed to be himself, and he could feel at home with Hughes as he never managed to feel with intellectuals, not to mention those denizens of show business of whom he had been seeing so much in London. The Orient he described in his pieces on Hong Kong and Tokyo was very much Richard Hughes's Orient. And it was with Hughes that he boarded the ferry S.S. *Takshing* at Hong Kong for the slow romantic trip of forty miles through the little islands to the Portuguese colony of Macao, oldest European settlement in China, important entrepôt for illicit bullion, and site of the celebrated nine-storey Central Hotel—the highest, if not the largest, house of ill-fame in the world, 'whose function and design', wrote Fleming, with his customary absence of humbug, 'I recommend most warmly to the attention of those concerned with English morals'.

Wisely he stayed at the graceful old Portuguese Bela Vista Hotel; his room had a balcony looking out over the estuary of the Pearl River, and on their first evening Hughes joined him there for a drink. The evening was warm and clear, the fishing junks were gliding in, silent as moths, and Fleming was visibly touched by the melancholy beauty of the scene. 'You know, Dikko,' he said, 'I suppose a man could be happier here than anywhere else in the world.' He paused, sipped his drink, and gazed at the boats tacking up-river. 'For about a fortnight,' he added.

But life was moving too fast now to allow him even a fortnight. A hurried visit to Tokyo, still with his 'comprador' Richard Hughes, was sufficient to overcome almost all his reservations—'during the war they had been bad enemies' —about Japan and the Japanese. Then it was time to battle on towards Honolulu, where he was horrified by the blue-rinsed elderly American matrons with their 'huge, blue-veined, dimpled thighs . . . and sagging bosoms garlanded with *leis*'; to Las Vegas, where he won three jackpots on the fruit machines; and to Chicago, where Ray Russell of *Playboy* magazine arranged for him to visit the scene of the St Valentine's Day massacre, the Chicago Art Institute, and the hottest striptease in town—'a display of positively exquisite boredom and lack of finesse'. Finally, his 'brains boiling with a fine confusion of impressions', he headed for New York and the next episode in the making of 'James Bond, Secret Agent'.

In just one essential, plans for the film were considerably clearer now than when he had left England five weeks earlier. Whittingham had finished the treatment and the few people who had seen it agreed that it was a winner. Otherwise the general situation was still dark. McClory, excited by what Whittingham had written, was thinking big and talking in terms of million-dollar budgets. Bryce, finally realizing the bitter truth that he stood to lose a considerable sum on *The Boy and the Bridge*, was getting nervous about such expensive talk and looking round for one or two Bond-struck millionaires whom he could bring in to cushion the risk. And Fleming, tired and still suffering the 'after-effects of jet travel—a dull headache and a bronchial breathlessness'— was fervently wishing that he had never became involved in the whole wretched business in the first place.

Discussions in McClory's hotel suite dragged on without any particular decision. At one point of impasse Fleming said he wanted a few words with Whittingham in private. They went into the bedroom and there Fleming wearily explained that he was afraid that the whole scheme, which had appeared so simple when it started, seemed to be getting completely out of hand. The plans for expensive stars and lavish underwater production were beginning to frighten him. He was worried that Bryce was going to lose a lot of money, and if this happened it would be all his fault. He insisted that James Bond could carry the film without their having to worry about big-name stars and expensive production. Whittingham shrugged and explained that he was a screenwriter, not a film producer. When they returned to the others it was decided that the film would go on. Whittingham was to go down to one of the Bryce homes at Nassau for further work on the script and would start looking for locations; Bryce would try for further backers.

For Fleming the next few weeks were hectic. When he found time to write to Bryce, at the end of December, it was to say that he had been 'completely submerged' in writing his series of round-the-world articles and in making arrangements to leave the *Sunday Times* staff and set up on his own account, with his own secretary and an office off Fleet Street. Under the highly amicable arrangement he made with Denis Hamilton, Fleming kept close links with the paper, being paid a retainer of £1,000 a year and still attending the Tuesday morning conference. When the business was concluded Hamilton sent him a prophetic wire:

By the New Year of 1960 affairs in London were reasonably
in order, and he planned to fly to Jamaica on January 4th
with Anne, Caspar and a governess. On the eve of his
departure he wrote to Bryce telling him that he had 'no idea
what is going on in the Xanadu film world' but that he had
managed to find time during the last breathless weeks for
a meeting with McClory. He had the impression that Bryce
might 'have gone a bit cold on the whole business. If so, I
shall perfectly understand and be most philosophical. The
idea of a \$3 million budget ... dismays me, although I'm sure
Kevin could help to make a James Bond film that would
please us both and bring in cash customers.'

He went on to repeat all his old doubts about show
business in general. In the light of what was to happen they
have an ominous ring:

Show-biz is a ghastly biz and the last thing I want is for you to
lose your pin-striped trousers in its grisly maw, however much
fun you may have in the process. Nor, of course, do I want the
first James Bond film to be botched, but the first consideration is
primary. If you decide to skip the whole thing, don't forget that
you have, or should have, a good saleable property in the script,
so all is not completely lost.

It was the confusion behind that last sentence which was to
cause all the trouble. When he arrived at Goldeneye he
began working on that year's book, *Thunderball*.

But the situation was not quite that simple, and there
were certain danger signals which Fleming, in his frenzy of
work, unaccountably missed. The chief of them was that the
screenplay was a collaboration between three people.
McClory had been working closely and enthusiastically on
the project for nine months and was now beginning, understandably, to feel insecure. It was at this moment that Ian
Fleming began to write that year's James Bond book, using
the plot which had gone into the film script of 'James Bond,
Secret Agent'. In a letter to Bryce he referred quite casually
to *Thunderball* as 'the book of the film'. And as was
acknowledged at the subsequent trial, Fleming was acting in
good faith and in what he honestly believed to be the best
interests of all concerned in the production of the screenplay.

By now he had found how easy it was to build his stories
out of his used or unused scripts for television. *Dr No*, it will

be remembered, began as a treatment for Henry Morgenthau III. Three of the five stories in *For Your Eyes Only* had begun as outline plots for C.B.S. With *Thunderball* he did much the same thing, and although he added the entire opening section on Shrublands, the nature cure clinic, and changed some of the characters, the finished version of *Thunderball* was still recognizably 'the book of the film'. He dedicated it: 'To Ernest Cuneo, Muse.'

Even at this stage everything would probably have worked out satisfactorily if he had kept his mind clear. All his life he had been in the habit of getting his own way without too much concern for the feelings of people with whom he failed to get on. At this point he was tired and unwell, he had been pushing himself too hard, he was bored with 'show-biz' and longed to be rid of anything that would further complicate his life.

That January McClory made a last visit to Jamaica to argue his case for being retained as producer of the James Bond film when it was finally made. But by now Fleming had made up his mind that he and Bryce should not be saddled with the worry and financial risk of producing the film on their own account. As he wrote to Bryce a few days before McClory arrived:

I am entirely in favour of you and I offering this script and a bit of capital and joining up with a big group such as Paramount and riding further on their backs . . . It would be good if Paramount would take on Kevin because he has thought a lot about this film, but he should be swallowed up in the Paramount machinery and not be coming to you the whole time.

When an anxious and aggrieved McClory arrived at Goldeneye to find out for himself what was going on Fleming decided that the time had come for some straight speaking. He described what happened in a letter to Bryce the following day:

Kevin went through the whole story—Ivar promised that I would be producer—we are partners in Xanadu and Xanadu engaged Jack, paid all salaries etc.—it was as if you had all lined up against me—no one would answer my letters—Ian, you must realize how far the script is away from your original treatment. It's really a different property altogether (I said so is Ben Hur and the Bible).

Anyhow, before my brains finally boiled out of my ears I managed to get this across to him and got his reluctant consent. I will take the script to Jules Stein (of M.C.A.) on behalf of me and you with our joint *recommendation* that Kevin should be the producer, which in the right hands I think he would do very well . . . If Jules says he has the company [to make the film] but they will not accept Kevin as producer we will rediscuss and tell Kevin that unless he can sell himself to the company in some role or other he can either back out or reach for his lawyers.

It was, no doubt, a very depressed Kevin McClory who left Jamaica after his conversation on the beach at Goldeneye. But there was not a great deal he could do.

With the benefit of hindsight, it was obviously the moment when the matter should have been put into the hands of some good lawyers for them to unravel.

But Fleming was impatient and excited and in no mood for caution. Everything was going his way, everyone was becoming interested in James Bond—even John Fitzgerald Kennedy. It was during this spring of 1960 that the two men met: a casual encounter but one which was to play its part in the strange and sombre story of Ian Fleming's last years.

II

Fleming never liked Washington—'it reminds me of one enormous Greek mausoleum'; New York was his city. On the way back from Goldeneye, however, he accepted an invitation from the *Sunday Times* correspondent in Washington, Henry Brandon, to stay for a couple of days with him at his house in Rodman Street. Brandon knew Fleming very well—they had worked together from the very earliest days of the Mercury Service. Brandon also knew Kennedy well, probably better than any other foreign correspondent in Washington at the time and suggested that Fleming might like to meet the Democratic presidential candidate-elect. But when Brandon telephoned Kennedy he was away campaigning. Brandon also rang Allen Dulles, Director of the C.I.A., on Fleming's behalf, but he was out of town.

But a meeting did occur between Kennedy and Fleming. When Fleming went to see his friend Mrs Marion 'Oatsie' Leiter on Sunday March 13th, she mentioned that she was dining with the Kennedys that evening. After lunch at her house on R Street she was driving Fleming through George-town in her white Chrysler when she spotted the Kennedys strolling along P Street. She stopped the car and asked them if she could bring a visitor to Washington to dinner with them that evening. As a matter of fact, he was with her right now.

'Who's that?' asked Kennedy politely.

She introduced the two men. 'Mr Ian Fleming—Senator Kennedy.'

Kennedy studied Fleming for a moment and said as they shook hands, 'James Bond? But, of course, by all means—do please come.'

They were seven for dinner at the Kennedys' house on N Street that evening, the guests being Mrs Leiter and Ian Fleming, the journalist Joseph Alsop, the painter William Walton, and a man from the C.I.A. called John Bross.

During dinner the talk largely concerned itself with the more arcane aspects of American politics and Fleming was attentive but subdued. But with the coffee and the entrance of Castro into the conversation he intervened in his most engaging style. Cuba was already high on the headache list of Washington politicians, and another of those what's-to-be-done conversations began to develop. Fleming laughed ironically and began to develop the theme that the United States was making altogether too much fuss about Castro—they were building him up into a world figure, inflating him instead of deflating him. It would be perfectly simple to apply one or two ideas which would take all the steam out of the Cuban.

Kennedy studied the handsome Englishman, rather as puzzled admirals used to study him in the days of Room 39. Was he an oddball or something more? What ideas had Mr Fleming in mind?

'Ridicule, chiefly,' said Fleming. And with immense seriousness and confidence he developed a spoof proposal for giving Castro the James Bond treatment. There were, he said, three things which really mattered to the Cubans: money, religion and sex. Therefore:

1. The U.S. should send planes to scatter Cuban money over Havana, accompanying it with leaflets showing that it came with the compliments of the United States.

2. Using the Guantanamo base, the U.S. should conjure up some religious manifestation, say a cross of sorts. in the sky which would induce the Cubans to look constantly skyward.

3. The U.S. should send planes over Cuba dropping pamphlets, with the compliments of the Soviet Union, to the effect that owing to American atom-bomb tests the atmosphere over the island had become radio-active; that radio-activity is held

344

longest in beards; and that radio-activity makes men impotent.

As a consequence the Cubans would shave off their beards, and without bearded Cubans there would be no revolution.

He kept his foot on the pedal for ten minutes, and it was a great success. If he could bring himself to take the trouble he could charm practically anyone. He laughed easily and infectiously, and there was something about his enjoyment to which Kennedy responded. He was impressed by the Senator's concentration on him and then the 'royal' dismissal as he turned to other guests.

Early the following morning Fleming left Washington for New York, but the evening at the Kennedys was to have its own hilarious postscript. Half an hour after Fleming had left, Henry Brandon was rung up by Allen Dulles. Already he had heard of the secret weapon for demolishing Castro and regretted that he wasn't able to hear about Fleming's ideas in person.

But the most important result of the evening was to come some months later; for the time being it was enough that Fleming had recruited his most important fan and that the Kennedys had been intrigued by the mystique which was already beginning to surround him. From then on Fleming maintained his connection with the family, sending suitably inscribed copies of his books to Kennedy himself, to Robert Kennedy and to their sister Mrs Eunice Shriver ('I wish someone else could read it also,' said a black-edged card written to Fleming in the spring of 1964 by the Attorney-General of the U.S., Robert Kennedy, thanking him for *You Only Live Twice*.) At the White House the new President would sometimes ask Brandon for news of Ian Fleming. 'Kennedy,' says Brandon, 'was fascinated by the line dividing Ian's real life from the fantasy life that went into his books. He often asked me how such an intelligent, mature, urbane sort of man could have such an element of odd imagining in his make-up.'

The cult of James Bond was growing, in the United States as well as in the United Kingdom. Yet for the rest of 1960 Fleming gives the impression of a man waiting impatiently at the mouth of a goldmine, wondering and asking if the strike is really a big one.

Thunderball was completed and duly dispatched to William Plomer with a depressed little note:

You may say that it needs drastic re-writing. I certainly got

345

This is the only bound copy of a short book I wrote on Kuwait in December 1960.

It was a condition of my obtaining facilities to visit Kuwait and write the book that the text should have the approval of the Kuwait Oil Company, whose guest I was.

The Oil Company expressed approval of the book but felt it their duty to submit the typescript to members of the Kuwait Government for their approval.

The Sheikhs concerned found unpalatable certain mild comments and criticisms and particularly the passages referring to the adventurous past of the country which now wishes to be "civilised" in every respect and forget its romantic origins.

Accordingly the book was stillborn.

The copyright is the property of the Kuwait Oil Company and may not be set up in print or quoted from without the written approval of the Company.

Ian Fleming.

The One Banned Book. The frontispiece to Fleming's unique copy of 'State of Excitement', about Kuwait. The book was never published

thoroughly bored with it after a bit, and I have not even been able to re-read it, though I have just begun correcting the first chapters. They are not too bad—it is the last twenty chapters that glaze my eyes.

He was feeling impatient and tense and worried about his health. On the other hand his departure from Gray's Inn Road gave him a lot of time for golf and for very long week-ends with Anne and Caspar at the Old Palace, the house which he had recently bought at Bekesbourne, near Canterbury; and there was no difficulty in his finding assignments to make up for the loss of a regular salary. In the light of what was to happen to the cult of the secret agent after his death the grounds on which he turned down a request from *Holiday* magazine to write a 'Portrait of an International Spy' are not without interest. 'If one goes on knocking one's own agents here—compared Carol Reed's "Our Man in Havana" with Hitchcock's "North by North-West"—one will end up by destroying the myth around which all my books are written.'

To his little office in Mitre Court came a suggestion in the autumn of 1960 which he was glad to accept. It was that he should spend two weeks in Kuwait as guest of the Kuwait Oil Company, collecting material for a short book on this small sheikdom the whole way of life of which had suddenly been transformed by oil. It was a theme after his own heart. He found that the place appalled and fascinated him. As a romantic it was inevitable that he should have preferred the piratical and blood-curdling Kuwait of the past to the little welfare state which the Sheikh of Kuwait had built in its place. He also found the pretensions of these Islamic *nouveaux riches* distinctly droll.

That December he wrote the little book for a fee of £1,000 and expenses. He called it 'State of Excitement' and treated his subject with a lightheartedness which few serious-minded Arabs could really be expected to share. The Kuwait Oil Company felt it would be tactful to make sure of the Kuwait Government's approval before they published it. They were wise. The Kuwait Government emphatically disapproved, and as a result 'State of Excitement' remains the one banned book Ian Fleming ever wrote. He kept a copy for himself and had it beautifully bound: as a book collector he appreciated its uniqueness.

It took him a little more than two weeks to write, and when it was finished he went off with Anne just before Christmas to Pontresina, in the Swiss Alps, to enjoy the snow and the winter sports. He found that he loved to be skiing again and forced himself to take almost as many risks as he had at Kitzbühel thirty years before. But the strain and sense of effort of the last few months clung to him obstinately, and what he most enjoyed was long expeditions with Anne by mountain railway. They would take a packed lunch from their hotel and stop off at small mountain villages they had never seen before. It was a nostalgic, strangely happy little interlude. When he returned to London he felt, hauntingly, as if something precious in his life was over for good.

'Gamblers just before they die,' he wrote in his notebook, 'are often given a great golden streak of luck. They get gay and young and rich and then, when they have been sufficiently fattened by the fates, they are struck down.'

CHAPTER TWENTY-FIVE

THE HOLLOW VICTORY

I

FOR Ian Fleming the twin gates of success and catastrophe flew open in the early spring of 1961. It was the sort of cruel joke that he always suspected life would play him. But not even in his blackest moments can he have anticipated that fate would have quite so bitter a sense of symmetry.

On March 17th James Bond had received the biggest boost of his career. In an article in *Life* magazine on the reading habits of President Kennedy ('his speed is at least 1,200 words per minute—the average person reads 250 words per minute'), Hugh Sidey gave an authorized list of ten favourite books of the President. It was an impressive affair, as it was presumably intended to be. Lord David Cecil's biography of Lord Melbourne headed it. Buchan's *Montrose* and Churchill's life of Marlborough followed. And just beating Stendhal's *Scarlet and Black* to ninth place was *From Russia, With Love* by Ian Fleming. He in turn had just been beaten by Peter Quennell, whose *Byron in Italy* came in eighth.

There is still a slight mystery about his appearance on this list and President Kennedy's much-advertised enthusiasm for his books. Arthur Schlesinger has hinted that it was little more than part of the publicity build-up of the new President, and it seems possible that when the Presidential Press secretary was compiling the list for Sidey he slipped in *From Russia, With Love* at ninth place to show that a president could be an egghead yet remain human.

Nevertheless, both the Kennedys had undoubtedly read and enjoyed the early Bond books. According to Allen Dulles it was Mrs Jacqueline Kennedy herself who introduced him to *From Russia, With Love* with the words, 'Here is a book *you* should have, Mr Director.' Anyhow, the Kennedy accolade was bestowed in the *Life* article, and it would be hard to over-estimate its importance in the development of the cult of James Bond in the United States. From that moment the American boom really began. It was what Fleming had worked for and longed for. But he was to have no real chance to enjoy it: for coincidentally with the appearance of the *Life* article Kevin McClory read an advance copy of *Thunderball*, which Cape was to publish early the following month. As he read it, all he could see was that Fleming had based it on the treatment which had been jointly devised for the film and that there was no acknowledgment to him or to Jack Whittingham. He took action. On the very day Fleming read the good news in *Life* Kevin McClory petitioned the High Court for an injunction to hold up publication of *Thunderball*. It was alleged that Fleming had infringed the joint copyright in a screenplay owned by himself, McClory and Whittingham by publishing, without their consent, a book based on it.

If Fleming had been expecting something to go wrong around this time, he had never foreseen this.

The feeling that morally at least he was in the right must have made the hearing in the High Court on March 25th, 1961, before Mr Justice Wilberforce, more of an ordeal than it seemed. Outwardly Fleming was his cool, blue-suited self, with a cheerful 'Good morning, Jack old boy' for Whittingham as they met at the entrance to the Law Courts. Inwardly he was loathing every second of it. He had a private horror of law courts and litigation. It had been bad enough turning up in court with his mother during her case. But now he was being virtually accused of plagiarism in public. It would have been an ordeal at the best of times, but he was tired now and the fight had gone out of him and the very idea of plagiarism matched his secret fear that perhaps he really was drying up.

During the hearing the defence set out to prove that so much was now at stake over the book that it would cause undue hardship to forbid publication. Wren Howard of Cape gave evidence that 32,000 copies of *Thunderball* had already been sent out to the booksellers and £2,000 spent on advance publicity. The judge decided to allow the book to be published, making it clear that his decision in no way prejudiced the applicants' forthcoming action. It was to be two years before the case came to a conclusion. Fleming relapsed into a mood of black melancholy.

But worse was to come. On April 12th he had driven to London for the usual Tuesday conference at the *Sunday Times*. He had been feeling unwell for some days, but he was anxious not to miss this particular conference because it was to be given an outline of the plans for the paper's new colour magazine, to be introduced early in the following year. Since Roy Thomson had taken over the Kemsley empire many things had changed, and soon Denis Hamilton was to take charge of the Tuesday morning conference. But this one was still held in Lord Kemsley's old office on the third floor, and when Fleming took his seat he was still in the place he had first occupied when he came to Kemsley House as Foreign Manager sixteen years before.

That morning he was unusually silent, looking down at the chairman's desk as he smoked through his long Edgar Wallace cigarette holder. The teddy-bear charm of Roy Thomson made it an easy meeting, and when a discussion on colour printing began to warm up he invited Fleming's views. Fleming haltingly made a few points then looked down at the desk again. It was Denis Hamilton who finally noticed that something was wrong. He exchanged a word with Fleming and in a sudden silence they left the room together. That afternoon Fleming was admitted to the London Clinic. He explained what had happened in a typically apologetic note of thanks dictated to Hamilton from the Clinic a week later:

Although neither of us knew it I am afraid that I was in the middle of a rather major heart attack this time last week. One never believes these things so I sat stupidly on trying to make intelligent comments about the thrilling new project about which I long to hear more. However a thousand thanks for noticing my trouble so quickly and for shepherding me away when the time came.

Alas this is going to mean at least another month in the Clinic without moving and then two or three more behaving like an old man. But after that I hope I shall be quite all right again, though I shall never be able to pack so much into my existence as I have foolishly been trying to do.

He had suffered from ill health for some time and the truth was that he was lucky to be alive at all, and the seriousness of the attack brought an immediate demonstration of affection from his friends. Lord Beaverbrook dictated a note for the diary in the *Evening Standard* blaming the trouble on excessive smoking, and privately he wrote from Cap d'Ail with his own unusual recipe for a swift recovery. Ian should cut out smoking and put his faith instead in strong drink which, unlike cigarettes, was good for heart trouble. His old chief and others had proved his point.

Somerset Maugham called at the London Clinic, to find that Fleming was asleep and could not be disturbed. The following day Fleming's secretary took a dictated note of thanks to Maugham: 'I was miserable to have missed you because of my siesta, but when you reach my age you will find that a rest after lunch is very beneficial, and I really don't think you ought to have been gallivanting around in the heat of the day.'

Certainly for his friends he put on as cheerful a show as possible about conditions in his 'mink-lined womb' in the Clinic. Thus to the American publisher Lawrence Hughes —Hugo Pitman's son-in-law—he wrote with Bond-like bravado, managing to echo the very words of Darko Kerim in *From Russia, With Love*: 'I am glad to say that while the iron crab made quite a sharp pass at me, he missed with the major claw.' And less than a fortnight after his attack he was telling Michael Howard (somebody had just sent him a copy of Beatrix Potter's *Squirrel Nutkin*, which he disdained except for the illustrations) that he had started writing a children's book—it later developed into the three volumes of *Chitty-Chitty-Bang-Bang*: 'So you will see that there is never a moment, even on the edge of the tomb, when I am not slaving for you.' He even managed to see the funny side of the macabre fate that befell the large jar of caviare sent him by Ivar Bryce. His next-door neighbour in the Clinic was the elderly Lord Dovercourt, and towards the end of April Fleming was writing to a friend, 'Poor old Dovercourt passed away in the next room to mine last Saturday. Our last connection with each other was a muddle over whose caviare it was in the fridge!'

But beneath the apparent high spirits his morale as well as his physique had taken a hard knock, and it was now that he gave the only sign of concern he ever made about the possible effect that James Bond was having on the world at large. In a letter to the Rev. Leslie Paxton, of the Great George Street Congregational Church, Liverpool, he revealed a side of himself few of his friends can have suspected:

I see from the public prints that the Sunday before last you preached a sermon against the leading character in my books, James Bond, and, presumably by association, against myself.

Now, having had a Scottish nonconformist upbringing and considering myself at least some kind of sub-species of a Christian, I am naturally very upset if it is thought that I am seriously doing harm to the world with my James Bond thrillers.

Would you be very kind and let me have a copy, if you have one, of your sermon, so that I may see the burden of your criticisms and perhaps find means of mending my ways if I feel that your arguments have real weight behind them.

I can, of course, myself see what you mean about my books, but it occurs to me that you may have put forward profounder arguments than those which are already known to me.

This unlikely mood of death-bed repentance did not last long. Mr. Paxton hastened to assure him that he had never implied that the creator of James Bond had done the world a serious disservice. Reassured, Fleming turned his thoughts once more to making the best of a distinctly straitened future. By the end of April he was telling Hugo Pitman that his doctors were delighted with him and 'I think I have only another two or three weeks here before being allowed to go down to Brighton to sit in one of those blasted shelters and look at the yellow sea.' And on the same day he sent off an unusual but strictly practical request to his friend and Churchill's son-in-law, the Minister of Agriculture, Fisheries and Food, Christopher Soames:

Now the point is that I am condemned for the rest of my life to three ounces of hard liquor per day, and since I have to be really rather careful about it I wish to concentrate upon the purest and finest liquor available in England. This vital piece of information will be known in your Ministry—i.e. which is the finest refined spirit, gin, whisky or brandy on the market at any price.

Do you think you could possibly extract this vital piece of information on the absolute understanding that it is for my private information only? I am sorry to bother you with this picayune inquiry, but it is just conceivable that you may also be interested in the reply.

The Minister's amiable but slightly baffled reply at any rate embodied the useful information that Green Chartreuse was the most alcoholic drink on the market.

Fleming left the London Clinic during the second week in May and duly arrived in Brighton to begin his convalescence; but he soon grew tired of gazing at the yellow sea from the 'blasted shelters' on the sea-front and before long was persuading Anne that he would get better far sooner on the French side of the English Channel. Their friend Edward Rice had a large house with a beautiful garden near Dieppe; and a few days later it was all arranged. Muffled against the Channel breeze and leaning heavily

353

upon a walking stick, Fleming crossed from Newhaven to Dieppe, and he and Anne spent some of the next few days wandering in the woods and collecting wild flowers. Even convalescence from a severe heart attack could be turned into something to be enjoyed.

Not that he ever deluded himself about the seriousness of his condition. By the beginning of June he was back in London and writing to his mother that he had just attended a 'giant meeting' of his various doctors and that they had seemed satisfied.

Though it does sound as if convalescence from one of these things is more or less endless and that I shall have to 'take care' for ever more, which is very much against my nature. However, as everyone says, it might have been much worse and you will be amused to hear that 'The Times' had actually written my obituary when it seemed that the tomb was about to yawn! I am doing everything I can to get a copy.

It was now that he and Anne decided to give up the house at Bekesbourne, near Canterbury. Anne had never liked Kent—'no architecture between Saxon and Subtopian'—and had always longed to be back in the Cotswold country where she had lived as a girl. After a long search they had finally found Sevenhampton House, near Swindon, a large, empty, originally Jacobean place which had latterly belonged to Lord Banbury. It was not too far from Huntercombe golf course, an easier course than Sandwich, and Fleming was longing to play again. Yet the house needed extensive rebuilding and he was in two minds about it—he still held to his lifelong prejudice against becoming encumbered with land and too much property. In the end he decided to go ahead, demolishing the Victorian part of the house, and as he wrote to his mother:

It will be a good solid base in the country . . . and I shall take to planting lupins or some other elderly and responsible pursuit, as it seems that strenuous golf is now out for always . . . I shall just have to adjust to 'growing old gracefully', which will be a most entertaining spectacle for my family and friends!

But growing old gracefully was beyond him, and he soon accepted the fact. He did his best to stop smoking, even attempting what he called a 'last-ditch operation at the hands of a hypnotist'. 'Unfortunately while he ineffectually tries to get me under, all I can think of are the rumblings of my stomach after too thin a lunch and the man's

Australian accent.' He also loathed the diet he was on now: no more sausages, no more scrambled eggs made to the butter-rich recipe of May Maxwell, the Bryces' housekeeper.

By the end of August, in an ominous note to Sir William Stephenson, he described himself as 'taking the whole thing very philosophically'. He went on:

In particular, I have not been seized by what they call 'coronary neurosis', which apparently is a very real consequence of one of these attacks. It results in people thinking of nothing except their health and going about as if they were made of spun Venetian glass. Such people are an infernal nuisance, and since my malady got into the newspapers I am regarded as fair game by all those morons who bore me to death with tales of their symptoms and of the pills and tests they have to take.

In other words, he was already doing his best to behave as if his heart attack had never occurred. Despite his gloomy words to his mother in June about planting lupins and not playing strenuous golf again he was now telling Stephenson that he was back in operation at the Royal St George's: 'My more relaxed golf swing and an increased handicap (I happen to be on the handicapping committee) have confounded my enemies.'

And that August Fleming received an additional incentive to start life again. After all the false alarms and disappointments from 'the ghastly world of show-biz' a big film deal materialized at last. Earlier, Harry Saltzman, a Canadian producer working in England, had taken an option on all available Bond novels. He had now joined forces with another producer, Albert Broccoli, of Warwick Films, who in turn had secured the backing of United Artists to film *Dr No*. Further options were paid for the film and television rights in the James Bond books—with the necessary exception of *Casino Royale*, which had been sold for a song back in 1955, and *Thunderball*—and Fleming was guaranteed a minimum payment of $100,000 a film plus 5 per cent of the producers' profit. The anxious agony of *Thunderball* had been completely unnecessary after all. But by now he had learned one lesson at least. With *Dr No* in the making he refused to become too involved with either the film or the film-makers. When the deal was announced the *Daily Express* ran a competition to find the ideal James Bond. After all the earlier talk of trying to persuade major stars like David Niven and Richard Burton to play Bond, it was now considered more sensible to find someone relatively unknown who could be groomed for the part, signed up for a series, and if possible projected as the public's idea of Bond.

There were 1,100 replies to the *Express* competition, including one from a man whose real name was James Bond. But none was considered suitable, and at the end of August Fleming wrote to tell Bryce:

Saltzman thinks he has found an absolute corker, a 30-year-old Shakespearian actor, ex-Navy boxing champion, etc., etc., and even, he says, intelligent. But in fact I am staying away from all this side of the business and dodging all those lunches and dinners at the Mirabelle and the Ambassadeurs which seem to be the offices for all this huckstering.

The name of Saltzman's discovery was Sean Connery. He was duly signed up, and his share of the profits of the first three films was to make him a very rich man. From now on the public image of James Bond was in Connery's hands, not Fleming's. The professional myth-makers had taken over.

This suited Fleming. Inevitably the heart attack had turned him back still further into himself. His capacity for new faces was down to a minimum. 'After a certain age,' he wrote now, 'one must not consort with persons who leave one with a bitter taste in the mind or on the palate. *Méfiez-vous du sang âpre.* Try and move among people—they may even be bores—who are *douce.*'

He wanted his few old friends. He wanted his golf. He wanted his long week-ends in the country with Anne and with Caspar when the boy was home from school. For now that the films were being made he had done all that was really required of him. He had no say in the scripts, no control over how Bond was presented, and with the real fame beginning his own role suddenly became a curiously passive one. There was nothing he really needed to do any more. He simply had to be Ian Fleming: Harry Saltzman and 'Cubby' Broccoli, geniuses at their job, would take care of all the rest.

It was a part he was good at. Over the years he had learned to play himself, and he was ready now for the photographers. Not even Edgar Wallace had excelled him in projecting the image of the famous thriller-writer. He posed sniffing the muzzle of a Beretta. Someone found a vintage Bentley with an Amherst Villiers supercharger, and he posed with that as well. The interviews began, particularly with American correspondents whose editors were hot to know the truth about the man behind James Bond. He used to talk to them in his elegant office in Mitre Court. It was boring, of course, but it passed the time, and it was strange how the very past seemed to become burnished up by the golden myth forming round him. Even something as painful as the memory of the failure at Sandhurst began to change. 'When I got my commission,' he told a man from the *New Yorker* in April 1962, 'they were mechanizing the army and a lot of us decided we didn't want to be garage hands running those bloody tanks. My poor mamma, in despair, suggested that I try for the diplomatic.'

It might seem strange that he still forced himself to go on writing his books. No longer an annual treat, they were becoming progressively more difficult now that the spark of his old enthusiasm for Bond had gone, and with the first film being made it might have seemed that money could no longer be a matter of serious concern. In fact, money was still an important incentive to the completion of each annual instalment of James Bond, and he never thought himself a rich man. When his mother sent him a cheque to help with the cost of his stay in the London Clinic there was genuine gratitude in his reply:

It was really angelic of you to send me that wonderful cheque . . . It has taken a great weight off my mind as finances really are quite a problem. You see, the Company (Glidrose) owns all my copyrights apart from serial and film rights which are assigned to the trust fund for Caspar. Now while the company pays me a salary of £2,000 a year and pays for all my personal travel abroad and part of the costs of my car in fact I get my hands on very little money from all these books. If I had lived in Edgar Wallace's day or in Somerset Maugham's I should be a rich man by now, but, alas, I just missed the boat.

The fact was that the books had become one of his habits. With age and illness, the accustomed routine of his life was more important than ever, and he was so used to writing his annual book during his two months' holiday at Goldeneye that it is hard to imagine what he could have done without the typewriter and the ream of blank foolscap and the target of seventy thousand words to be finished by the beginning of March. He took as much trouble as ever with the plot of *On Her Majesty's Secret Service*, which he wrote at Goldeneye at the beginning of 1962. Although *The Spy Who Loved Me* was not published in England until that

April he already sensed that his experiment of telling the story in the first person through his heroine and of leaving Bond offstage until well over halfway through was not what his public wanted. *O.H.M.S.S.* was to be a return to the traditional James Bond formula. Blofeld's Alpine hideaway was suggested by the luxurious Corviglia Club, near Geneva, which he and Anne had visited when he was writing about Geneva for the European part of the 'Thrilling Cities' series. To make sure that the genealogical details of the book were right he spent several afternoons at the College of Arms in Queen Victoria Street. This was when he learned that the motto of the Bond family was 'The world is not enough'. It pleased him and he saw the irony of it. For by now he had clearly decided that the hollow, bitter game of life could no longer be won. The odds against him were too high. To express his feelings he adapted John Gay's epitaph:

> Life's a cheat and all things show it.
> I thought so once and now I know it.

If he had stopped smoking and drinking, if he had stuck to planting his lupins and growing old gracefully, he could have survived, but he had been living out the dream of James Bond for so long that gardening and the life of a semi-invalid would be the final insult. By early autumn Broccoli and Saltzman had completed the film of *Dr No*, and it was clear already that it would be a runaway success. Fleming attended the première, but afterwards, at the film party at the Milroy, his friends saw him standing on his own and it was as if the success and the congratulations had nothing to do with him. They were eighteen months too late.

And it was now that he saw his old friend Amherst Villiers again. He had known him first when as a very young man in the early 1930s Villiers had been designing the superchargers for Tim Birkin's Bentleys. 'He is, you know,' Fleming told his friend David Bruce, U.S. Ambassador in London, 'an engineer of the highest quality and his was the Amherst Villiers supercharger for the 4½-litre Bentley which James Bond used to drive!' Since the war Villiers had worked as an engineer in California and as a hobby had studied portrait painting under Annigoni. Now that he was back again and living in London, Fleming asked him if he would care to paint his portrait. As it grew it began to show a sad face, and Villiers suggested that perhaps he should make the set of the mouth a shade happier. 'No,' said Fleming. 'Leave it as it is.' He bought the portrait for £500 and reproduced it in the limited edition of *On Her Majesty's Secret Service*.

Soon after this he decided that instead of growing old gracefully with the lupins he wanted a longer look at Japan than he had had time for three years before. Clearly there was a book in it—M. would have to send James Bond to Japan for his next assignment. It would also be a chance for Fleming to see his old friend Richard Hughes again. From the detailed itinerary which he sent in advance to Hughes it is clear that the entire action of *You Only Live Twice* was worked out to give him a chance to see all the things in Japan that appealed to his macabre imagination.

After perhaps a couple of days in Tokyo, I would like us to take the most luxurious modern train down south to the inland sea . . . I would also like to see pearl girls diving—my heroine will be a beautiful *ama* girl who has learned to speak English working on an underwater film in Hollywood—and hot baths, a live volcano for suicides, and any terrifying manifestation of the horrific in Japan.

The third member of the party was Torao 'Tiger' Saito— destined already for the part of Tiger Tanaka, head of the Japanese Secret Service—architect, editor, formerly a crack Japanese war correspondent, and a great friend of Richard Hughes's. Fleming had met him on his previous visit to Tokyo.

With Glidrose Productions footing the bill, the three of them made the James Bond twelve-day tour of Japan. It was a great success. The simplicity of the Japanese, their oddity, their obsession with death all fascinated Fleming. But Hughes could hardly fail to notice the difference between Fleming now and the Fleming of three years before, and he detected something desperate in his eagerness to feel and understand everything through the eyes of James Bond. At Mikimoto's pearl island Fleming pushed through the crowd of sightseers watching the girls diving and carefully placed his hand on a startled shoulder as a girl emerged from the water. 'You must *touch* to get the precise texture of wet feminine skin,' he explained seriously.

He tried drinking hot *saké* at meals and after dinner and grew to like it so much that when he returned home he tried to import a regular supply from Japan. Otherwise he drank bourbon, carrying his own private supply in his suit-case. Hughes asked him if he really preferred it to Scotch and was given an explanation a little reminiscent of the advice Fleming had received from Lord Beaverbrook. 'The cardiac muscles expand under bourbon, Dikko, but they contract under Scotch.' Hughes noticed that he was still smoking as heavily as ever and asked him about that as well. Fleming insisted, deadpan, that bourbon also helped to correct the effects of nicotine.

'In other words,' said Hughes, 'the more bourbon you drink and the more cigarettes you smoke, the better for your heart?'

'Come, come, Dikko. A little common sense. You are not writing a news story for the *Lancet*.'

He had sufficient common sense himself to know what he was up to, and soon after his return to London, when he found himself absolutely exhausted, he received a card from some friends announcing the death of their nineteen-year-old son, who had been drowned at sea off the coast of California. Printed on the card was this unascribed quotation:

I would rather that my spark should burn out in a brilliant blaze than it should be stifled by dry rot. I would rather be a superb meteor, every atom of me in a magnificent glow, than a sleeping and permanent planet. The proper function of life is to live, not to exist. I shall not waste my days in trying to prolong them. I shall use the time.

The words seemed appropriate, and he used the last two sentences, without acknowledgment to Jack London, for the short obituary Mary Goodnight was to write of James Bond at the end of *You Only Live Twice*. But they applied still more closely to himself. For instead of wasting time on bitterness or despair or the mere prolonging of his days he was trying to live now as James Bond would live. 'I do not want to be a different person,' he told one of his friends. He would enjoy life as long as life permitted him to.

While he was finishing *You Only Live Twice* at Goldeneye early in 1963 he heard with emotion of the death of one of his oldest friends, Duff-Dunbar. 'I am now vividly concerned about all my friends,' he wrote to Ivar Bryce, adding the slightly desperate injunction, 'after fifty, one must really *love* every day—if one is allowed to.'

Not that it was always easy. As he neared the end of writing *You Only Live Twice* he sent Richard Hughes a card from Jamaica:

I'm grinding away at Bond's latest but the going gets harder and harder and duller and duller and I don't really know what I'm going to do with him. He's become a personal—if not a public—nuisance. Anyway he's had a good run, which is more than most of us can say. Everything seems a lot of trouble these days—too much trouble. Keep alive.

Hughes sent a stern reply, saying that he would never answer another letter which ended 'Keep alive'. A week later another postcard arrived from Fleming: 'Dikko: I promise. Don't worry. I'm not worrying any more. Down with death!'

But death was not to be dismissed so lightly. That summer another friend died—Hugo Pitman. Fleming went to the funeral and was very moved and upset. 'Friends dwindle rapidly at our age,' he wrote to Hilary Bray, 'and Duff and Hugo were a bad left-and-right.'

For the rest of that summer he did his best to put such thoughts out of his mind. From Sevenhampton he would drive his new black Studebaker Avanti to Huntercombe golf course, where his Grandmother Fleming, in her black button boots, had given him his first golf lesson when he was sixteen. He began seeing more of his brother Peter now, though their affection for each other had been lifelong, and a number of his earliest friends, including Selby Armitage. He enjoyed meeting them and playing golf and was soon starting yet another of his routines: every Saturday he would lunch with Sir Jock Campbell (now Lord Campbell), who had also been at Eton, at his house near Nettlebed. Campbell was chairman of Booker Brothers, McConnell, the big Commonwealth merchants; as a Socialist he was also chairman of the *New Statesman*, the journal which had carried the angriest attack ever made on James Bond and the books. In the not very distant future he and Ian Fleming were to do a little business together.

Another source of pleasure now to the creator of Bond was the money which had begun to flow with such startling rapidity since the film of *Dr No* had appeared the previous autumn, though British taxation and his serious heart condition made it not a great deal of use to him. Practically the only treat he bothered to give himself was his super-charged Avanti car. But at least the treasure *had* finally been cracked and he was happy that Bond was steadily stacking up hard cash. He liked to be reassured about it and during that summer of 1963 would often ring up his film agent, Robert Fenn, to ask, 'How's Bond doing? What're we making now?'

Bond was doing magnificently. Between 1960 and 1964 Fleming's earnings increased more than tenfold and the book rights alone netted more than a quarter of a million pounds. It must all have seemed oddly unreal to Fleming, for just as the sheer volume of Bond's earnings had already turned money into something abstract to be discussed by tax advisers and accountants and agents, so the whole new Bond cult, with the films and the international publicity, was taking place in a world he had nothing to do with. His private daydreams had become a world phenomenon, but he had very little contact with it all now.

One of the few occasions when he did was the première of the second James Bond film, *From Russia, With Love*. It took place in October 1963, and he and Anne felt that perhaps they should hold, after the performance, a separate party at home for their own friends. Anne afterwards regretted suggesting a menu called *From Russia, With Love*, with only caviare to eat. The idea appealed to Ian Fleming, who had just won £500 at Le Touquet, and to Anne's dismay he insisted on spending the whole sum on the best Beluga imported to Paris. They went from Le Touquet to Paris, arriving rather late and uncertain where to find the finest caviare. They telephoned Nancy Mitford; she told them to go to Petrossian's in the boulevard de la Tour Maubourg; and next day Anne was given the job of bringing two extremely large containers back to England—he was flying the car from Le Touquet.

'What happens if they try charging me customs duty on it?' she asked.

'Tell them it's for James Bond,' he replied.

But at the party not even £500-worth of caviare could make Ian Fleming into James Bond; and there was a terrible contrast between the young superman whom everyone had just seen on the screen, potent, violent, battling with Donovan Grant aboard the Orient Express, and the man who once dreamt it all. Haggard and unwell, he received his guests, declined his own caviare, and made off to bed soon after midnight. The refrigerator at 16 Victoria Square was full of the stuff for weeks.

Fleming explained his deathly appearance at the party in a letter to William Plomer, written soon after it: 'I am now winding myself up like a toy soldier for this blasted case with McClory that starts on November 19th and may last for as much as ten days. I dare say that a diet of T.N.T.

pills and gin will see me through, but it's a bloody nuisance.'

Ivar Bryce was sued with him as a defendant; and Fleming was right about the duration of the action. As he sat in court day after day, swallowing the nitroglycerine pills prescribed to prevent another heart attack and listening to all those old arguments again, he must have told himself how unnecessary it all was, how easily it could all have been avoided.

As the long, expensive speeches dragged on for ten days in that wintry court it was not hard for McClory's counsel to establish that the original theme and ideas put forward by McClory and by Whittingham had been reproduced in *Thunderball*—in the circumstances it was enough. Bryce decided that he would settle rather than allow things to drag on any longer. Fleming bitterly agreed, and after negotiations the settlement of the action was announced in open court. McClory acknowledged the good faith both of Fleming and his publishers, Fleming acknowledged that the novel *Thunderball* was based on a screen treatment which was the joint work of Kevin McClory, Jack Whittingham and himself, and there was to be an acknowledgment to that effect in all future editions of and references to the novel. Payment was made to Fleming for his share of the film rights in the novel and his interest in the screenplay. McClory, who thus got all the film rights in *Thunderball*, disclaimed any further interest in the novel. Fleming paid his own costs. McClory received £35,000 damages from Ivar Bryce in full settlement of all his claims against him, and Bryce was to pay McClory's costs as well as his own. The costs bill for all parties was estimated just after the case at £80,000.*

II

The Bond boom went on. Fleming watched it with a mixture of satisfaction and detachment. It was all out of his hands now. In August 1963 he and Anne had gone off on holiday to Montreux, and while they were staying at the Montreux Palace he went to see Simenon, who lives in a château outside Lausanne. Fleming recalled the first Simenon stories he had come across—he had 'absolutely adored them' and had read nearly fifty more since. But

* The film was released in 1965 and was a phenomenal success at the box-office. It was produced by Kevin McClory.

Simenon had never read any of Fleming's books and seemed to have only a dim notion of the whole Bond business. They recorded a talk about their ways of working, Simenon being characteristically contemptuous of 'literary' novels and Fleming showing charming deference to his old hero by his witty self-disparagement.

Then in December, after the 'Thunderball' case, he went to Bad Nauheim for a couple of days to see a new and highly recommended heart specialist, whose findings were not over-encouraging: 'coronary and aortic sclerosis—signs of moderate myocarditic damage—intermittent coronary insufficiency.' He was strongly urged to lead a more moderate life, to avoid smoking and over-exertion and to take long periods of rest and relaxation. Alcohol was not forbidden —he could take small amounts of whisky, brandy, and wine.

This specialist would hardly have approved of the effort Fleming was to put into writing *The Man with the Golden Gun* at Goldeneye, but nothing would stop him; he kept at it stubbornly even though he could do no more than an hour at a time. But he was grateful to be back and enjoyed the flowers and the birds and the fish more than ever. Soon the Flemings were joined by the most restful of all their friends, Hilary Bray and his wife—Ian and Anne were both devoted to them—and their presence at Goldeneye helped him to forget that fate was now pressing him so hard. There was also another distraction at Goldeneye that year. James Bond called. The ornithologist who wrote Fleming's favourite *Birds of the West Indies* was visiting Jamaica with his wife, and far from being annoyed at what had happened to his name since Fleming first borrowed it without permission, invited himself to lunch. Fleming thought the Bonds 'a charming couple who are amused by the whole joke'.

This was to prove Fleming's last winter in Jamaica. He returned home to grapple with the tax problems of Glidrose Productions, his Bond company. He was advised that his success made it impossible to keep it a private one, and certainly a sale had attractions, as it would give him what he had always wanted, a sizeable tax-free capital sum. Anne's recollection is that Rothschild's had expressed an interest, and indeed there was always the possibility of auctioning it round the City. Anne herself was in favour of this, but Fleming did not have the vitality to explore the auction possibilities and, against her advice, he sold it to his golfing friend, Sir Jock Campbell. The announcement came at the end of March 1964. Booker Brothers, Campbell's company, had acquired 51 per cent of Glidrose for a straight capital payment of £100,000.

For even now the real treasure was to slip through Fleming's fingers—after his death the £100,000 was to go in death duties*—and it was Booker Brothers rather than Ian Fleming himself who ended up with the golden egg. Apart from the fantastic sales of the books in paperback the 'merchandizing' of James Bond shirts and shoes and drinks and toys and all the rest of it was really getting going.

When the deal with Booker Brothers was announced Fleming's boyhood friend Selby Armitage met him at Huntercombe, and they went back and sat beneath the lime trees in Armitage's garden. They talked about the old days, and Armitage said, 'Ian, what is it like, what is it really like, to be famous? Ever since I've known you it's what you've really wanted. Are you enjoying it now you've got it?'

Fleming's face fell, and he looked very sorry for himself. 'Well,' he said at last, 'I suppose it was all right for a bit—nice being known in restaurants and having people take notice of you. But now, my God! Ashes, old boy—just ashes.' He paused and stared across the garden. 'You've no idea how bored one gets with the whole silly business.'

Only his friends and his golf still offered some relief. This was presumably why he insisted on driving over to Huntercombe the Sunday after the Easter holidays despite a bad cold and a temperature and all Anne's efforts to stop him. 'But what is there to do at home on a Sunday?' he had said, and drove off in the rain. It rained all through his game, and afterwards he drove on to London in soaking golf clothes. Two weeks later the cold had become pleurisy, but although he was very weak it was as much as anyone could do to persuade him to enter King Edward VII's Hospital

* Ian Fleming left £302,147 (gross), £289,170 (net). Estate duty already paid amounts to over £210,000, but the final figure will depend on valuations still being calculated. Under his English will his wife Anne was the principal immediate beneficiary. He also left £19,275 in real estate and £1,625 in personal funds in Jamaica and made a Jamaican will. He did not benefit spectacularly under the will of his mother, Mrs Evelyn Fleming, who left £101,000 on her death (over £90,000 net): her main beneficiary was her adopted daughter Amaryllis. But his mother's will was, of course, made in the knowledge that, on her death, Fleming came into his own substantial share of the inheritance under his father's will.

for Officers, otherwise Sister Agnes's, in Beaumont Street.

He immediately hated the small room he was given—he said it gave him claustrophobia. Before the doctor arrived he begged Anne to take him away. When he got to know the doctor and matron he liked them both, but he was still determined to leave, and he did so before he should have done.

After a short stay at home at Victoria Square he went off to the Dudley Hotel, Hove, with a devoted nurse, to recuperate once again by the 'yellow sea'. This time there was no question of a jaunt across the Channel; a local doctor was in permanent attendance, and human contact exhausted him profoundly. He ate little, smoked constantly, and usually sat on the same bench staring at the sea. By a strange twist of fate he was a few hundred yards away from his mother; after the death of Lord Winchester in 1962 Mrs. Val, very old and frail, had returned to England, and now she was dying in an hotel on the front at Brighton. But although he had been a dutiful son during the last few years he was too ill to be able to comfort her. Apart from Anne the only visitors he enjoyed seeing were William Plomer, Cyril Connolly, and Alan Ross. Once a week his devoted secretary Beryl Griffie-Williams would arrive and he would dictate a few important letters to her.

One of these was a reply to Somerset Maugham, who had just written a sad little note of thanks for his copy of *You Only Live Twice*.

Forgive me for not having acknowledged it before but I have been very seedy and distraught. I have just returned from Venice, but with the realization that my travelling days are over—it is a great grief to me . . . I think of you with great affection and would like to see you once more.

Fleming did his best to reply with his usual cheerfulness:

Cease at once being 'seedy and distraught'. Move about as much as you can, even if it's only short distances, and don't forget that today's news wraps tomorrow's fish. I have been seedy, but without being much distraught, with pleurisy and shut up in Sister Agnes's for two or three weeks. I am going to try and persuade Annie that we might fly down to Nice and invite ourselves to you for a week-end, if you will have us . . .

Now please don't treat yourself like a piece of Venetian glass. It is not your style at all, and you have always had the courage and fortitude of ten.

So had Fleming; and he decided that the days of treating

himself like spun glass had gone on quite long enough.

On July 24th his mother died in the hotel just along the front from him. Anne and Dr Beal both told him that it was madness for him to think of attending the funeral at Nettlebed, but he insisted. Although in the past he had shown no love for family gatherings he seemed to find a certain comfort in this one. Sad though the occasion was, he was grateful for the sight of familiar places and fortified by a feeling of family solidarity. And even a funeral was better than the desolation of Hove.

One thing which the excursion did for him was to convince him that he was ready to leave Hove. Again Dr Beal advised caution and again he ignored his advice. At the beginning of August he drove home to Victoria Square. Caspar was there and he was glad to see him. But one thing about him really frightened Anne. In the past sun and light had been vital to him. Now he longed for the dark. He spoke little. When he did it was with a despairing impatience that he had to get back to life, or else . . .

For sick as he was he was still tormented by the old dream of freedom and action that he had put into Bond. 'I must be able to live as I want, with no restrictions, or I don't want to live at all,' he had told Robert Fenn, and it seemed a mockery to him that he could no longer swim, no longer drink what he wanted or travel or climb mountains, things that the creator of James Bond should do.

But there was still one thing he was determined to do—spend August at his favourite hotel, the Guilford at Sandwich Bay. He had not been able to revise and rewrite parts of *The Man with the Golden Gun* as he had intended but it couldn't be helped. He was to be the next captain of the Royal St George's golf club, and that was more important now than all the vast and meaningless success of his books. 'Have booked at the Guilford for all August,' he wrote to Hilary Bray and his wife, 'and the wild garlic and Nick and you both will certainly hoist me out of this stupid valley I have got into.' Nick was another friend, Wing Commander H. D. Nicholson, the secretary of the club.

But neither golf nor friends nor wild garlic were enough. On August 11th he forced himself to attend a committee meeting at the club and to stay on to lunch afterwards. it was too much for his heart. 'That night,' says Anne, 'he was in great despair,' and by the following evening the haemorrhage was so severe that he had to be taken to

Canterbury Hospital. He died there at one the following morning.

All that day the flag of the Royal St George's flew at half mast. Ian Fleming, only begetter of James Bond, was dead. Already his books had sold more than 40 million copies, and the 'great splurge' of sales he had foreseen had only just begun. He had not seen the film of *Goldfinger*, but it was nearly finished and would soon be seen by millions. Already Bond was a world-wide cult and his creator had become a myth in his own lifetime.

But none of this mattered now, and the Royal St George's would have to find itself a new captain for the autumn. Once again, despite all the success, life had cheated Ian Fleming of the one thing he had set his heart on, and James Bond had finally destroyed his only flesh-and-blood victim.